FROM
MAHAN
TO
PEARL
HARBOR

FROM MAHAN TO PEARL HARBOR

The Imperial Japanese Navy and the United States

SADAŌ ASADA

NAVAL INSTITUTE PRESS
Annapolis, Maryland

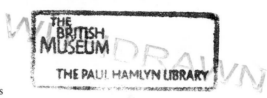

Naval Institute Press
291 Wood Road
Annapolis, MD 21402

This book has been brought to publication with the generous assistance of Edward S.
and Joyce I. Miller.

ISBN-13: 978-1-55750-042-7

Library of Congress Cataloging-in-Publication Data
Asada, Sadao, 1936–
  From Mahan to Pearl Harbor: The Imperial Japanese Navy and the United States /
Sadao Asada.
     p. cm.
  Includes bibliographical references and index.
  ISBN 1-55750-042-8 (alk. paper)
  1. Japan—History, Naval—1868–1941.   2. Japan. Kaigun—History—20th century.
  3. Japan—Foreign relations—20th century.   4. World War, 1939–1945—Japan.
  5. Mahan, A. T. (Alfred Thayer), 1840–1914. I. Title.
  DS839.7.A87 2006
  359.00952'09041—dc22

                                                                    2006015540

Printed in the United States of America on acid-free paper ∞
12 11 10 09 08   9 8 7 6 5 4 3 2

To My Esteemed Friend *Robert H. Ferrell,*
and to the Memory of Our Great Teacher
Samuel Flagg Bemis (1891–1973)

CONTENTS

TABLES

PREFACE

After many years of research into Japanese and American sources—I confess I am close to retirement from Doshisha University in Kyoto—I offer the present essay on the Imperial Japanese Navy spanning the half century preceding Pearl Harbor. It is, of course, a saddening account of a great navy with a tradition and authority that became alienated from and finally clashed with the navy of a neighbor separated by the nine thousand miles of the Pacific Ocean.

To trace the genesis of antagonism I go back to the American ideologue of sea power, Alfred Thayer Mahan; his sea power doctrine; and its influence on the Japanese navy. In 1906–1907 the two navies, as if in a mirror image, began to see each other as hypothetical enemies. During a happy interlude, the Washington Conference of 1921–22, the Japanese navy under the charismatic leadership of Admiral Katō Tomosaburō cooperated with the United States to dispel a war scare and frame the Washington system of naval limitation. What followed in Japan after Katō's untimely death in 1923 was a revolt against the Washington naval treaty, disintegration of the naval tradition, and degeneration of naval leadership until it virtually collapsed in 1941.

I tell the story from the perspective of my own country, but I have been much influenced by my long experience in the United States, where I studied at Carleton College and then, the academic experience of my life, with the late Samuel Flagg Bemis of Yale University. I was Bemis's last doctoral student before his retirement, and I shall never forget his instruction and especially his kindnesses, which were innumerable. He introduced me to a fine dissertation topic, "Japan and the United States, 1915–25," centering on the Washington Conference. This was the start of the pages that follow.

Setting out this large portion of history from 1890 to the fateful day of 7 December 1941 has involved many difficulties. Research in Japanese sources has been formidable, especially in the magnificent and hitherto untapped collections of documents on the Washington, Geneva, and London naval conferences. Alas, the naval and army archives for 1931–41 suffered systematic destruction at the time of Japan's surrender in August 1945 by the highest naval and military leaders, who hastily burned any confidential records that might implicate them in the postwar war crimes trials. I once stated—to be sure, helplessly—that the act constituted a crime against history. Nonetheless I have managed to put history back together by supplementing the surviving official records from private sources—manuscript collections, diaries, memoirs, and interviews as well as multivolume official war histories.

Sadao Asada
7 December 2005

ACKNOWLEDGMENTS

Over the years I have profited from interuniversity research projects and Japanese-American historical conferences, most importantly the Kawaguchiko Conference held in July 1969 under the leadership of Hosoya Chihiro. The late Nomura Minoru of the National Defense College (director of the Second Division of the War History Office, the Defense Agency) and the late Admiral Suekuni Masao, also of the War History Office, were of great assistance. The late Admiral Tomioka Sadatoshi, Chief of the Operations Division and, after the war, President of the Historical Sources Research Society, was generous with his time. The late Enomoto Jūji, Senior Councilor to the Navy Ministry, kindly invited me to examine his unparalleled collection of interwar naval conference materials at his house in 1975. Hatano Sumio helped me obtain copies of important diaries.

American and British scholars also guided me during their stays in Kyoto. The late Arthur Marder, then working on his *Old Friends, New Enemies* (1981), befriended me; it was a pleasure to contribute to his Festschrift. He was greatly helpful with a Mahan anthology I was editing and translating. The late British political scientist Joseph Frankel carefully commented on one of my papers from the viewpoint of decision making. In London, D. C. Watt and Ian H. Nish commented on several of my chapters.

My friends in America have done everything in their power, which is a great deal, to be of help. I am especially grateful to Robert H. Ferrell, the most distinguished of Bemis's students, for constantly encouraging and helping me by commenting on and improving my English-language publications. For more than ten years, Edward S. Miller has provided me with friendly support, and he made a generous endowment to the Naval Institute Press on behalf of this book. Robert J. C. Butow took pains to improve the manuscript even though he was so busy with his *F. D. Roosevelt and Japan*. Dean Allard, Former Director of Naval History, Department of the Navy, was always helpful. It is impossible to name all those to whom I am indebted, so I shall confine myself to several more friends who read and commented on this book manuscript either in part or entirely—James Auer,

Michael A. Barnhart, Waldo H. Heinrichs, Charles E. Neu, Ronald H. Spector, and the late David A. Titus.

In acknowledging the help I received I must also include experiences with such people as Mrs. Theodore Roosevelt Jr. who invited me to her mansion ("Old Orchard") on Long Island to examine the papers and diary of her husband and even to be an overnight guest. I fondly recall how I entered the world of the Theodore Roosevelts, *pere et fils*. That was back in 1959. My years in America included a notable visit in Washington with Ambassador Stanley K. Hornbeck, long of the State Department, where he was Far Eastern adviser to Secretary of State Cordell Hull. He not only let me see portions of his papers in his apartment but also introduced me to Ambassador Joseph C. Grew, my benefactor who made my college education in America possible.

I am grateful to Paul Wilderson, former Executive Editor of the Naval Institute Press, for his constant encouragement, and new editor Eric Mills for his help in the final stage of revising and editing the manuscript. Peter Mauch of Ritsumeikan University helped proofread the manuscript. Nakatani Tadashi was helpful in multiple ways as my graduate assistant. Among my former students, Ken Yoshimura has taken the greatest interest in the completion of this book. It goes without saying that errors of omission and commission or remaining stylistic infelicities are solely mine.

Gratefully I dedicate this book to Samuel Flagg Bemis and to his memory, which I warmly share with Robert H. Ferrell.

A Note on Translation   Japanese documents are incredibly difficult to translate. In addition, national policy papers in the years in which I have been working were studies in deliberate ambiguities, being products of tortuous interservice compromises. Rear Admiral Tomioka wrote in his memoirs *Kaisen to Shūsen* that "the Japanese language is so ambiguous, vague, and pregnant with meaning that it is not suited to operational planning." Usually I trusted my own translations, but when English translations existed, I sometimes gratefully availed myself of them, with minor changes for stylistic consistency.

In accordance with the established convention in academic works, Japanese names are presented with the family name preceding the given name. Because my account deals with history before World War II, I have spelled place-names in their contemporary form.

PART ONE

THE

GENESIS

OF

ANTAGONISM

CHAPTER ONE

MAHAN AND JAPANESE-AMERICAN RELATIONS

The Birth of an International Classic

On 12 May 1890, Theodore Roosevelt wrote to Captain Alfred Thayer Mahan, "During the last two days I have spent half of my time, busy as I am, in reading your book, and that I found it interesting is shown by the fact that having taken [it] up I have gone straight through and finished it. . . . It is a very good book—admirable; and I am greatly in error if it does not become a naval classic."[1] The book praised so extravagantly was, of course, *The Influence of Sea Power upon History, 1660–1783.*[2] Overnight its publication transformed an obscure naval officer into a world authority on naval and international affairs.

This book also caused a sensation among foreign leaders precisely because it was a timely publication that met their respective political needs. The British Admiralty, augmenting the building program of 1889, welcomed Mahan's forceful exposition of the importance of sea power.[3] In Germany, Kaiser Wilhelm II, who was about to launch an overseas career, wrote that he was "just now not reading but devouring Captain Mahan's book and am trying to learn it by heart. It is a first-class book and classical in all points." Recently lured to the sea, the young kaiser was determined to lay the foundations of a great navy, a navy that could challenge British sea supremacy.[4]

Japanese leaders responded to Mahan's work with equal alacrity. Baron Kaneko Kentarō, former minister of agriculture and commerce, who happened to be in the United States on a fact-finding tour, hastened to peruse it. A graduate of Harvard Law School, Kaneko was a leading Westernizer and importer of American ideas to Japan. He immediately recognized the universal implications of Mahan's sea power doctrine. In the apt words of naval historian Roger Dingman, "It brought to him something akin to a burst of Zen enlightenment."[5]

Upon his return to Japan, Kaneko had the book's introduction and first chapters translated, and he showed them to Navy Minister Saigō Tsugumichi, who gave them to Suikōsha, the professional association of navy line officers, to be published in its journal. When the complete translation came out in 1896 from the Oriental Association in Tokyo, the publisher enthusiastically wrote Mahan that "several thousand volumes were sold in a day or two" and that the Naval and Army Staff Colleges later adopted it as their textbook. Copies were presented to the emperor and the crown prince and received "the honor of Their Majesties' approval."[6] Mahan later recollected with pleasure, "[My] theme brought me into pleasant correspondence with several Japanese officials and translators, than whom none, as far as known to me, have shown closer or more interested attention to the general subject; how fruitfully, has been demonstrated both by their preparation and their accomplishments in the recent [Russo-Japanese] war."[7]

Mahan also noted that more of his works were translated into Japanese than into any other language. In 1899 he wrote to Minakami Umehiko, the translator of *The Interest of America in Sea Power, Present and Future* (released, significantly, under the title of "On the Sea Power in the Pacific"), "I trust that your undertaking may promote the interest of the Japanese nation in the subject, and so may advance Japan farther in that career of national development, in which she has already made such remarkable progress."[8]

What Mahan did not realize was that the Japanese were quick to appropriate his messages to enhance their own sea power, which would one day come to clash with that of the United States. In the preface to the Japanese translation of *The Influence of Sea Power*, Soejima Taneomi, an influential member of the Privy Council, declared, "Japan is a sea power." He argued, "Japanese leaders must carefully study Mahan's doctrines to secure command of the sea; Japan would then be able to control the commerce and navigation in the Pacific and gain sufficient power to defeat any enemy." Later, in his introduction to the Japanese edition of Mahan's *The Interest of America in Sea Power*, Kaneko proclaimed, "The Japanese empire is the foremost sea power in the Pacific." Like Soejima, he urged Japanese leaders to obtain the key to the command of the sea by assiduously studying Mahan's writings.[9] Ironically, at the same time that Mahan was so pleased with the attention given to his books in Japan, some Americans (Mahan included) were beginning to perceive a menace in a modernized and expanding Japan.

This chapter will discuss (1) Mahan's early contacts with and impressions of Japan; (2) his doctrine of sea power; (3) his views on expansion into the Pacific and East Asia; and (4) his "yellow peril" notion as it affected Japanese-American relations.

MAHAN'S FIRST IMPRESSIONS OF JAPAN

Although Alfred Thayer Mahan was born into "the mainstream of the American military tradition," his early career showed little promise.[10] When Alfred applied for admission to the Naval Academy at Annapolis, his father, Dennis, a professor of engineering at West Point, warned him that he was more suited for a civilian career than a naval one. Years later in his *Recollections of Naval Life*, the son acknowledged that his father had probably been right.[11] It was not as a fighting admiral or even as a competent captain that Mahan would distinguish himself. By his own admission he did not excel in sea duty and after minor shipboard mishaps, he came to dread the possibility of a major accident. Whenever possible he attempted to postpone or evade sea duty.

Yet in all fairness it must be pointed out that he had more than his share of overseas experiences that influenced his later ideas. Of particular interest for our purpose was his cruise around the world in 1867 on board the steamship USS *Iroquois* when he was twenty-seven years old. It was sheer curiosity and love of adventure that compelled young Mahan. The *Iroquois* took nine months to reach Japan via the "roundabout road"—West Indies, Brazil, South Africa, the Persian Gulf, India, Singapore, Hong Kong, and China. In his memoirs Mahan fondly wrote that the voyage to Japan and China was "the dream of years to me."[12] His firsthand observations in Japan and China were also important as harbingers of the interest he later explored in his *Problem of Asia* (1900).

The *Iroquois* stayed in Japanese waters for more than a year, protecting American interests and lives in the newly opened treaty ports. As he recollected, "Japan had not entered upon the path of modernization." It had been only fourteen years since Commodore Matthew C. Perry had extorted a treaty that opened Japan. In 1867–68 Japan was in the midst of a civil war. In his letters to his family and friends, Mahan vividly described his impressions of Hiogo (Kobe) and Osaka—cities that were in political turmoil following the opening of Japan.[13] The disorder was partly caused by resentment against the presence of foreigners. Rioters succeeded in driving foreigners from Osaka, whereupon a landing force supported by guns of foreign ships extracted concessions from Kobe.

To understand what he saw, Mahan "hurriedly and nervously" read *The Capital of the Tycoon* by Sir Rutherford Alcock, the first envoy from England,[14] but the complexities of Japanese domestic politics eluded his understanding. He could understand, however, that Japan was going through a "revolutionary transition"; its far-seeing leaders realized that the days of seclusion were over and there was no choice but to meet the inevitable and "develop the nation to equality with foreigners in material resources."[15]

On the street Mahan saw two-sworded samurai, with their stern bearing, "as thick almost as blackberries." Even when the country became safe and the *Iroquois*'s officers were permitted to go ashore, they were ordered to carry revolvers. But Mahan found the Japanese people "perfectly civil and respectful; I don't think there is any more danger than in walking in New York at night."[16]

When conditions eased, Mahan enjoyed long hikes in the mountains near Kobe and he rhapsodized, "The country is more beautiful than anything in our own land. Just between Kobe and Osaka is one of the loveliest, if not the loveliest rural view I have ever seen." Naval lore had it that the valley he "discovered" came to be known as "Mahan's Valley" to subsequent naval visitors. "But I have never heard it has been so entered on the maps," he wistfully recalled. In his memoirs, written some forty years later, he expressed concern that modernization would wipe out the charms of his favorite valley. "If the march of improvement has changed that valley, Japan deserves to be beaten in her next war." Some reason for "beating" Japan![17]

The young Mahan took an instant liking to Japan. "I think I shall like Japan; all agree in representing the people as amicable and good-natured to the utmost." "The people seem exceedingly good humored—inquisitive about us but not impertinently so—rather in awe of us I think and not venturing on liberties; but they act as though glad to see us." He wrote about the "smiling affability characteristic of all classes in Japan." His general impression of Japan, viewed from the cultural "distance," was "very pretty, like a stage scene."[18]

These idyllic impressions are interesting in light of the ambivalent images of Japan that came to dominate his views after the 1890s: a favorable view of Japanese culture and the Japanese people, and the yellow peril notion about Japanese expansionism in the Pacific and immigration to the United States. As the modern Mahan biographer Robert Seager II has written, his experiences on board the *Iroquois* "led him, for the rest of his life, to fancy himself as a leading authority on Japanese history and American-Japanese relations."[19]

From 1877 to 1880, when Mahan taught gunnery at the Naval Academy, he came to know personally several Japanese midshipmen being trained at Annapolis under an 1868 agreement with the Japanese government. One of them was Uriu Sotokichi, who graduated with the Class of 1881. Bright and well versed in English, he was "the most outstanding Japanese student ever sent to Annapolis."[20] (Mahan would take pride in Uriu's exploits as commander of a division of cruisers under Admiral Tōgō Heihachirō during the Russo-Japanese War. Uriu later rose to the rank of full admiral.)

GOSPEL OF SEA POWER

In early 1885 President Stephen B. Luce of the newly established Naval War College invited Mahan to teach naval history and strategy. His lectures on the rise and fall of sea powers resulted in *The Influence of Sea Power upon History, 1660–1783*. In this book Mahan drew panoramic pictures of the great European sea battles of the seventeenth and eighteenth centuries fought among Britain, Holland, France, and Spain. Its central theme was how England, through sea power, attained its hegemonic position in the world. The lesson for the United States was obvious: "The United States is to all intents an insular power, like Great Britain." This dramatic conceptualization of the United States as one huge island washed by the Atlantic and the Pacific was to become central to his philosophy of sea power.[21] Like Britain, the United States must have an offensive navy and colonies. Through writing his *Influence of Sea Power*, Mahan, a onetime anti-imperialist, was "converted" to the gospel of imperialism.[22]

Familiar as they may be, for our interpretive purposes we will summarize here the salient points of Mahan's sea power doctrine that would in time come to influence—in fact, dominate—Japan's strategic thought and naval policy.

In the first chapter of *Influence*, Mahan gave his analysis of "Elements of Sea Power." These were (1) geographical position (insular position); (2) physical conformation (coastlines with abundant natural harbors); (3) extent of territory (a territorial base for wealth and resources); (4) population (a seafaring, shipbuilding, and trading people); (5) national character (aptitude for pursuing maritime and commercial pursuits); and (6) character of the government (a form of government or institutions that can intelligently direct seagoing energies). Mahan claimed that the United States possessed the potential for fulfilling these requirements to become a great sea power; all it needed was proper leadership, national will, and energy to achieve its seafaring destiny.[23] In this sense, what Mahan offered was less a naval strategy than "a national policy for the pursuit of national greatness."[24]

Mahan's thought fell under two rubrics: a theory of naval strategy, pure and simple, and a theory of commercial expansion backed by sea power—"mercantilist imperialism," in the words of naval historians Harold and Margaret Sprout.[25] When these two theories converged, Mahan's doctrine partook of a kind of determinism that postulated that the U.S. Navy was bound eventually to clash with competing naval powers.

Central to Mahan's strategic thought was the idea that "if the true end [of the navy] is to preponderate over the enemy's navy and so control the sea, then the enemy's ships and fleets are the true objects to be assailed on all occasions." Again: "War, once declared, must be waged offensively, aggressively. The enemy must not be fended off, but smitten down." The aim of a naval engagement was the total annihilation of the enemy fleet in a decisive battle. His strategic doctrine put a premium on command of the sea and the concentration of battleships that alone, he stressed, could destroy the enemy fleet. Mahan postulated that a fleet must never be dispersed and broken into pieces by a superior enemy force. Steaming out to meet the enemy, with a fleet at least as large as the opposing armada, the American navy would engage in a brief and decisive battle.[26]

Perhaps the most lasting legacy of Mahan's strategy as it bore on Japan was his fixation on the battleship and a decisive fleet engagement. As I will elaborate in later chapters, this same obsession would govern the Japanese navy until the Pearl Harbor attack and beyond. Naval historian Ronald H. Spector has written, "The Japanese navy was a faithful mirror image of its American opponent in strategy. Japanese naval officers, too, had inhaled deeply the heady, if somewhat musty, fumes of Mahan's classic brew of imperialism and salt water."[27] George W. Baer, a naval strategy specialist, goes as far as to say, "Japan's naval strategy was more Mahanian than America's." In addition to Mahanian influence, he points out that "principles of naval warfare would force maritime states to think alike." An enemy's strategy and force structure would be governed by the objective of fleet concentration for decisive battle. This added to a mirror image shared by both navies.[28] And it was precisely this mirror image that came to characterize Japanese-American naval confrontation.

To buttress his case for a large battleship navy, Mahan marshaled political-economic arguments. He posited three links on which naval dominance rested: production, shipping, and colonies. In particular he emphasized the commercial component of sea power. "The tendency to trade, involving of necessity the production of something to trade with, is the national characteristic most important to the development of sea power."[29]

On the relationship between naval power and commerce, Mahan was often ambivalent and his reasoning circular. Mahan's main purpose in writing *The Influence of Sea Power* was, of course, to provide a rationale for a strong battleship navy: the book has been called an "apologia for naval appropriations."[30] At times, however, he argued that promotion of overseas commerce required naval supremacy; the navy was to be the spearhead of commercial expansion. Mahan's theory of commercial and colonial expansion has been reinterpreted by the "new left" school of historians, notably Walter LaFeber. Expansionists like Mahan argued that a vast industrial surplus at home demanded outlets in the form of overseas markets and colonies and that commercial expansion in turn called for sea power.[31] Like many naval officers, Mahan came to believe in the imperatives of economic prosperity at home that dictated overseas expansion. This economic argument assumed that other powers would also aspire to international economic preeminence. A corollary of this assumption was the belief that commercial rivalry would inevitably bring the United States into conflict with a competitor.[32]

America's navalists deduced from this assumption that they would come to armed conflict with Japan over trade with China. Perpetuating the myth of the China market, navy men in America took it for granted that the United States would fight Japan in order to protect the Open Door in China. They seemed to be oblivious to the fact that the United States and Japan were natural trade partners. As I shall describe in later chapters, Japan's navalists came to postulate from Mahan's economic and commercial doctrine a form of economic determinism that held that the irrepressible urge of capitalist America dictated expansion into China, threatening Japan's vital interests. In time it became an article of faith in Japanese naval circles that America's "economic penetration" of China, supported by a superior navy, would lead to Japanese-American war.

EXPANSION IN THE PACIFIC

After the publication of his *Influence of Sea Power* made him a world figure, Mahan was frequently asked to write on current international events. While keeping in close touch with Theodore Roosevelt and his fellow expansionists, Mahan wrote many articles exhorting the nation to build up sea power and to expand in the Pacific. His most comprehensive attempt to address American expansionism was a polemical essay titled "The United States Looking Outward" that appeared in the *Atlantic Monthly* in December 1890. In this often-quoted article, he called for vigorous efforts to compete in world trade and to penetrate overseas markets to solve the problem of domestic overproduction. The theater of international action, he emphasized, was moving from the Atlantic to the Pacific. The threat to the United States henceforth would come from Japan. In this connection, Mahan had already warned that "internal troubles were imminent" in Hawaii and that "no foreign influence" must be allowed to intervene.[33]

When the Hawaiian revolution broke out in January 1893, Mahan hastened to publish an article titled "Hawaii and Our Future Sea Power," arguing the case for its prompt annexation. On 16–17 January a small minority of American residents in Honolulu seized control of the islands from Hawaii's Queen

Liliuokalani with the aid of armed sailors and marines from the USS *Boston* and the encouragement of John L. Stevens, the expansionist American minister. A provisional government immediately sought annexation to the United States. Such a prospect strongly appealed to Mahan. The Hawaiian Islands, only two thousand miles from the American West Coast, were the key to the control of the Pacific, vitally important for strategic and geopolitical reasons. They would also provide stepping-stones for further expansion in the Pacific and a way station en route to the coveted China market. All in all, their possession would offer the United States commercial and maritime control over the Pacific.[34] In an article he published shortly thereafter, Mahan paid homage to American imperialism in social Darwinist terms: "The issue of annexation cannot be dodged. . . . If we do not advance we recede." Such a notion called for a navy sufficiently large to assert American "preponderance" in its "sphere of influence," by which he meant the eastern Pacific as well as the Caribbean and the approaches to the Isthmus.[35]

Signs of American expansion in the Pacific naturally alarmed the Japanese government. Tokyo was sensitive to the rights of its nationals in Hawaii, who constituted roughly 40 percent of its population and ten times the population of whites. The government decided to dispatch its newest and most powerful battle cruiser, *Naniwa*, commanded by Captain Tōgō Heihachirō, to Honolulu as a demonstration to protect the rights of Japanese residents. But this naval action backfired, only provoking American annexationists. However, in the end President Grover Cleveland, an anti-imperialist, repudiated the treaty of Hawaiian annexation. Nevertheless it was portentous that the first clash between American and Japanese expansionism occurred over Hawaii.

Mahan's advocacy of the annexation of Hawaii did much to arouse the American public and congressional opinion.[36] "Hawaii and Our Future Sea Power" raised for the first time the specter of yellow peril. Curiously, this time it was directed against the Chinese before it was targeted against the Japanese. In 1893 Mahan feared that "the vast mass of China" was overrunning the Hawaiian Islands. What Mahan dreaded was "invasion" of Hawaii and the West Coast by the "teeming multitudes" of Asians. "It is a question for the whole world and not for the United States only," Mahan wrote, whether Hawaii would in the future remain "an outpost of European Civilization, or of the comparative barbarism of China." The United States, as "a great, civilized, maritime power," must "take a firm hold of the Sandwich Island." He added that "the United States by her position must be one of the frontiers from which, as from a base of operations, the Sea Power of the civilized world will energize." This called for "a great expansion of our naval power."[37]

When the second crisis over Hawaii erupted in 1897, the focus on Mahan's yellow peril had shifted to Japan. By then, Japan stood second only to Britain as a Pacific naval power, and two Japanese battleships on order from Britain would outclass every ship in the American fleet. The emergence of Japan posed a new threat to American (white) supremacy in the Hawaiian Islands. Flushed by its recent victory in the Sino-Japanese War of 1894–95, Japan had been expanding in the Pacific by promoting immigration to Hawaii. The attempt by the Hawaiian government, dominated by the whites, to prohibit further Japanese immigration and to restrict the treaty rights of Japanese residents brought about the second Japanese-American crisis. The Japanese government made shrill protests in defense of the right of its nationals, claiming that maintenance of the status quo in the Pacific was essential to the preservation of friendly Japanese-American relations. The Tokyo government again dispatched the battle cruiser *Naniwa* to Honolulu with a special commissioner. The conduct of the Japanese on *Naniwa* was exemplary, but American naval officers and annexationists hinted darkly of possible foreign intervention in the islands. There was no doubt, however, that the second dispatch of the *Naniwa* unwittingly provided Mahan and his fellow expansionists with further ammunition to push for Hawaiian annexation.

A genuine war scare was in the making. Mahan warned Roosevelt, now Assistant Secretary of the Navy, of a "danger of trouble with her [Japan] toward Hawaii, I think beyond doubt." Roosevelt sent to the Naval War College the "Special Confidential Problem," stated as follows:

1. Japan makes demands on Hawaiian Islands.

2. This country intervenes.

3. What force will be required to uphold intervention, and how shall it be employed?

At Roosevelt's request, the Naval War College prepared the first strategic plan for operations against Japan. The navy's objective was to destroy the Japanese fleet, presumably in the vicinity of the Philippines. President William McKinley stood ready to go to war.[38] On 1 May 1897 an alarmed Mahan wrote Roosevelt a "personal and private" letter: "Of course Japan is a small and poor state, as compared to ourselves; but the question is are we going to allow her to dominate the future of those most important islands because of our lethargy. It may very well happen, if we shut our eyes. . . . Take [Hawaii] first and solve [political questions] afterwards."[39]

Roosevelt replied that he absolutely agreed with Mahan: "If I had my way, we would annex those islands tomorrow." He added that with respect to Hawaii, he was "fully alive to the danger from Japan." He subsequently wrote Mahan, "I agree with all you say as to what will be the result if we fail to take Hawaii. It will show that we either have lost, or else wholly lack, the masterful instinct which alone can make a race great."[40] Mahan later restated the case for annexation of Hawaii to counter "military danger" from Japan: "Hawaii is now exposed to pass under foreign domination—notably Japan—by a peaceful process of overrunning and assimilation. This will inevitably involve its possession by a foreign power—a grave military danger to us—against which preoccupation by the United States is, in my judgment, the only security."[41]

Mahan was called before the Senate Committee on Foreign Relations "to prove that the possession of Hawaii was essential for the defense of the Pacific coast." Senator Henry Cabot Lodge included lengthy excerpts from "Hawaii and Our Future Sea Power" in the committee's record. Citing Mahan, the committee stated, "The present Hawaiian-Japanese controversy is the preliminary skirmish in the great coming struggle between the civilization and the awakening forces of the East and the civilization of the West. The issue is whether, in that inevitable struggle, Asia or America shall have the vantage ground of the control of the naval 'Key of the Pacific.'"[42] The idea of struggle between Western and Eastern civilizations definitely bore Mahan's stamp; he had been urging that the United States, as the champion of Western civilization, annex Hawaii to forestall its possession by Japan.

Mahan now saw the Pacific Ocean as the arena of America's naval and national destiny. Since the Sino-Japanese War, Mahan had been sensitive to the steady growth of Japan's naval power. Convinced that the main threat to the United States lay in the Pacific, Mahan wrote Roosevelt about "the need of strengthening our Pacific squadron." He added, "In building war ships, build on the Pacific side. . . . Also your best Admiral needs to be in the Pacific, for much more initiative *may* be thrown on him than *can* be on the Atlantic man." Departing from the traditional naval concentration in the Atlantic, Mahan seemed to be prematurely advocating a Pacific-first strategy. In fact, he confided to Roosevelt in May 1897, "In my opinion we have much more likelihood of trouble on that side [the Pacific] than in the Atlantic. . . . In Asia, not in Europe, is now the greatest danger to our proximate interests." He repeated that there was "a very real present danger of war" with Japan. Not coincidentally, in June 1897 the first thoughts on the possibility of war with Japan appeared in a study prepared at the Naval War College. Occasioned by the Hawaiian crisis and the visit of the *Naniwa* to Honolulu, this study was a precursor of the famous War Plan Orange ("Orange" being a code name for Japan).[43]

In 1897 William McKinley, whose platform was akin to Mahanian expansionism, was elected president of the United States. That same year, Mahan retired from the navy, but he maintained a liaison with the Naval War College, attended conferences, and offered strategic advice. Now released from restrictions incumbent upon an active naval officer, he could write more freely on a wide range of subjects, assuming the pontifical role of a leading publicist and propagandist.

MAHAN THE IMPERIALIST

"A Twentieth Century Outlook," appearing in September 1897, marked this departure. From a viewpoint of world history that was at once broader and more pessimistic, Mahan tried to predict the shape of the coming century in terms of a collision between Western and Asian countries. In view of "a rapid closing together of the vastly different civilizations," he said that the central question of the twentieth century was "whether the Eastern or Western civilization is to dominate throughout the earth and to control the future." To prepare for such a showdown, he urged the United States to act as a protector of Western civilization—by acquiring outposts in Hawaii and the Caribbean, building an Isthmian canal, and expanding U.S. naval power. Pervading his article was a brand of fatalism that reflected the fin de siècle mood prevalent among East Coast intelligentsia. Previously Mahan had subscribed to the dynamic, vigorous, and optimistic version of Manifest Destiny, which preached spreading a "superior" Anglo-Saxon civilization to backward areas of the world. Now he believed that the mission of the United States was to defend Western civilization from hordes of Asiatic invaders. Given such a Weltanschauung, it seemed obvious that America's external relations would revolve around the Pacific Ocean. "It is in the Pacific, where the westward course of empire again meets the East, that their relations to the future of the world become most apparent."[44]

Mahan noted in particular "the astonishing development" of Japan. "The appearance of Japan as a strong ambitious state, resting on solid political and military foundations, has fairly startled the world." Mahan applauded Japan's "quick acceptance" of the material civilization of the West but pointed to "the diverse evolution of racial characteristics radically different" from those in the West. What was required, then, was to bring about the "*conversion* of Eastern civilizations," by which he meant the penetration of Asia with the spiritual and religious civilization of the West.[45] Only such a "conversion" could prevent invasion of the West by hordes of Asiatic barbarians.

In the aftermath of the Spanish-American War in 1898, the United States acquired the Philippines and Guam. The United States was now in a strategic position to expand its oceanic frontier to the western Pacific and assert itself in East Asian international politics. Although Mahan was a leading expansionist of the day, he later confessed that when the Spanish-American War erupted, "the Philippines, with all they mean, had not risen above my mental horizon." Mahan's imperialistic vision went no farther than Hawaii. He wrote, "I looked with anxious speculation toward the Chinese hive; but I never dreamed that in my day I should see the U.S. planted at the doors of China." Although he had vigorously called for the annexation of Hawaii, which had been attained during the Spanish-American War, his feeling as to the Philippines was "much more doubtful." At first he was skeptical about even the annexation of Luzon, but he would take only Luzon as a "wise compromise," leaving the rest of the Philippines to Spanish hands.[46] He was realistic enough to fear that if the United States annexed the entire archipelago, defending it from Japan would be impossible. The Philippines, which could not be defended by the Pearl Harbor–based squadron, would become a diplomatic pawn, a hostage, or an "Achilles heel" (in Theodore Roosevelt's later words) in the power game with Japan.

Mahan had finally come around to accepting annexation of the entire Philippines because he subordinated realistic strategic considerations to the ideology of Manifest Destiny. He wrote, "Our nation will be forced to feel that we cannot abandon to any other the task of maintaining order in the island in which we have been led to interpose. 'Chance' said Frederick the Great. 'Deus vult' [God wills it] say I. It was the cry of the Crusaders and the Puritan, and I doubt if man ever utters a nobler [word]."[47]

On another occasion he spoke of the Philippines as a "task" or "charge" to which God has "led" the United States. It was out of the question, he declared, to give independence to these backward people who were not fit for self-government. For Mahan the direct occasion for annexation of the entire archipelago was "the refractoriness of the insurgents themselves." An escalating jungle war with local guerrillas fighting for independence, led by the Philippine leader Emilio Aguinaldo, had become totally unmanageable. Thus began America's first involvement in an Asian war that a later generation would call a "war of national liberation."[48]

Once he had reconciled himself to the annexation of the entire Philippines, Mahan saw a magnificent vista of possibilities. In a memorandum to Secretary of the Navy John D. Long, he wrote that Manila was "very centrally situated" as a base of operations in the Asia-Pacific regions, "which owing to unsettled political conditions, and our having great political and commercial interests in them, are liable to become scenes of war." The Philippines thus assumed "miraculous importance" strategically, commercially, and politically in defending American interests in China.[49]

At the same time, Mahan noted with satisfaction the remarkable improvement of relations with Japan. Less than four years earlier Japanese leaders had warned the United States that they could not remain indifferent to any annexation of Hawaii, but now they had come round to welcoming American possession of the Philippines. The Japanese government, increasingly concerned about the "slicing" of China by the major powers, wanted to cooperate with the United States to prevent that from happening and to see the Philippines in the hands of the United States, rather than any other power.

THE PROBLEM OF ASIA AND THE OPEN DOOR

For Mahan, as noted, the greatest source of "anxieties" lay in East Asia. He was alarmed at "the collapse of the organization in all its branches [in China] during the late war with Japan." Faced with these developments in 1899–1900, he concluded that the United States must play a leading role in Chinese affairs. "The future of China is the most interesting commercial question of the Pacific to us at the present moment," he wrote. *The Problem of Asia and Effects upon International Policies*, published in 1900, was a running commentary on current events: Russian-American rivalry in China, John Hay's Open Door notes of 1899–1900, the Boxer Rebellion of 1900, and the siege and relief of foreign legations in Peking.[50]

Mahan's conceptual framework was a geopolitical notion, a perspective he had developed four years before Sir Halford Mackinder, famous English geopolitician, had done likewise. According to Mahan, the sea power that had dominated world politics since 1500 was now being replaced by a massive land power, the Russian Empire, whose "aggressive advance moves over the inert Asiatics like a steam-roller."[51] To contain Russia, Mahan now emphasized "the solidarity of interests" among the four "maritime states"—the United States, Great Britain, Germany, and Japan. He explained to Vice President Roosevelt that these commercial powers should regard the teeming Yangtze Valley as their common base from which to protect themselves against Russian expansion. Mahan, who had been alarmed by the Japanese peril in Hawaii, was now willing to include Japan

in the common front against Russia. Jointly with Japan he would support the
Open Door in China as a means of preventing its control by Russia. Such a
vision of a de facto American-British-Japanese entente against Russia became
so appealing to the U.S. Navy that its war planners now viewed the Japanese
navy as a worthy potential ally.[52]

Second, Mahan reinforced his geopolitical notion with racial, or more accurately racist, theories. He saw the problem of Asia in terms of a three-cornered
conflict among the Asiatic, Slavic, and Teutonic races. He painted an alarmist picture of "such a vast mass as four hundred million Chinese equipped with modern appliances, and cooped within a territory already narrow for it." For Western
civilization, Mahan warned, there would soon be "a day of visitation."[53]

On the other hand, although Mahan admired a "progressive" Japan, his views
of Japan were ambivalent. Shelving for the moment his yellow peril notion, he
praised Japan for having accepted not only the "material improvements" of
Western civilization but also its "ideals, intellectual and moral." In this respect,
Mahan seemed almost willing to regard the Japanese as a Teutonic race, perhaps as an "honorary Aryan" (as Hitler would call his Axis partners during
World War II). Mahan wrote, "In their immediate interests, the Teutonic group
and Japan are at one." Mahan even credited Japan for having participated in
"the spirit of the institutions of Christendom." In this "conversion" Japan was
"repeating the experience of our Teutonic ancestors, as they came into contact
with the ancient Roman policy and the Christian Church."

This is not to say that Mahan held no reservation about Japan's
Westernization. He reminded his readers that Japan still suffered from intellectual and moral indigestion in partaking of Western civilization. And Mahan
never entirely shed his fear of an eventual racial conflict with Japan.
"Differences of race characteristics, original and acquired, entail divergence of
ideal and of action, with consequent liability to misunderstanding, or even collision." Yet in *The Problem of Asia* he minimized his anti-Japanese racism. He
rhapsodized, "Japan has established and maintained its place as a fully
equipped member of the commonwealth of states, under recognized international law." In other words, Japan was a peaceful "partner" of the family of
advanced Western nations. Mahan earnestly hoped Japan would "pass" on to
China the "example" of its successful Westernization. In short, Japan was to
become the champion of Western civilization to the rest of Asia.[54]

Mahan assured his readers that the United States would not have to worry
much about Japan as an enemy. The limit of its territorial size and population
as well as its insular location precluded "distant enterprises," and its ambitions

of territorial acquisition on the Asian continent would be limited. Such a bland view of Japan soon evaporated and gave way to Mahan's habitual suspicion of that nation.

MAHAN AND THE JAPANESE IMMIGRATION CRISIS

When in 1903 the General Board of the U.S. Navy, its highest advisory body responsible for advising the secretary of the navy on naval policy, asked Mahan's views about fleet distribution, he surprised many admirals by recommending fleet concentration on the Pacific coast, not on the Atlantic, as had been the practice. Mahan based this advice on political rather than strategic considerations. A threat from Europe was unlikely, whereas the Far Eastern situation was highly volatile; therefore "taking the offensive" in the Pacific might become necessary. He advised the General Board, "To remove our fleet—battle fleet—from the Pacific would be a declaration of policy and a confession of weakness. It would mean a reversion of a policy narrowly American, and essentially defensive, which is militarily vicious. . . . The Pacific and Eastern [sic] is the great coming question, as long as we can easily foresee."[55]

However prescient Mahan's vision of a transpacific threat may have been, the navy's leaders, wedded to an Atlantic-first strategy and considering Germany the hypothetical enemy number one, rejected Mahan's advice and kept the fleet concentrated on the Atlantic Coast.

The outbreak of the Russo-Japanese War on 8 February 1904 caught Mahan totally by surprise. Regarding Russia as a menace in Manchuria, Mahan cheered for the underdog, Japan. He saw a "brilliant success" in Japan's surprise attack on the Russian fleet at Port Arthur. The Japanese navy, he was pleased to note, had incorporated his doctrines, especially that of tactical concentration. And he had befriended a core of Japanese officers at Annapolis, including Admiral Uriu Sotokichi. Mahan also counted among his disciples Commander Akiyama Saneyuki, a brilliant staff officer in Tōgō's Combined Fleet, who had visited him and sought his personal advice in New York in 1897.[56]

Mahan dashed off a couple of articles ("Some Reflections" and "Retrospect") on the naval battles of the Russo-Japanese War. He expressed pleasure that his strategic doctrines were vindicated by the Battle of the Sea of Japan. The primary lesson to be learned from Tsushima, Mahan wrote in 1906, was never to divide the battle fleet: the Russian navy had made the fatal mistake of dispersing its battleship strength among the Pacific fleet (based in Port Arthur and Vladivostok), the Black Sea fleet, and the Baltic fleet, which had steamed all the way from Europe. Emphasizing his doctrine of concentration, he asked readers "to substitute therein, in their apprehension, Atlantic for Baltic, and Pacific for Port Arthur." Later, in his *Naval Strategy* (1911), Mahan devoted two chapters to praising the Japanese navy for having adhered to his dicta that the sole purpose of the navy was to have command of the sea and that the aim of a navy was annihilation of the enemy navy. "[Contrary to the Russians] Japan appears fully to have grasped, and to have acted upon, the principle that the one object of a navy is to control the sea; the direct corollary from which [is] that its objective is the enemy's navy—his organized force afloat."[57]

Japan's victory at Tsushima ended the bogey of czarist Russia overrunning China, and replaced it with the fear of Japan's newly enhanced naval power. This fear, when combined with hysterical alarms over Japanese immigration on the Pacific Coast, escalated into a major nightmare. Mahan's "great coming question" in the Pacific was sparked in 1906, when the San Francisco school board decided to segregate Japanese pupils into a separate school. The Tokyo government vigorously protested that this instance of racial discrimination was a violation of the equal treatment clause of the 1894 Japanese-American treaty. This triggered a war scare. On 14 June 1907 President Roosevelt asked Admiral George Dewey to devise a strategy in case war broke out with Japan over the immigration question. Responding to the Japanese-American crisis, Mahan revived the yellow peril notion he had held during the Hawaiian crisis. He was in all seriousness concerned about the "Japanizing" of America, or at least the western part of it. He sounded almost as shrill as anti-Japanese agitator on the West Coast when he wrote, "Open the doors to immigration, & all west of the Rocky Mountains would become Japanese or Asiatic. It is not a question of superior or inferior race; but of races wholly different in physical get-up, and in traditions wholly separate during all time, up to a half-century ago."[58]

The image of Japan as a probable enemy began to congeal in War Plan Orange, first drafted in 1906. War with Japan had become for the first time a real possibility, and the weakness on the Pacific Coast due to the fleet's Atlantic concentration became intolerable to Mahan. The problem of strategic fleet movement had become a genuine conundrum.[59] In July 1907, when the Japanese immigration crisis reached a boiling point, President Roosevelt announced the audacious plan to send the entire American battleship fleet, composed of sixteen battleships, on a cruise around the world. Although Roosevelt's avowed purpose was "pacific" and was primarily meant to be a "practice cruise," it was also intended as a demonstration of naval power in the Pacific, which had been enlarged under his administration. Roosevelt believed that the fleet movement was "absolutely necessary for us to try in time of peace to see just what we can do in the way of putting a big battle fleet in the Pacific."[60] In his public writings Mahan wholeheartedly supported the cruise of the "Great White Fleet" (so called because the ships were painted white).[61]

To the Japanese it looked like an intentionally visible show of Roosevelt's "big stick." The Japanese naval attaché in Washington, Commander Taniguchi Naomi, warned that "the cruise [of the Great White Fleet] was aimed at not only enhancement of military efficiency in time of war but also implicitly at intimidating Japan." He sent a worried report about the war scare to Chief of the Naval General Staff Tōgō Heihachirō. Taniguchi wrote, "Among those military men who openly discuss a Japanese-American war in journals is Admiral Mahan; I have reason to believe that he and other naval officers secretly regard our Empire as an enemy."[62] Mahan, whom the Japanese Naval Staff College had once considered inviting as a visiting professor, was now regarded as a spearhead of the Japanese-American war scare.

In his article titled "The True Significance of the Pacific Cruise" (December 1907), Mahan denied that the cruise of the Great White Fleet was an act of hostile demonstration toward Japan, but he, like Roosevelt, linked sea power in the Pacific to the problem of Japanese immigration. While denying that either the United States or Japan wanted to fight, Mahan wrote to an English friend that the conflict over the Japanese immigration question was unsolvable because "there is raw human nature, irrepressible". "So long as you and we have big navies, and Japan is in a financial hole, the Jap will do his best to keep his people in order; but weaken our navy, and fill the Jap treasury, and it will no longer [be] worth while for them to be unpopular with their own people. When the people of two nations are antagonistic, because of clashing interests, the peace can only be kept by force."[63] Pending the completion of an Isthmian canal, Mahan felt it was especially urgent for the United States to demonstrate to Japan its ability to move an undivided battle fleet over immense distances from the Atlantic to the Far East quickly and efficiently.

As stated, Commander Taniguchi had warned the naval authorities in Tokyo that the transpacific cruise of the sixteen American battleships was intended as an act of "intimidation." Eager to dispel war clouds over the Pacific, the Tokyo government, in a moment of inspiration, decided to invite the Great White Fleet to visit Japan, where the officers and crew would be lavishly entertained. Navy Vice Minister Katō Tomosaburō was appointed chairman of the committee to welcome the fleet, in which capacity he did his best to turn an American "provocation" into an occasion for jovial exchange. This dramatically dissipated the war clouds and seemed to bring back friendly relations. But in Japanese naval circles many, like Ōsumi Mineo (a future navy minister with a hard-line outlook of the United States), continued to feel rancor against the Great White Fleet as an act of intimidation.[64] It is also significant that shortly after the Great White Fleet left Japan, the Japanese navy conducted the first large-scale exercise south of Kyushu that was aimed against the hypothetical enemy, the United States.

In Mahan's mind the "threat" presented by the Japanese navy and the "danger" posed by Japanese immigration were inseparably intertwined. In 1910 he wrote, "The Pacific coast intrinsically is more exposed, in greater danger from an enemy, than either of the others. There is also much more imminent danger of hostilities in that sea than in the Atlantic, because of the doubtful issue of the Open Door, and the inflammable prejudice of our Pacific population towards the Japanese resident."[65] This perception of twin dangers from Japan persisted in the supposition of War Plan Orange.

In 1913 the second immigration crisis arose over the California alien land law that denied the Japanese the right to own land. Mahan's position had been that "free Asiatic immigration to the Pacific coast" would mean "Asiatic occupation—Asia colonized in America." In June 1913 Mahan wrote a lengthy letter to the editor of the London *Times*. Obviously a racist, Mahan asserted that "the Japanese racial characteristics" could not be changed by the Westernization of Japan in two generations, and for this reason Japanese immigrants remained unassimilable. "The virile qualities of the Japanese will still more successfully withstand assimilation."

On the other hand, he fondly recalled his youthful visit to Japan on board the *Iroquois*, during which he saw much of the old Japan then on the point of vanishing. He loved the "charming geniality and courtesy of her people." During the subsequent forty years, he had followed Japan's modernization with "admiration." The question, he emphasized, was not a matter of superiority or inferiority. Rather, he believed the problem was one of "physical set-up" that prevented assimilation. The presence of a racial group in the United States that was unassimilable remained a source of trouble with Japan. Mahan wrote, "Should these words fall under the eyes of any Japanese, I trust he will accept these sincere assurances, and will himself sympathize, as far as may be, with the difficulties of the United States in the particular instance."[66]

Japanese readers, however, reacted violently. Tokutomi Sohō, the leading spokesman of the nationalist camp, responded, "Admiral Mahan says that

Japanese must be excluded because they cannot assimilate. It all boils down to this: The only sin the Japanese have ever committed is that of being Japanese. If this is the case, we must break down the white domination [of the world]." The learned politician Kodera Kenkichi translated Mahan's *Times* letter and presented his criticisms. Mahan's stark racism further alienated the Japanese from the United States.[67]

The immigration crisis of 1913 caused a war scare in American naval circles. As usual the navy indulged in saber rattling. Rear Admiral Bradley Fiske, Chief of Naval Operations, warned that since the United States was containing Japan in both Asia and the Pacific, a further blow to its "racial pride" would result in a Japanese attack on America. Japan would find in the California land law a perfect casus belli for seizing the Philippines and Hawaii. The General Board advised the new assistant secretary of the navy, Franklin D. Roosevelt, to take measures "in preparation for possible war." However, President Woodrow Wilson squelched the navy's provocative move and the war scare soon petered out.[68]

MAHAN AND THE PACIFIC STRATEGY

As noted, at the height of the California crisis of 1906, the United States hurriedly drew up War Plan Orange, directed against Japan. On its part, Japan formulated in 1907 the Imperial National Defense Policy, sanctioned by the high command, in which the navy designated the United States as its hypothetical enemy. There was, however, a certain asymmetry between the outlooks of the two navies. Mahan and Theodore Roosevelt believed that the immigration issue, combined with the lack of American naval preparedness, would someday trigger a Japanese-American war. In fact, Japanese exclusion was one of the three policies—the others being the Monroe Doctrine and the Open Door—for which the naval planners assumed the United States would fight Japan.[69] However, at no time did Tokyo seriously consider war over the immigration question. It was merely a matter of "face," not a vital interest. The Japanese navy's primary concern was to maintain a semblance of naval balance with the United States that would allow supremacy in the western Pacific as well as prevent the United States from forceful intervention in China. But the immigration question undeniably antagonized the Japanese navy and colored its threat perception regarding the United States.

On matters of strategy, the Naval War College and the General Board continued to ask Mahan to comment on their war plans, especially War Plan Orange.

He insisted on a navy strong enough to protect the Open Door and the Monroe Doctrine and to exclude Japanese immigrants. In September 1910 Mahan advised, "To cover the Pacific coast against a landing, and at the same time protect our other interests in the Pacific—the Open Door, the Philippines, Hawaii—Pearl Harbor should receive the development now contemplated, and Guam should be constituted a kind of Gibraltar. . . . No situation in our possession equals Guam [for] protect[ing] every interest in the Pacific." Such a buildup would some day enable the American fleet to defend the Philippines and deter a Japanese intrusion into the eastern Pacific.[70]

In February and March 1911 Admiral Raymond P. Rodgers, President of the Naval War College, asked Mahan to comment on War Plan Orange of that year. The plan assumed that Japan would overrun the Pacific, conquering the Philippines and probably Guam, Samoa, and even Hawaii. The strategy Rodgers favored was to advance through the central route; to recapture Hawaii and advance through the central Pacific to seize the Marshalls and the Carolines (in those days German territory); to recapture Manila; and to control Japan's home waters (Okinawa and Formosa) and strangle Japan by blockade. The plan envisioned that the U.S. Navy would seek in East Asian waters a decisive fleet action against the outnumbered Japanese navy. (The plan, in its acceptance of the initial loss of the Philippines and its scenario of the island-hopping campaign, was prophetic of the naval campaign of the Pacific War.)[71]

In his detailed response, Mahan rejected this central approach to the Philippines. Instead, the demigod of sea power supported a "northern route": he would move the main force to Kiska in the Aleutians and from there strike Guam, and then use Guam as a base for a direct attack on the Ryukyu islands and a blockade of Japan's home islands. In Mahan's mind, Guam was the key to the Pacific campaign. Underlying this strategy was his conviction that "blows must be straight, rapid, and decisive." Although Mahan left the fact unstated, the northern route had the advantage of being short, an important factor given Mahan's passion for a short war. He was certain that the American public would not tolerate a war of one or two years' duration.[72]

His advice was brilliant.[73] However, the Naval War College rejected his plan, reprimanding its mentor. His northern route was deemed too dangerous and too uncertain from the viewpoints of climate, logistics, and navigation. The central approach was said to be safer. In his second reply to Rodgers and the Naval War College, Mahan wrote, "I do not believe it practicable for Orange to occupy all possible bases [in the Pacific]." Although Mahan's particular critique was rejected, his broad strategic outlook was in accord with the basic concept of

War Plan Orange, which would dominate American naval strategy over the next thirty years. The scenario of the 1911 plan—annihilating Japan's fleet in a main fleet engagement, securing command of the sea in the western Pacific by a concentrated U.S. fleet, and blockading Japan's homeland to force its defeat— may be considered an application of Mahanian doctrines to the Pacific.

Mahan repeated his conviction that America's next war would be with Japan. Because of a possible clash with Japan over the Open Door in China, the "inflammable" issue of Japanese immigration, and the exposed position of Hawaii and the Philippines, he warned Secretary of the Navy George von L. Meyer and the members of the General Board that "invasion of the Pacific coast is a possibility." In order to protect the Open Door from violation by Japan, he urged the United States to reinforce its advance bases and maintain a powerful navy in the Pacific. Interestingly, Mahan warned about Japan's surprise attack, "Orange will not make formal proclamation before striking."[74]

By this time Mahan had grasped the global balance of power as a mechanism that underwrote American security. In an essay published in 1910, he explained that the Open Door in China rested on the balance of power in Asia and the Pacific, which—through the Anglo-Japanese Alliance—rested on the balance of power in Europe. In the likelihood of a European war, British and German naval power in the Pacific would be called back to Europe at once, leaving Japan and the United States directly confronting each other across the Pacific. To maintain a commercial Open Door, the two powers would have to create a new regional balance of power. Faced with the new reality of sea power, Mahan retreated from the position he had taken ten years earlier in *The Problem of Asia*. The United States should no longer seek "supremacy" in the Pacific, but secure only its possessions in the Pacific and its approaches to them. He suggested a new balance of naval power in which the United States would dominate the eastern Pacific (Hawaii) and Japan the western Pacific. And he repeated that "the Pacific rather than the Atlantic [should] be the station for the United States battle fleet."[75]

After 1913 it was the younger Roosevelt, Franklin Delano, newly appointed assistant secretary of the navy, who turned to Mahan for advice on naval matters. He had been an avid reader of Mahan ever since Christmas 1897, when on his fifteenth birthday he received from Theodore a gift-wrapped copy of *The Influence of Sea Power upon History*. On his next birthday he received Mahan's *Interest of America in Sea Power*. The historian William Neumann writes that Mahan understood that "he had an apt pupil in the younger Roosevelt." Soon Franklin was citing the books in a debate at Groton.[76]

The Mahan-Roosevelt correspondence in 1914 on the eve of World War I focused on the danger of war with Japan. On 26 June Mahan wrote, "Personally, I feel that our danger in the Pacific much exceeds that in the Atlantic. [Japan] feels as an insult what we regard as essential to national security in forestalling and avoiding a race [immigration] problem." Because of this danger from Japan, Mahan emphasized the utmost importance of building up military installations on the Pacific Coast for maintaining and repairing the American fleet.[77]

Mahan worried that eruption of a European war would have immediate repercussions on the Pacific, causing a dangerous turn in relations with Japan. On 15 August, when Japan presented an ultimatum to Germany, he again wrote Franklin Roosevelt, expressing concern that once war broke out, Japan might seize the German insular possessions in the central Pacific north of the equator, including the Marianas. Some of these islands flanked America's route to the Philippines and Guam. Mahan wrote, "Japan, going to war with Germany, will be at liberty to take the German Islands, Pelew, Marianna, Caroline, and Samoa." It was one thing to have them in the hands of a power whose main strength was in Europe, and quite another to have them passed into the hands of Japan. Looking to the future peace conference, Mahan worried that these islands would become Japan's "territorial possessions." He wrote to Roosevelt to plead for a vigorous protest throughout London, warning of the "very critical" situation the United States would face if Japan permanently possessed the islands.[78] With regard to China, Mahan warned that Japan might develop "that sense of proprietorship" that "easily glides into the attempt at political control that ultimately means control by force." He thus predicted Japan's forceful presentation of the Twenty-One Demands to China in January 1915 that jeopardized China's sovereignty.

Once the European war broke out, Mahan's Anglophilia drove him into a corner. President Woodrow Wilson appealed to the American people to remain strictly neutral. Wilson blamed rampant "navalism" as one of the causes of the war. Mahan's outspoken support of Britain flew in the face of Wilson's appeal to the American people to be "impartial in thought as well as in action." President Wilson forbade naval officers, active or retired, to publicly discuss the military and political situation of the European war. Mahan's plea for exemption was denied by Secretary of the Navy Josephus Daniels. His family and close friends believed that this incident hastened Mahan's death on 1 December 1914. Others believed that Mahan was inwardly tortured by an awareness that his doctrine of sea power had intensified an Anglo-German naval rivalry that led to war. No doubt, apprehensions about Japanese-American relations also pre-occupied Mahan's mind in the months before his death.[79]

In the final analysis, Mahan was a successful—too successful—propagandist of sea power and imperialistic expansion. His influence on England and Germany has been noted, but no scholar has examined, except in passing, his influence on the Imperial Japanese Navy. American historian Richard W. Turk has written, "Nowhere was Mahan's strategic doctrine pursued in purer form than in the Imperial Japanese Navy."[80] My task in the next chapter is to examine how true such a generalization is.

CHAPTER TWO

MAHAN'S INFLUENCE ON JAPANESE SEA POWER

Nature of Influence

J apanese leaders, civil and military, were quick to note the contemporary relevance of Mahan's *Influence of Sea Power upon History*. The navy found in this book both a uniquely American doctrine (a national policy of greatness through overseas expansion) and universally applicable naval theories (strategic principles). As to the former, Japanese leaders said Mahan's works must be carefully studied for what they revealed about the direction of American national policy. In particular, *The Interest of America in Sea Power, Present and Future* (1897) was an "ideal weathervane for the secret of America's national power and its future projections abroad."[1] This may be called an "American studies" approach to Mahan.

Naval leaders saw in Mahan's works more than guidebooks to American expansionism. They were keenly aware that his works formulated universally applicable strategic doctrines. They believed they could extract "certain immutable principles." Kaneko Kentarō had this in mind when he introduced *Influence of Sea Power* to Japan. He urged readers of the Japanese translation "to study it carefully and strive so that the Japanese Empire can secure sea power in the Pacific." Concerning the universality of Mahan's strategic teachings, Fleet Admiral Tōgō Heihachirō of Tsushima fame later paid this homage: "Naval strategists of all nations are of one opinion that Admiral Mahan's works will forever occupy the highest position as a world-wide authority in the study of military science. I express my deep and cordial reverence for his far-reaching knowledge and keen judgment."[2] Moreover, as we will see later, Mahan's *Influence of Sea Power* in Japanese translation provided a weighty and sophisticated theory that Japan's navalists could use to assert their primacy in budgetary appropriations in competition with the army. The sea power doctrine provided navy leaders such as Admiral Yamamoto Gonbei with a bureaucratic rationale for planning a naval buildup.

Mahan's writings became canon in the navy, but did its officers really read them? Mahan's convoluted prose must have seemed formidable. Even Admiral Suzuki Kantarō, one of the three most illustrious naval theorists (the other two being Akiyama Saneyuki and Satō Tetsutarō, discussed shortly) who taught in the Naval Staff College in the early twentieth century, confessed that the English original of *Influence* was beyond him and that he waited for a Japanese translation. But even the Japanese version, written in florid and long-winded prose, was hardly readable. Lieutenant Commander Ogasawara Naganari found it necessary to write a simplified version, *Teikoku kaigun shiron* (On the History of the Imperial Navy), using examples from Japanese naval history. In its preface he wrote, "Mahan's book [*Influence*] is not only too technical but its argumentations too profound and erudite to be understood by our youth."[3]

Most officers absorbed Mahan's doctrines through the lectures and writings of their instructors who had come under Mahan's influence. We shall examine three of them: Ogasawara, Akiyama Saneyuki, and Satō Tetsutarō. None of them was Mahan's understudy; they each brought their own individual and national perspectives to bear on their commentaries on sea power.

While basically agreeing with Ronald Spector that Japanese officers had "inhaled deeply the heady . . . fumes" of Mahan's doctrine,[4] I must caution the reader that it is a tricky business to weigh the international "influence" of a seminal thinker like Mahan. As I pointed out in Chapter 1, the shared objectives of fleet concentration and a decisive battle forced two maritime powers to think alike, projecting a mirror image between the two navies.[5] One must be careful to separate such built-in mirror images from Mahan's personal and doctrinal influences. To be influenced by Mahan's writings was one thing; to use his sea power doctrine to enhance the navy's bureaucratic interests—fleet expansion—was quite another. Keeping in mind these caveats, let us trace Mahan's influence on the Imperial Japanese Navy.

OGASAWARA NAGANARI (1867–1958)

The first Japanese naval officer to introduce Mahan's theory of sea power was Ogasawara, an intelligence officer, the official historian of the Sino-Japanese and Russo-Japanese Wars, and later a biographer of Fleet Admiral Tōgō (1926). He was commissioned by Admiral Itō Yūkō, Chief of the Naval General Staff, to write a popular naval history in order to win public support for a policy that gave precedence to the navy in budgetary appropriations. In 1898 he published his *Teikoku kaigun shiron* (On the History of the Imperial Navy), a popular account of Japanese naval history. It was first presented to the Meiji Emperor and then published and distributed to secondary schools all over the country. In this book he stated, "From olden times the rise and fall of sea power has gone hand-in-hand with the ebb and flow of national power and prestige." Basing his account on the first chapter of Mahan's *Influence*, he argued that Japan at one time in the past had developed its sea power as the natural result of geographic position, insularity, and national character. These elements of sea power had enabled Japan to embark on overseas ventures before it ill-advisedly went into seclusion from the world in 1633. Ogasawara faithfully echoed Mahan when he argued that sea power was necessary "not only to annihilate the enemy fleet and obtain hegemony in wartime but to maintain the safety of our sea lanes, while always securing communication between colonies and the home country."[6]

According to Ogasawara, Japan's victory in the Battle of the Yalu River during the Sino-Japanese War in September 1894 dramatically demonstrated the validity of the Mahanian concept of command of the sea. However, because of Japan's maritime weakness, it was forced, in 1895, to retrocede to China the prize of the strategic Liaotung Peninsula through the Triple Intervention of Russia, France, and Germany. The goal was obvious: "to maintain sea power superior to our enemy (enemies)." As a result of the China war, Japan became a proto–maritime empire with the acquisition of Taiwan as a colony, which marked the beginning of Japan's expansion in the Pacific, especially the immigration to Hawaii that would soon alarm Mahan.

Ogasawara was appointed instructor at the Naval Staff College, and in his lectures, published in 1904 as *Nihon teikoku kaijō kenryokushi kōgi* (Lectures on the History of the Sea Power of the Japanese Empire), he stressed the importance of Mahanian sea power, which consisted of both naval power and commercial power.[7] During the Russo-Japanese War he served as an important intelligence officer and after the war served in the Naval General Staff. Having risen to the rank of vice admiral, he was placed on the reserve list in 1921. Thereafter he wrote a number of popular books serving the navalist cause. In 1930 Ogasawara joined Fleet Admiral Tōgō (he became Tōgō's secretary), Imperial Prince Fushiimi, and their entourage, particularly Admiral Katō Kanji, Chief of the Naval General Staff, in opposing the 1930 London naval treaty. He remained a rabid navalist throughout his life.

In his declining years Ogasawara actively participated in naval politics, serving as Tōgō's crony in the appointment of Prince Fushiimi as chief of the Naval General Staff and of Ōsumi Mineo as navy minister.

AKIYAMA SANEYUKI (1869–1918) AND MAHAN

Known as the father of modern Japanese naval strategy, Akiyama began his professional naval career as a disciple of Mahan. Brilliant, imaginative, and resourceful, he was not only a seminal naval theorist but also a renowned hero of the Russo-Japanese War, in which he had played a crucial role as a senior staff officer of Admiral Tōgō's Combined Fleet. His impact on Japanese strategic thought was such that every important staff officer and fleet commander who fought in the Pacific War was likely influenced by his teaching.

Akiyama graduated from the Naval Academy at the top of his class in 1890, barely ninety days after Mahan's *Influence of Sea Power* was published. In June 1897 the young Lieutenant Akiyama was chosen for a two-year tour of duty in the United States as a part of the navy's program to make its officer corps more professional. He was instructed by Navy Minister Yamamoto Gombei to devote himself to the study of Western naval strategy. Already deeply knowledgeable of Mahan's *Influence* to the point of having memorized portions of it, he naturally wished to go to Newport to study under Mahan. However, he could not enroll in the Naval War College, which had closed its doors to foreign students to protect secrecy relating to national security in areas such as war planning. The ever-resourceful Akiyama visited Mahan twice in his New York home to seek his advice on how to advance his professional training. Mahan told him that several months of course work at the Naval War College would hardly suffice; instead, he urged Akiyama to read the literature of Western naval and military history, both classical and modern, as widely as possible. Mahan gave him a list of basic works on strategy and tactics, starting with Antoine Henri Jomini's *Art of War*. He also provided an introduction to the Navy Library, then on the third floor of the Navy Department in Washington. In its spacious reading room, Akiyama immersed himself in books on military and naval history and strategy.[8]

Reporting on the progress of his work, Akiyama wrote to Captain Katō Tomosaburō (acting head of the Naval Affairs Section), "Captain Mahan says the subject of naval strategy is too profound to be grasped by mere academic studies. I agree with him that it is all important to take part in naval actions." A splendid opportunity presented itself when the Spanish-American War broke out in April 1898. Through the intercession of the Japanese legislation, Akiyama received permission to join the American forces sailing from Tampa Bay to Cuba. In Santiago he observed how Admiral William T. Sampson blocked Admiral Pascual Cervera's Spanish fleet in Santiago and destroyed it.[9] His comprehensive intelligence reports to Tokyo on this operation became legendary for their "accuracy, insight, and polished prose." Akiyama believed that his report of the Battle of Santiago would some day prove useful to the Japanese navy.[10] (Indeed, during the Russo-Japanese War, he drew on the lesson of Santiago when he drafted the plan to sink the Russian Pacific Fleet by blocking the entrance to Port Arthur Harbor.)

From February to May 1899 Akiyama was allowed to board the armored cruiser USS *New York,* the flagship of the North Atlantic Fleet, for practical experience, and traveled to the West Indies and the coast of South America. He became well acquainted with Chief of Staff French E. Chadwick, whose knowledge of naval history and diplomatic history was well known.

Upon his return to Washington, Akiyama learned that the Japanese Naval Staff College was considering hiring Mahan for three years as visiting professor of strategy. The idea apparently had originated with Captain Serata Tasuku, Section Chief of the Naval Affairs Bureau, whom Mahan had befriended while studying at Annapolis. Serata's suggestion was approved by Navy Minister Yamamoto Gombei, and instructions concerning the plan were cabled to the naval attaché in Washington. At the same time, Akiyama's friend Lieutenant Commander Yamaya Tanin, an instructor at the Naval Staff College, wrote to him, asking for a frank opinion of Mahan. Akiyama replied, "Although I do not necessarily admire all of his views, judging from his words and deeds, he appears to be a meticulous nervous [spirited] strategist who combines a philosophical brain with a logical mind. He is a spiritualist—a pretty rare bird among Americans. . . . Mahan has come a long way since he authored *The Influence of Sea Power;* he has deepened his knowledge and ideals. There is much to be learned from his recent writings."[11]

Akiyama was alluding to Mahan's influential articles that had recently been collected in his *Interest of America in Sea Power.* Akiyama continued, "Mahan entertains definite strategies and national ambitions, and I believe we must keep a watchful eye on this old man." Keeping in mind America's recent annexation of Hawaii and its decision to acquire the Philippines, Akiyama had become wary of the American ambition to advance into East Asia.[12]

Although the plan to invite Mahan never materialized, the episode shows how highly he was regarded in Japanese naval circles, and it indicates the great respect the Japanese navy had for the Naval War College at Newport. It is interesting to speculate how different the course of Japanese-American relations might have been in the unlikely event that Mahan had gone to teach at the Naval Staff College.

Akiyama returned to Japan in 1900, and following a stint as a staff officer, he was appointed to be a senior instructor of the newly established course on naval tactics and strategy at the Naval Staff College in 1902. One of the first things he did upon his appointment was to introduce advanced war gaming and tabletop map exercises, which he had observed at Newport. While studying in America, Akiyama had written Commander Yamaya describing in great detail the war games conducted at Newport in a required course. He wrote that war games "enhanced student-officers' resourcefulness, power of observation, and quick decision [making]."[13] The tabletop maneuvers, which had been refined during Mahan's presidency at Newport, used large tables, game boards, ship models, and markers to simulate real combat with the hypothetical enemy. These war games provided the Japanese navy with the same sort of organized, practical application of naval theory that informed American planners. This injected an additional element of mirror image between the two navies.[14]

As to Akiyama's lectures, according to one student, they "marked an epoch in the teaching of naval science in the Imperial Navy."[15] In his lectures on fundamental strategy, he categorically stated, "The main object of battle is attack. The main element of fighting power is offensive power. The battleship is the fighting unit that controls naval battles."[16] Akiyama's strategic thought became the basis of the Naval Battle Instructions (*Kaisen yōmurei*) of 1910, which through five revisions remained the fundamental manual for Japanese naval actions until the mid-1930s. The instructions declared, "Decisive engagement is the essence of battles. Battles must be offensive. The aim of a battle is to annihilate the enemy speedily. . . . The essential points of the battle are forestalling and concentration." Mahanian doctrines resounded throughout, especially with regard to the concentration, the importance of the offensive, the emphasis on the battleship, and the decisive fleet engagement.[17]

During the Russo-Japanese War, Commander Akiyama played a central role as a senior staff officer to Admiral Tōgō Heihachirō's Combined Fleet. Shimamura Hayato, Akiyama's immediate superior, stated, "There was not a single major operational plan of the war that was not drafted by Akiyama." When the Japanese navy concentrated its fleets and won a decisive battle in Tsushima Strait that annihilated Russia's Baltic Fleet, Mahan applauded the Japanese strategy as vindication of his principle of fleet concentration.[18]

From December 1905 to February 1908, Akiyama again taught naval strategy at the Naval Staff College. This period is known as the "golden age of the Naval Staff College." In addition to Akiyama, Captain Satō Tetsutarō lectured on naval history and Captain Suzuki Kantarō lectured on torpedo tactics. Akiyama devoted his full attention to devising a strategy against the United States, which was then emerging as the Japanese navy's hypothetical enemy.

Formulating a war plan against the United States, separated from Japan by nine thousand miles of the Pacific Ocean, so severely taxed Akiyama's resources that his colleague Satō Tetsutarō began to worry that Akiyama had become mentally deranged.[19]

As noted, Akiyama was no uncritical follower of Mahan. He fully took into account Japan's peculiar geopolitical condition and modified Mahan's teachings with ideas drawn from Japan's maritime tradition as well as his own battle experiences. He contended that Mahan's concept of command of the sea needed a clearer definition; it ignored the practical difficulties involved in securing complete control of the vast expanses of the Pacific. He also departed from Mahan's overriding emphasis on annihilation of the enemy fleet, arguing that victory could be achieved by "breaking the enemy's will to fight and forcing it to succumb rather than literally annihilating its fleet."[20] The strategy that brilliantly succeeded at Tsushima was "ambush operations" against Russia's Baltic Fleet, which had traveled all the way from Europe in 220 days. But how could an ambush strategy work against the superior American fleet, which would travel only six thousand miles from a base in Hawaii? Akiyama and his colleagues devised a prototype of "interceptive operations (*Yōgeki sakusen*)." As later formulated, interceptive operations consisted of lying in wait for the American fleet to reach Japan's home waters and then engaging in a climactic Mahanian encounter. Interceptive operations would become the centerpiece of Japanese strategy for more than three decades.

After 1909 Akiyama forsook Mahanian navalism, increasingly turning his attention to China. He said, "Enough of the navy; henceforth our tasks must be China and Greater Asia." After taking a fact-finding tour of Manchuria in 1909, he came to emphasize the special importance of Manchuria. Its diplomatic background was of the Taft administration's bold projection of "dollar diplomacy" into Manchuria to "smoke out" Japan's special interests there. Now Akiyama gravitated toward the policy of expanding Japanese influence in China. Increasingly he emphasized the prospect of conflict with the United States over the China question. At the same time, Akiyama developed a racist notion (in a way, an obverse of Mahan's racism) of a clash between the "white race" and the "colored race." It was Japan's responsibility, he said, to free the colored race in Asia from domination by the white race.[21]

When World War I broke out, Akiyama proposed an "offensive-defensive alliance" with China, directed against the United States.[22] In 1913–14 Akiyama supported Sun Yat-sen in his "revolution" against Yuan Shikai, but in the end Sun's attempt failed.[23] Akiyama's involvement in political activities in China incurred the displeasure of Navy Minister Katō Tomosaburō, who forbade further intervention in Chinese affairs.

In 1916, when the United States embarked on a plan to build a "Navy Second to None," the greatest naval expansion plan up to that time, Japanese navy men were alarmed, fearing that it was directed against Japan. But Akiyama remained confident. He said, correctly, that the American building plan was occasioned by the European war. American naval expansion was nothing new, and "forerunners like Mahan [had] been clamoring for it for decades." He dismissed the Japanese-American war scare as nonsense. On the other hand, he took seriously the "risk of coming to a clash with the United States over the China question." During his 1916 visit to America, he said in a press interview, "If a foreign power, be it the United States or any other power, should infringe on our traditional rights in East Asia and jeopardize the existence of our Empire, we will fight to the last ship to resist such an attempt."[24]

Akiyama died in 1918 at age fifty, leaving behind him a rich legacy of strategic thought. Akiyama was a unique individual: he was the only Japanese naval officer to have enjoyed extensive contact with American naval officers and naval operations, in both peacetime and wartime. He became the first Japanese naval officer to observe Western sea power in action. And the Naval Battle Instructions, which were based on his precepts, became the core of Japanese strategic thought in the mid-1930s.[25]

SATŌ TETSUTARŌ (1866–1942) AND NAVY-FIRST IDEOLOGY

Satō Tetsutarō adapted Mahan's sea power theory to Japan's geopolitical situation and strategic realities, recasting it as Japan's own doctrine of naval defense. Just as Mahan had been handpicked by Admiral Stephen B. Luce, President of the Naval War College, to become an ideologue of sea power, so was Satō chosen by Navy Minister Yamamoto Gombei to become a leading theorist and propagandist for a navy-first policy.

Traditionally, the navy was distinctly subordinate to the army in power and influence. In 1898 Yamamoto, engaged in a bureaucratic battle with Army Minister Katsura Tarō, attempted to reverse the priority of defense spending. His aim was to establish a national policy that would "make the navy the more important branch of national defense." He attempted to present to the Diet a bill intending to establish the navy's primacy, but he met with defeat.

Yamamoto's second plan to boost the navy was more successful in the long run. In May 1899 he sent Lieutenant Commander Satō Tetsutarō, then a relatively obscure officer in the Naval Affairs Bureau, to England to study naval strategy and history. After a year and a half in London, Satō traveled to the United States, where he stayed for eight months and fell under the "decisive influence" of Mahanian navalism.[26] Like Akiyama, Satō steeped himself in naval history books. He returned to Japan in October 1900 and was appointed instructor at the Naval Staff College. On Yamamoto's orders, in November 1901 Satō presented the fruits of his study abroad in a strategic manifesto titled *Teikoku kokubōron* (On Imperial National Defense). In this volume he opposed the army's continental expansion and argued the navy's case for equality with the army in budget appropriations. He emphasized that Japan must use its insular condition to become a maritime power.

On 14 January 1901, Satō had an audience with the emperor, to whom Yamamoto dedicated a copy of *Teikoku kokubōron*. Yamamoto also arranged for it to be published by Suikōsha, the influential association of naval officers. Yamamoto hoped that the book would sway the government, the Diet, and public opinion in favor of naval primacy. However, the blatantly partisan nature of Satō's navy-first arguments only provoked the army, especially its head Field Marshal Yamagata Aritomo, and caused heated controversies.

After serving as the senior staff officer of the Second Fleet during the Russo-Japanese War, Satō was promoted to captain and in 1907 was again appointed to be an instructor at the Naval Staff College, where he taught a course on the history of naval defense. One of his former students, Admiral Yamanashi Katsunoshin (himself an avid reader of Mahan), later recalled,

> Admiral Satō in his lectures frequently referred to Captain Mahan's doctrine, often quoting from his writings. Mahan may have been a great scholar, but he had no real combat experience. On the other hand, Admiral Satō was both an excellent scholar and an able staff officer and commander. This is where he differed from Captain Mahan.... He interfused his history with his actual battle experiences.[27]

On Mahan's authority Satō warned that no nation, however rich, could maintain both a first-class army and a first-class navy. Declaring the navy to be Japan's "first line of defense," he attacked the army's program of continental expansion even to the point of suggesting the withdrawal of troops from Korea and Manchuria. "History proves that since time immemorial there has been no nation that became a world power without oceanic expansion."[28]

In 1908 Satō expanded his lectures, added profuse historical examples, and spiced them with his own battle experiences to write his massive tome *Teikoku kokubō shiron* (History of Imperial Defense). Nearly nine hundred pages long and written in formidably arcane prose, the book nevertheless became a great classic. Evans and Peattie call this volume "the most extended and comprehensive essay ever formulated by [the] Japanese on the relationship of sea power to the Japanese situation."[29] Few important Japanese officers failed to come under Satō's influence, whether in person or in print.

In this tome, Satō fiercely attacked the "excessive emphasis" that the army had placed on "continental conquest" since the Russo-Japanese War. He argued that Japan must "take advantage of its geographic situation to expand its sea power." To buttress his arguments, Satō quoted extensively from Mahan on the importance of the command of the sea, fleet concentration, decisive fleet encounters, and the need to take the offensive.[30] Citing Mahan almost verbatim, he wrote, "The object of a wartime navy is, first and foremost, to break up the enemy fleet, thus securing command of the sea. For this purpose, our navy must concentrate its sea power to annihilate the enemy fleet."[31]

Although Satō stressed the importance of taking the offensive, the navy's planning for war with the United States was essentially defensive: waiting for the approach of the American fleet into the western Pacific, where Japan would seek a decisive fleet encounter. This "ambush strategy" was based on the regional advantages of the Japanese navy in East Asian waters.

At times, however, Satō was carried away by Mahan's vision of imperial navalism and wrote about global "oceanic expansion." "Now is the time for our Empire to attempt world-wide expansion, and our world-wide expansion must of necessity depend on oceanic expansion." He also wrote, "Japan must control world trade, and for this purpose it is absolutely necessary to obtain command of the sea, and this in turn necessitates the building of sea power capable of annihilating the enemy fleet."[32] These were brave words, but Japan simply did not possess the "three links" that Mahan had postulated for a great sea power: production, commerce, and colonies. Satō probably did not seriously believe that Japan was capable of global maritime expansion, but instead sensed that contending for it would provide a bureaucratic rationale for establishing the navy's primacy over the army. In reality, Satō's vision of maritime expansion was limited to East Asia and, later, Southeast Asia (especially the Dutch East Indies)— vital areas for Japan's "political, commercial, and colonial" expansion.

One interesting example of Mahan's influence on Satō was the idea of a hypothetical enemy. In "Preparedness for Naval War" (1897), Mahan wrote, "It is not the most probable of dangers, but the most formidable, that must be selected as measuring the degree of military precaution."[33] Similarly, Satō conceived of a hypothetical enemy not in terms of its *intention* or *probability* of war but in terms of its *capability*. He defined a hypothetical enemy as "any one power, whether friendly or hostile, that can confront Japan with the greatest force of arms." If he regarded the United States as Japan's "hypothetical enemy," he merely meant it to be a "standard of naval armaments."[34] This notion of a hypothetical enemy was handed down to his successors and provided a lever for contending for large naval budgets.

In *Teikoku kokubō shiron*, Satō had not yet conceived of the United States as a *probable* enemy. Referring to the crisis over the immigration question and the war scare in the United States in 1906–8, Satō wrote, "Of late the United States seems to be suffering from morbid oversensitiveness. There are signs, it is said, that the American people are looking at our country with belligerent feelings. But I wish to believe that there is no possibility of war with the United States in the near future." Although America, with its "formidable national power," posed a far greater *potential* threat to Japan than any other powers, Satō believed it unwise to "maintain a naval power on a par with such a rich nation." "*Therefore, it is absolutely necessary to continue the friendly relations with that power that exist today.*" The United States, then, was a "hypothetical enemy" only in the sense that it was a standard against which to maintain Japan's minimum force level.[35]

Satō's views on the United States took a pessimistic turn in 1912, when he wrote "Kokubō sakugi" (Plans for National Defense), a confidential memorandum for limited circulation within the Navy Ministry. He argued that Japanese-American antagonism had become a serious issue because of the immigration crisis in California and conflict of policy in China. As to the former, he observed that "the United States is actively oppressing Japan to bring us to our knees." He felt bitter about the Mahanian version of the yellow peril, which held that because Japanese immigrants could not assimilate, the two nations would sooner or later clash. Satō now saw anti-Japanese agitation in California in the context of war with the United States.[36]

Another and more recent cause of conflict with the United States was America's "dollar diplomacy," which challenged Japan's position in Manchuria. Based on the economic determinism that he read into Mahan's writings, Satō was now convinced that the United States "absolutely requires expansion of its China market" and that "it is determined to monopolize all interests in China." He cited America's role in the four-power consortium in China in 1912, warning that if the "United States freely exerts its power in the Orient, a clash of interests with Japan will become inevitable."[37]

Like Akiyama, Satō attached increasing importance to the China question, but unlike Akiyama he never forsook his navalism. The possibility of war with the United States over the Manchurian question gave Japanese navalists an additional rationale for fleet expansion. In 1913 Satō and three associates wrote "Kokubō mondai no kenkyū" (A Study of the National Defense Problem). Among other things, they contended that "the first nation that will obstruct our trade in China will be the United States, and it is our navy that can prevent it from doing so."[38]

In arguing that Japan and the United States would clash, Satō's arguments reflected neo-Mahanian determinism, which postulated an inevitable war between the two powers. Because the expansion of the Japanese empire must be sought in the Pacific Ocean, he wrote, "Japan and the United States are destined to contest for naval supremacy in the Pacific." The United States seemed "intent on monopolizing the interests in the Pacific basin, making it an American lake by means of naval and commercial expansion." For this purpose, he observed, the United States was "building up Hawaii as a base and fortifying the Philippines, and it may be that there is no way to avoid war unless we abandon our China market and our interest in the South Seas."[39] He had come a long way since 1908, when he had denied the possibility of war with the United States.

Satō is often called "the Mahan of Japan," but definite differences existed between the two. Mahan advocated expansion backed by a "preponderant navy" that would share global command of the sea with Britain. For Japan, Satō wanted "a naval force sufficient to control Far Eastern waters." Satō was aware of the great disparity in economic and military strength between the two nations. His vision, therefore, rarely went beyond naval superiority in East Asia (later, also Southeast Asia). Consequently, because Japanese and American visions for sea power and overseas expansion were fundamentally different, the applicability of the Mahan doctrines to the Japanese navy was limited.

After Japan entered World War I and suddenly accelerated its expansionist program in China, Satō publicly denounced the army's expansion and deplored that his country had become vaingloriously entranced with the idea of a continental state, forgetting the far more important task of naval defense.[40]

Unlike Mahan, Satō climbed to a high position: in August 1915 he was appointed vice chief of the Naval General Staff. But his overzealous navalism irritated Navy Minister Katō Tomosaburō. When Satō pestered Katō to speed up completion of the ambitious "eight-eight fleet" program (consisting of eight battleships and eight battle cruisers), the latter snapped back sharply, "That I can't do; you do it when you become navy minister."[41] Satō later incurred Katō's wrath by plotting to expand the authority of the Naval General Staff at the expense of the navy minister. Satō's maneuver angered Katō so much that he demoted Satō to president of the Naval Staff College.[42] Unlike some of his colleagues, Satō was not allowed to go on a fact-finding tour of Europe and the United States during and after World War I, so he missed the opportunity to observe the revolutionary changes that had been taking place in naval warfare. Satō's outlook on naval warfare remained embedded in the "lessons" of the Russo-Japanese War. At the time of the Washington Conference of 1921–22, Satō argued that Japan must not succumb to "the unreasonable demands" of the United States; rather, he said, Japan must "throw in the sponge and return home." Incensed by Satō's belligerent posture, Navy Minister Katō placed him on the reserve list in the personnel retrenchment that followed the Washington Conference.[43]

Throughout his life Satō remained a staunch lobbyist for naval budgets. In 1936, after the Washington and London treaties expired, the navy quoted from his *Teikoku kokubō shiron* (1908): "In the course of history one cannot find an instance of a nation ever having gone bankrupt and ruined as the result of excessive expenditure on naval armaments."[44] Thus Satō abetted the ensuing naval race with the United States, which placed Japan in an increasingly difficult position. (See Chapter 8.)

KATŌ KANJI (1870–1939) AND NAVALISM

After Satō Tetsutarō, the Japanese navy, instead of merely being influenced by Mahan, increasingly set out to use the Mahanian doctrine to justify the navy's interest in fleet expansion. A case in point was Katō Kanji, who succeeded Satō as president of the Naval Staff College in 1920. He seemed to have deeply absorbed Satō's "blue water" navalism. The leading opponent of naval arms limitation throughout the 1920s and the first half of the 1930s, Katō served successively as vice chief of the Naval General Staff (1922–23), commander of the Second Fleet (1923–24), commander of the Combined Fleet (1926–28), chief of the Naval General Staff (1930), and Supreme Military Councilor (1930–35). (The Supreme Military Council was composed of the highest-ranking admirals and generals, who had authority to sanction the navy's and army's decisions.) He linked his navalism to the army's continentalism in such a way as to rationalize naval expansion against the United States.

Unlike Akiyama and Satō, Katō was no disciple of Mahan. In fact, we do not know that he steeped himself in Mahan's writings, although he may have absorbed Mahan's ideas through his predecessor Satō. The navalist ideology that he developed in the 1920s and early 1930s definitely bore the stamp of economic determinism in the tradition of Mahan. The United States was an inevitable enemy, with deep-rooted economic, cultural, and military antagonism, because it had unjustly denied Japan the equality of armament it deserved, imposing an inferior status.

Let us push back history and begin at the point of first contact between Katō's navalism and Mahan's doctrine, because Katō's early experience influenced his later views of the United States. In February 1893, when Mahan was writing "Hawaii and Our Future Sea Power," the young Ensign Katō Kanji was on board the cruiser *Naniwa*, commanded by Captain Tōgō Heihachirō, which was speeding to Honolulu. Its alleged mission was to protect Japanese nationals in Hawaii. As noted, this naval demonstration backfired, provoking American naval expansionists to increase pressure for the annexation of Hawaii. Some thirty years later, Katō bitterly recollected, "There was hardly anybody in Japan at that time who talked about the value of Hawaii—the Gibraltar of the Pacific." No Japanese, even in the navy, warned that Hawaii in American hands would tip the balance of naval power enough to pose a strategic threat to Japan.

In retrospect, what smote Katō most was the thought that Japan had high-speed cruisers such as the *Naniwa* and the *Takachiho*, which were far superior to any American ships, and that "given America's weak international position at the time, it was in Japan's power to keep Hawaii at least neutral, especially if Great Britain could be won over to Japan's side."[45] (Katō was indulging in sheer hyperbole, of course, because the Japanese navy at that time was in no position to support naval actions nearly five thousand miles away.) Katō was further embittered by the American annexation of the Philippines and Guam after the Spanish-American War. In not opposing their secession, Japan repeated its mistakes and left "a greater cancer at the forefront of Japan."

As with Satō, Katō's feelings toward the United States were inflamed by the anti-Japanese agitation on the Pacific Coast. In 1907 he visited the United States on his return journey from England, at the height of the crisis triggered by the San Francisco school board incident. He was exposed not only to the jingoistic press but also to a "widespread feeling" in American naval circles, Mahan included, that Japan was the future enemy.[46]

When the second immigration crisis occurred in 1913 over California's alien land law, Katō, then Vice President of the Naval Academy, expressed his sentiments in a letter to a friend:

> Having foreseen the Californian question several years ago, our military and naval authorities have not been caught unaware. Our fully trained crack contingents are prepared at any moment to rush to any needed areas, whether for demonstration or actual combat. . . . If we are to advance, the clash of interests

must occur to the east and south of the Pacific. I believe that Japan must develop and guide China to establish a great union in which Japan will be the leader with the guiding principle of a Monroe Doctrine in the Eastern Hemisphere. The violent explosion of [anti-Japanese] Californians may force us to rally to create a union of Japan and China.[47]

The California crisis incited both naval and continental expansionism, driving Katō to confront the United States in both the Pacific and China. Significantly, for Katō, the Mahanian sea power doctrine, expansionism in China ("great Asianism"), and anti-Japanese movement in California all converged to a confrontational posture toward the United States.

Katō's experience at Tsushima and the perceived lesson of Jutland convinced him beyond any doubt that Mahan was right about his fixation on the battleship and the overriding importance of main-fleet engagement. The supreme importance he attached to command of the sea, involving contests between battle fleets, was also Mahanian.

In 1921–22 Katō attended the Washington Conference as the navy's chief adviser. As described in Chapter 5, his intransigent demand for a 70 percent fleet ratio in capital ship strength against the United States was squelched by chief delegate Katō Tomosaburō. Throughout the 1920s and the early 1930s, Katō Kanji was the most spirited opponent of the Washington naval treaty, and during this period he formulated his navalist thought in a series of speeches and memoranda. Echoing Mahan, he argued that the "rise and fall of sea power determines the destiny of nations." The "irresistible lure of the Pacific" spelled a naval showdown between Japan and the United States, in which each side would contend for its economic stake in China. Reflecting Mahan's economic determinism, Katō argued that as the leading "capitalistic-imperialistic nation," the United States was bound to find an outlet for its expansive energies where it would meet the least resistance—the Pacific Ocean. This not only caused "economic warfare over China" but would "sooner or later" plunge the two nations into war over China.[48]

Katō and his kindred spirits emphasized how "deep-rooted" was "the American advance into the undeveloped China market." Indeed, he historically traced American expansionism to Secretary of State William H. Seward, who had predicted in the mid-nineteenth century that "the Pacific Ocean would become the arena of fierce economic competition among the powers." More recently, the United States had annexed the Philippines, and Secretary of State John Hay had proclaimed the Open Door policy. Behind these historical milestones Katō detected an "American intention to open up and control the China market and its determination to achieve this goal by whatever means."

Neo-Mahanian economic determinism seemed to be particularly applicable in the 1920s, when the American economy was enjoying unprecedented prosperity. "For the Republican administration to maintain this prosperity, the United States must export its surplus products." To find an outlet for these products, the United States was rushing into China, Katō wrote. (Japanese officers believed that American commercial expansion in China would bring war. Of course, the American government ruled out war with Japan to defend the Open Door policy.) To support its China policy, the United States was building an "offensive navy" and developing operational plans to advance its fleet to Far Eastern waters. Japan's continental policy was thus gravely threatened.[49] To counter the American thrust, Japan needed to build up its naval armaments. This desire for fleet expansion to back up commercial and naval rivalry was, of course, another application of Mahanian theory. These arguments were repeated ad nauseam by Japan's navalists until the arguments became an article of faith with them, as we shall see in later chapters.

MAHANIAN STRATEGY IN TRIUMPH

The Mahanian strategy, which put a premium on the battleship fleet and on decisive engagement, continued to dominate Japanese naval thinking in the interwar period. For example, a memorandum from Navy Minister Ōsumi Mineo, prepared in connection with the 1935 London Naval Conference, stated, "Some argue that in future wars a decisive fleet engagement will never take place, but didn't Admiral Mahan, venerated by American strategists, declare that the primary aim of naval power is annihilation of the enemy fleet in a decisive encounter?"[50]

Japanese naval officers continued to peruse Mahan's works in the 1930s. The Japanese translation of Mahan's *Naval Strategy: Compared and Contrasted with the Principles of Military Operations on Land* (1911) was published in 1932 at the height of the crisis over the Manchurian Incident. The translator, Ozaki Chikara of the Naval General Staff, wrote in the preface, "The publication of this book is most timely and significant; it gives a good idea of naval strategy according to which the offensive actions of the United States navy will be conducted."[51]

Interestingly, this book was reprinted in July 1942. In the preface of the reprinted edition, Lieutenant Commander Tominaga Kengo of the Publicity Division of the Naval General Staff asserted, "If there had been no Mahan, perhaps the Greater East Asian War would never have taken place. At least there would have been no Hawaii operation." Tominaga quoted Mahan as allegedly saying, "Hawaii was the starting point of the American attempt to make the

Pacific its own lake." After the annexation of Hawaii, Tominaga wrote, "American extension of bases, so essential for command of the sea, has faithfully followed Mahan's wise counsels." Then Tominaga speculated how Mahan would have reacted to the Pearl Harbor attack had he been alive: Mahan would have been "thrown into consternation" and soliloquized, "The object of the navy is to destroy the enemy fleet. There never was and there never will be such perfect demonstration of this [as the Pearl Harbor success of Japan]."[52]

By the time Tominaga wrote that "Mahan's book is a required reading to reconfirm our understanding of the importance of command of the sea," the Japanese navy had been defeated in the Battle of Midway. Mahan's disciple President Franklin D. Roosevelt saw his mentor's strategic doctrine applied by Admiral Ernest King in his transpacific operations that would lead to victory over Japan. Military historian Russell F. Weigley wrote, "The American victory over Japan was a Mahanian triumph of sea power, that power rendered immensely more formidable through its acquisition of aerial and amphibious dimensions." The U.S. Navy fought the Pacific War essentially in accordance with Mahan's sea power doctrine, which held that it was necessary first to secure undisputed command of the sea.[53]

MAHAN AND THE MIRROR IMAGE

Mahan was primarily a propagandist, perhaps a too-successful one internationally. This view is inescapable when one sees Mahan and his legacies in the context of Japanese-American confrontation. It is possible to argue that precisely because the Japanese and American navies shared the same Mahanian strategic doctrine—fixation with the battleship and obsession with the main-fleet engagement—they pursued a collision course eventually leading to Pearl Harbor. The American navy was quite aware of Mahan's influence on the Japanese navy. For example, William H. Gardiner, president of the powerful Navy League, who had access to the inner circles of the navy's officialdom, wrote in a letter to Admiral William S. Sims, President of the Naval War College in 1920–21: "I warrant every Japanese flag officer knows [Mahan's books]. . . . Mahan is a perfect guidebook to the imperial policy of Japan and to me the wonder is that we are blind to the fact that her overseas expansion is an exquisite adaptation to her entourage of the overseas expansion of England—without England's mistakes. We talk about her Prussianized army, but of what infinitesimal danger is that to us or even to continental Asia, without her sea power, naval and mercantile?"[54]

About the same time, an American naval attaché in Japan was reporting, with some exaggeration, "Through the writings of Admiral Mahan it has become common knowledge not only to the man on the street but even the schoolboy, that to an Island Kingdom a foreign war is only possible by having command of the seas."[55] The unease in American naval circles about Japan's adoption of Mahan's doctrines presents another interesting case of a mirror image.

The United States and Britain saw a periodic recurrence of the "devil" theory of Mahan, which indicted him as an incendiary, a philosopher of death and destruction, and the mastermind behind the naval race between Britain and Germany before World War I.[56] But Mahan's influence in Japan seemed to be the most devastating.

One middle-echelon officer who carried Mahanian navalism to the extreme was Captain Nakahara Yoshimasa, nicknamed "the King of the South Seas" because of his ardor for southern expansion. On 3 September 1939, the day Britain declared war against Germany, Nakahara wrote in his diary in large letters: "The important thing now is to take this opportunity to reorient Japan as a sea power and concentrate its efforts on naval expansion." He essentially restated Satō Tetsutarō's brand of navalism when he wrote, "If our sea power is expanded, the East Asian continent will automatically be stabilized and Japan will be able to expand its interests there. However, even if continental interests are expanded, there is no way to increase production unless sea communications are secured. . . . What is sea power? It consists of the following elements: shipping and maritime transportation; protection of shipping which is the task of the navy; bases for the protection of maritime transport; resources, etc."[57]

Nakahara continued, "The history of the East and West, both ancient and modern, more than amply testifies that expansion of continental interests, not based on sea power, is ephemeral. Nay, the existence of continental interests itself depends on sea power." In September 1939 he declared that the most important thing for Japan was to take advantage of the European war to quickly expand its sea power. And he insisted that Japan "like lightning must advance to the South Seas," specifically the Philippines, Borneo, Celebes, New Guinea, and the Solomon Islands. "Today is the moment for maritime Japan to carry its flag as far as to the Bay of Bengal." To attain this objective, Japan "should not flinch from even fighting Britain and the United States." Although cautious navy leaders rejected such a drastic policy, it revealed Mahanian navalism run amok, threatening to play havoc with relations with the United States, especially after September 1940, when Japan marched into northern Indochina.

As the example of Nakahara shows, the Japanese navy's adoption of
Mahan's ideas was highly selective and arbitrary. The Japanese navy was not
only influenced by Mahan's strategic doctrine, but also used his sea power theory as a rationale for fleet expansion. Those who had originally introduced
Mahan to Japan were careful to point out these two aspects of his doctrine: it
was a uniquely American doctrine of overseas expansion and a universally applicable strategic theory. However, later generations of Japanese navalists ignored
these aspects, interpreting Mahan's writings at will and holding one-sided views
of them. Misuse and misapplication of Mahan's doctrines that ignored differences in the geopolitical positions of the two nations were of course recipes for
catastrophe. For example, Admiral Inoue Shigeyoshi, one of the few leaders of
"liberal" persuasion, wrote after the war that Japan lacked most of the elements
of great sea power (as spelled out by Mahan) that were required to wage war
with the United States, namely (1) a secure territorial position; (2) human
resources (size of population, national character, and so on); and (3) material
resources (natural resources, industrial power, and so on).[58]

As noted, Japan's prime Mahanian strategist, Satō Tetsutarō, sometimes
confused Japan's regional superiority with a global Mahanian mission. And the
navy's use of the Mahanian theory of sea power as a lever to win its budgetary
fight proved to be the undoing of the Imperial Japanese Navy. As I will explain
in later chapters, this one-sided interpretation of Mahan's doctrine by Japanese
navy men prodded them on their course to Pearl Harbor.

It has been suggested that cultural exchange causes people to become more
sensitive to each others concerns, thus reducing the danger of war between
them. In a different context, John L. Gaddis has pointed out that there is little
historical evidence to validate this thesis.[59] The influence of Mahan on the
Imperial Japanese Navy is an example that supports this point.

PART TWO

PACIFIC

RAPPROCHEMENT

CHAPTER THREE

FROM ENMITY TO DÉTENTE

Foundations of Japanese Naval Policy

T he year 1907 marked a significant turning point in the history of the Imperial Japanese Navy. In that year Japan's highest military authorities— the ministers of the army and navy and the high command—decided on the Imperial National Defense Policy (*Teikoku kokubō hōshin*), which was sanctioned by the Meiji Emperor.[1] This document was accompanied by the General Plan for Strategy (*Yōhei kōryō*) and the Naval Strength Requirement (*Kokubō shoyō heiryoku*).

From this point forward Japan's naval policy was defined by the following basic doctrines: (1) the concept of the United States as the navy's "hypothetical enemy"; (2) the need for a 70 percent fleet ratio against the U.S. Navy as a strategic imperative; and (3) its corollary, a program for building a first-line "eight-eight fleet" consisting of eight modern (dreadnought) battleships displacing 20,000 tons and eight armored cruisers (later, battle cruisers) displacing eighteen thousand tons.[2] These doctrines were, of course, interrelated.

The concept of the United States as the navy's hypothetical enemy first appeared in the National Defense Policy of 1907. (The army's hypothetical enemy was Russia.) The policy stipulated that "of all hypothetical enemies the most important from the viewpoint of naval operations is the United States." At that time, however, it amounted to little more than a "budgetary enemy," a target for building a large fleet. Recall that Satō Tetsutarō, in his treatise *Teikoku kokubō shiron* (1908), used the term "hypothetical enemy" as a "standard for armaments," a bureaucratic rationale for building appropriations. This definition of a hypothetical enemy mirrored Mahan's dictum that the standard of naval preparedness should take into account "not the most probable of dangers, but the most formidable." Similarly, Japanese naval strategists defined their "hypothetical enemy" as "any one power, whether friendly or hostile, that can confront Japan with the greatest force of arms."[3] However, the National Defense Policy did state that although friendly relations with the United States must be maintained, there was a possibility of "a violent clash some day because of geographic, economic, and racial reasons." The last reason given—the immigration crisis in California and the war scare it generated—seemed ominous. The seeds of Japanese-American antagonism had been planted. By the time the Imperial National Defense Policy came up for revisal in 1918, the prospect of a "violent clash" with the United States had come to revolve around the conflict over China policy.

The idea of a 70 percent naval ratio as Japan's minimum defense requirement against the United States had been jointly worked out around 1907 by Akiyama Saneyuki and Satō Tetsutarō, when both were instructors at the Naval Staff College. This ratio rested on the basic premise that "an approaching enemy armada would need a margin of at least 50 percent superiority over the defending fleet." If the Japanese navy had 70 percent strength against the United States, it would correspond to 143 percent for the American navy—not quite enough for launching a successful attack on Japan. If the Japanese navy had only 60 percent, the American navy's strength would amount to 166 percent, which was deemed sufficient for attacking Japan. To put it another way, with a 70 percent ratio, Japan's chance in a war with the United States would be fifty-fifty according to Akiyama and "slightly in Japan's favor" according to Satō. However, the 70 percent figure was not based on any strict mathematical calculation.[4] On the American side, distance, as Mahan said, was a factor equivalent to a number of ships.[5] The Philippines were three thousand miles from Hawaii. American naval planners used the rule of thumb that a battle fleet would lose 10 percent of its fighting efficiency as it cruised each one thousand miles from its Hawaiian base because of wear and tear, bottom fouling, the enemy's attacks en route, and declining morale of officers and men. This accounted for the operational strength of 70 percent upon arrival in the western Pacific, and it would give the American navy a "sporting chance."[6]

To the Japanese navy, the seemingly minor margin between 60 and 70 percent made the difference between victory and defeat. The notion of the 70 percent ratio—"insufficient to attack (in transpacific operations), sufficient for defense (in Japan's home waters)"—was reinforced by war games, tabletop maneuvers, and fleet exercises, and it crystallized into a firmly held consensus—even obsession—within the Japanese navy until the eve of the Pearl Harbor attack.

The Naval Strength Requirement that accompanied the National Defense Policy stipulated that Japan's naval armaments should be "sufficient to take the offensive against American forces in Far East waters [the Asiatic Fleet]."

The Battle of the Sea of Japan had established the primacy of the battleship. By 1907 the Japanese-American naval race was on. Whereas in 1901 Japan possessed twelve battleships and armored cruisers and the United States possessed a mere seven ships, by March 1907 Japan had become the inferior party with twenty-five ships compared to thirty-five ships for the United States.

With an eye to attaining 70 percent of U.S. strength, the Japanese navy drafted the "eight-eight" fleet plan, an ambitious building program consisting of eight battleships and eight armored cruisers (later, battle cruisers), all no more than eight years old, together with auxiliary ships.[7] Japanese planners believed that this level of force would deter the United States from risking war with Japan. The eight years spanning 1914–21 may be called "the age of the eight-eight fleet." This building plan became the focal point of Diet debates in which Navy Vice Minister Katō Tomosaburō brilliantly defended the government's naval expenditures. Through the navy's public relations efforts, the eight-eight plan became widely known to the Japanese people.

The General Plan for Strategy that accompanied the National Defense Policy of 1907 was still in its embryonic stage. It merely stipulated in abstract Mahanian terms that "the principal object is to take the offensive to annihilate enemy naval forces." But it gave no further provisions, except to say, "subsequent operations should be planned according to the requirements of the moment."[8] Because no record exists of the navy's operational plans, they must be reconstructed from such fragmentary sources as the naval maneuvers of November 1908 and the map exercises conducted at the Naval Staff College in 1911.

Because the navy did not have the material strength to carry the war to America's shores, it would have to fight an essentially defensive war near Japan's home waters. For the first time, in 1908, the navy conducted a large-scale exercise with the United States as its hypothetical enemy. Naval leaders assumed that the American fleet would capture the Japanese base in Amami-Oshima and head north; the Japanese navy would counter it south of Shikoku in a decisive fleet engagement. The first concrete study of a Philippine operation is found in the map maneuver conducted at the Naval Staff College in 1911. Japan would capture Luzon island in the Philippines and destroy the American base there before intercepting the U.S. fleet.[9] This exercise established the principles of "big battleships and big guns (*taikan khonōshugi*)" interceptive operations, and the decisive fleet encounter—the three principles that became fundamental strategic doctrines until the eve of the Pearl Harbor attack.

On the basis of these records we can piece together Japan's operational plan as follows. At the outset of hostilities, the Japanese navy would conduct offensive operations against the Philippines, neutralizing American naval forces there and occupying Manila. It would then lie in wait for the American battle fleet advancing westward across the Pacific to reclaim the Philippines. When the American fleet approached Japan's home waters, the navy would intercept and then annihilate it in a decisive battle west of the Bonins, just as it had destroyed Russia's Baltic Fleet in the Tsushima Strait. Japan would have the geographic advantage because of its proximity to the main theater of operations, and there would be a quick showdown. The winner of the decisive battle would obtain command of the sea and dictate peace. This strategy set a pattern for interceptive operations that governed Japan's Pacific strategy for more than three decades.

In 1906, after Japan's victory in the Russo-Japanese War, Japan emerged as the U.S. Navy's hypothetical enemy in War Plan Orange, a war plan drawn up in the midst of the Japanese-American war scare that was triggered by the immigration crisis in San Francisco. The American war scenario roughly paralleled that of Japan: it included recapture of the Philippines, destruction of the Japanese battle fleet in its home waters, and the complete commercial isolation of Japan. In 1911 Raymond P. Rodgers, President of the Naval War College, restating the Orange situation, predicted that the Japanese fleet would attempt to drive the United States from the western Pacific by overrunning the Philippines, Guam, and perhaps Hawaii. To counter Japan, the U.S. fleet would steam from the Pacific Coast and then advance along the "central route," recapturing Hawaii and Guam, and strike into the Philippine Sea. There the American fleet would engage and defeat the Japanese fleet. If Japan still refused to surrender, the American navy would isolate and strangle Japanese commerce.[10] By 1914, it seems, the American navy had worked out its operational plan in greater detail than the Japanese navy had.

By this time the Japanese navy had been provoked by the bold diplomatic initiatives the United States had taken to neutralize Manchurian railways and "smoke out" Japan from Manchuria. In 1910 Navy Minister Saitō Makoto stated in his proposal for a naval increase that Japan must be "alert to the policy of the United States that has recently shifted from the Monroe Doctrine to imperialism and intervened in the Manchurian question." He wrote that the United States was speeding up its construction of the Panama Canal, maintaining the Hawaiian base, building up the Philippines, and expanding its fleet. When these objectives were attained, he wrote, "The Empire's policy would frequently encounter formidable difficulties." In 1913 the Naval Staff College, provoked by the American intervention in Manchuria and the recurrent immigration crisis in California,

demanded a "sea power that can defy the United States." It pushed for early completion of the eight-eight fleet program, but that program was overstraining
Japan's financial capability.[11] In 1914 the opening of the Panama Canal revolu-
tionized the strategic prospect of a Japanese-American war, greatly facilitating the
transfer of American battleships from the Atlantic to the Pacific. They no longer
had to travel ten thousand miles across the globe to join the fleet on the Pacific
Coast; the distance to the Philippines was reduced by half. As Mahan once
remarked, distance was a factor equivalent to a number of ships, and the drastic
reduction of strategic distance enhanced the threat the Japanese navy perceived.[12]

MOUNTING TENSION IN THE PACIFIC

The outbreak of the European war in August 1914 proved Mahan's predic-
tions correct: the great war destroyed the multilateral balance of power in East
Asia and left Japan and the United States directly confronting each other across
the Pacific. Upon Japan's declaration of war on Germany, the Japanese navy hastened to occupy the German islands in Micronesia (the Marshalls, Carolines, and
Marianas) that flanked America's line of communications running from Hawaii
through Guam to the Philippines. For the Japanese navy this meant a sudden
expansion of its defense perimeter and a step toward realizing southward
expansion, as Satō Tetsutarō had envisioned. Katō Kanji, Captain of the *Ibuki*
and Chief of Staff in the Second Fleet, which was then operating in the South
Seas, urged the naval authorities in Tokyo that the "time has come for Japan to
conduct active southern operations with a view to expansion in the south."[13]
The Japanese occupation of the German islands would mean acquisition of
advanced posts in the mid-Pacific—a prospect that had alarmed Mahan.
Shortly after Japan presented its ultimatum to Germany, Mahan had urged
Franklin D. Roosevelt, Assistant Secretary of the Navy, to warn Britain (Japan's
ally) that Japan's seizure of the islands would cause outrage among Americans.
American naval men reacted strongly: "Too much stress cannot be laid on the
dangers of the foothold the Japanese are gaining in the South Pacific Islands,
and the possibility of their extension of operations all over the Pacific." The
navy's General Board warned that Japanese possession of these islands would be
a "perpetual menace to Guam and to any fleet operations undertaken for the
relief of the Philippines."[14] The American navy's fears never materialized, however. As it turned out, the mandated islands worked to America's advantage. At
the Paris Peace Conference, Japan, upon being awarded these islands as mandates of the League of Nations, pledged not to fortify them. Unfortified, these

islands became "hostages" of the U.S. Navy, which could use them as way stations in its transpacific campaign.[15]

Japan's second move to take advantage of the European war was to impose the Twenty-One Demands upon China in January 1915, which jeopardized China's sovereignty. The imperialistic actions of Japan in China (and later in Siberia) provoked sharp reaction in American naval circles. In June 1915 Lieutenant Commander Harry E. Yarnell wrote in his report to the Naval War College that Japan had "impressed her suzerainty upon a helpless nation of 300,000,000 souls." If successful, he warned with a touch of Mahanian racism, Japanese control would lead to "the strangulation of foreign trade [and] the final elimination of the white race from the Far East." There was an increasing awareness that a clash with Japan was likely. In February 1916 the War Plans Division stated, "Japan is generally credited with a desire to extend her dominion to the Philippines, Guam and Honolulu and possibly to . . . other U.S. possessions in the Pacific." In the following month the Office of Naval Intelligence observed, "Assuming that she [Japan] has determined to attack us, it is more than a probability that she has been preparing to do so for the last two years, and that she will strike suddenly when ready."[16]

To counter the perceived Japanese threat, the U.S. Navy's General Board, in January 1917, urged the need "for American naval domination of the western Pacific." The mission of the U.S. fleet was to strike immediately to secure control of the western Pacific and to cut Japan's overseas communications by dispatching a superior fleet to the Far East.[17] In January 1917, in response to Secretary of the Navy Josephus Daniels, the General Board presented a plan titled "Strategic Problem, Pacific." It represented the fullest survey yet completed. To secure naval domination of the western Pacific, the board calculated that the U.S. Navy required a fleet twice the size of the Japanese fleet. As naval historian William R. Braisted observed, "The Board proposed in 1917 to provide the United States with unprecedented military power in the Far East, but it would also practically deprive Japan of [the] capacity of independent self-defense."[18]

The Japanese navy was keenly aware of the dynamic, and apparently offensive, war plan being worked out by the U.S. Navy. An increasing number of Japanese officers regarded the United States as more than a mere "budgetary enemy." A significant memorandum prepared in March 1916 by Rear Admiral Takeshita Isamu, head of the Operations Division, stated, "The nation with whom a clash of arms is most likely *in the near future* is the United States." He noted, "The United States is rapidly expanding its naval armaments and it is building its military installations in the Pacific, thereby trying forcibly to impose its national policy on Japan." Takeshita concluded with a neo-Mahanian brand of economic determinism: "With its vast resources and newly acquired colossal financial power, the United States is invading the Oriental market. It is blocking our national expansion and depriving us of our interests [in Asia]. In addition, it is rapidly expanding its naval strength and completing its military facilities in the Pacific, thus forcing its national policy on us."[19]

Takeshita's memorandum was important, because he participated in the 1918 revision of the Imperial National Defense Policy. Similarly, a secret report submitted by the Naval General Staff to former Navy Minister Saitō stated, "The Japanese-American crisis stems from the American effort to unjustly obstruct Japan's development. . . . If the United States truly wants to avoid war, it must refrain from threatening Japan by building bases nearby. Otherwise war is inevitable."[20] Such perceptions must have affected naval leaders who were revising the National Defense Policy. It was sanctioned in June 1918, but its text has not yet been discovered. In light of the Takeshita memorandum, however, the revised defense policy likely defined the United States as the hypothetical enemy with which a clash was likely "in the near future." This is corroborated by a working paper prepared by the Naval Staff College in 1918 that stated, "The rivaling nation with which the clash is most probable on account of the China question, in other words the hypothetical enemy, has become the United States." This document continued:

> Although the government in its explanations to the Diet has never openly indicated which nation is our hypothetical enemy, if under the existing circumstances the question is raised, it will not be unreasonable to state that the United States is the foremost hypothetical enemy. . . . The United States has excluded Asiatic immigrants and clamored for the Open Door in China. More recently there are many among its intellectual classes who violently oppose Japanese occupation of South Sea [German] islands and openly call Japan their hypothetical enemy. Also the United States is rapidly expanding its navy, carefully preparing for [a Pacific] campaign. These facts obviously bespeak its policy of intimidation in the Orient.[21]

However, Navy Minister Katō Tomosaburō would not accept such a redefinition of a "hypothetical enemy." In a cabinet meeting on 26 July 1917, he stated that it was "from the viewpoint of naval armaments that America is regarded as hypothetical enemy number one."[22] Katō's statement reflected the traditional concept of the United States as a target for naval buildup. As far as he was concerned, the revised National Defense Policy of 1918 expressed Japan's desperate effort to maintain a semblance of naval balance with the United States. President Wilson had announced in August 1916 a building program that included ten superdreadnoughts and six battle cruisers to be completed in three years. This plan for a "Navy Second to None" was by far the largest rapid building program up until that time. Although the plan primarily was directed toward dangers in the Atlantic, Japanese navy men saw it as directed against them.

As the naval journalist Itō Masanori has written, the two naval powers that were least damaged by (or, most profited from) World War I—Japan and the United States—entered into a Mahanian naval race "as if preordained by Fate."[23] The appearance of the post-Jutland superdreadnought intensified the race. In 1921 Hector C. Bywater, a famed British naval journalist and American, attracted international attention by publishing *Sea-Power in the Pacific,* in which he astutely dealt with the "naval resources" of the United States and Japan and the strategic problems that such a war would present.

Facing the dangerous situation in November 1918, shortly after the armistice, Katō observed at the Advisory Council on Foreign Relations (Japan's highest advisory body on foreign policy) that if the huge American building plan was completed, "It will result in such an extreme disparity as to reduce the Pacific Ocean to an American lake."[24] To counter such a fear, the Naval Strength Requirement that accompanied the revised National Defense Policy of 1918 provided for an "eight-eight-eight fleet" plan that would add eight capital ships or battle cruisers (all no more than eight years old) to the existing eight-eight program. The new plan consisted of *three* battle fleets of eight warships each. To complete this program, Japan would have to launch three battleships or battle cruisers every year. The naval historian Nomura Minoru commented that "the weight of these battleships would have, so to say, sunk the Japanese archipelago."[25] From the beginning there was little hope of obtaining budget appropriation for the eight-eight-eight fleet program. The shares of naval appropriations in the total national budget for 1919, 1920, and 1921 were 23.4 percent, 26.5 percent, and 31.6 percent, respectively. (See Table 1.)

Mutual antagonism between the two navies had been rapidly increasing. As early as 1917 the Japanese navy had obtained a generally accurate picture of War Plan Orange. The Japanese asserted that U.S. war plans were stolen, but without resorting to clandestine operations, the Japanese navy could have deduced American plans from geography, war objectives, and relative strength. It was a matter of mirror imaging. Whatever the source of the information, Japan knew that the United States would advance its fleet to the mid-Pacific (Hawaii, the Carolines, and the Marshalls), recapture Guam and the Philippines, and, after victory in a climactic Mahanian engagement in the western Pacific, cut off Japan's seaborne traffic, blockade its home islands, and starve it into submission. In October 1920 Tokyo clandestinely acquired an operational study on a transpacific campaign jointly drafted by three brilliant planners, Harry E. Yarnell, Holloway H. Frost, and William S. Pye.[26] Japanese admirals noted that the American strategy corresponded with their plan to intercept the U.S. fleet in the western Pacific. Meanwhile the American navy surmised, correctly, that the Japanese strategy was to wait until the U.S. fleet, because of the difficulties of a transpacific passage, had sufficiently lost its strength (about 30 percent) before conducting a decisive fleet engagement near Japan's home waters.[27] The mirror image was noted by both navies.

To counter America's forward strategy, the Japanese navy reformulated its General Plan for Strategy in 1918. The plan consisted of two parts: (1) the navy would stage a bold offensive at the outset to destroy America's much inferior Asiatic Fleet, to capture Luzon, and to obtain command of the western Pacific; and (2) as the U.S. main fleet approached Far Eastern waters, the Japanese navy would deliver a decisive blow in a climactic main encounter. It was assumed, rather too optimistically, that the winner of the decisive battle would obtain command of the sea and end the war.[28]

In the U.S. Navy, the scenario worked out by the Plans Division (newly created in 1919) projected a three-phase operation: (1) during the first phase, the United States would concentrate its main battleship forces in the eastern Pacific; (2) during the second phase, the U.S. fleet would occupy points in the Japanese mandates in the mid-Pacific and recapture the Philippines and Guam; and (3) during the third phase, the U.S. fleet would defeat the Japanese fleet in a decisive battleship encounter and pressure Japan through blockading and occupying the Japanese territories. A key paper, "Strategic Problem, Pacific," adopted by the Joint Board in December 1919 assumed that Japan would acknowledge defeat only after the United States had effectively blockaded its homeland and captured the outlying islands. Such operations presupposed American domination of the western Pacific. This in turn required battleship superiority of at least three-to-two over Japan.[29]

LESSONS OF WORLD WAR I

What kind of armaments would Japan require in this new age of total war? Conflict over this question was at the heart of the dissension concerning strategy, armaments, and policy toward naval conferences throughout the 1920s and beyond.

The "clash between the two Katōs" at the Washington Conference—Navy Minister Katō Tomosaburō and Vice Admiral Katō Kanji (no relation)—will be described in the next chapter with all its drama and human poignancy.[30] Here I will simply contrast their views on naval defense. Cognizant of the new realities of total war, Navy Minister Katō Tomosaburō held a modern view of naval defense that saw national security in relation to economic, technical, political, and diplomatic factors. In a new age heralded by World War I, "National defense is no longer the monopoly of the military," he declared. No amount of armaments would be adequate unless backed by total national strength, which essentially consisted of industrial and commercial power. Squarely facing Japan's limitations in this respect, he believed that the nation would have to be content with "peacetime armaments commensurate with its national strength, if it were to avoid financial ruin."[31]

In sharp contrast, Vice Admiral Katō Kanji, who had served almost exclusively on the Naval General Staff and in the fleets, drew a diametrically opposed lesson from the recent war. Ignoring the requirements of total war, his thinking was embedded in military-strategic considerations of a limited war. "The cardinal lesson" of the world war, he held, was the vital importance of effecting a decisive fleet engagement early in the war before the United States could mobilize its formidable industrial potential. Failure to execute a quick and short war would turn the conflict into a war of attrition, to Japan's mounting disadvantage. He wrote, "One of the most important lessons we have learned from the Great War was the need of 'quick encounter, quick showdown.'" And the decisive fleet engagement was predicated on "the principle of big battleships and big guns."[32]

Katō Kanji held that the United States, with its "huge wealth, resources, and gigantic industrial power," could quickly turn its military potential into a formidable fighting force once war broke out. It thus could meet its security needs, he argued, with peacetime preparation equal to or even less than that of a "have-not" nation like Japan. Conversely, Japan's security required a large peacetime armament, he concluded.

However, some naval officers recognized the importance of preparing for a total war. They realized that "determination and preparation to endure a protracted war will be required." One of them was Commander Niimi Masaichi, who had been sent to England to study the lessons of World War I. He submitted reports on such subjects as "Economic Warfare and the Navy" and "Preparations for a Protracted War." These officers also realized that battles like Tsushima and Jutland were unlikely.[33] However, such perceptions never took root in the Japanese navy. The majority, wedded to the doctrine of "quick encounter, quick showdown," focused their attention on a decisive battleship engagement at an early stage, instead of preparing for a total war that entailed a protracted conflict.

Thus the Japanese navy faced the dilemma of expecting the next war to be a protracted one while reckoning that its only chance of success lay in a quick showdown. This meant that Japan would have to prepare for the type of warfare that it could least afford to fight.

Ironically, Katō Tomosaburō—the architect of the eight-eight fleet plan—was the first to recognize that this building program was bound to exist only on paper. Although the appropriation for the eight-eight fleet plan, to be completed in 1927, was finally approved in 1920, he saw that the plan was beyond Japan's financial capability. He had his subordinates—Captain Yamanashi Katsunoshin, Section Chief of the Naval Affairs Bureau, and Commander Hori Teikichi of the same bureau—estimate the costs of maintaining the eight-eight fleet program, and they found that the fleet program alone would require one-third of the government's budget—and Japan was already suffering a serious postwar recession.[34] At the budget subcommittee meeting of the Diet in February 1919, Katō admitted, "Even if we should try to compete with the United States, it is a foregone conclusion that we are simply not up to it. . . . Whether the United States, with its unlimited wealth and resources, would continue its naval expansion is up to that country. My policy is to build up an adequate defensive force within the limits of Japan's national power."[35]

In late 1920, Katō gathered leaders of the navy ministry—the navy vice minister, the chief of the Naval Affairs Bureau, and the chief of the Naval Construction Department—for secret consultation at his official residence. The gist of his talk was as follows:

> Since I became navy minister six years ago, the trends of public opinion and in the Diet have changed a great deal. In the olden days Diet members and other dignitaries were delighted to be invited to the Yokosuka naval yard and drink a toast at launching ceremonies. They congratulated me, saying Japan is becoming a great naval power. But during the past year or two they keep on asking about the costs of construction or maintenance, launching ceremonies, and maintenance of new ships. Our national wealth has simply not increased in proportion to naval expenditure, and we cannot proceed at the present pace. I am at my wit's end.[36]

About the same time, a desperate appeal came from Nishihara Hajime, Vice Minister of Finance. He told Katō and the sixty assembled naval officials,

"Our financial position is fast becoming hopeless; whether it will be ruined or not is entirely up to you navy people. . . . We'll have to give up in despair. Please put your heads together about this."[37]

The thankless task of scuttling the eight-eight fleet plan fell on Katō Tomosaburō. Drastic mutual reduction, he realized, was the only way to stop the arms race and save Japan's financial situation. On 18 January 1921 Navy Vice Minister Ide Kenji, under Katō's direction, told the *New York Tribune* that Japan would voluntarily reduce the eight-eight plan if a proper balance was maintained with the Anglo-American powers. Then on 14 March Katō himself told an Associated Press correspondent that Japan would not insist on completing the eight-eight fleet program if the powers could find a "suitable formula" for a "dependable" international agreement to limit their navies.[38] He made it quite clear that Japan was not attempting to compete with the U.S. Navy. This was the first signal to the world that Japan was prepared to discuss naval arms limitation. For Katō, who was hoping to halt the dangerous arms race, the American invitation to the Washington Conference that arrived on 11 July 1921 must have seemed a godsend. He later confided to Shidehara Kijūrō (who became his co-delegate to Washington), "There was no chance of building an eight-eight fleet, so I want to scrap it when given a chance."[39]

THE WAR SCARE OF 1920–21

The immediate background of the Washington Conference was an acute war scare that had developed in both Japan and the United States in 1920–21. The American navy became haunted by the vision of war with Japan. It was largely rooted in the "security dilemma" between the two navies: the Japanese would view a navy strong enough to protect the Philippines and the Open Door as a threat to their security. Conversely, Americans would view a navy powerful enough to defend Japan and its policies as a threat to the Philippines and other national interests in the Far East.[40]

The Japanese navy was more alarmed than ever by America's accelerated efforts to build a "Navy Second to None." The Japanese also nervously noted the creation, in 1919, of an imposing battle fleet in the Pacific. The United States placed half its fleet, with more than half its naval firepower, in the Pacific; and the enlarged Pacific Fleet was at least equal to the Japanese fleet. This clearly indicated that, as Mahan had, the Pacific had become of greater strategic importance than was the Atlantic. Fearing that the United States was about to establish its naval dominance in the Pacific, Japan responded by increasing its naval budget nearly fivefold between 1917 and 1921. Leaders of both countries denied that their building programs were directed against each other, to little avail. Captain Malcolm D. Kennedy, a British officer stationed in Japan since 1917, noted, "In Japan war with the United States was discussed as though it were inevitable and even to be welcomed."[41]

On the American side, Secretary of the Navy Daniels told the House Naval Affairs Committee in 1920 about "the necessity of being prepared if [Japan] should attack."[42] In February 1920 Director of Naval Intelligence Albert P. Niblack wrote the General Board, "During the past year Japan has been making strenuous preparations for war. These preparations are frankly directed against the United States." The Office of Naval Intelligence had "conclusive information" that Japan was "exerting every endeavor to prepare for war at the earliest possible date."[43]

On 14 July 1921, a few days *after* the United States had invited Japan to the Washington Conference, Theodore Roosevelt Jr., Assistant Secretary of the Navy, wrote his wife, "The best authority whom I have met says that Japan is preparing for war in time of peace more systematically and more thoroughly than any other nation in modern history. . . . I think it probable that Japan's war appropriations are simply incident to her desire to maintain absolute sway in Asia. . . . With the Philippines and our Asiatic relationships, I can easily imagine how, even with Asiatic dominance as her sole policy, unavoidable friction might ensue."[44] Apparently, in an instance of selective perception, the American navy had failed to need Navy Minister Katō's statement in March 1921 that Japan was willing to cut back its eight-eight fleet program.

Meanwhile, the American navy had conjured up an elaborate picture of the yellow peril that was inherited from Mahan's age. In 1921 the General Board and the War Plans Division prepared a number of reports about Japan, from which it is possible to extract American admirals' Weltanschauung. They saw in Japan a strategic, economic, political, ideological, and racial threat to the United States. The General Board feared that Japan sought not only territorial expansion and commercial domination of China but also political control of East Asia and the Pacific. The specter of a gigantic racial conflict seemed to alarm American admirals most. They feared that control and exploitation of China's resources and manpower would enable Japan to attain a "unification of the yellow race" that would "sweep over the world." The "rising tide of color," advancing eastward over the Pacific, would threaten not only white supremacy but the security of the United States itself.[45] This lurid yellow peril image essentially reiterated Mahan's nightmare of the clash of the Eastern and Western civilizations.

As during earlier war scares, the crisis of 1920–21 was accompanied by a resurgence of the immigration question. Japan resented the passage in 1920 of a new alien land law in California that made it totally impossible for Japanese to own land. The immigration issue, while not a casus belli for Japan, exacerbated Japanese resentment. Warlike propaganda ran rampant on both sides. The Japanese government was especially concerned about an inflammatory book by Lieutenant General Satō Kōjirō, *If Japan and America Fight.* The American public was treated to equally sensational fare that included such titles as *The Menace of Japan, The Rising Tide of Color, The New Japanese Peril,* and *Must We Fight Japan?*[46] Overall, in 1920–21 Japan and the United States seemed to be moving toward a head-on collision.

THE ROAD TO WASHINGTON

Behind the Japanese-American naval race were the shared Mahanian doctrines of the supremacy of the battleship and the clash of rival battle lines in a decisive fleet encounter. This mutually shared doctrine had originally incited and later intensified the competition between the two navies over the capital ship ratio,[47] as noted by Vice Admiral Katō Kanji, the dogged opponent of naval limitation. He later wrote, "The Japanese navy's studies on strategy tallied exactly with their American counterparts." It was natural, he noted, that "strategic planning in any nation, even that bearing on the secret aspects of national defense, should lead to identical conclusions if based on the same premises and reliable data." The two navies based their conclusions on Mahanian sea power doctrine, reinforced by map maneuvers, large- and small-scale exercises, and study of naval history. Noting a mirror image, Katō Kanji explained, "This is precisely the reason why the United States has been trying to impose a 60 percent ratio on us and why we have consistently demanded a 70 percent ratio."[48]

The Japanese navy's study of naval limitation began as early as June 1919, when Navy Minister Katō Tomosaburō appointed a special committee, under his direct control, to study the matter. (Originally navy leaders anticipated that the problem of naval limitation would come up in the League of Nations.) The formula this committee presented became the guideline for the navy's position at the Washington Conference. Chaired by Rear Admiral Abo Kiyokazu, head of the Operations Division, this committee consisted of captain-rank officers from both the Navy Ministry and the Naval General Staff, including Yamanashi Katsunoshin, Nomura Kichisaburō, Kobayashi Seizō, and Suetsugu Nobumasa—all of whom were to participate in the three naval conferences of the 1920s. The committee's report, presented to Katō on 21 July 1921, shortly after Japan had received the invitation to the Washington Conference, stated, first, that "Japan does not persist in building the eight-eight fleet as long as it can keep balance with the Anglo-American powers." This was a retreat from an earlier committee report of June 1920, which had stated that an eight-eight fleet was the minimum requirement. Second, and more important, it confirmed the earlier report's assertion that Japan "absolutely required" a ratio of 70 percent or more against the U.S. Navy. "There can be absolutely no room whatsoever for compromise on this ratio," the report categorically stated. This was, of course, a restatement of the long-standing naval conviction about minimum security needs.[49]

The demand for a 70 percent ratio was based on a prerequisite: prohibition of further U.S. fortification of the Philippines and Guam. (American bases there were not yet adequately equipped to repair and maintain ships, much less to accommodate a large fleet.) Any buildup of bases on these islands, the research committee stated, would eliminate Japan's geographic and strategic advantage that had hindered U.S. plans to wage a transpacific offensive. On the other hand, if a base in Guam were reinforced, a great American fleet could anchor and be repaired there. "Should this [fortification] problem fail to be satisfactorily resolved," the report warned, "naval arms limitation would not only be meaningless but may conceivably prove suicidal to Japan." However if the United States refrained from building up these bases, its badly damaged battleships would have to return to Hawaii, and the danger of such a long passage would be prohibitive. Navy Minister Katō agreed with the report. Apparently he regarded the fortification problem as more crucial to Japan than hair-splitting bargains over fleet ratios. If the United States built impregnable fortresses in the Philippines or Guam and obtained footholds in the western Pacific, Japan's fleet ratio would become meaningless. On the ratio question, therefore, he would take a flexible stand at the Washington Conference.[50]

The naval limitation committee presented its report as a resolution embodying the navy's consensus. Although Katō Tomosaburō, who was appointed chief delegate to the Washington Conference, did not officially endorse the resolution regarding the 70 percent ratio, he could not entirely ignore the firmly held naval consensus. Katō Tomosaburō told Vice Admiral Katō Kanji, President of the Naval Staff College, who accompanied him to Washington as a chief naval expert, that the committee's reports and resolutions should guide the negotiations at Washington.[51] However, Katō Tomosaburō did not consider himself bound by these reports.

As the head delegate, Navy Minister Katō resolved to have a completely free hand at the coming conference, and he had Prime Minister Hara Kei's full support. He had already been navy minister for six years and his position was second only to the prime minister. He was ideally suited to head the Japanese delegation in Washington.

The government's instruction to Katō was carefully drafted to give Katō maximum discretion. Significantly, it did not mention the ratio question. Instead, it contained a flexible provision requiring naval strength "sufficient at least to maintain a rough parity with the effective operational strength that the United States can command in Far Eastern waters." The instruction directed the delegates to preserve the status quo in Pacific fortifications. Above all, the instruction stated, "The [Japanese] Empire must attach special importance to maintenance of friendly relations with the United States"—a condition to which Katō Tomosaburō paid close attention.[52]

Shidehara later recalled that from the beginning, Katō seemed to have decided that Japan could negotiate on the basis of a 60 percent ratio, although he did not tell this to anyone. Katō said, "A well fortified Guam would be as impregnable as Heligoland in Germany. If the status quo is agreed on Pacific fortifications, Japan can fight the United States with a 60 percent ratio."[53]

The stage was now set for negotiations in Washington. Japanese-American relations had already reached such a critical state that both sides fretted about whether the Washington gathering would be able to dissipate war clouds. The assembled leaders felt that the only way to reach a naval agreement was to treat it within a broader political context. Putting my conclusion first, the Washington experiment showed that successful naval limitation must include an across-the-board adjustment of political questions of the Pacific and the Far East. Before discussing the naval negotiations in the next chapter, I will digress and briefly trace the process of Japanese-American détente as it related to the naval issue.

DÉTENTE IN THE MAKING

Political scientist Hedley Bull wrote, "Armaments are causes as well as effects, and shape political motives and intentions as well as express them." To put it differently, naval arms limitation depends on the wider context of political agreements and accommodations among the participating nations.[54] None recognized this better than Charles Evans Hughes, American Secretary of State and Chairman of the Washington Conference. The Washington naval treaty did not stand by itself; it was part of "the Washington system," a cooperative framework that defined naval, political, and economic relations among Japan, the United States, and Great Britain in East Asia and the Pacific.[55] Unlike subsequent naval conferences, the Washington Conference succeeded because its delegates recognized this relation between naval and political issues.

Thus the American invitation to the Washington Conference called for discussions "to seek ground of agreements as to principles and their application to find a solution of Pacific and Far Eastern problems." President Warren G. Harding, Secretary Hughes, and his fellow delegates stressed the linkage between the naval treaty and Far Eastern political settlements. As long as Japan and the United States feared going to war over the China problem, naval arms limitation was out of the question.[56]

When Tokyo received America's invitation to the Washington Conference, many Japanese were alarmed by such a linkage; they suspected that the naval limitation proposal merely camouflaged an attack on Japan's position in China.[57] However, the influential segment of the Japanese government recognized that a basic reorientation of its China policy was imperative to prevent further diplomatic isolation and deterioration. A Foreign Ministry memorandum crisply stated, "Necessity to shift our policy. Otherwise, the fear of total isolation and a Japanese-American war."[58] Shidehara, ambassador to Washington and the foremost advocate of peaceful economic policy, pleaded with Tokyo for a "constructive" policy to stabilize East Asia. He assured Tokyo that because the conference sought naval limitation and general détente in the Pacific and East Asia, Japan had nothing to fear.[59]

As Shidehara had surmised, the Harding administration, with its ties to business interests, had a great stake in improving relations with Japan. Hughes told Shidehara in preconference conversations, "The United States desires to eliminate all the sources of conflict and misunderstanding in the Far East in a frank and friendly spirit." Shidehara saw that the American government was primarily interested in the success of naval limitation and that it would be satisfied with a reasonable compromise regarding East Asian problems.[60]

However, one anticipated stumbling block was Japan's resistance to a categorical restatement of the Open Door in China. Hughes had been warned by State Department officials that Japan would insist on confirming its special interests in Manchuria. In a perceptive memorandum to the American delegation, Edwin L. Neville of the State Department's Far Eastern Division pinpointed America's weak position: "Our Open Door policy cannot be sustained without force," but the United States had never been willing to supply force. "Besides, we have at different times even recognized the special interests of Japan."[61] Chandler P. Anderson, a member of the American delegation, handed Hughes a copy of a letter President Theodore Roosevelt had written to warn his successor, William H. Taft, in 1910: "As regards Manchuria, if the Japanese choose to follow a course of conduct to which we are adverse, we cannot stop it unless we are prepared to go to war."[62]

Hughes carefully noted that the American people overwhelmingly demanded naval limitation, while few took serious interest in East Asian issues. It followed that he could not afford to antagonize Japan regarding East Asian questions, for fear of jeopardizing the naval negotiations. On the other hand, he feared that the U.S. Senate might never ratify a naval treaty if East Asian political problems were left unsolved.

Advisers' recommendations all pointed to the wisdom of handling Japan with kid gloves. Hughes opposed Japan's "aggressive" policy of "political domination" but he was willing to recognize "natural and *legitimate* economic opportunities for Japan."[63] Regarding Japan's "legitimacy," however, the American delegates held differing opinions. Herbert C. Hoover, Secretary of Commerce and a member of the advisory committee for the American delegation, admired the Japanese and sympathized with their plight. He emphasized that given its vital dependence on China's resources and market and faced with the chaotic condition there, "Japan certainly had legitimate reasons" for its continental policy.[64] Elihu Root, one of the American delegates and an elder statesman of the Republican Party, was the most outspoken in defense of Japan. He held Japan in high regard as a peacekeeping and stabilizing power in East Asia, and he believed that Americans must recognize the cold logic of Japan's position there. Believing that the moderate liberals controlled the Tokyo government, Root advocated a manifestly friendly policy calculated to strengthen this group.[65]

The most comprehensive examination of the conference strategy was presented by J. Reuben Clark, Special Council to the State Department and Hughes's assistant. His memorandum included the following points.

1. America's "only prime and great concern" is the "security" of the United States in the Pacific region. The problem of naval limitation is of vital importance, but Far Eastern questions are only secondary.

2. This conference must do the utmost to take away from Japan its distrust and fear of the United States.

3. The doctrine of "special relationship" must be agreed upon. Japan is right in its claim that it has a special relationship in China.[66]

In giving priority to America's security in the Pacific, emphasizing the primacy of naval limitation, and calling for recognition of Japan's special interests,

Clark was clearly in line with Rooseveltian realism. Most of the points he raised in this memorandum were incorporated in Hughes's diplomacy at the conference.

Hughes gave his views in his instruction to the American delegation: "He had gone along on the theory always that this country would never go to war over any aggression on the part of Japan in China, and that consequently the most that could be done would be to stay Japan's hand."[67] Like Root, Hughes pursued a friendly policy intended to bolster liberal moderates who supported naval limitation. The stage was set for Japanese-American détente at the Washington Conference.

COMPROMISE SETTLEMENT AND
THE WASHINGTON SYSTEM

The Washington Conference started its sessions on 12 November 1921. Hughes took a bold initiative on the opening day, proposing a drastic naval reduction. He calculated that his proposal would instantly receive such overwhelming support, not only from the American people but also from world public opinion (including Japan's), that Japan would have no choice but to accept it. Japan would not dare take an obstructionist position that would torpedo the conference, because it would be denounced by the whole world. Hughes was proved right. Japan's chief delegate, Admiral Katō Tomosaburō, was greatly moved by the enthusiastic reception that greeted the Hughes was proposal and concluded that Japan "must pay dearly for opposing it."[68] (See Chapter 4.)

In his conference strategy Hughes had linked the naval question with Far Eastern issues. If naval limitation were jeopardized by Japan's intransigence regarding Far Eastern problems, Japan would be condemned by the whole world, so it would have to cooperate regarding Far Eastern questions. Hughes's strategy worked beautifully. The most important tasks for the Japanese delegates were to wipe out the stigma of a "militaristic" and "aggressive" nation and extricate Japan from diplomatic isolation. Each time a deadlock over a Far Eastern issue (especially the Shantung question) threatened the success of the naval treaty, the Japanese delegates tried to save the conference, entreating Tokyo to make one compromise after another. The Japanese delegates, like their American counterparts, understood that naval arms limitation depended on a wider context of political accommodation.

Hughes's larger design was to start the process of Pacific détente. First, the United States took the initiative by demonstrating its friendly and peaceful posture. As Root secretly apprised a Japanese delegate, the United States had proposed drastic naval limitations at the outset of the conference in order to assure Japan that it held no hostile intentions.[69] Throughout, Hughes was careful to avoid any overt threat, relying on diplomatic persuasion and the force of public opinion. In this respect, Hughes's success was nearly complete.

In contrast to his dramatic appeal for naval limitation, on Far Eastern problems Hughes secretly negotiated with Japanese delegates to reach quiet compromise settlements. He entrusted the pro-Japanese Root to keep close liaison with a Japanese delegate. Root said he was going to help Japan "to extricate itself from the present difficulties," such as the Shantung question. As for Manchuria, he anticipated that the Japanese "would undoubtedly insist upon maintaining their hold on [Manchuria]," admitting that "a good deal was to be said" in favor of Japan's position.[70]

When he drafted the Root Resolution that became the basis of the Nine-Power Treaty relating to China, Root quietly inserted the so-called security clause: a pledge committing the signatories to refrain "from *countenancing action inimical to the security of [signatory] powers.*" It was an implicit concession to Japan's traditional contention that its special interests in Manchuria were vital to its "national defense and economic existence." Furthermore, Root secretly reassured the Japanese delegates, "There will be no change in Japan's present position in Manchuria."[71]

America's navy men were quick to note the relation between the Nine-Power Treaty and the naval treaty. Because the General Board regarded the fifteen unfinished American battleships, earmarked for scrapping, as the "very potent argument" with which to force Japan into a Far Eastern settlement, it recommended that the naval treaty "be not signed until a satisfactory solution regarding Far Eastern Questions has been embodied in a treaty and signed." The navy men felt that, because the naval treaty drastically reduced American influence in the Pacific, the United States must obtain political compensations that would protect its interests in the Far East.[72]

Regarding the Shantung question, the Tokyo government firmly opposed any American intervention, claiming it was a "problem of sole concern to Japan and China." But Shidehara urged Tokyo to recognize that "it was extremely important to solve the Shantung question," which had become a crucial political issue for the United States because of the controversy over the ratification of the Versailles treaty.[73] Hughes was careful to avoid confrontation with Japan over Shantung lest naval negotiations be jeopardized. Unless the Shantung question was solved, however, he feared the Senate would refuse to ratify the naval treaty.

Shidehara, fully aware of the political significance of Shantung to the Republican administration, warned Tokyo that if the Shantung negotiations ruptured, the Senate would not ratify the naval treaty, and Japan would be blamed for the subsequent failure of the conference. Like Hughes, Shidehara linked the Shantung question to the naval issue and tried to solve both questions in a broad context of Japanese-American détente. His repeated entreaties finally moved the Tokyo government.[74]

Admiral Katō Tomosaburō confidentially reported to the naval authorities in Tokyo that the American delegates, especially Elihu Root, were "extremely friendly to Japan," while they were responding to China's concrete proposals "merely with harmless resolutions." This unexpectedly friendly attitude of the United States encouraged Katō to redouble his efforts to come to agreement on the naval issue.[75]

Termination of the Anglo-Japanese Alliance was another important prerequisite for a naval limitation treaty. As long as this alliance remained, the United States would have to expand its navy to protect against a joint Anglo-Japanese naval confrontation. Hughes held that naval limitation depended on termination of the Anglo-Japanese Alliance. But this alliance was not even on the conference agenda, and it would have been tricky for a third party to demand its annulment. Having accepted the drafts of Shidehara and the British chief delegate, Arthur Balfour, as the basis of negotiations, and careful not to offend Japan, Hughes skillfully transformed these drafts into the Four-Power Treaty, "a general and harmless international agreement" among the United States, Japan, Britain, and France. Hughes limited the scope of its application to the Pacific islands, guaranteeing the status quo of the Pacific and the security of the Philippines.[76] For the United States the Four-Power Treaty was a diplomatic triumph: it gracefully terminated the Anglo-Japanese Alliance, demilitarized the western Pacific, and facilitated a nonfortification agreement regarding the Pacific islands that was stipulated in the naval treaty. Along with the naval treaty, the Four-Power Treaty was a part of a Pacific security system. Japan and Britain accepted the treaty because they gave priority to naval limitation and improved relations with the United States. Japan lost the alliance, but it was assured its position as a member of the Washington system.[77]

Henceforth peaceful cooperation became the mainstream of Japanese foreign policy. This historic turnabout hinged on a remarkable improvement in Japanese-American relations. The Japanese delegates were relieved at the unexpectedly "sympathetic attitude" of the Americans and appreciated their efforts "not to hurt our feelings or honor." Shidehara declared, "There is no doubt that Hughes has respected Japan's position so far as possible."[78] Regarding the naval negotiations (which will be covered in the next chapter), Katō Tomosaburō cabled the government, "Here in Washington we delegates scarcely imagined such things as Anglo-American oppression." Eager to emphasize this point, he declared at the dinner that Prime Minister Takahashi gave to welcome back the delegates, "There are some prejudiced people who claim that Japan had been oppressed by the Anglo-American powers, but I can categorically declare that those of us who negotiated the treaties at Washington assure you that this was not the case."[79]

Hughes emphasized the importance of mutual trust and friendly rapport that went beyond individual treaties, which he called the "spirit of the Washington Conference."[80] Admiral Katō Tomosaburō, known for reticence, spoke with equal eloquence: "The conference succeeded because the participating nations agreed on the pressing need to establish world peace and alleviate the burden [of armaments]. And these two aims can be accomplished only by freeing ourselves from the old system of exclusive competition among the powers and by creating a new world of international cooperation."[81] The American naval attaché in Tokyo reported how completely the Washington Conference had dispelled the "war psychology": "I have told members of the Cabinet and other Government bodies repeatedly that prior to the Washington Conference, whether rightly or wrongly, there existed a war psychology and consequential war talk. The Washington Conference has dispelled these war clouds.... It is truly as important as any treaty and agreement reached there. It is our mutual duty to see that this mental attitude is maintained and bettered on both sides of the Pacific."[82]

The naval treaty succeeded largely because it was integrated into the Washington treaty system, which rested on an across-the-board adjustment of political questions. However, as we shall see in the next chapter, from the time of the treaty's inception, a strong undercurrent of opposition to the Washington system ran through the navy. The malcontents, particularly those on the Naval General Staff, led by Katō Kanji, reacted violently against the naval treaty, regarding it as a flagrant Anglo-American imposition of an inferior naval ratio on Japan. Preoccupied with strategic imperatives, they did not comprehend the broad political considerations that had brought about Pacific détente. The enemies of the naval treaty were determined to scrap the Five-Power Treaty just as soon as soon as they seized power. This split between the pro-treaty and anti-treaty forces plagued the Japanese navy during the 1920s.

CHAPTER FOUR

THE WASHINGTON CONFERENCE

Katō Tomosaburō's Leadership

A
dmiral Katō Tomosaburō was one of the most powerful leaders in the history of the Imperial Japanese Navy. The political considerations behind his appointment as chief delegate to the Washington Conference tell a great deal about his leadership qualities as well as the nature of civil-military relations under the Meiji Constitution. (This constitution made no stipulation for civilian control.) Prime Minister Hara Kei chose Katō because he was the only individual capable of "controlling" the navy. When Hara approached Katō to be chief delegate, Katō demurred, saying that he was a man of few words, was not good at English, and had no previous diplomatic experience. Hara reminded him, "What we expect of you is not oratorical skill at the conference table; Shidehara will handle that. We badly need your service in order to control the navy." Civilian delegates not only would be powerless to restrain the navy but would likely provoke the navy's opposition.[1] Paradoxically, only the powerful head of the navy—the navy minister and a full admiral on active duty—could be expected to exercise control over unruly subordinates; one might call it "civilian control by proxy." Before accepting the mission, Katō consulted Fleet Admiral Tōgō, who said nobody was better qualified.

Prime Minister Hara had absolute trust in Katō, who had had a superb career as both a fighting admiral and a naval administrator. In 1894, in the midst of the Sino-Japanese War, he was called back to serve in the First Section of the Naval Affairs Bureau, the locus of naval policy making. In 1900, he became chief of that section. After gallantly serving as Admiral Tōgō's chief of staff in the Battle of the Sea of Japan, he was promoted to head of the Naval Affairs Bureau; in 1906–09 he served as navy vice minister. In these crucial years after the Russo-Japanese War, he frequently appeared at the Diet as the government's spokesman for the eight-eight fleet program. Promoted to full admiral in 1915, he was appointed navy minister, serving three successive cabinets (headed by Ōkuma Shigenobu,

Terauchi Masatake, and Hara Kei). As navy minister he also attended the Advisory Council on Foreign Relations after 1917. Over these years he had acquired a broad international outlook that earned him acclaim as an "admiral statesman" among the foreign delegates and journalists gathered at the Washington Conference.

Captain Yamanashi Katsunoshin, who worked closely under Katō at the conference, later reminisced that he was "a man of iron nerves and great self-possession." His brain was "razor-sharp, but as supple as a school boy's and it cut straight to the heart of any problem." At meetings he rarely said anything on non-naval matters, but when he spoke up, he was always to the point, giving only his terse conclusions.[2] One commentator wrote, "Katō possesses not only ample combat experiences but rich administrative experiences. He is thoroughly informed about national defense, yet he is capable of taking a large view of things. . . . *His mentality is largely civilian* and he is the only naval statesman in the Imperial Japanese Navy."[3] Itō Masanori, a naval journalist who was acquainted with Katō, wrote, "Katō does not waste his time with petty details and tedious processes, but at once gets to the heart of important questions. By taking a large and prescient view, he will reach compromise settlements."[4]

Indeed, Katō Tomosaburō was *the* dominant figure presiding over the naval establishment. A charismatic leader of towering prestige and unquestioned authority, he concentrated power in his hands. He belonged to that rare class of Japanese leaders who resolutely acted on their own authority, ignoring their subordinates' dissenting views. In Washington he was determined to take full responsibility for his decision making. These qualities created optimum conditions for rational decision making.

U.S. Navy leaders took full measure of Katō's character. Captain Luke McNamee, Director of Naval Intelligence, reported to Admiral Robert E. Koonz, Chief of Naval Operations, that Katō "is the strongest man in the cabinet, next to the Prime Minister." "He will go [to the conference] as a cabinet minister and not as a naval officer or in connection with the naval delegates."[5] An attaché report from Tokyo stated, "He will consider the question of disarmament from the standpoint of the wider interest of the nation rather than from a narrow professional standpoint." Another report contained this significant account: "Japan's navy minister is not only a man of proven caliber, but he is a statesman of achievement. . . . His strongest recommendation is that of being a man of decision who will not hesitate to assume responsibilities at important moments without reference to the home government."[6] Captain William V. Pratt, who came to know Katō in Washington, wrote, "My admiration for Kato was great. I have always looked upon him as one of the world's leading statesmen.

He was a man of great character."[7] Such favorable estimates of Katō boded well for successful naval negotiations.

The American attaché was less charitable to the junior Katō, Vice Admiral Katō Kanji, who accompanied the delegates as chief naval adviser. Among his fortes, the attaché reported that he was "alert, energetic, decided, a man of action, opinionated, independent, and likes to talk. . . . Man of marked initiative. . . ." Less flatteringly, the attaché reported that "[Katō]'s enemies call him narrow-minded and radical. . . . Is quite fearless and does not hesitate to attack both seniors and juniors personally. . . . For the above reasons he is gradually losing his former popularity with both older and younger officers." The American navy greatly underestimated him. He was a rising star in the Japanese navy. As for his views of America, he frankly supported continental expansion and opposed America's meddling with it. According to a report that the Chief of Naval Intelligence received, Katō was quoted as saying, "Japan . . . must have an opportunity to expand on the continent of Asia, and America must not endeavor to restrict Japan's expansion so long as America herself is not affected." He would oppose any American attempt to meddle with Japan's continental expansion.[8] This posture sharply contrasted with Tomosaburō's view that emphasized, above all, the improvement of Japanese-American relations.

Before Katō Tomosaburō's departed for Washington, Captain Yamanashi, his close subordinate, lectured him on the importance of public opinion in the United States: "You are always grumpy and very unpopular with newspapermen, but remember, America is a country where public opinion is largely swayed by newspapermen and ladies." Katō protested that he was not good at courting press people.[9] Yet he was mindful of his subordinate's proddings. He found moments during his voyage to the United States on board the *Kashima Maru* to read the recent English translation of Count Sergei Y. Witte's memoirs, paying special attention to Witte's efforts during the Portsmouth Peace Conference in 1905 to swing American opinion in favor of Russia through a press campaign.[10] Katō Kanji, who had separately boarded the *Corea Maru* in advance of the main delegation, was reading a war scare book by Walter B. Pitkin, *Must We Fight Japan?*

Secretary of State Hughes had cautioned Ambassador Shidehara (soon to be appointed one of the delegates) that "very likely it might be well not to have Admirals and Generals on the delegation" because this was a conference of arms limitation.[11] Obviously, Hughes did not understand Japan's peculiar mode of "civilian control by proxy," which was aimed at controlling the naval establishment by appointing the highest naval leader. Anxious to remove Hughes's misapprehension, Katō Tomosaburō told Ambassador Charles Warren that he was not a "militarist" and that he was going to Washington not as navy minister but as a statesman.[12] The American naval attaché reported that in Japan, too, criticism was raised on the grounds that "having a naval man [as chief delegate] would create a bad impression in America and Europe and confirm the prevailing belief that Japan was militaristic."

To dispel any possible misunderstanding, Ambassador Shidehara cabled Katō, imploring him "to don civilian clothes, bow and smile, and wave your hat to the cheering crowd when you arrive in Washington." Katō, who was close to Shidehara, could not ignore this plea. So the usually tight-mouthed Katō did his very best to be affable in Washington. Indeed, he was so successful at this that he won an accolade, perhaps to his own surprise, as "the charming admiral"![13] This episode symbolizes the differences in the civil-military relations of the two nations. During the conference Katō never wore his navy uniform. Katō's press conferences were so well attended that people jostled for seats in a fully packed hall. American reporters were impressed with his prompt, candid, and clear-cut responses to even the most pointed questions. Some even wrote that they were "deeply attracted" by Katō.[14]

KATŌ'S REACTION TO THE HUGHES PROPOSAL

In the days before the conference, a visiting journalist found the prevailing mood in Washington "one of intense nervousness, even anxiety."[15] Rumors circulated about the U.S. proposal. The Japanese delegation spent a considerable sum of secret funds, to no avail, to find out about it. Only Hughes and three American admirals knew the content of Hughes's proposal. At first, Katō had ruled out as unrealistic any plan to scrap ships under construction, not to mention existing ships; he assumed the conference would deal only with plans for future construction. He quickly sensed, however, that the American government was planning a far-reaching proposal to scrap ships that were completed or under construction. Accordingly, on 5 November, Katō ordered his senior aide, Captain Nomura Kichisaburō, to cable Navy Vice Minister Ide Kenji, directing him to prepare for substantial cuts in naval personnel and shipyards. These retrenchments were to be treated as purely "domestic matters" so that they would not hamper the Japanese delegates in Washington in their negotiations.[16]

The Washington Conference sessions opened on 12 November 1921 in Continental Hall, which belonged to the Daughters of the American Revolution. Its white panels shone brilliantly, left unadorned by colorful decorations. Nearly a thousand invited guests filled the hall. The wives of American delegates and advisors and the diplomatic corps occupied the boxes. The galleries were packed with members of Congress and other guests.[17] It was the greatest diplomatic gathering held in the United States up to that time.

In the opening session Hughes, as chairman, broke all diplomatic protocol by presenting a far-reaching proposal: (1) a ten-year "naval holiday" during which each power would cease construction; (2) limitation of the fleets of the great powers by tonnage according to the naval ratio of 10:10:6 for the United States, Britain, and Japan; and (3) an itemized plan for scrapping ships in accord with a "stop now" formula.[18] Hughes's "bombshell proposal" came as a breathtaking surprise. Yamato Ichihashi, a Stanford assistant and Katō's translator, observed, "It electrified the calm session. Some were shocked, some were even alarmed, but the others were pleased."[19] Theodore Roosevelt Jr., chief American naval expert, had been studying Katō's expression, but, as he recorded in his diary, Katō hid his agitation "under his immovable face looking straight ahead."[20] In reality, the proposal dumbfounded the normally self-possessed Katō. He was deeply moved to see the audience galvanized by Hughes. During Hughes's speech Shidehara heard "a commotion as if a bomb had been thrown into the Continental Hall."[21] Then and there Katō decided that Japan had no choice but to accept Hughes's proposal in principle: "It is simply impossible to oppose the American plan. If we oppose it, we'll have to pay a heavy price. World public opinion would not allow it."[22]

In his car on his way back to the Shoreham Hotel, where the Japanese delegation was staying, Katō was in a state of meditation, occasionally hitting his knees with his hands and nodding his head. Secretary Hughes had taken a unilateral initiative for détente in the Pacific, and Japan must respond to it positively and quickly. At the hotel, Katō assembled the delegation to tell them that he considered the American proposal "reasonable." He told Shidehara, "The Hughes proposal clarifies the situation. It takes away fears and suspicions on both sides. As far as Japan and the United States are concerned, there is a good prospect of concluding a [naval] agreement." What struck Katō most was the power of American public opinion.[23] He told Itō Masanori, a naval journalist, "What do you make of what happened in the conference hall today? I instinctively felt that Hughes' proposal represented the voice of all Americans. This is clear from the enthusiastic applause given by senators and congressmen. That applause represented the opinion of the entire American people. It's a formidable force."[24] Only a few hours later Katō cabled his government, "Hughes' proposal made such a powerful appeal to American public opinion that it gave the impression that any opposition would be tantamount to opposition to justice."[25]

On the same day, 12 November, Katō hurried to cable Vice Minister Ide a top-secret message describing the enthusiastic reception of the Hughes proposal: Hughes's address was frequently greeted with passionate applause and, above all, when he declared that the United States would scrap the fifteen battleships under construction, the whole audience stood up and their applause and cheers lasted for a long while. The fervent applause of the members of the House and Senate, who occupied the second floor, attracted his particular attention. "And the contents of the Hughes proposal are believed to be generally reasonable, so I believe that the Imperial Government must resolutely respond." He underscored that if Britain supported the Hughes proposal, forging Anglo-American unity, Japan would be compelled to follow suit. "We must accept the proposal by taking a broader view of things." Because the negotiations were likely to take a sudden turn, Katō asked for discretion. In response, Ide assured Katō of full support.[26]

Thereupon Katō opened an active publicity campaign. At a press conference, he stated as his personal opinion that "Japan will make every effort to fulfill the aims of the [Hughes] proposal."[27] At a party that Shidehara gave for reporters, Katō declared, "There is no doubt that a perfect understanding can be reached as far as Japan and the United States are concerned."[28] On 14 November, Katō again cabled Foreign Minister Uchida, "I am convinced that the Imperial Japanese Government must promptly and decisively resolve to accept the American proposal." Katō had made this decision all by himself. As Captain Nomura testified, Katō did not consult with his naval advisers when he made up his mind.[29]

At the plenary session of 15 November, Katō accepted the Hughes proposal "in principle," adding that "a few modifications will be proposed with regard to the tonnage basis" in light of Japan's "security requirement." And in a statement that came back to Japan in 1935 (during the Second London Conference of 1935), he made a ringing declaration: "Japan has never claimed nor had any intention of claiming to have a naval establishment equal in strength to that of either the United States or the British Empire."[30] Because a widespread rumor existed that Japan would not accept Hughes's proposal, Katō's speech was greeted with a standing ovation, with Hughes himself rising to his feet.

70 PERCENT RATIO VERSUS 60 PERCENT RATIO

On the following day, in a surprising turnabout, Katō Tomosaburō let chief naval adviser Katō Kanji present, at the first meeting of the naval advisers, a demand for a 70 percent ratio and retention of the battleship *Mutsu*, which had been earmarked for scrapping. Katō Kanji stated that Japan's "absolute" demand for the

70 percent ratio was based on "national security needs," declaring that with anything less, Japan would be unable to "obtain security and defense."[31] The American representative rejected Japan's bid for a 70 percent ratio on the grounds that it negated Hughes's whole proposal. Heated discussions ensued on the ratio question.

The *Mutsu* was a highly prized post-Jutland battleship mounting eight 16-inch guns with good armor protection. It was faster than any U.S. battleship. This latest superdreadnought was the symbol of the Imperial Japanese Navy. (Even schoolchildren had donated their spending money toward its completion.) The Americans argued that it was only 98 percent completed, and hence must be scrapped, but the Japanese argued that it had already completed a trial cruise and was fully commissioned, thus falling outside the category of warships to be scrapped.[32]

The ratio issue was far more serious. Why had Katō Tomosaburō deviated from his initial reaction to the Hughes proposal even though he must have anticipated that the United States would object to the demand for a 70 percent ratio? For one thing, Katō chose not to reject the navy's "established policy" regarding the 70 percent ratio outright. Perhaps he meant to placate and save the "face" of his intransigent naval advisers, headed by Katō Kanji, who absolutely opposed the 60 percent ratio. At any rate, Katō Tomosaburō was determined to make the final decision himself on the ratio matter.

Second, he had to consider domestic political factors.[33] In an unguarded moment at the Advisory Council on Foreign Relations, he had once stated that a 70 percent ratio was required for national defense. A telegram from Vice Minister Ide reminded Katō that the members of the Advisory Council were attacking him for reneging on his "pledge."[34] Prime Minister Hara had promised before his departure to protect Katō from precisely this sort of domestic complication but Hara was assassinated on 4 November, a week before the Washington Conference opened. With Hara gone, Katō felt totally lost. At home the antigovernment members of the Advisory Council had become unmanageable. The succeeding cabinet of Takahashi Korekiyo was too weak to control the obstructionists. Katō began to wonder whether the Privy Council would ratify any naval treaty he would present.

At a Big Three meeting (of Hughes, Katō, and Arthur Balfour, British head delegate) on 19 November, Hughes opposed the Japanese demand for a 70 percent ratio as undermining his whole proposal. He insisted that no agreement could be reached on the basis of security needs and that the 10:10:6 ratio was based on the existing strength of the three powers. Failing to agree, the Big Three entrusted the naval subcommittee with devising an acceptable formula.

In this subcommittee, which dealt with technical matters, the United States was represented by Assistant Secretary of the Navy Theodore Roosevelt Jr., and Japan by Vice Admiral Katō Kanji, both strong-willed men. Roosevelt wrote in his diary that Katō posed as a "samurai gentleman" whose "eyes lit as he spoke of the samurai and the samurai songs." Thirty-four-year-old Roosevelt, son of the former president, was an army veteran of the world war and one of the founders of the American Legion. The two often met in the privacy of Roosevelt's residence. Katō told Roosevelt repeatedly, "I pledge you my word as a two-sword man that what I tell you is the truth." He gave Roosevelt the impression of being "a great fighter." He claimed that according to Japanese calculation of the "existing strength," Japan's strength came somewhere between 69 and 86 percent.[35] (In fact, the U.S. Navy's General Board, using completed capital ships as a measure, had calculated Japan's relative strength to be 68 percent as of January 1922.) Roosevelt countered that according to the American formula, which included ships under construction, the Japanese ratio was below 60 percent.

Japan and the United States clashed over what constituted the "existing strength"—the yardstick that Hughes had proposed as the basis of reduction. Katō Kanji complained that no mutually acceptable definition existed. Hughes calculated the "existing strength" by including all dreadnoughts, superdreadnoughts, and capital ships under construction to the extent that they were completed. On the other hand, Japan wanted to include predreadnoughts but exclude all ships under construction because such uncompleted ships could not yet undertake a battle cruise. The following table represents the Japanese calculation presented by Katō Kanji:[36]

Japan calculated an 83 percent ratio for superdreadnoughts and a 70 percent ratio that included those under construction. Even accepting the American

Category	United States	Japan — Japanese Classification	Japan — U.S. Classification
(1) Predreadnoughts, dreadnoughts, superdreadnoughts	100%	76%	69%
(2) Dreadnoughts, superdreadnoughts	100%	70%	61%
(3) Superdreadnoughts	100%	86%	86%

Note: (1) is based on the Japanese view that predreadnoughts ought to be included.
    (2) is based on the American view that predreadnoughts ought to be excluded.
    (3) is based on calculations that included only superdreadnoughts.

method of computation, Katō declared that Japan's strength would be well over 70 percent. On the other hand, Hughes stated that Japan's "existing strength," according to *his* calculation, amounted at best to 48 or 50 percent, but "to be on the generous side" he proposed a 60 percent ratio.[37] Aside from the calculation of the existing strength, Katō persisted throughout that a 70 percent ratio was needed for Japan's security, the position Hughes had firmly rejected.

At one point, when Katō was being particularly obstinate, Roosevelt declared that if he was judging the situation correctly, they were both willing to fight each other at any time over the interests of their respective countries. As a "samurai gentleman," Katō thanked Roosevelt for his "reception" and intimated that he would have to commit suicide if he had to go home with anything less than 70 percent.[38] (A rumor in Tokyo suggested that Kanji had actually performed *hara-kiri* in Washington!) He exceeded his authority as a naval adviser, however, when he alluded to the possibility of a breakup of the conference. But the bluff was wasted on Roosevelt, who doubted that Japan would dare to defy world public opinion.[39]

Hughes had to avoid confrontation with Japan because he was also engaged in negotiations on delicate political questions concerning East Asia. His ways of applying subtle pressure on Japan without coercing it were fourfold. First, he obtained British support for the American position. In fact, more than two weeks before the conference opened, Admiral Earl Beattie, Britain's chief naval adviser, had assured Roosevelt that Britain and the United States could dictate to the Japanese any terms within reason. Now, in response to Roosevelt's appeal, Rear Admiral Ernle Chatfield, a member of the British naval subcommittee, unequivocally backed up the American views in front of the Japanese, which Katō Kanji feared might develop into "an Anglo-American oppression of Japan." Later, Britain's chief delegate Balfour supported the American position. He agreed with Hughes: "If the American people should feel that Japan had improperly refused to agree to a fair naval ratio, they would vote for the building of a navy of any size asked for." The Japanese delegates were alarmed to see their British ally siding with the Americans because this threatened Japan with isolation. Their original instructions had stated that they must "maintain full consultations with the British," but the Japanese delegates, taking for granted their British ally's friendly support, had not even informally discussed the matter with the British delegates.[40]

Second, Hughes redoubled diplomatic pressure through Ambassador Charles B. Warren in Tokyo. On 19 November Warren was instructed to tell Foreign Minister Uchida that Japan would have to either accept the American terms or "go back to competitive building." This was a strong warning. On 3 December,

Hughes stepped up pressure on Tokyo through Warren: "There was no hope for Japan to better the existing ratio as the United States could build as rapidly as Japan."[41]

Third, Hughes brought the pressure of public opinion to bear on the Japanese. In the words of Harold and Margaret Sprout, Hughes's initial address had been "a masterpiece of political strategy calculated to mobilize public opinion behind the American proposal."[42] Hughes assumed that his proposal would win over world public opinion so strongly that if Japan remained intransigent, it would be censured internationally and become completely isolated. He felt that Japan would go a long way to avoid such a predicament. Katō Tomosaburō told Itō Masanori, "When two thousand or more American newspapers supported Hughes' plan without a single dissenting voice, this struck me as a very heavy pressure."[43]

Fourth, the American delegates tried to influence the Japanese through the Japanese business and financial leaders who had gone to Washington as "unofficial delegates." On 30 November Elihu Root saw Fred Kent, a New York banker, and explained that the breakup of the conference on the rock of Japanese intransigence would mean the loss of all Japanese trade, not only with the United States but with England, France, and Italy as well, and that such a boycott and embargo would spell Japan's economic ruin. Kent, who had personal connections with Japanese financiers, notably Shibusawa Eiichi and the Mitsui interests, immediately talked the matter over with them.[44] Kent's efforts were apparently successful, because in the telegram that reached Washington on 7 December, Vice Minister Ide reported to Katō that a majority of Japanese businessmen and financiers were coming around to accepting the 60 percent ratio.

Accumulating pressures placed the Japanese government in a difficult predicament. Because deliberations at the technical naval subcommittee had failed to resolve the Japanese-American impasse, the matter was thrown back to the Big Three on 30 November. The last days of November were a critical period in the naval negotiations. In its instruction on 22 November, the Tokyo government had urged its delegates to stand firm by the 70 percent ratio, and repeated that it attached utmost importance to Katō's previous "pledge" regarding this ratio.[45] On 30 November Roosevelt noted in his diary that for the first time, Hughes appeared worried, but on the following day he saw signs that the Japanese delegates were more willing to come to an agreement.[46] This impression was confirmed when Japanese diplomatic dispatches were decoded by the American "Black Chamber"—the Cryptographic Bureau headed by Herbert O. Yardley—and turned over to the American delegation.[47] The telegrams revealed that the Japanese delegation was weakening and that with one more push, Japan would yield. (Not suspecting Japanese dispatches were deciphered, Katō Kanji recalled later that the chief delegate's telegrams to Tokyo were mysteriously leaked to the American delegation.)

DECISION MAKING IN WASHINGTON

Unknown to Americans—and Japan's naval advisers—chief delegate Katō Tomosaburō had been in close communication with Vice Minister Ide to forge a compromise among the highest navy leaders in Tokyo. In an important telegram to the government on 23 November, Katō outlined the following four options:

1. Persist in the Japanese demands of the 10:7 ratio and the retention of the *Mutsu;*
2. Accept the 10:6.5 ratio in return for retention of the *Mutsu;*
3. Accept the 10:6 ratio in return for retention of the *Mutsu;*
4. Accept the 10:6 ratio and the scrapping of the *Mutsu.*[48]

Katō urged that he be authorized to opt for Plans 2 and 3 and, if absolutely necessary, Plan 4. "Taking a larger view of the conference," he wrote, "if Japan should clash with the United States on naval limitation and thus cause its miscarriage, it will be as clear as day that the onus will fall on us." It was therefore "absolutely necessary" to reach an agreement with the United States.

This cable, on its face, seems like a request for a fresh instruction from the government, but it was merely a formality aimed at appeasing both Katō's subordinates in Washington and his political foes in Tokyo. He was determined to make his own decision and take full responsibility for it.[49]

On 26 November Katō, in an urgent telegram, directed Vice Minister Ide and Abo, Vice Chief of the Naval General Staff, to explain his decision to the highest naval and government leaders. The naval leaders, from Fleet Admiral Tōgō Heihachirō of Tsushima fame on down, agreed that if it was necessary to save the conference, the navy would consent to lower the 70 percent demand, but they wished to avoid Plan 4 by all means. This Naval Opinion, stated in an important memorandum, spelled out the navy's position as follows: "While the Navy considers the ratio of 10:7 as absolutely mandatory, it also deems the successful conclusion of the conference absolutely imperative. If the conference should break up as a result of Japan's absolute insistence, naval building competition, far keener than at present, will inevitably ensue. It is obvious that the Empire cannot compete with the United States numerically. Taking a large view of the future of our nation and trusting our delegate, we accept as unavoidable a decision to lower our ratio below 70 percent."[50]

The Naval Opinion was discussed at the Supreme Military Council (the highest advisory body to the throne on military-naval affairs, composed of two service ministers, two service chiefs, and several designated councilors). Fleet Admiral Tōgō powerfully backed up Katō, declaring that "a margin of 10 percent or so should not concern us much." When Admiral Nawa Matahachirō objected to it for fear of sapping the navy's morale, Tōgō sharply retorted, "Such an argument simply does not stand to reason since the responsible navy minister himself has judged a 60 percent ratio to be acceptable." He said he could not help expressing "full sympathy with Katō's painful predicament and all his efforts."[51] At the request of Admiral Yamashita Gentarō, Chief of the Naval General Staff, Vice Minister Ide cabled Tōgō's words to Katō, adding, "Please set your mind at ease on this score." These assurances must have been encouraging to Katō, who had served as Tōgō's chief of staff in the Battle of the Sea of Japan. Tōgō in turn trusted Katō.

Tōgō's view was significant in light of his later reversal of his position, at the time of the London Conference of 1930. In 1921 he held that the navy minister was responsible for advising the emperor in both high command and administrative matters. "As long as Navy Minister Katō Tomosaburō says the 60 percent ratio does not endanger our national defense, those charged with high command must accept this naval strength and work for the security of national defense. They must not evade their responsibility by saying that they could not fight a war with the given strength."[52] The significant telegram to Katō on 28 November, based on the Naval Opinion, dwelled on the importance of avoiding a clash with the United States and directed Katō to make a final effort to carry through Plan 1. But if it failed, he was to negotiate on the basis of Plan 2. If further concession became necessary, the delegate must take "a broad consideration of Japan's interests" and accept the 10:6 ratio, provided the Anglo-American powers agreed to reduce or at least maintain the status quo with respect to fortifications in their Pacific island possessions. The paramount consideration, Tokyo reminded the delegate, was to retain a naval "balance" by "reducing operational power of the American fleet in the western Pacific," in accord with the original instruction.[53] On 1 December, Katō received the telegram from Ide conveying the reassuring message from Tōgō: "A difference of 10 percent or so does not concern us much. . . ." with the caveat, "However, if all of our revised proposals were to be rejected and there is no way but to accept the American proposal in toto, this would have a grave impact on our public opinion, the future of the government, and the morale of the navy. At the same time, I wish to express full sympathy for the delegates' difficulties and all their efforts."[54]

On the same day, 1 December, an agitated Balfour approached Katō. His voice trembling, the British head delegate feared that unless the United States and Japan could agree on the 10:6 ratio, the whole naval agreement would go overboard, with disastrous repercussions on the Far Eastern questions being discussed. He emphasized the interrelatedness between the naval and Far Eastern issues, and ominously warned that if the conference failed because of Japan's insistence on a 70 percent ratio, the United States would begin a large-scale building program that would reduce Japan's strength to far below 60 percent within five years. Katō feared that if the British openly sided with the United States, Japan would be totally isolated.[55]

Convinced that "naval limitation must succeed whatever it takes" and wanting to break the deadlock, Katō broached the question of the status quo regarding fortification of the Pacific islands, which he said could not be considered separately from naval limitation. He explained to Balfour that if the United States, as reported in the press, was spending a colossal sum to build mighty bases in the Philippines and Guam, Japan would be greatly threatened.[56] Thereupon Balfour, acting as an honest broker, conveyed Katō's proposal to Hughes and on the following day the Big Three met to discuss the Pacific fortification issue.

Hughes said the United States did not wish to take up the nonfortification issue unless Japan agreed to a 60 percent ratio. In addition, he proposed a new treaty that would dissolve the Anglo-Japanese Alliance and demilitarize the western Pacific. (This resulted in the Four-Power Treaty already discussed in Chapter 3.) The United States would discuss the naval treaty and Pacific nonfortification issue only as parts of a comprehensive Pacific security system that included the Four-Power Treaty. Hughes stressed that American willingness to forgo further construction of fortifications and naval bases in the western Pacific was contingent on Japan's entry into the Four-Power Treaty.[57] In effect, this nonaggression treaty was a corollary of naval arms limitation. As noted, this interconnection of agreements was the hallmark of the Washington system. However, Katō for some reason was cautious about Hughes's new proposal linking the Pacific nonfortification issue to the Four-Power Treaty that would abrogate the Anglo-Japanese Alliance. Katō merely replied that he was not prepared to go into details, so there was no further discussion on the matter at that time.[58]

On 4 December, Katō sent an important telegram to Tokyo that began with a review of the changing American attitude toward Japan:

> At the present conference the United States is taking as sympathetic an attitude as possible toward the Empire's position. For example, going against its public opinion, the U.S. immediately began discussing naval arms limitation, while relegating Far Eastern questions to a secondary place. . . . Newspapers, with the exception of the Hearst press, have generally taken a friendly attitude [toward Japan] to date. . . . Such improvement of American feelings seems to be motivated by a desire to produce a successful conference. However, in view of the proclivities of the American people, if Japan posed an obstacle, their attitude toward Japan would suddenly change.[59]

Katō informed the Tokyo government that Balfour had for the first time come out openly in support of the 60 percent ratio and was pressuring Japan "to accept the American plan by arguing that our insistence on the 70 percent ratio would wreck the whole treaty." In that case the resulting naval arms race would progressively lower Japan's ratio. "The present situation must be regarded as a turning point in the future of our Empire. I am extremely worried." Finally, Katō conveyed to Tokyo his fear that domestic advocates of the 70 percent ratio seemed intent on controlling the Japanese press. "If public opinion should be allowed to be inflamed, the Japanese government will be placed in a most inimical position both internally and externally."[60]

On the same day, 4 December, Katō sent a second telegram to Tokyo: "In discussing national security in the broad sense of the word I believe we must consider not only naval strength but many other factors." "From the standpoint of strictly naval defense the navy's traditional position [70 percent ratio] is correct and I am second to none in eagerness to have it accepted [at the conference]. However, from a broader standpoint, it is necessary to cooperate with the Anglo-American powers, obtain international understanding, and improve the Empire's position, thus securing our nation's future and its safe development." Judging from the firm position of Hughes and Balfour on the ratio matter, Katō decided that further argument on the ratio issue would be futile and would only antagonize the American public. His "back against the wall now," Katō felt that this was the moment of his final decision.[61]

In a strongly worded and important telegram he sent to Tokyo on 5 December, Katō warned that Japan would be held responsible for a collapse of the conference and would be forced into total isolation. If Japan accepted the 60 percent under the circumstances, Japan would seem to have surrendered to coercion, and this would inflame the Japanese public so much that it might jeopardize Japan's relations with the United States. If the conference failed and the naval race accelerated, Japan was certain to lose. Katō assumed that the United States would complete its current building program by 1924 and embark on a fresh construction plan, whereas Japan would not be able to complete its eight-eight fleet plan until 1927. Therefore Japan would progressively fall behind the United States and end up far below 60 percent. Katō asked Ide to show his telegram to the prime minister, the foreign minister, Fleet Admiral Tōgō, Chief of the Naval General Staff Yamashita, and the members of the Supreme Military Council. In this telegram he asked for "the final instructions" from his government to accept the 60 percent ratio.[62]

Why did Katō, determined to make his own final decision and supported by top navy leaders, request a second instruction from the government at this time? According to Enomoto Jūji, a senior councilor of the Navy Ministry who assisted Katō, it was purely a formality; he was merely trying to save the "face" of the government. In particular, Katō worried about the confusion within the governing Seiyūkai party, which had been floundering since Hara's assassination.[63] He also had to be wary of the opponents in the Advisory Council on Foreign Relations. He later explained in the secret "Katō message" to Vice Minister Ide that he might have "appeared to be evading responsibility," but he "took the final measure to appease domestic political forces." On 10 December Yamashita Gentarō, Chief of the Naval General Staff, gathered Fleet Admiral Inoue Yoshika (Tōgō was traveling) and the members of the Supreme Military Council to explain Katō's most recent telegram, and they all agreed that acceptance of the 60 percent ratio could not be helped.[64] Thus reassured by the top navy leaders, Katō stated at the Big Three meeting on 12 December that he would accept the 60 percent ratio in return for agreement on Pacific nonfortification and retention of the post-Jutland battleship *Mutsu*.[65]

The most incisive expression of Katō's views on naval limitation appears in the now-famous "Katō message," a confidential message dictated to Commander Hori Teikichi, who carried it to Tokyo and delivered it to Vice Minister Ide.[66] In this message Katō stated, "What intuitively governed my thinking at the conference was [the importance of] improving Japanese-American relations. It was from this viewpoint that I made 'my final decision' on any question." Katō was going to effect a 180-degree swing from a dangerous naval race (a system of mutual distrust) to arms limitation and Japanese-American détente (a system of mutual trust). For this purpose, he subordinated military-strategic needs, however imperative, to broader political considerations. He declared, "Avoidance of war with America through diplomatic means constitutes the essence of national defense." In extremely forthright language he asserted, "To speak plainly, we cannot fight a war without money. The United States is the only country with which war is probable, but it is also the only country where we can float foreign loans. Therefore, the conclusion is that we cannot fight a war with the United States." Avoiding war with the United States while enhancing commercial and industrial power was at the core of Katō's convictions on national defense. This realism, based on the exigencies of total war, underlay his decision to accept the 60 percent ratio.

Katō's decision-making style was highly personalized. Remaining cool-headed, he thought through the issues at hand and, as the highest authority, he "intuitively" came to his conclusions. He thus circumvented the bureaucratic and organizational channels of the navy and the foreign ministry, not to mention the Advisory Council on Foreign Relations. In the annals of Japanese diplomatic and naval history, such individualized decision making was atypical, perhaps unique. The closest parallel was Secretary Hughes. Similarities between these two leaders did not escape the attention of a contemporary reporter of *Yorozu Chōhō:* "Hughes is a typical American statesman who always maintains certain convictions and directly pushes them forward in a commonsensical way. Admiral Katō is a typical warrior who also holds firm convictions and presses them. They are similar in that they do not indulge in petty political tricks. This perhaps was the reason why there always was a measure of mutual understanding between the two men."[67]

KATŌ KANJI'S INTRANSIGENCE

In his telegram to Ide, Katō Tomosaburō succinctly spelled out his differences from Katō Kanji: "The insistence of the chief naval advisor [Katō Kanji for the 70 percent ratio] is in line with our traditional policy and is quite proper if viewed only from the standpoint of naval defense. In holding this position I am second to none. However, it is of utmost importance for the security of our nation to take a larger view of the matter and insofar as possible to take the initiative to improve the Empire's international position and promote cooperation with the United States and Britain." To reiterate, it was not that Katō Tomosaburō considered the American proposal "satisfactory". In light of Japan's limited resources, which precluded a naval race, he decided that "it would be to our advantage to put up with the 60 percent ratio." In accepting a

60 percent ratio, he considered such factors as economic, political, and diplomatic realities, as well as the vital need to improve relations with the United States. His decision was bound to provoke strong opposition from Katō Kanji, who, as chief naval adviser, saw Japan's security needs from a strictly military-strategic viewpoint.

Why did Katō Tomosaburō choose Katō Kanji, then President of the Naval Staff College, as his chief naval adviser when he must have been aware of Kanji's hard-line position? In the past Tomosaburō had contended with Kanji's proclivity for unauthorized arbitrary action. The senior Katō must have anticipated a violent clash with Kanji in Washington, given their differences in views on national defense and naval limitation, and attitudes toward the United States. He may have chosen the junior Katō to accompany him to Washington so that he could directly and personally control his intransigent stand against naval limitation. Also, it was impolitic to bypass Kanji, who had been gaining ascendancy and had an increasing voice in matters of strategy and operations.

Katō Kanji's intransigence was famous. Tokutomi Sohō, the leading journalist of the day, wrote, "Katō is, on the one hand, impulsive and simple-hearted, and on the other hand, fearless and daring. He eliminates any obstacle and fearlessly pushes forward according to his convictions. It is unavoidable, therefore, that he should create friction. He is not the kind of person who patiently waits until a persimmon ripens and drops to the ground; rather he will strike it down with a pole even if it is not ripe yet."[68]

The differences between the two Katōs predated the Washington Conference. Unlike the senior Katō, Kanji had a modicum of experience in the Navy Ministry, being a typical "sea warrior."[69] A few episodes shortly after World War I illustrate their contrasting approaches to international issues as they bore on the navy. When the Russian Revolution broke out in 1917, Katō Kanji was dispatched to Vladivostok as commander of the Fifth Squadron. Time and again he urgently requested permission from Navy Minister Katō Tomosaburō for military intervention to eliminate the Bolsheviks and establish Japan's "leading position in the Orient." Tomosaburō firmly rejected Kanji's plea, saying that such a landing party would lead to a large-scale expedition to Siberia with attendant international complications.[70] In 1919 Katō Kanji led the navy's investigative mission; in Germany he overstepped his authority and negotiated a clandestine submarine agreement with the German navy minister. (See p. 167.) Katō Tomosaburō, afraid that such an agreement violated the Versailles Peace Treaty and would antagonize the United States, Britain, and France, peremptorily ordered Kanji to cancel the agreement. Kanji felt compelled to submit a tentative resignation as a way to take responsibility, but he was somehow allowed to remain.[71] Kanji was obsessed with strategic-technical-military advantages, whereas Tomosaburō put great store in broader political and international considerations.

The two men were antithetical in personality as well. Tomosaburō was always cool-tempered and rational, whereas Kanji openly admitted that he was "a man of emotion." Harada Kumao, Prince Saionji's secretary, later called Kanji "a very simple-minded and emotional man." Admiral Suzuki Kantarō said Kanji was "headstrong and emotional, thus hard to deal with."[72] Given such a background, it was inevitable that the two Katōs would collide in Washington. Kanji's habit of going off the deep end and his clandestine, arbitrary ways of conducting naval affairs were disturbing.

Kanji's intransigent stand on the 70 percent ratio went beyond strategic considerations; it was grounded, as already noted, on his twin doctrines of the "equality of armament" and "points of national honor." He argued that Japan, as a sovereign nation, was inherently entitled to "parity"—"a ratio of 10:10." Viewed this way, a 70 percent ratio already constituted the maximum concession and compromised Japan's "national prestige." A 60 percent ratio was out of the question. Furthermore, the "stop now" formula of the Hughes proposal, though seemingly fair, hid a selfish desire to freeze a status quo that favored the United States, enabling it to perpetuate its naval predominance in the Pacific. To impose such "inequality and fetters" was an act of "intimidation committed only by the victor" that utterly disregarded Japan's national prestige.[73]

Katō Kanji was convinced that the American proposal, "under the cloak of righteousness and humanity," camouflaged an intention to "deprive the Imperial Navy of its supremacy in the Far East" and replace it with America's own "hegemony." He was particularly incensed by the statement made by Admiral Hilary P. Jones, Commander in Chief of the Atlantic Fleet, that "the United States absolutely requires keeping Japanese naval forces below a 60 percent strength to be able to bring Japan to its knees over the China question."[74] On 27 November and 4 December, Katō Kanji dispatched urgent, top-secret telegrams to the navy vice minister and the vice chief of the Naval General Staff, warning them that the United States was "dictating in a most high-handed manner that Japan abandon its legitimate rights of self-defense." If Japan conceded the 60 percent ratio, it would be "tantamount to surrendering" to the United States.[75]

Embittered to see British delegates now aligning with the Americans, Katō Kanji warned that "Anglo-American oppression" not only would be an "unbearable humiliation" but would result in "the most serious threat" to Japan's security. "Whether or not Japan abandons the right of self-defense depends on [the navy's] determination." Whereas Katō Tomosaburō saw a crisis in the escalating naval race, Katō Kanji saw one in "American imposition" of the 60 percent ratio. Whereas the elder Katō keenly felt the "silent pressure" of American public opinion in support of naval limitation, the junior Katō cabled to Tokyo the importance of firming up domestic public opinion behind a 70 percent ratio. In a secret dispatch dated 4 December, Katō Kanji warned the naval leaders in Tokyo: "The United States and Great Britain are banding together in oppressing Japan. Mutual compromise and give-and-take are something these powers simply don't have in mind. In our view, their intention obviously is to deprive the Imperial Navy of its predominance in the Orient. They are threatening Japan by holding it responsible for wrecking the conference. To yield to such an overbearing attitude is an utter humiliation. The future of the Empire and the morale of the navy rest entirely on the resolve of the government."[76]

Katō Kanji felt so strongly that the situation was critical that he sent a second telegram on the same day: "The whole matter involves Japan's right of self defense." If the government accepted the Hughes proposal, "the game is up: Japan would succumb to American domination." "Unless we firmly resolve to reject American 'dictates,' the future of our nation will become precarious, indeed. Whether or not to abandon our legitimate right of self defense as a nation will depend on this resolve. We are in the last five minutes of the battle."[77]

These strongly worded views were, of course, diametrically opposed to those of the senior Katō. In his confidential message to Vice Minister Ide, the senior Katō cabled, "The American way is on the whole fair-minded." "Anglo-American oppression is something we delegates at Washington have never imagined."[78]

The impetuous Katō Kanji remonstrated with the elder Katō, sometimes tearfully. The latter, a controlling figure, simply ignored any challenge from subordinates. But he met Kanji's violent opposition with cogent arguments. What was the mathematical basis, he demanded, for asserting that a 70 percent ratio could "absolutely" guarantee Japan's security, whereas a 60 percent ratio "absolutely" undermined it? Kanji and like-minded advisers were hard put to answer. "As a naval officer," Katō Tomosaburō said, "I can certainly understand the demand for a 70 percent ratio, but it is not acceptable to American and British politicians and diplomats. We must come up with an argument that will persuade them."[79] This reasoning, however, failed to persuade Katō Kanji. The elder Katō knew that behind the "impulsive" Kanji were even more stalwart navalists led by Captain Suetsugu Nobumasa, who was known for his ability to pull strings. The senior Katō scolded Kanji: "Now that you are a vice admiral, you must learn to control your subordinates."[80] After one late-night session in which he had upbraided Kanji with unusual severity, Katō Tomosaburō quietly looked into Kanji's room for fear he might have killed himself in a fit of anger.

The senior Katō had been Kanji's gunnery instructor in the Naval Academy and, as such, felt entitled to a measure of deference. Elsewhere I have written, "Katō Kanji always retained a sense of respect for his superiors. Theirs was an honest difference of opinion."[81] This would have been a nice way to end our story, but the recently published diary of Katō Kanji reveals that he harbored deep personal animosity, even venom, toward the senior Katō. On 12 January 1922 Kanji wrote, "Now I know how crafty he is. He is not the kind of person one can work with." A week later he wrote, "The way he curses the Advisory Council of Foreign Relations is unspeakable. He is hardly a big man."[82] Kanji openly defied Tomosaburō. He incurred the latter's wrath on 28 November when he told the Associated Press that Japan would withdraw from the conference if denied a 70 percent ratio.[83] A violation of service discipline, Kanji's political statement overstepped his authority as a technical adviser and incurred Tomosaburō's wrath.

Such acts of insubordination did not in the slightest affect the elder Katō's command of the situation, nor could Kanji's distractions confuse or mislead the top naval authorities in Tokyo. As noted, with his usual precaution Katō Tomosaburō through Ide had obtained approval of his decision from top naval leaders, especially Fleet Admiral Tōgō. So when Katō Kanji protested, saying Fleet Admiral Tōgō would never condone such a compromise, Katō Tomosaburō laughed and said he had already obtained Tōgō's approval.

But Katō Tomosaburō had reason to worry about his political opponents at home, so he decided to set the record straight. The government was under attack because a series of concessions in Washington were expected to come up at the forty-fifth Diet, scheduled to open on 21 January. As stated on 27 December, when the naval negotiations were near completion, he sent back to Tokyo his trusted subordinate, Commander Hori Teikichi, bearing the "Katō message" to Navy Vice Minister Ide. In this confidential message, Katō declared that he took full responsibility and would not evade it by saying he was following instructions from the government.[84]

Katō Tomosaburō ordered Kanji to be present when he dictated this "message." In the "appendix" to this message, Kanji stated his position: "Although the navy has definite reasons [to demand a 70 percent ratio], the chief delegate has forcefully carried out his convictions. Upon return to Japan I shall have occasion to express my views as the chief naval advisor. So I refrain from saying anything now." This was an admission of total defeat on Kanji's part.[85]

IMBROGLIO OVER PACIFIC FORTIFICATIONS

Although Katō Tomosaburō's handling of the ratio decision was masterful, his negotiation concerning the status quo of Pacific nonfortification was not. In July 1921 the report of the research committee on naval limitation had clearly stated that nonfortification was essential to a *70 percent ratio*. Now that Japan had conceded a 60 percent ratio, obtaining a nonfortification agreement was all the more imperative. The government's initial instruction to the delegates contained an explicit stipulation regarding Pacific fortifications.

Katō was uncharacteristically slow in raising this issue; he did not broach it until his meeting with Balfour on 1 December. Conceivably he could have broken the impasse over the ratio issue earlier by proposing Pacific nonfortification in return for a 60 percent ratio. He later explained that from the beginning, the question of Pacific nonfortification was ever present in his mind, but he had his own ideas about the timing of such a proposal. He feared that a premature introduction of the issue might further complicate the ratio negotiations; he felt it imperative to reach an agreement on the all-important ratio problem first. The government had given Katō wide latitude in naval matters, but he did not always show diplomatic finesse in his negotiations of Pacific fortifications. Whatever reasons existed for his ineptitude, on 2 December Katō finally raised with Hughes the question of fortifications and bases in Hawaii, Guam, and the Philippines. Hughes immediately excluded Hawaii but saw "no difficulty in providing for the status quo of Guam and the Philippines." At the same time, Hughes demanded and Katō agreed to treat the nonfortification issue as part of a comprehensive Pacific security system, including the Four-Power Treaty that demilitarized the Pacific.[86]

As expected, American admirals, who had not been consulted at all, violently opposed the Pacific nonfortification agreement. They had warned Hughes that such an agreement would be "fatal to the security of our position in the Western Pacific." The U.S. Navy, in the tradition of Mahan, regarded Guam as the key to any successful Pacific campaign. American admirals did not believe that in the Four-Power Treaty, Japan was promising to respect American sovereignty in Guam and the Philippines.[87] Independently Hughes had solicited the opinion of Professor George H. Blakeslee of Clark University, a Far East expert, who said on the authority of Mahan that Guam was a "lancet pointed to Japan's side." Hughes agreed that relations with Japan had deteriorated so much that the relations would not have peacefully survived had Guam and the Philippines been left free to be fortified.[88]

With Hughes willing to accept Katō's proposal on the nonfortification of the Pacific, the prospect of arriving at a naval treaty looked promising. After Katō obtained approval of the naval leaders in Tokyo, the principal delegates came to a provisional agreement on the naval treaty on 15 December. It stipulated the 10:10:6 ratio; substituted the battleship *Setstu,* an older ship, for the *Mutsu;* and specified nonfortification of the Pacific islands.

Unexpectedly, difficulties erupted from Tokyo. The provisional agreement had stated that the Pacific nonfortification agreement did not apply to "the islands composing Japan proper." But what were the islands constituting "Japan proper"? The Tokyo government held that the Bonins and Amami-Oshima were an integral part of "Japan proper" and thus fell outside the scope of the nonfortification agreement, contrary to Hughes's understanding.[89] Japan contended that its people would never understand why fortifications in Amami-Oshima, an island close to Japan proper, should be restricted while outlying Hawaii, two thousand miles from the American Pacific Coast, should remain unrestricted. Involving Japan's image, the issue became emotionally heated. Katō advised his government that the matter was not strategically significant. In fact, he had stated at a meeting in early December that he did not object to restrictions on the fortifications of the Bonins and Amami-Oshima.

Apprehensive about the worsening American attitude toward Japan, Katō begged his government to forgo an uncompromising stand. The political foes of the Takahashi cabinet, entrenched in the Advisory Council on Foreign Relations, were again resorting to obstructionist measures to embarrass the government, and Katō believed he was being made a domestic plaything. In early January 1922 the Tokyo government instructed its delegates to make no further concessions, arguing that they would inflame public opinion at home, jeopardize ratification of the naval treaty by the Privy Council, and endanger the future of Japanese-American relations: "Thus the naval agreement, which professedly aims at the maintenance of peace, might be interpreted in Japan as an oppressive Anglo-American measure directed against Japan; and this would in the future have irradicable harmful effects on the sentiment of our people toward these two nations. . . . If the voices for peace should turn into cries for vengeance, Japan's destiny will be fearfully affected."[90]

On 14 January, Foreign Minister Uchida sent a categorical instruction to adhere to the government's rigid position; otherwise Japan must refrain from signing the naval treaty. The issue, Uchida explained, was no longer a matter of national security; it had instead become "a grave issue affecting the feelings and morale of the Japanese people." "[Compromise on the nonfortification issue] is bound to kindle violent feelings of the Japanese people. They will regard the arms limitation treaty, aiming at the maintenance of peace, as nothing but an Anglo-American oppression of Japan. . . . [If Japan's demand is not accepted], the national opinion will reach a boiling point, provoking violent antipathies against the Anglo-American powers and jeopardizing the ratification of the naval treaty at the Privy Council."[91]

Katō refused to carry out this instruction. Failure of nonfortification would be nothing to the Anglo-American powers, but it would be "a great blow" to Japan. Worse, it would torpedo the whole naval treaty. Rather than taking responsibility for causing the failure of the conference, he cabled that he would resign as chief delegate,[92] emphasizing the folly of jeopardizing the future of the nation on account of petty domestic considerations.

Navy Vice Minister Ide did his best to dissuade Katō from resigning. Fortunately, in the end, moderate council prevailed in Tokyo and Japan accepted the nonfortification agreement that became Article XIX of the Five-Power Naval Treaty, signed on 6 February 1922. The United States promised to maintain the status quo regarding bases in the Philippines and Guam, and Japan agreed not to fortify the Kurile Islands, the Bonin Islands, Amami-Oshima, the Ryukyus, Formosa, and the Pescadores.[93]

Under Article I of the Five-Power Treaty, Japan was allowed ten capital ships including the *Mutsu* (a total of 301,320 tons) and the United States eighteen ships (a total of 500,650 tons). The maximum tonnage and gunnery allowed for ships other than the capital ships was 10,000 tons, and 8-inch guns were the maximum gunnery permitted. Two years' notice was required for abrogation of this treaty; otherwise the treaty would last permanently.

The Five-Power Treaty made it extremely difficult, if not impossible, for the U.S. Navy to wage offensive warfare against Japan in the western Pacific. In the event of war with Japan, the United States would have to fall back on the Hawaiian Islands as its base of operations. Japan would have enough strength to defend itself, but certainly not enough for offensive operations across the Pacific. Together with the Four-Power Treaty, which forestalled the possibility of Anglo-American navies joining forces against Japan, the Five-Power Treaty left the Japanese navy dominant in Far Eastern waters. The Washington system effectively replaced the "security dilemma" or zero-sum game with a regime that simultaneously enhanced the security of *both* the United States and Japan. From the viewpoint of naval strategy, the settlement was a great success for Japan.

LIMITS OF KATŌ TOMOSABURŌ'S ACHIEVEMENTS

The most notable feature of Katō's decision making (with the exception of the nonfortification negotiations) was the extent to which he bypassed the naval and foreign ministry bureaucracies in Tokyo and suppressed his unruly subordinates in Washington. His highly personalized decision making—quite unusual in Japan, where consensus building was (and still is) the norm—was effective in coping with a crisis. It was a triumph of rational decision making over bureaucratic politics.[94]

But it had the drawback of overburdening a single leader. Already suffering from colon cancer, Katō endured excessive strains that shortened his life. It taxed him almost beyond endurance to counter Katō Kanji's opposition in all-night sessions, communicate with Tokyo, conduct daily negotiations, and prepare for the following day's session. In addition, during the early phase of the conference, he had to take over the negotiations of the Far Eastern question because Shidehara had fallen seriously ill. Upon his return to Tokyo, he confided to Admiral Saitō Makoto, his former superior and onetime navy minister, "I really felt I was going to die in America."[95]

Another disadvantage was that no matter how powerful a leader he was, his individualized decision making went against the organizational norms of the naval establishment. Thus Katō's decision was destined sooner or later to be challenged by malcontent subordinates and eroded from within the navy once his commanding presence was gone. As the clash between the two Katōs has shown, the elder Katō squelched the junior Katō's spirited opposition, but the latter remained unpersuaded and unreconciled to the 60 percent ratio.

On the day Japan accepted the 60 percent ratio, Katō Kanji was seen shouting, with tears in his eyes, "As far as I am concerned, war with America starts now. We'll get our revenge over this, by god!"[96] Kanji scribbled in his diary on 30 December, "We must not compromise on the basis of the American proposal unless there is a guarantee that war between Japan and the United States would never materialize." He also added, "The China problem may have been settled for the moment, but there is no telling what will happen tomorrow." He did not believe in the efficacy of the Washington treaty system. He consoled himself, "One can never tell how the international situation will change ten years hence; therein lies an opportunity to alter [the naval ratio]." His diary conveys his sense of desperation: "How lamentable for Japan's future!" "Unspeakable agony!"[97]

It remained uncertain whether the elder Katō's policy and philosophy on naval limitation would take root among Japanese naval men. The junior Katō's fulminations were an ominous sign. As far as he and his subordinates were concerned, the new treaty strengthened their obsession with the 70 percent ratio and their notion of an inevitable war with the United States. The elder Katō was, of course, aware that this policy rested on his leadership and would erode once he disappeared from the scene. Already during the Washington Conference this awareness had caused him to contemplate drastic institutional reforms, including "a system of civilian navy ministers—after the British pattern." In the "Katō message" he ordered Vice Minister Ide to begin preparing such a reform.[98] Apparently he had been contrasting the Anglo-American type of civilian control with Japan's anomalous system, which imposed on him, a full admiral and navy minister, the onerous task of going against the organizational mission of the service he headed. Another reform Katō "emphatically urged" was a clear subordination of the Naval General Staff to the Navy Ministry. Did Katō foresee, ever so dimly, the collision that would occur at the time of the 1930 London Naval Conference?

In later years the division within the Japanese navy revolved around conflicting positions on the Washington naval treaty. At the time of the Washington Conference, however, no clear-cut line of conflict had yet emerged between the Navy Ministry and the Naval General Staff. Yet, significantly, the rebels against the Washington naval treaty centered in the Naval General Staff, with Captain Suetsugu now heading its Operations Section. "Hot-blooded young officers" whose influence grew in the years after the London Conferences of 1930 were the disciples or followers of Katō Kanji and Suetsugu.

Officers in the Navy Ministry who had assisted Katō Tomosaburō became his self-conscious "heirs." They remained committed to his policy of arms limitation and avoidance of war with the United States. The conventional interpretation (to which I once subscribed) holds that the elder Katō's views on naval limitation and national security were handed down through these heirs as the "naval orthodoxy" during the 1920s and 1930s.[99] Viewed in the foregoing context, however, a somewhat different picture emerges. After all, the elder Katō had abandoned the three guidelines of the Japanese navy that had been tradition since the Imperial National Defense Policy of 1907: a 70 percent ratio, an eight-eight fleet program, and the notion of the United States as the hypothetical enemy. In particular the claim for the 70 percent ratio became a rallying point for opposing the Washington treaty. Henceforth it became an obsessive goal that governed the hard-line elements of the Japanese navy. Katō Kanji and his followers in the Naval General Staff soon claimed to be the "mainstream." Katō Tomosaburō's legacy of not going to war with the United States was handed down to the magnificent triumvirate of Yonai Mitsumasa, Yamamoto Isoroku, and Inoue Shigeyoshi in the 1930s, but the three men represented the minority of the isolated few.

MAHAN REPUDIATED?

Together with the Four-Power Treaty, the Washington naval treaty facilitated Japan's command of the sea in the western Pacific and regional supremacy in the Far East. The nonfortification provision neutralized American bases in the Philippines and Guam, guaranteeing Japanese supremacy in East Asian waters. Under the new terms, neither the United States nor Japan could launch a naval offensive across the Pacific. As for the United States, the Washington treaties confirmed its traditional policy that it would not fight Japan to enforce the Open Door. The American policy and interests in the Far East thus became "hostage to Japanese restraint."[100]

This "new order of sea power" must be understood in the broader context of Japanese-American rapprochement. As American delegates claimed, the naval treaty would have been impossible without the new cooperative relations created by the Four-Power Treaty and the Nine-Power Treaty; conversely, without an accord on naval limitation, these treaties would never have been concluded. The Washington Conference thus proved the premise, advanced by political scientists, that "just as it is futile to attempt to settle the problem of arms limitation without reference to all other political issues, it is also impossible to resolve these issues without balancing relative naval power."[101] This explains why the Washington Conference succeeded; indeed, it was the only naval conference in the interwar period that truly succeeded.

The U.S. Navy did not hold this view, however. If Mahan had been alive, he would no doubt have strenuously opposed the Five-Power Treaty. He always felt strongly about the right of a sovereign nation to employ naval force as a means of self-preservation and advancement of its interests. The idea of arms limitation perturbed him, because he thought it weakened the prerogatives of national sovereignty. Mahan would also have argued that naval retrenchment induced national lethargy and stagnation, a weakening of the national muscle.[102] Disciples of Mahan in the U.S. Navy were upset by the Five-Power Treaty. William O. Stevens, one such disciple, was distressed with the battleship limitation ratio, protesting that it threw "overboard [Mahan's] whole philosophy of sea power." The treaty, Stevens felt, left the nation naked in the western Pacific in the face of an aggressive Japan.[103] Also repudiated was the Mahanian doctrine that had linked the navy to America's commitments in the Pacific and East Asia—the Philippines, Guam, and China.[104] The Washington treaties amounted to declaring that the Open Door was not worth a war with Japan— a position that would have distressed Mahan, who had written so passionately about the Open Door in his *Problem of Asia*.

In particular, the General Board reacted vigorously against Hughes's decision to scrap the fifteen modern capital ships under construction, because doing so made the United States "impotent to restrain [Japan's] aggressive plans in the Far East." The board in particular opposed the Pacific nonfortification provision because it negated the fleet's ability to "cross the Pacific and operate in Far Eastern waters." In this sense, the Five-Power Treaty repudiated Mahanian strategy in the Pacific.[105]

Naval historian William R. Braisted wrote that the U.S. Navy "emerged from the Washington Conference psychologically bruised and physically curtailed."[106] A classic naval critique of the conference was Captain Dudley W. Knox's *The Eclipse of American Naval Power* (1922). Undaunted, however, the American navy soon set about to offset the work of the architects of the Five-Power Treaty. In the 1922 and 1923 versions of War Plan Orange, the U.S. Navy continued to envision "an offensive war, primarily naval, directed toward the isolation and harassment of Japan, through control of her vital sea communications and through offensive sea and air operations against her naval forces and economic life." The United States was to "establish at the earliest date American sea power in the Western Pacific in strength superior to that of Japan." Nor did the board abandon its assumption that the United States would "go to war to enforce the Open Door."[107] This assumption contradicted the thinking of the American (civilian) architects of the Washington treaty system. In a report on Pacific strategy in April 1923, the planners emphasized the enhanced importance of the Philippines. An American base there was absolutely necessary to protect American interests in Asia, including access to the China market. In July 1923 the General Board defined the initial mission of the navy as "[establishing] at the earliest date American sea power in the western Pacific in strength superior to that of Japan." The Washington treaties had apparently made no difference in the strategic outlook of the U.S. Navy. Perhaps Mahan had not been repudiated after all.

PART THREE

COMPROMISE

AND

REACTION

CHAPTER FIVE

REVOLT AGAINST THE WASHINGTON TREATY

The Aftermath of the Washington Conference

hen Katō Tomosaburō returned from Washington on 10 March 1922, he received a hero's welcome from senior naval leaders, especially Fleet Admiral Tōgō. The naval *genro* (elder statesman) showed Katō "grandfatherly affection" and showered him with hearty thanks for his efforts in Washington. When the unreformed Katō Kanji blurted out that with a 60 percent ratio the navy could not assume responsibility for national defense, Tōgō sharply reprimanded him, "As long as the responsible navy minister says the 60 percent ratio poses no threat, those in charge of naval command must secure Japan's national defense with the given naval strength. You must not evade responsibility by saying you cannot fight a war with inferior strength."[1]

On 12 June 1922 Katō Tomosaburō was appointed prime minister in recognition of his achievements in Washington. The same sense of duty that had driven him to extremes at the conference moved him to serve concurrently as navy minister. His immediate task was to implement the Washington treaties, but his more intractable problem was to reform the navy and revise the Imperial National Defense Policy to agree with the vision he had brought back. At the Washington Conference he had entertained the idea of civilian navy ministers and a no-war policy toward the United States. Alas, his health, so taxed in Washington, failed him, and his death on 25 August 1923 doomed all but the first of these tasks.

Faithful to the Washington treaty, Japan abandoned the eight-eight fleet plan and scrapped two 48,000-ton battleships and four 46,000-ton battle cruisers. It also canceled plans for four battleships and four battle cruisers. The nation was left with only a "six-four fleet" (six battleships, four battle cruisers), to be supported by three carriers. When earmarked battleships were sunk as targets of gun and torpedo practice, officers and crew who had once manned them tearfully gave them full funeral rites. Captain Takahashi Sankichi, hard-line chief of the Operations Section, recalled later, "It was natural that our navy men harbored profound resentment of the Anglo-American powers."[2] Lieutenant Commander Inoue Shigeyoshi, a moderate officer who accepted the 60 percent ratio, nevertheless was "deeply chagrined to see one warship after another scrapped," and he was mortified that a dozen of his Naval Academy classmates were dismissed.[3] None could deny, however, that the Washington treaty saved Japan financially by allowing it to drastically cut its naval budget in 1923. The percentage of naval expenditures in the national budget, which was 31 percent in 1921, dropped to 26.5 percent in 1922 and 21 percent in 1923. National financial bankruptcy was averted and the Washington naval treaty helped Japan more than other signatories. (See Table 1.)

The drastic personnel retrenchment, amounting to 1,700 officers and warrant officers and 5,800 petty officers, caused great shocks. Nine out of ten vice admirals, the generation that had served in the Sino-Japanese and Russo-Japanese Wars, were retired. It was rumored that Katō Tomosaburō got rid of those whom or whose policies he disliked. (Satō Tetsutarō, who was mentioned in Chapter 2, was one of them.) Even those who remained in the navy lost their chances of promotion and commanding a ship. The trauma caused by enrollment reduction at the Naval Academy was profound: the entering class of 1922 numbered less than one-fifth of the previous class. The students were advised to consider returning to civilian life and to discuss it with their parents when they went home for summer vacation. The demoralizing effect was deep. It was no accident that four of the young naval officers later implicated in the "May 15 [assassination] Incident" of 1932 came from the classes affected by the Washington Conference.

The second task, institutional reform, had little chance of success, because objection loomed not only from the Naval General Staff but from the army. Katō Kanji, promoted to vice chief of the Naval General Staff in May 1922, absolutely opposed any system of civilian navy ministers. The elder Katō, in response to Diet questioning, pleaded for time while he investigated the matter. In November 1922, Rear Admiral Nomura Kichisaburō, head of the Intelligence Division, told the British naval attaché, Captain R. M. Colvin, that "fierce political agitation" was anticipated at the Diet session over the matter of civilian navy ministers. Nomura, Katō's former aide, questioned Colvin about British staff organization and the power of the First Lord of the Admiralty.[4]

To forestall any plan for civilian navy ministers, Katō Kanji ordered his protégé Takahashi Sankichi, Head of the Operations Division, to draft a counterplan to expand the jurisdiction of the chief of the Naval General Staff so that there would be little fear even if the system of civilian navy ministers did materialize. The plan envisioned transferring from the Naval Ministry to the Naval General Staff authority over armaments, personnel, and even education. However, Kanji did not dare submit such a plan to the elder Katō, who used to say, "As long as I am alive and kicking, I will never allow the Naval General Staff to have its own way."[5]

THE NATIONAL DEFENSE POLICY OF 1923

Katō Tomosaburō's third and most important agenda was revision of the Imperial National Defense Policy so that it would agree with the course he had set at the Washington Conference. However, he failed to incorporate his guide-line—avoidance of war with the United States—into the revised defense policy. In fact, only after the Naval General Staff (led by Vice Chief Katō Kanji and Chief of the Operations Division Suetsugu) and the representatives of the Army General Staff had decided on the new defense policy was it shown to the ailing Katō Tomosaburō, who had no choice but to acquiesce. Concerning the General Plan for Strategy that accompanied the new National Defense Policy, he fared even worse: he had been excluded from its formulation on the grounds that it was a highly confidential matter pertaining only to the high command.[6]

Sanctioned in February 1923, the revised Imperial National Defense Policy[7] negated the elder Katō's principle of avoidance of war with the United States and substituted Katō Kanji's notion of inevitable war. This top-secret document for the first time singled out—at the navy's insistence—the United States as "hypothetical enemy" number one for *both* the navy and the army. (Russia, the army's traditional enemy, had been weakened by the Bolshevik Revolution, the Siberian intervention, and its aftermath.)

The new defense policy's underlying view of the international situation went counter to the views of Katō Tomosaburō and the liberal diplomat Shidehara Kijūrō (soon to be appointed foreign minister), who envisioned a regime of peaceful cooperation under the Washington treaties. In short, the new defense policy negated the Washington system. It viewed the East Asian scene as riddled with conflict. The focus of "economic warfare" was China—"the greatest mar-ket in the whole world teeming with a population of hundreds of millions." It reflected the neo-Mahanian economic determinism.

> The United States, with its recent enhancement of national power and unlim-ited resources, is following a policy of economic invasion of China, menacing the position of our Empire and threatening to exceed the limits of our

endurance. . . . In addition, anti-Japanese agitation in California, spreading to other states, is growing in strength. . . . The Californian exclusion of the Japanese is becoming more deep-rooted. Nor does the problem of Japanese in Hawaii leave room for optimism. The longstanding embroilment, rooted in economic problems and racial prejudice, is extremely difficult to solve, and the conflict of interests and estrangement of emotion will become increasingly serious in the future. . . . Such being the Asiatic policy of the United States, which maintains bases in the Pacific and the Far East and possesses powerful armaments, a clash with our Empire will become inevitable sooner or later. In short, the Imperial National Defense Policy must be primarily directed against the United States, a power which is most likely to come to clash with us and which also possesses the greatest national strength and armaments.[7]

The motifs of neo-Mahanian economic determinism and a fatalistic belief in war with America unmistakably bore the stamp of Katō Kanji, vice chief of the Naval General Staff, with his ethnocentric perspective on the external world. To Katō the United States was not a mere "budgetary enemy" but *the* archantagonist with whom hostilities were unavoidable "in the near future." Japan now defined the United States as its foremost enemy in terms of both its *capabilities* and its *intentions*. A supreme irony of the Washington treaty was that Japan's National Defense Policy adopted the idea of inevitable war precisely when that treaty had reduced the Japanese and American navies so that neither could conduct offensive operations.

The internal background to these developments was the remarkable ascendancy of Katō Kanji. Outmaneuvering his mild-mannered chief, Admiral Yamashita Gentarō, he wielded such power that, according to his official biography, the Naval General Staff became Katō Kanji's one-man show. "He often tended to overwhelm the administrative branch [the Navy Ministry]."[8] He was aided by his protégé Captain Suetsugu, newly promoted to chief of the Operations Division, and Takahashi Sankichi, chief of the Operations Section.

The General Plan for Strategy that accompanied the new National Defense Policy reflected Katō Kanji's obsession with "quick engagement, quick showdown."[9] He ignored the exigencies of total war that pointed to any future war being a prolonged conflict. In keeping with his perceived lesson of World War I, Katō Kanji was preoccupied with a decisive main-fleet encounter, which he expected at an early stage of war. It was generally projected that the Japanese navy would complete the Philippine operations within a month and that a decisive battle would materialize within forty-five days after the opening of hostilities. Suetsugu also held, "One of the greatest lessons Japan learned from the great war was 'quick encounter, quick decision.' Unless we launch a positive offensive, the war would become prolonged with the result that both sides will lose, regardless of which side wins."[10] Although the National Defense Policy of 1923 referred to "the need for determination to endure a prolonged war," Katō Kanji's whole strategic idea ran counter to it. And the General Plan for Strategy of 1923 essentially restated its 1918 version: "At the outset of hostilities the navy will speedily devastate the enemy fleet [the much inferior Asiatic Fleet] in the Far East and, in cooperation with the army, will destroy the enemy's naval bases in Luzon and Guam. As the enemy's main fleet comes steaming to Far Eastern waters, the navy will gradually reduce its strength en route by repeatedly attacking and at an appropriate moment our main fleet will annihilate the enemy fleet."[9]

As a result of the Washington ratio of 60 percent, the new strategic plans spelled out for the first time the attrition strategy (*Zengen sakusen*) as an essential preliminary to interceptive operations and a decisive fleet encounter. The attrition strategy aimed, through repeated torpedo attacks by submarines, to whittle down the enemy's main fleet on its transpacific passage. In addition, the capture of Guam was a new feature of this strategic plan. In short, the plan consisted of three stages: scouting, attrition strategy, and a decisive fleet encounter. Like its earlier versions, the General Plan for Strategy of 1923 did not spell out what further actions would be required after the destruction of the enemy's fleet; it merely stated that further operations would be determined "according to the requirements of the moment."[10] The assumption seems to have been that even the United States with all its industrial power would take many years to rebuild a new battle fleet, enabling Japan to choose an appropriate moment to seek favorable terms. This continued to set the pattern for Japanese strategic thought into the late 1930s.

The strategic plan of 1923, with its emphasis on "quick engagement, quick showdown," contradicted the stipulation in the revised National Defense Policy that Japan "must be prepared for protracted war." This awareness of the exigencies of total war, however, did not take root in the Japanese navy.[11]

AFTER KATŌ TOMOSABURŌ

Despite naval dissatisfactions beneath the surface, the aftermath of the Washington Conference brought forth an era of good feelings in relations between the two navies. Admiral William T. Pratt, who unlike most American navy officers trusted Japan, wrote in a personal letter in September 1922, "I feel that if she [Japan] adopts a policy of close cooperation with Great Britain and with ourselves, particularly the United States, she will through cooperation with these two countries gain more than she will by playing a lone hand. I followed the course of the Conference very carefully and it seemed to me that this was beginning to be a dominating note in Japanese policy. The appointment of Baron Kato as Premier only seems to be a step in this direction."[12]

Arthur Balfour, British chief delegate at Washington, also admired Katō. In June 1922 he wrote to Charles Eliot, new ambassador to Japan, "I cannot but welcome [Katō's appointment as Prime Minister], since I believe that his influence in Far East politics will be on the side of peace and harmony, that he will have the courage of his opinion . . . and be a statesman of eminently practical, sensible and moderate views. . . . I greatly appreciated his readiness to take a broad-minded and independent point of view."[13]

The news of Katō Tomosaburō's untimely death on 25 August 1923 was a devastating blow to Pratt. Significantly, Pratt perceived the effect of Katō's death on Japanese-American relations. Shocked to hear of Katō's death, Pratt sent a letter of condolence to his old friend, Rear Admiral Nomura Kichisaburō, Katō's aide at the Washington Conference, whom he had known since his attaché days in Washington:

> I feel that not only Japan lost one of the greatest broad-minded men but that we in the United States have lost a sincere friend and a man who understands us far better than the average man can. During the course of the conference in Washington I watched Baron Kato very closely. I wanted, if possible, to find out the kind of a man he was. . . . I became thoroughly convinced in my mind at that time that Baron Kato was one of the finest, biggest, and most courteous gentlemen that I ever had the honor of meeting. I felt that so long as he had the direction of affairs in his hands no misunderstanding could arise between your country and mine which could not be settled through amicable arrangements.[14]

Pratt also wrote in his unpublished autobiography, "I have always looked upon him as one of the world's leading statesmen. He was a man of great character."[15] Other American admirals shared Pratt's sentiment. For example, Lyman A. Cotton wrote in his diary, "[Katō] was a man of splendid character and excellent brains. A real leader of his people, and one that can be spared with difficulty."[16]

Pratt worried whether Katō's successors would uphold the cooperative policy he had established at the Washington Conference. As Pratt feared, Katō's death, which removed the suppression of insurgent elements in the navy, caused a breach in the Washington treaty system. Admiral Yamanashi, a faithful heir to Katō, reflected after the war, "If Fleet Admiral Katō Tomosaburō [he was made a fleet admiral after his death] had lived several more years, Japan would never have placed itself in the position to plunge into the Pacific War."[17] The succeeding navy minister, Admiral Takarabe Takeshi, who served from 1923 to 1927 and again from 1929 to 1930, did not possess the kind of leadership and broad international outlook that were the hallmarks of Katō Tomosaburō. It is not clear why a man of Takarabe's caliber was appointed to head the navy for so long. He had risen through the ranks with unusual rapidity—"like an imperial prince"—because of, it was rumored, the clout of his father-in-law, Admiral Yamamoto Gonbei, former navy minister and prime minister.[18]

Katō Tomosaburō seemed to have intended as his successor his Vice Minister Ide Kenji, who had ably assisted him at the time of the Washington Conference. Ide's friends remembered him as "a man of exceptional brilliance, determined character, and keen political sense." However, disgruntled old officers who had been retired under the Washington treaty made Ide a scapegoat, because they would not dare openly attack the great Katō Tomosaburō. Vice Admiral Yamanashi believed that "if Ide had not fallen from power but remained in the Navy Ministry, the subsequent course of the navy would have been different."[19] With Katō gone and Ide victimized, naval intellectual Rear Admiral Takagi Sōkichi wrote, "the navy's leadership shifted from truly outstanding individuals to institutionalized authority," and "competition among mediocrities" came to the fore. At the same time, Takagi held Katō Tomosaburō responsible for his failure to groom his successors: "When power is concentrated in one individual, it is the iron law of history that his successors will be mediocre; they become mere administrators."[20] This statement could be applied to all five of the navy ministers who succeeded Katō Tomosaburō: Takarabe, Murakami Kakuichi (1924), Abo Kiyokazu (1930–31), Ōsumi Mineo (1931–32, 1933–36), and perhaps Nagano Osami (1936–37).

Katō Kanji had been building a powerful coterie. He and Suetsugu appealed for the support of "hot-blooded" young officers in the Naval General Staff who opposed naval limitation. In the Navy Ministry, Abo and Ōsumi were Katō's allies in opposing the Washington treaty system. Against this backdrop, let us now examine the Japanese navy's preparations for the next naval conference.

THE RACE IN AUXILIARY SHIPS

At the Washington Conference, Charles Evans Hughes had declared that the Five-Power Treaty "ends, absolutely ends, the race in the competition of naval armaments."[21] Katō Tomosaburō, however, had been more realistic. In his "message" to Vice Minister Ide, he had stated, "Don't have false hopes: the naval limitation conference at Washington is not going to be the last one."[22]

After Washington the arms race revolved around auxiliary ships (defined in the Japanese navy as all units other than battleships and aircraft carriers)—especially heavy cruisers replacing 10,000 tons and mounting 8-inch guns. They were called "treaty cruisers" because they represented the maximum displacement and gunnery allowed under the Washington treaty. During the treaty era, Japan took the world lead in heavy cruiser design. Its heavy cruisers were faster, had a greater cruising radius, and were more heavily gunned than their American counterparts. The Japanese navy intended these heavy cruisers to be "substitutes" for battleships, whose construction was prohibited under the Washington treaty. Thus the heavy destroyers were expected to play a crucial role in a decisive fleet encounter.

After the Washington Conference, harmony and cooperation prevailed within the Japanese navy in its effort to build a treaty navy. The British naval attaché observed, "The ship's company are cheerful, clean, and healthy, and discipline is as near perfection as possible. There are no defaulters."[23] But sooner or later a second naval conference was anticipated. Assuming that the United States would propose a second conference, the navy's research committee on arms limitation drafted a study in 1925. This study began, appropriately enough, with a discussion of "Lessons of the Washington Conference."[24] The first lesson was that Japan's "failure" in Washington, as Katō Kanji and kindred minds saw it, was due to inadequate preparations. For the next conference, Japan must establish "a firm, concrete, and clear-cut policy" well in advance and demand preliminary negotiations to obtain prior acceptance of Japan's demands. There was a general feeling that the Japanese navy, having backed down in Washington in 1922, *must* stand firm the next time, whatever the risk.

The second lesson was that the navy's position must be publicized at home to "educate, unify, and firm up" domestic public opinion in support of Japanese demands. This point was particularly stressed by Katō Kanji; he recalled how he had been "handicapped" by the lack of domestic support in Washington.[25] A third lesson was that "the utmost caution must be taken never again to be confronted by joint Anglo-American coercion." The Japanese navy feared that these two powers would pressure Japan again by threatening a ruinously expensive naval race if the conference broke up.[26]

Japanese planners assumed that the Americans would call a second conference to extend the Washington ratios of 10:10:6 to auxiliary ships. In fact, as early as June 1922, the General Board of the U.S. Navy had recommended, "Maintain 5–3 ratio with Japan in all classes of fighting ship."[27] The Japanese navy was "absolutely opposed" to such a ratio and planned to declare at the outset that it must be regarded as a "separate" gathering, not an extension of the Washington Conference.[28]

As to the all-important ratio question, the report, echoing Katō Kanji's view regarding "the right of equality," stated that Japan would be justified in proposing the "principle of parity" (10:10), but anticipating Anglo-American opposition, would compromise with, say, an 80 percent ratio. Some members argued that with an 80 percent ratio in auxiliaries, Japan would achieve a roughly overall ratio of 70 percent against the United States. This idea, however, was rejected by those committed to the long-standing consensus on a 70 percent ratio.[29] The final point was the timing of the next conference. Japan would have an advantage if the conference could be synchronized with the completion of the current "auxiliary replacement plan" in 1928. To place itself in an advantageous position at the next conference, the Naval General Staff urged acceleration of the building program, and by 1927 Japan's auxiliary strength actually surpassed 70 percent of the U.S. Navy's.

Before we examine the Geneva Naval Conference of 1927, it is appropriate to examine weaponry and strategic development during 1922–27.

STRATEGY IN THE PACIFIC

Japan's construction program was noteworthy for its special emphasis on the large submarine. The Washington Conference had reduced Japan's naval strength to a "six-four fleet" (six battleships and four battle cruisers) against an American fleet of fifteen battleships and three carriers. Efforts to redress this imbalance had produced major innovations in Japan's technology and strategic planning. A new feature of the General Plan of Strategy of 1923 was an attrition strategy to precede interceptive operations. It depended on large, high-speed submarines whose mission would be to whittle down the American fleet on its transpacific passage and attack American battleships in the decisive fleet encounter. The "uniquely innovative" strategist Rear Admiral Suetsugu worked out this attrition strategy as commander of the First and Second Submarine Divisions in 1923–25.[30] He has rightly been called "the father of Japanese submarine strategy." During World War I he had studied German U-boat operations as a naval observer on board HMS *Queen Mary*, Admiral David Beatty's flagship, in the North Sea, and he believed that the submarine offered the best hope of countering America's battleship superiority. It was "the weapon of the weak party."

After the mid-1920s, Japanese submarines were to scout the enemy fleet upon its sortie from Pearl Harbor, shadowing and keeping it under surveillance, and repeated relentless attacks to "gradually reduce" the enemy's strength by about 30 percent before staging a decisive fleet encounter. For this purpose Japan built, after 1924, a large number of oceangoing "fleet submarines" with a cruising radius of twenty thousand miles (sufficient to reach California and return without refueling) and a surface speed of 20 knots (sufficient to accompany a battleship). And they were equipped with reliable torpedoes.[31]

In the mid-1920s, for both navies, the radius of action and line of naval defense had been extended by rapid advances in technology and weaponry. War plans became more concrete on both sides of the Pacific. Shortly after the Washington Conference, the Japanese navy seemed to have clandestine access to a confidential paper on America's Pacific strategy. It revealed that the U.S. Navy would advance across the central Pacific and commandeer Japan's mandated islands (unfortified, these island were "hostages" to the U.S. Navy). Using these islands as a base, the American fleet would recapture the Philippines and then move to the western Pacific for the climactic Mahanian battle. The confidential paper indeed matched American planning. The War Plan Orange of 1924 envisioned the following scenario. The main objective of the U.S. Navy was to obtain command of the sea in the western Pacific as soon as possible, by seizing the Japanese mandated islands, recapturing the Philippines, and building an advanced base to accommodate the entire fleet. Thus fortified, the American fleet would seek a main-fleet encounter with the Japanese navy and control its vital sea communications, isolating Japan and forcing it to surrender by means of a blockade and attacks on its commerce.[32] As if in a mirror image, Japan's naval planners anticipated such an American scenario.[33] But they disagreed over the timing of the American advance to the western Pacific. The dominant view of the Naval General Staff, represented by Katō Kanji, was that Japan's capture of the Philippines would enrage the American people and compel a rapid thrust westward of their battle fleet to avenge the loss of the Philippines.[34]

However, as Edward S. Miller's study of War Plan Orange shows, America's Pacific strategy had two variations. The strategy supported by what he calls the "thrusters" ("Through Ticket to Manila" strategy) would quickly rush the U.S. fleet to the western Pacific to recapture the Philippines. This strategy held out the hope of a short war; the American people would not be willing to endure a long war. Had Mahan not taught, "War once declared must be waged offensively, aggressively"? On the other hand, the "cautionary" strategy foresaw a stepwise advance along the central Pacific route. This strategy held that Americans would accept a long war only for a righteous cause. In the 1920s the former option, a rapid thrust to the Philippines and Guam, seemed increasingly difficult. Instead, an island-to-island campaign in the central route to obtain forward bases was thought necessary before challenging Japan to a main battle-line engagement.[35]

Unaware of the debates within the U.S. Navy, Katō Kanji assumed that the American navy was committed to the rapid-thrust scenario. He observed, "The fundamental guideline of American strategy is the principle of the quick encounter, quick showdown. It is bent on promptly forcing an engagement with the Japanese fleet, thus deciding the issue in one stroke." In the 1920s the ratio of American and Japanese shipbuilding capacity was estimated at three or four to one. Therefore Japan would have the advantage if a quick showdown materialized before the margin of American industrial power became even more overwhelmingly against Japan's odds. If a crushing blow was dealt to America's main fleet early in the war, Katō was certain that even the United States, with its great industrial might, would take a long time to build enough battleships to attempt another decisive battle. Meanwhile Japan would search for acceptable peace terms.[36]

Once again, a certain mirror image appears between the Japanese and American war scenarios. Both navies anticipated an initial Japanese seizure of the islands in the western Pacific, including the Philippines. Both antici-pated an eventual effort by the numerically stronger U.S. fleet to fight its way across the Pacific and stage a climactic battle fleet engagement near Japan's home waters.

But there were dissenting views. A minority of Japanese planners ques-tioned whether the American navy would oblige Japan with a quick westward dash. What if the United States decided to bolster its main fleet until it had built up an overwhelmingly superior power and the essential logistic support? In that event, Japan's efforts to maintain its fleet ratio against the United States would be fruitless. Japan had no means of forcing a decisive fleet encounter with the U.S. Navy. Even in the event of a big battle, the war games and map maneuvers conducted in the late 1920s showed that Japan's chances were ques-tionable. Rear Admiral Takagi Sōkichi, who graduated from the Naval Staff College in 1927, recalled that unless the umpires of war games rigged them and made special allowances—for additional fuel oil, logistical advantages, or repairs—the bulk of the Japanese fleet would sink even before engaging the U.S. main fleet.[37] This problem was not solved in the 1930s, either.

To overcome Japan's inferior fleet ratio, Katō, appointed Commander in Chief of the Combined Fleet in December 1926, with Takahashi Sankichi serv-ing as his chief of staff, ordered the fleet to engage in relentless close-in night exercises that were "more heroic than under actual battle conditions." (When a dejected Katō Kanji had returned from Washington and tearfully apologized for failing to obtain a 70 percent ratio, Fleet Admiral Tōgō had cheered him up, saying, "The treaty places no limitation on drills, does it?") No other navy held such rigorous drills. Night exercises were so risky, carried out at full speed and without lights, that two cruisers and two destroyers collided one moonless night of 21 August 1927 off Mihogaseki in the Sea of Japan near northwestern Honshu, resulting in 120 casualties. Instead of acknowledging his responsibility for the errors, Katō attributed the disaster to the Washington treaty. He grimly addressed the assembled commanders: "We must devote ourselves more and more to this kind of drill, to which our navy has applied all its energies ever since the acceptance of the 10:10:6 ratio." He continued, "With a 10:6 ratio, unsurpassed training is required to prevail in battle." This language was calculated to inflame feelings against the Washington treaty. The 60 percent ratio had crystallized into the conviction that "only through these hard drills can we expect to beat America!"[38]

The U.S. Navy added to such resentment in Japanese naval circles. During the first half of 1925, the commander in chief of the U.S. fleet, Admiral Robert E. Coontz, led 145 ships, including twelve battleships, and 24,500 men in extensive maneuvers west of Hawaii, followed by a spectacular cruise to Australia and New Zealand. These maneuvers were the largest ever conducted up to this time and, indeed, the greatest voyage ever attempted before the Pacific War.[39] Held in the middle of a war scare prompted by the passage of the Immigration Act of 1924, the maneuvers seemed like a naval demonstration against Japan. Indeed, they were targeted against the Orange enemy, Japan. (Admiral Coontz was determined to sail westward quickly in the event of war with Japan.) Although the fleet refrained from a trial run to the Philippines out of deference to Japan, the cruise provoked Katō and kindred minds, who saw the maneuvers as a dress rehearsal for transpacific operations. A secret report of the Naval General Staff stated:

> The United States Navy, conducting the exercise of a large-scale transoceanic operation, is engrossed in undisguised building [of] armaments against Japan. . . . It is building forward bases in Hawaii and the Panama canal zone while reinforcing its bases on the Pacific coast. . . . In short, U.S. naval strategy is not a passive one of merely relieving the Philippines and Guam from Japanese control but it is a more positive and aggressive one of attacking Japan's coast, occupying strategic points in Japan's home waters or air-raiding Tokyo, Osaka, and Nagoya, thus forcing a decisive battle with the Japanese fleet. If our fleet does not come forward, the U.S. fleet would cut Japan's vital communications and force it immediately to succumb.[40]

The disquietude and alarm that had been building among fleet officers ever since the Washington Conference found expression in a letter of protest written by Admiral Yamamoto Eisuke (no relation to Yamamoto Isoroku) to Saitō. As the nation's first line of defense, he said, the fleet engaged day and night in relentless exercises to overcome treaty deficiencies in armaments. But the top leaders of the navy ministry were all too ready to make political compromises when confronted with budgetary difficulties, oblivious to the serious defects in armaments they had created. These moderate leaders in Tokyo, he charged, resembled "civilian desk officers" rather than real "sailor-warriors." Venting his resentment, Yamamoto traced this "deplorable" condition to the Washington Conference, and accused Katō Tomosaburō of maintaining a "despotic" rule that "emasculated" the navy by dismissing senior officers who went against him.[41]

These sentiments reflected a division among naval officers into two groups. On the one hand, "sea officers," led by Katō Kanji and his kindred spirits in the Naval General Staff and fleets, were called the "command group." These commanders sensed a growing crisis regarding the "grave defects in national defense." On the other hand was the "administrative group," composed of "desk officers" who excelled in administrative work and held key posts in the navy ministry. The former opposed the Washington treaty, whereas the latter adhered to Katō Tomosaburō's legacy of naval limitation and the Washington system. The demarcation between the two groups became clear at the time of the London Conference of 1930, and a major conflict would explode over the London treaty. Before this impasse came an interlude in 1927 when Japan participated in a second naval conference at Geneva.

PREPARING FOR THE GENEVA
NAVAL CONFERENCE

On 10 February 1927, President Calvin Coolidge invited Japan, Britain, France, and Italy to a naval conference in Geneva. France and Italy refused to participate, and it became a three-power conference. Its aim was to extend the Washington capital ship ratios of 10:10:6 to auxiliary ships. The Japanese government, headed by Wakatsuki Reijirō, wanted to participate because it was suffering from an economic depression and put a premium on cooperation with the United States, but the government asked for the navy's view before responding to the invitation to Geneva. The navy took a very strong position. Fleet Admiral Tōgō had reversed his support for naval limitation after the Washington Conference, apparently due to the influence of Katō Kanji and Tōgō's crony Vice Admiral Ogasawara Naganari.

Tōgō stated, "We might consent to participate but we must be absolutely deter-mined to withdraw from the conference unless we can carry through our demands."[42] The navy had been making all-out efforts to build auxiliary ships, having obtained from the Diet, in late 1926, an approval for a plan that would ensure a ratio of more than 70 percent strength.

What was the position of the U.S. Navy? The General Board had not changed its views about Japan's aggressive policy. Because Japan's goal was "the political, commercial, and military domination of the Western Pacific," the board felt that the basic clash of interests could still lead to war.[43] Anticipating the Japanese demand for a 70 percent ratio, American admirals declared that "the desire of Japan for the security of her sea lines of communication is in conflict with the American desire for security of sea lines of communication to China and the Philippines." The board believed that the U.S. Navy had greatly weakened its position in the Pacific after the Washington treaty and to further "weaken our position . . . would not conduce to peace but would have the opposite effect by giving greater security to Japan in furthering of her policies and plans adversely affecting the United States." Rear Admiral Hilary P. Jones, co-delegate at the Geneva Conference, held that a large number of 8-inch-gun cruisers was necessary for fleet operations against Japan. He was more Mahanian than Mahan himself would have been. Thus a Japanese-American clash at Geneva seemed inescapable.[44]

As it turned out, however, the parley at Geneva was so plagued with Anglo-American differences over cruiser types and tonnages that a Japanese-American conflict never surfaced. As the civilian delegate Ishii Kikujirō reflected, "Had the negotiations continued for a little while longer, at the least a violent controversy with America over the ratio issue would have become inescapable."[45] This was cor-roborated by Commander Nomura Naokuni, a naval member of the delegation: "Although Japan had taken a very rigid stand [on the ratio issue], Anglo-American antagonism so dominated the conference that it broke up without going into the issues at stake with Japan."[46] As far as the Japanese navy was concerned, therefore, the 1927 conference amounted to a skirmish with the United States, a prelude to a major confrontation that would occur at the London Conference.

The Geneva Conference ran aground on the shoals of the Anglo-American clash over the cruiser question. The United States, possessing few bases outside home waters, required heavy cruisers capable of transoceanic passage, whereas Britain, with bases and colonies around the world, demanded a large number of smaller cruisers. The U.S. Navy needed heavy cruisers (10,000-ton vessels armed with 8-inch guns) for operations against Japan across the Pacific. The General Board was particularly insistent that distances and lack of bases necessitated heavy cruisers. So in roundabout fashion, Japan became an integral part of the three-cornered impasse that developed in Geneva. Using the Japanese naval record, it is now possible to examine for the first time Japan's policy at the Geneva Conference.[47]

One of the "lessons of the Washington Conference," as the 1925 report had emphasized, was the need for adequate preparations, and naval leaders took this to heart. Preparatory discussions began in late March 1927 under the direction of Navy Vice Minister Ōsumi Mineo, but the wide divergence of opinions soon became unmanageable. Ōsumi, an ally of Katō Kanji, adamantly clamored for a 70 percent ratio. He resented the "most high-handed imposition of the Washington treaty on Japan."[48] On the other hand, Vice Chief of the Naval General Staff Nomura Kichisaburō, faithful to the legacy of Katō Tomosaburō, took "a large view," and asserted that a 60 percent ratio in auxiliaries should be accepted if necessary to prevent an unlimited naval race with the Anglo-American powers. Nomura was contradicted by "hawks" such as Captain Nakamura Kamesaburō, chief of the Operations Section, who asserted that "in the near future Japan will have a 70–80 percent ratio as regards the cruiser and that it actually surpasses their [Anglo-American] strength in the newest type cruiser."

Confusion reigned when it came to drafting instructions to the chief naval adviser, Vice Admiral Kobayashi Seizō, who handled the negotiations in Geneva. Having served as head of the Naval Affairs Bureau since 1923, Kobayashi was a strong leader of the "administrative group" and was known for his political acumen. A nephew of Katō Tomosaburō, he hoped to complete the work of the Washington Conference. Like Tomosaburō, Kobayashi had served for many years in the navy ministry.[49] At the meeting of 8 April 1927, attended by Navy Minister Okada Keisuke and Chief of the Naval General Staff Suzuki Kantarō, the naval leaders discussed the draft instructions that contained a demand for a 70 percent ratio. The meeting was thrown into confusion when Rear Admiral Hara Kanjirō, chief of the Operations Division, remarked, "The actual truth is that Chief of Naval General Staff Suzuki Kantarō says 60 percent is all right." An exasperated Kobayashi asked where the wishes of the Naval General Staff lay.[50]

On the same day, Navy Vice Minister Ōsumi asked Lieutenant Commander Satō Ichirō of the Naval General Staff to prepare a memorandum to help him draft instructions to Kobayashi. Satō stressed the "importance of making as clear as possible the demands of the government, so as to provide the delegates with a firm basis of negotiations." He emphasized that unlike at the Washington Conference, Japan's fleet strength was now "very advantageous, so the delegates must take the initiative and come forward with an initial proposal at the conference."[51]

On 11 April the naval leaders gathered again at the navy minister's official residence to explain the draft instructions to the assembled admirals and the members of the Supreme Military Council.[52] Lieutenant Commander Satō's report
throws much light on bureaucratic politics within the navy. The original draft
instructions, prepared by Iwamura Seiichi of the Operations Division, were emasculated by the Naval Affairs Bureau. The revised instructions failed to give what
Vice Admiral Suetsugu Nobumasa, head of the Education Bureau, had demanded:
a clear-cut and forceful instruction on a 70 percent ratio. Lieutenant Commander
Satō complained, "There is just too much rhetoric about easing economic burden
and saving government expenditure. Almost nothing is said about the needs of
national defense." The draft instructions were to be revised again.

The following day, altercations occurred between Kobayashi and the leaders
of the Naval General Staff, Vice Chief Nomura and Chief of the Operations
Division Hara. When Kobayashi questioned them about the minimum tonnage
acceptable, Nomura and Hara "floundered through their answers." Kobayashi
finally lost his temper: "I cannot help but note that the Naval General Staff
has no firm convictions on the force level required for national defense!" He
added, "It has become clear that the naval authorities do not possess any concrete plan. This being the case, we cannot expect to conduct negotiations at
Geneva."[53] While Navy Vice Minister Ōsumi continuously insisted on the 70 percent
ratio, both the Chief and Vice Chief of the Naval General Staff, Suzuki and
Nomura, were initially prepared to settle for 60 percent. Having encountered
strong resistance from their subordinates, however, they equivocated.

The instructions finally given to Japan's chief delegates, Admiral Saitō
Makoto and Ishii Kikujirō, contained no mention of ratios, vaguely directing
them "not to lower the relative ratio below the requirements of our security."
specific instructions handed to chief naval adviser Kobayashi stated that heavy
cruiser strength must be no lower than 70 percent.[54] However, Saitō and Ishii
interpreted the 70 percent ratio as "a mere criterion for negotiations," and not
as a "strict mathematical figure absolutely required for national defense."[55]

As at the Washington Conference, much depended at the Geneva Conference
on the chief naval delegate—his personality, leadership, and international outlook. The great importance Prime Minister Wakatsuki attached to the conference, rendered all the more urgent by a financial crisis in March 1927, was clear
from his selection of Admiral Saitō. The admiral had a long and distinguished
career, especially in administrative posts on shore, having served for eight years
as a navy vice minister and eight more years as minister, and he was incumbent
governor-general of Korea. The seventy-year-old Saitō was respected as "a great

figure of superdreadnought caliber." However, considering his post in Korea to be his last calling, he declined to go to Geneva, so Vice Admiral Yamanashi, a former aide to Saitō, went to Seoul to persuade him that his presence at Geneva was absolutely necessary.[56]

The move to appoint Saitō alarmed the Combined Fleet commander, Katō Kanji. One sleepless night, he impulsively wrote a long and presumptuous letter, urging Saitō to turn down the mission. (In view of its delicate nature he wrote in the margin, "Please burn this letter upon reading.") First, he argued that the appointment of a lightweight such as Hugh Gibson as America's chief delegate would likely doom the conference to failure. Second, Katō invoked the "bitter lesson" of the Washington Conference. "From the navy's standpoint," he opined, "it is undesirable to appoint a great naval figure as the head delegate to discuss naval questions." Apparently, Katō's greatest fear was that an admiral-statesman such as Saitō might overrule the narrow strategic views of his naval advisers to reach a political compromise, just as Katō Tomosaburō had done in Washington. Third, Katō emphasized the importance of leaving substantive matters to the naval experts, for they were experienced in the give-and-take of international conferences. Disingenuously he wrote that this was where Katō Tomosaburō had his greatest difficulties. Obviously the junior Katō underestimated Saitō's diplomatic acumen.[57]

In the negotiations in Geneva, Saitō commanded the respect of the American and British delegates for his impartiality and devotion to naval limitation. The American navy considered Saitō "a good patriot and a fair-minded man," and also noted that he was somewhat pro-American. The British ambassador, John Tilley, reported that Saitō "has the reputation of being a man of decided views and not easily turned from his path." Under Saitō's leadership, assisted by his chief adviser Kobayashi, the naval members of the Japanese delegation worked in harmony.

On their voyage to Geneva on board the *Awa-Maru*, the naval members argued over conference strategy. Hard-liners, reflecting Katō Kanji's views, maintained that Japan, "instead of stooping low and fawning on America and England, must forestall these powers, resolutely declare a concrete proposal, and adhere to it even at the risk of breaking up the conference." Lieutenant Commander Satō drafted a hard-line memorandum for his superiors, in which he said, "Even if the conference should fail, there is no fear of Japan getting into financial difficulties. If the Empire's legitimate demands are not accepted, we must be prepared to furl the flag and return home."[58]

Saitō scolded the hard-liners. It would be impolitic for Japan to bluff, he said. Preparedness consisted of gradually enhancing national strength—economic and industrial power—while "winning greater respect and understanding from the rest of the world." In view of limited resources, he warned, it would arouse antipathy if Japan "demanded parity or some preferred ratio. . . . We should not opportunistically attempt a sudden expansion of our navy in one conference or two." Saitō's words settled the argument, and they reminded the delegates of Katō Tomosaburō's broad views on national defense.[59]

Like Katō, Saitō controlled the naval members of the delegation, but unlike Katō he could not persuade Navy Vice Minister Ōsumi, who adamantly demanded a 70 percent ratio. The delegates' work at Geneva was hampered by lack of coordination with the naval authorities in Tokyo. Departing from the procedure set at the Washington Conference, the naval authorities decided that instructions should be sent from Vice Minister Ōsumi to the chief naval expert Kobayashi, not directly to the head delegate. Ōsumi's instructions on the crucial ratio question were secretly drafted within the confines of the navy and were not discussed in cabinet meetings. Therefore, technical-strategic considerations dominated Tokyo's instructions to the exclusion of broader political views.[60]

Navy Vice Minister Ōsumi was Katō Kanji's confidant. Regarding the Washington Conference as "a most flagrant oppression," he harbored a distrust of the United States that went as far back as the cruise of the Great White Fleet in 1908. On the other hand, chief naval adviser Kobayashi was a man of broad international outlook, similar to his illustrious uncle Katō Tomosaburō. Both men had the ambition of becoming navy minister. Friction between them would complicate communication between Geneva and Tokyo.[61]

COMPROMISE RATIO

The Geneva Conference opened on 20 June 1927 at the Palais des Nations, headquarters of the League of Nations. Emulating Hughes at the Washington Conference, Hugh Gibson, head American delegate and chairman of the conference, presented the initial proposal, which was an extension of the Washington ratio of 10:10:6. The issue had thus been drawn between the United States and Japan. Unlike in Washington, however, the American position was weak in auxiliary vessels, especially cruisers, both built and planned. The Japanese navy had made all-out efforts to build auxiliary ships, having obtained from the Diet, in late 1926, approval for a plan that would ensure a ratio of 70 percent strength. Japan demanded its tonnage on a status quo ("existing strength") basis; the United States would then have to greatly increase its tonnage to achieve a 10:6 ratio superiority. And the United States could offer Japan no political compensations in return for naval concessions. Political questions on the Far East were carefully excluded, and the conference became a strictly technical one dominated by naval experts. The United States could offer neither a diplomatic carrot nor a naval stick.

In comparison with other delegations at the conference, America's head delegate, Gibson, was only forty-four years old and minister to Belgium; his sole credential was that he had served as the American representative on the League Commission on Disarmament. He could hardly be compared with Hughes. He had little knowledge of naval affairs and was overshadowed by his co-delegate, Rear Admiral Hilary P. Jones. An old sea dog and a member of the General Board, Jones was reputed to "see the world through a porthole."[62] On 3 June, shortly after the conference opened, Jones, a strong Mahanian, met Saitō and blurted out a threatening remark: "Since the United States restricted its Philippine and Guam fortifications, it will have to operate in the western Pacific with only half of its existing force. . . . If the application of the 10:10:6 ratio should fail to materialize, the United States will achieve it through a naval arms race backed by its unlimited wealth." He insisted that "a quota of 50 percent would practically assure Japan a parity in its home waters because the United States could effectively utilize only one half of its fleet in the event of operating in the western Pacific." So the 60 percent ratio was overly generous. A 70 percent ratio was simply out of the question, because it would destroy the naval balance. The United States did not wish to give Japan superiority in the western Pacific, the anticipated theater of operations.[63] This was, of course, the position of the U.S. Navy throughout the 1920s, but never had it been so bluntly stated by its ranking officer to a Japanese naval leader.

From the beginning, the Japanese delegates proposed to take, as the standard of reduction, Japan's existing strength plus its building program, which would place its ratio at above 70 percent of the United States but about 65 percent of Great Britain. But they carefully avoided publicly mentioning a 70 percent ratio for fear of rousing Anglo-American opposition. It would also "excite Japan's naval circles as well as the Japanese people" by reviving memories of the Washington Conference.[64]

It would be tedious to detail the Anglo-American-Japanese talks. Far more interesting and relevant for our purposes are various moves within the Japanese delegation. Middle-echelon naval members were angered that Vice Admiral Kobayashi was all too eager to find the right moment to retreat. Flying into a rage, Lieutenant Commander Satō told Kobayashi, "It is wrong to make one-sided compromises. You say they are only partial retreats, but when you add them all up, you lose the whole case."[65] Up until this time, the Japanese delegates had been so preoccupied with their ratio question that they did not recognize how serious the Anglo-American impasse had become. They had an excessive fear that the British would yield to the Americans and then form a joint Anglo-American front to impose a 60 percent ratio on Japan—a fear inspired by the memory of the "joint coercion" in Washington.

Japanese delegates entered into talks with the British, who seemed more flexible on the ratio issue, to work out some formula that might break the three-cornered deadlock. On 16 July a broad Anglo-Japanese "compromise formula" emerged out of informal exchanges between Kobayashi and the British delegate, Vice Admiral Frederick Field, and Saitō endorsed it.[66] This compromise formula provided Japan with 315,000 tons and the British with 325,000 tons in "surface auxiliary vessels" (cruisers and destroyers), which meant a ratio of 65 percent for Japan.[67] Most members of the delegation approved it, although not all young officers did. Lieutenant Commander Nomura Naokuni was greatly upset, shed tears, and refused to eat.[68]

Why did the delegates propose a 65 percent ratio, despite the renewed instruction from Navy Vice Minister Ōsumi "to do their utmost" to obtain the 70 percent ratio? According to Kobayashi's report, the delegates believed it urgent to remove the Anglo-American "fixation" with the Washington ratio and reach any agreement above it, be it 62 or 63 percent, which would do away with their obsession with a 60 percent ratio. The delegates had admitted that Japan's strength was about 65 percent of Britain's, so reaching parity between Britain and the United States would mean a 65 percent ratio against the United States as well. Computing from a 65 percent ratio for surface auxiliaries and parity of 60,000 tons for submarines, the Japanese delegates calculated that Japan's overall strength for auxiliary ships would amount to 68.7 percent—merely 1.3 percent short of their original instructions.[69]

On Saitō's behalf Kobayashi hastened to cable Vice Minister Ōsumi a recommendation, listing four reasons for accepting the compromise:

1. Naval limitation on the basis of the Anglo-Japanese plan would not be disadvantageous to Japan's national defense.

2. Breakdown of the conference would inevitably accelerate a naval arms race, causing international uncertainty.

3. If Japan took the lead in the breakup of the conference, its international position would be adversely affected.

4. A more favorable opportunity for reaching a naval limitation agreement would not recur in the near future.[70]

This "wide view," emphasizing political reasons for accepting a compromise, bore a remarkable resemblance to Katō Tomosaburō's position at the Washington Conference.

ŌSUMI REJECTS COMPROMISE

Not surprisingly, the naval authorities in Tokyo flatly rejected compromise with exceptional severity. Any formula that even slightly deviated from their original instructions on the 70 percent ratio was unacceptable. Ōsumi was known for his "intransigence and dogged determination that defied any placation once he had made up his mind." He ordered the delegates in Geneva to withdraw the "compromise formula" at once. He rebuked the luckless Kobayashi: "We feel it most deplorable that the delegates have proposed to sacrifice the 70 percent ratio which has been Japan's long-cherished desire. It will bring about grave consequences not only on our national defense but on other problems." The proposed concession would be "painful especially from the viewpoint of our relations with the United States." It would "gravely jeopardize national defense and would be a national disgrace." "The delegates must persist to the bitter end in their demand for a 70 percent ratio. If this demand cannot be met, public opinion will of course be inflamed to a boiling point, and the resultant treaty will have little chance of being approved by the cabinet or being ratified by the Privy Council. . . . Depending on the attitude of Britain and the United States, the worst contingency might arise, ultimately forcing us to resolve to *fight to the death* [*gyokusai*]."[71] In these scathing words, Kobayashi later wrote bitterly, Ōsumi had "rebuked and denounced me as if I were a traitor who endangered Japan's national defense."[72]

The reprimand from Ōsumi mortified the naval advisers in Geneva. On 20 July, Kobayashi sent a long telegram to Ōsumi "for his eyes only." It began by reminding him that before the delegates' departure, Vice Chief of the Naval General Staff Nomura "had agreed not to base the ratio question on a strictly strategic viewpoint but on broader considerations for Japan's international position." He had been doing his best to improve Japan's international position, and he had hardly imagined that the naval authorities in Tokyo "would consider our negotiations as something essentially endangering national defense." "When the time comes to negotiate the ratio question directly with the United States, we anticipate an even more difficult situation, and over this issue it might very well become necessary to withdraw from the conference. This being the case, is it your present stand that the Empire cannot possibly agree to a solution unless it is above 70 percent?"[73]

A dejected Kobayashi also drafted a cable tendering his resignation. Bitterly he wrote, "Because of my thoughtlessness I gave wrongful advice to the delegates and made them think that a 65 percent ratio vis-à-vis Britain is sufficient strength. Furthermore I profoundly regret the difficulties caused by my negotiations with Admiral Field. Because the matter is of the gravest concern to the nation's foreign relations, if you think my actions have led the nation astray, I desire you to discharge me as with the single stroke of a sword." Kobayashi was, however, persuaded to shelve this telegram pending Ōsumi's reply to his earlier message, so it was tabled.[74]

Chief delegates Saitō and Ishii were not to be deterred by Ōsumi's rejection of Kobayashi's recommendation of the 65 percent ratio. On 24 July, Saitō and Ishii proposed to go even below 65 percent. They cabled Tokyo their fear that the time was fast approaching when Japan would have to confront the United States over the ratio issue. (Unknown to the Japanese, two days earlier Gibson had wired Secretary of State Frank B. Kellogg that discussion of the ratios with the Japanese would be necessary "at a very early date.")[75] The Japanese delegates were sure that the United States would demand 63 percent if not 60 percent. Here was the dilemma as they saw it: if Japan rejected the American demand, Japan would be blamed for the breakup of the conference; on the other hand, if Japan yielded, an impression of surrender would be created at home, aggravating relations with the United States. The only way out, the delegates urged Ōsumi, was "to reach a compromise on the maximum ratio acceptable to the United States," which in their view was 63 percent. Warning that "we are now facing a great divide," the delegates asked that the timing of their proposal be left to them.[76]

As expected, Ōsumi's reply was a flat refusal: "If such is the case, the game is up; there will be no room for further negotiations whatsoever." If the Japanese demand for a 70 percent ratio were rejected, "the resentment of our people would become an eternal source of future trouble [with the United States] and the concession cannot but destroy the morale of our navy."[77]

From the beginning the Anglo-Japanese compromise was doomed, because it would have encountered opposition from the United States. As the Japanese delegates correctly surmised, the American naval advisers firmly opposed the 65 percent ratio as "gravely endangering America's position in the western Pacific." Gibson wired Secretary of State Frank B. Kellogg that his naval advisers "believe that no departure from the 5–3 ratio should be permitted."[78] However, the American delegates "evaded" Japanese attempts to ascertain their position on the ratio issue. The Japanese sensed the ploy: for now the Americans needed

Japan's cooperation in countering Britain's demands, but once Britain yielded, the United States would seek British support and together they would "turn all out against Japan to impose a 60 percent ratio." Here again the Japanese underestimated Anglo-American differences.[79]

In the end the United States never fought it out over the ratio issue and the Japanese narrowly escaped from a collision with the United States, because of the latter's clash with Britain. This was fortunate for Japan, as Gibson confided to a member of the Japanese delegation: "Anglo-American disputes occur all the time but never become very serious because of racial affinity. Japanese-American disputes are quite a different matter. They immediately inflame the passions of the two peoples and this leads to grave diplomatic difficulties. If the present conference must break up, it would be better to say it collapsed because of Anglo-American differences."[80]

The breakup of the conference allowed Saitō to act as an honest broker between the United States and Britain. After the conference, Vice Admiral Yamanashi paid him this tribute: "Your fair-mindedness enhanced Japan's international prestige and position; you accomplished great and magnanimous work between the world's two greatest powers."[81] On the public scene in Geneva, at least, the Japanese delegation narrowly managed to hold on to the legacy of Katō Tomosaburō.

Why did the naval authorities in Tokyo take such an inflexible stand on the 70 percent ratio? The division and confusion among naval leaders, very much in evidence in their preparations for the conference, account for this. According to Admiral Takarabe's testimony, the Anglo-Japanese compromise formula caused "tumultuous controversies" that became unmanageable. Upon Saitō's return, Yamanashi vaguely intimated that "knotty circumstances and irresistible pressures" accounted for the lack of coordination between Tokyo and its delegation.[82] Presumably these "pressures" had to do with the exigencies of bureaucratic politics. As stated, Ōsumi and Kobayashi were rivals and held the ambition of becoming navy minister.[83] Although some of the moderate leaders—Okada Keisuke, Nomura Kichisaburō, and Yamanashi—supported naval limitation and the Washington system, their collective influence could not emulate Katō Tomosaburō's leadership at the Washington Conference. Under such circumstances the opponents of naval limitation—Katō Kanji, Suetsugu Nobumasa, Takahashi Sankichi (chief of staff of the Combined Fleet), Yamamoto Eisuke (head of the Naval Aviation Department), and their associates—rallied behind Ōsumi. And Ōsumi had the strong backing of Fleet Admiral Tōgō, who "absolutely" opposed any compromise.

The balance between the two groups was precarious. Before it came to a show-down at the London Conference in 1930, the moderates attempted to reassert themselves.

KATŌ TOMOSABURŌ'S LEGACY RESTATED, 1928

Two months after the Geneva Conference, Navy Minister Okada ordered the committee on arms limitation to prepare a comprehensive study that would not only guide preparation for the next conference but also naval policy building programs in the broad context of Japanese-American relations. Headed by Vice Admiral Nomura, this committee was dominated by supporters of naval limitation: Vice Admirals Yamanashi, Kobayashi, and Sakonji Seizō, and Commander Iwamura Seiichi—all followers of Katō Tomosaburō and supporters of the Washington system. The confidential report, known as the Nomura report, that was submitted to the navy minister in September 1928, was an authoritative document that provided the basis for future naval policy.[84]

The Nomura report reaffirmed the Washington treaty system and Katō Tomosaburō's philosophy of naval limitation. Ōsumi's rigid stand at the time of the Geneva Conference notwithstanding, thinking in the upper echelons was still fluid. Under existing conditions, the report stated, the Washington naval treaty was "on the whole advantageous" to Japan, strategically as well as financially. Besides, the nonfortification agreement of the Five-Power Treaty regarding the Philippines and Guam "somewhat facilitated Japanese operations" in the western Pacific. Katō Tomosaburō's views regarding naval security in the age of total war were clearly restated in the following passages: "Vis-à-vis great industrial powers like the United States and Britain, the utmost effort must be made to avoid war whose outcome would be decided by an all-out contest of national strength. . . . Since Japan's national strength in relation to the Anglo-American powers is vastly inferior, it will be to our advantage to keep them tied down to the [capital ship] ratio of 10:10:6, even though Japan was assigned an inferior strength."[85]

Again like Katō Tomosaburō's thinking, the report was mindful of the exigencies of total war. "The United States with its vast economic power may very well decide to fight a protracted war and exhaust us in a war of attrition."[86] To fight against the United States (and Britain) "we must be prepared to fight virtually against the whole world." The Nomura report saw Japan's naval arma-ments as a "silent power" with which to deter the United States from "obstructing" Japanese policy in China. It reiterated Katō's view of the navy as an instrument of deterrence, not war.[87]

The Nomura report presented a realistic view of Japanese-American relations. Its premise was that since the time of the Washington Conference, relations had so improved that problems that would provoke a war no longer existed. As for China, Americans were awakening to its "chaotic and hopeless condition" and becoming sympathetic with Japanese policy. "Therefore the United States is quite unlikely to collide head-on with our efforts to make peaceable inroads into China." And the report emphasized the importance of closer economic relations with the United States.[88] Such views negated neo-Mahanian economic determinism and inevitable war between the two powers. Instead, they were almost identical to the peaceful cooperative outlook that informed Foreign Minister Shidehara Kijūrō's policy.

The dissenting opinion attached to the Nomura report (drafted by the hawkish Captain Nakamura Kamesaburō and Lieutenant Commander Yamaguchi Tamon of the Naval General Staff, among others) echoed Katō Kanji almost word for word. Its neo-Mahanian economic determinism restated the 1923 National Defense Policy, maintaining that conflict over the China market would "lead to the outbreak of war between Japan and the United States." At the height of prosperity in the 1920s, the United States was "increasingly showing its true colors as an economic imperialist in China," and it "frontally obstructed" Japan's continental policy. The dissenting opinion stated that if the United States should "excessively interfere with the Empire's Manchurian-Mongolian policy, eventually war will break out."[89] The minority report linked opposition to arms limitation with a belief in a Japanese-American war over China, again in line with Katō Kanji.

LOOKING TOWARD THE LONDON CONFERENCE

While the Nomura report and the dissenting opinion were diametrically opposed in their estimates of Japanese-American relations, both agreed on the need for a 70 percent ratio. This position did not necessarily contradict Katō Tomosaburō's acceptance of the Washington naval treaty. As the report explained, in Washington Japan had accepted a 60 percent ratio in capital ships only *in return for* the nonfortification agreement. Therefore it had not "abandoned" its demand for a 70 percent ratio. This subtle point became a standard argument for claiming a 70 percent ratio for auxiliary ships. The Nomura report confirmed that a 70 percent ratio for auxiliary ships was "absolutely necessary for the nation's defense, nay, for its very existence." There could be no bargaining on this at the next conference. A 70 percent ratio was especially important for 10,000-ton heavy cruisers armed with 8-inch guns (the maximum allowed under the Washington treaty), because the navy saw them as quasi battleships. As for the submarine, Japan would demand the tonnage it required for its operational needs; it was "the weapon in the hands of an inferior party." Anticipating that the United States would oppose these demands, Japan "must be prepared, depending on the circumstances, to cause the breakdown of the conference." The important thing was to determine a firm policy in advance of the conference.[90]

Meanwhile, Katō Kanji had become convinced that from a strategic viewpoint, "even the 70 percent ratio was not sufficient." He now realized the error of "relying too heavily on intangible forces," by which he meant the excessive drills that had resulted in the 1927 accident off Mihogaseki.[91] The occasion for his rethinking was the emergence of the 10,000-ton, 8-inch-gun cruiser as the prop of auxiliary strength. The Japanese navy, like the U.S. Navy, recognized the superiority of this class of cruisers. These ships would accompany the battleship fleet in any decisive engagement in the western Pacific.

A lengthy staff study, prepared in late 1929 by the Operations Division, spelled out in detail the "formidable power" of 10,000-ton cruisers. They excelled in speed; they were equipped with great striking power (8-inch guns had 2.5 times the range of 6-inch guns); and, most important, their cruising capacity was vital for transoceanic operations. In America's hand, these heavy cruisers could "run wild in all directions" in the Pacific without refueling, intercept Japan's sea communications, and destroy its morale.[92]

According to this study, America's remote strategic outposts—the Philippines and Guam in the west, Hawaii in the center, Samoa in the south, and the Aleutians in the north—could now be linked, thanks to the heavy cruiser. And these bases constituted "a strategic chain of encirclement of much of the Pacific Ocean." Thus the Pacific had "seemingly been reduced to an American lake." Japan was losing its geographic-strategic advantage that made it easy to defend and difficult to attack. The planners took it for granted that the American navy would deploy heavy cruisers to join in a decisive fleet engagement, but first they would run amok all over the Pacific, making surprise attacks to cut Japan's seaborne communications, thus threatening Japan's lifeline.[93] At the next naval conference, therefore, Japan would place particular emphasis on a 70 percent ratio for the heavy cruiser.[94]

Whereas ratio was all-important with regard to the heavy cruiser, total tonnage strength (irrespective of the ratio) was paramount with respect to the submarine. Unlike the heavy cruiser, the submarine was never meant to fight the enemy's counterparts but to pare down the enemy's fleet on its transpacific passage and then join the battleship engagement. Japan would demand 78,000 tons, which would be it's submarine strength upon the completion of the current building program at the end of fiscal 1931. This submarine strength was required for the surveillance, chase, and attrition of the American fleet's advance from Hawaii to the mandated islands; scouting the enemy fleet from Marianna to the Bonins; and finally join in big-battleship engagement.

The coming London Conference would be a denouement of the force and counterforce, compromise and reaction that had been building ever since the Washington Conference.

CHAPTER SIX

THE DENOUEMENT: THE LONDON NAVAL CONFERENCE

Failure of Preliminary Negotiations

The London Naval Conference of 1930 marked a turning point in Japanese naval history. It brought into the open a violent split within the navy between the supporters and opponents of naval limitation. Although the Navy Ministry's upper echelons had successfully steered the treaty to conclusion, the Naval General Staff, headed by Katō Kanji, claimed that the treaty caused grave deficiencies in Japan's naval strength compared to the United States, jeopardizing national defense. The internal division over the treaty was accompanied by a head-on collision between the government and the navy. This in turn brought about a major political crisis that triggered a series of assassinations, starting with the attack on Prime Minister Hamaguchi Osachi in November 1930. The domestic commotion further enhanced the power of the treaty's enemies. Viewed this way, the success of the moderate leadership in concluding the London treaty was a Pyrrhic victory. In addition to these consequences, the distinguished naval journalist Itō Masanori emphasizes as "the greatest tragedy in Japanese naval history" the controversy over the "supreme command," discussed shortly. Itō also argues that the London Conference and its aftermath became "one of the remote causes of the war with the Anglo-American powers."[1]

The navy's preparation for the coming conference, based on its attrition-interceptive strategy, began early. On 28 June 1929, Navy Minister Okada obtained the cabinet's approval of the Three Basic Principles that would guide the conference: (1) an overall 70 percent ratio against the United States in total auxiliary tonnage; (2) the special importance of the 70 percent ratio with regard to the 10,000-ton, 8-inch-gun cruiser; and (3) a submarine strength of 78,000 tons. Whereas a 70 percent ratio for total auxiliary strength had been Japan's policy at the Geneva Conference, now premiums were attached to the heavy cruiser and the submarine, on which the overall ratio of auxiliary ships

126

was to be predicated. Okada explained that the 8-inch-gun cruiser would serve as "a quasi-capital ship" in a decisive fleet engagement; herein lay the importance of its *relative* strength. Katō Kanji, chief of the Naval General Staff, claimed that in the heavy cruiser category, Japan already possessed more than 80 percent of the naval strength of the United States. As for the submarine, Japan's demand for 78,000 tons was based on map maneuvers conducted numerous times for attrition strategy. This tonnage was also the projected naval strength at completion of the current building program.

By late July 1929 the navy feared that the Anglo-American powers would again collude to impose a 60 percent ratio on Japan. Therefore, they held that it was all-important to obtain an "understanding" on the 70 percent ratio prior to the conference.[2] When Japan received an invitation to the London Naval Conference on 7 October, the navy demanded Japan's position be acceded to through preliminary negotiations and with this condition the government accepted the invitation.

Thus Foreign Minister Shidehara took an unusually stiff position in his efforts to obtain such a prior "understanding" with the Anglo-American powers.[3] Admiral Katō Kanji had been pressuring Shidehara. In November 1929 Katō stated that there was absolutely no room for compromise on the 70 percent demand: "We must hold a hardline position to the end and must be prepared to break up the conference as the result of our strong position."[4] And behind Katō's firm stand was Fleet Admiral Tōgō. When Katō met with Prime Minister Hamaguchi on 18 November, he conveyed to him Tōgō's conviction that "the compromise ratio of 70 percent was the absolute rock bottom demand, which is a matter of life and death to our navy; if an agreement cannot be reached on this demand we must resolutely withdraw from the conference."[5]

In Washington, Ambassador Debuchi Katsuji made no headway in his efforts to win Secretary of State Henry L. Stimson's acceptance of the 70 percent ratio. Parallel efforts were being made in London by Ambassador Matsudaira Tsuneo (soon to become one of the delegates), with equally negative results. On 11 December he warned the government that the coming conference would break up if Japan insisted on its demand for a 70 percent ratio in relation to the United States. He recommended that it would be to Japan's advantage to reach an understanding on a compromise proposal and asked if the government was preparing such a proposal.[6] The preliminary negotiations in Washington revolved around how to interpret the Five-Power Treaty of Washington. Stimson, who became America's head delegate, chided Japan for having "changed" its position: Whereas at the Washington Conference chief delegate Katō Tomosaburō had stated that he would "gladly" accept a 60 percent ratio (apparently including the auxiliaries), Japan now demanded a higher ratio. Debuchi, saying he had himself attended that conference, retorted that Japan had never abandoned the 70 percent ratio demand; it had instead agreed to the lower ratio only in return for the Pacific nonfortification agreement.[7] The matter was not solved when the Japanese delegates Wakatsuki Reijirō and Takarabe Takeshi stopped in Washington in December on their way to London. Wakatsuki told Stimson that anything less than a 70 percent ratio would "disturb Japan's sense of national security," but Wakatsuki failed to persuade Stimson.[8]

In closing the preliminary negotiations, Wakatsuki cabled Tokyo, "If we were to push the matter to extremes, we must be prepared for a quarrelsome parting."[9] Ambassador Matsudaira was even more pessimistic: "If it is the policy of the government not to make the slightest concession concerning the 70 percent ratio, I believe there is no way out but to break up the conference." He asked whether the government was willing to settle for a lower ratio.[10]

Shidehara harshly rejected what he took to be counsels of despair.[11] Why did Shidehara, a liberal diplomat who advocated cooperation with the Anglo-American powers, take such a firm stand on the 70 percent ratio? He feared that if Japan could not obtain a prior agreement, the navy might boycott the conference. And, as noted, he was under pressure from Katō Kanji. Uppermost in Katō's mind was a determination "never to repeat the mistake of the Washington Conference"; Japan must forestall "joint Anglo-American coercion."[12]

KATŌ KANJI STANDS FIRM

Katō Kanji had been stepping up his pressure on the government. On 18 November 1929, he told Prime Minister Hamaguchi that he felt that even 70 percent was not sufficient for Japan's defense, so the 70 percent ratio was absolutely minimal and constituted "a matter of life or death for our navy." This goal had "stiffened the navy's morale and sustained its determination through unspeakable hardships" ever since the Washington Conference. Japan would "rather do without any new treaty" than yield on the 70 percent.[13] On 26 November, Katō told Lieutenant Colonel Hata Shunroku, chief of the Army's Operations Division, that he would risk his position as chief of the Naval General Staff to uphold the 70 percent demand.[14]

To back up his case, Katō told Shidehara and Hamaguchi that Fleet Admiral Tōgō, venerated as the Nelson of Japan, had declared, "Not even an inch should be yielded on the ratio question. If England and America do not accept [our demands] in the preliminary negotiations, we will simply refuse to participate in the conference this time." He said that Japan surpassed the United States and Britain in cruiser strength.[15] In 1922 Tōgō had supported Katō Tomosaburo's decision for a 60 percent ratio at the Washington Conference, but since that time he had reversed his position, perhaps under Katō Kanji's influence. As he advanced with age (he was now eighty-three), he became more embittered by his memories of the Washington Conference. Going further back, he recalled the "outrageous treatment" meted out by Americans when, as captain of the cruiser *Naniwa*, he visited Hawaii in 1893 (and later in 1897) in the midst of the Hawaiian Revolution. "America is a recalcitrant country," he said.[16]

Katō anticipated that the United States and Britain would argue that because a 60 percent ratio had been acceptable to Japan at the Washington Conference, there was no reason why it should not be at London. Katō contended that, on the contrary, because an unacceptable capital ship ratio had been imposed in Washington, it became all the more imperative for Japan to obtain a 70 percent ratio in auxiliary strength. Besides, he pointed out, Japan now possessed 80 percent of U.S. auxiliary strength (including ships under construction). In a letter to Makino Nobuaki, Lord Keeper of the Privy Seal, Katō warned about America's ulterior motives. Apparently, he counted on Makino, in a position to advise the emperor politically, to convey his warning to His Majesty. Katō said, "Ever since the Washington Conference, attaining a 70 percent ratio has been the navy's conviction to which we have devoted all our energies. It is indeed a matter of life and death for our navy.... The United States is persistently insisting on construction of eighteen 10,000-ton, 8-inch-gun cruisers precisely because it is preparing for offensive operations against Japan.... The United States desires to maintain a decidedly superior force that would assure victory without fighting."[17]

Echoing the by-now-familiar neo-Mahanian determinism, Katō claimed that the American effort to capture the China market would spell an eventual clash with Japan. The United States under the Republican administration would be compelled to expand its China market as an outlet for its surplus products. "Its economic penetration" of China was destined sooner or later to cause a violent collision with the Japanese navy. Were not U.S. naval officials arguing that the defense of the Open Door in China required an offensive navy in the Pacific?[18] Katō warned Hamaguchi and Shidehara, "Diehards [in the United States] are clamoring that the China question must be forcibly settled by naval power." America's real intention at the coming conference, he maintained, was to commit Japan to an inferior naval ratio so that it could pursue its "domination" of China.[19] As Katō told Shidehara, "The real intention of the United States is to impose on Japan a naval ratio that spells defeat for Japan, thereby becoming a hegemon in China."[20] Both Katō and Tōgō argued that to forestall such an eventuality, Japan absolutely needed to maintain a 70 percent ratio compared to the United States.

In December 1929 Katō had the Operations Division prepare a lengthy study, titled "U.S. Naval Armaments Since the Washington Conference," that explained the need for a 70 percent ratio from the strategic viewpoint. Katō was convinced that the U.S. Navy would seek an all-out engagement with the Japanese fleet in a "quick encounter, quick showdown" after recapturing the Philippines and Guam and occupying strategic points in Japan's home waters. Katō asserted that only by maintaining a 70 percent ratio could Japan prevent America's offensive operations.[21] In another confidential memorandum Katō emphasized that the increase in the cruising capacity of capital ships and heavy cruisers had rendered it much easier for the attacker, the American navy, to take the offensive against Japan. The memorandum recapitulated Japan's three-stage operational plans to counter the American offensive: the attrition strategy, interceptive operations, and the main-fleet encounter. For such a strategy to succeed, the memorandum concluded, a 70 percent ratio in heavy cruisers and the requisite tonnage in submarines were absolutely essential.[22]

For Katō, however, the "absolute" demand for a 70 percent ratio went beyond strategic considerations. Ever since the Washington Conference he had held fast to twin "convictions": the doctrine of "the equality of armament" and Japan's "national prestige." He held that because Japan as a sovereign nation was entitled to a ratio of 10:10, a 70 percent ratio would already be a significant concession. He wrote to Makino that the more humbly Japan acquiesced in the 70 percent ratio despite its sovereign right of equality, "the more flagrant the United States would become in flaunting its high-handed and coercive attitude of forcibly imposing the 60 percent ratio."[23] In similar vein Katō wrote to Admiral Abo Kiyokazu, the highest naval adviser at the London Naval Conference, "The real issue at stake is no longer our naval power per se but our national prestige and credibility." He asked Abo to send home "more and more telegrams about Anglo-American oppression," which would help stir up public sentiment in Japan and "spur the government to stiffen its attitude."[24] In a letter he wrote to a friend in January 1930, Katō said that "a free and unrestrained navy that can flexibly utilize Japan's limited national power is better than a 70 percent ratio that rests on Anglo-American superiority. This being the case, I would rather desire the rupture of the conference."[25]

For Katō the root of all evils was the weak-kneed policy pursued by the Hara cabinet at the time of the Washington Conference. (Even now he would not dare openly criticize Katō Tomosaburō by name.) As he wrote to Kaneko Kentarō, a member of the Privy Council, the Hara cabinet's "timid" diplomacy made the U.S. government glory in its own success and look down on Japan, so much so that in 1924 it passed the Immigration Act excluding Japanese immigrants and injuring Japanese national honor. It was all-important not to repeat the mistake of the Washington Conference. "If the conference at London should fail because of American rejection of our demands, it will not be our fault but the result of American selfishness."[26] Katō expressed his warped view of the United States in a long letter he wrote to Admiral Abo on 5 February 1930 when the negotiations at London had reached an impasse:

> If they [Americans] turn a deaf ear to the small addition of 10 percent that Japan is requesting and thus break up the conference, Japan will gain the sympathy of the world. Because of the Kellogg-Briand Pact, the United States will perhaps be in the impossibly awkward position of feeling too ashamed to undertake any large naval expansion in the future. Even if it builds a "top fleet" and expands its navy to many times that of Japan. . . . the effect will be that Britain and Japan will draw together and the United States will become another Germany.
>
> We cannot say that out of these difficulties some fortunate result may not come. For instance, suppose Japan does not yield one inch in its just demands but breaks up the conference with an attack upon America's violation of the spirit of the Anti-War Pact. If that were to happen, the Puritans and pacifists in America would wish to cooperate with Japan and repress the imperialists.[27]

THE MAKEUP OF THE JAPANESE DELEGATION

A severe financial crisis had struck Japan two years before the U.S. stock market crash in October 1929 precipitated the Great Depression. Prime Minister Hamaguchi's foremost tasks were financial retrenchment and cooperation with the Anglo-American powers, and from the outset he was determined to conclude a naval treaty. His outlook on national defense reminds one of Katō Tomosaburō. He had always admired Katō "for his wide view, clear head, and resolve": "There are both broad and narrow views on national defense. The narrow view is merely concerned with the size of armaments, whereas the broad view takes into consideration not only armaments but also friendly international relations and the enhancement of national resources. . . . If we take too adamant a position on armaments and cause the naval treaty to fall through, it will jeopardize our national defense in the broad sense of the word."[28]

Hamaguchi chose Wakatsuki Reijirō as the head delegate to the conference. As a two-time finance minister (1912–13, 1914–15) and onetime prime minister (1926–27), Wakatsuki was a very strong civilian leader and he was determined to support Hamaguchi's policy wholeheartedly. In 1921–22 he had welcomed the Washington treaty, aware that the limit of Japan's financial capabilities ruled out a naval race. At the coming London Conference he felt it would be "unwise to persist uncompromisingly in the 70 percent ratio." Rather, he would conclude a treaty "within negotiable limits, say 65 or 67 percent. We are nonplused a great deal by the navy's clamoring for a 70 percent ratio no matter what." In his memoirs he recalled, "On the basis of the many years I spent in the ministry of finance, I fully knew that Japan's financial power could not stand the burden of [competitive] naval building. So at bottom my belief was that it was to Japan's advantage to stop competitive building by naval arms limitation."[29]

The choice of Wakatsuki as the chief delegate alarmed Japan's navy men, who did not like to have a party leader as head delegate. Although the navy chose its minister Takarabe Takeshi as its delegate, there was a fear that Takarabe would be outsmarted by Wakatsuki, who would be assisted by Kaya Okinori (a secretary to the finance minister in charge of naval armaments, later to become finance minister). In naval circles Takarabe was regarded as "unreliable," "irresolute," and lacking in leadership, but he was all too eager to go to London.[30] Fleet Admiral Tōgō was furious about Takarabe's decision to take his wife to London. Tōgō considered a naval conference to be a battlefield in peacetime.[31] In London, Takarabe did not actively participate in meetings of the delegates. He had much free time, and enjoyed sightseeing and shopping. Even at critical stages of the negotiations he remained strangely inert, making himself unpopular with hawkish naval subordinates.[32] Before departing for London, Takarabe had promised Fleet Admiral Tōgō and Admiral Prince Fushimi Hiroyasu that he would not retreat an inch from the Three Basic Principles.[33] Prince Fushimi, a cousin of the emperor, a senior admiral, and a member of the Supreme Military Council, had been on close personal terms with Katō Kanji since their Naval Academy days and shared his hard-line views.

Katō Kanji, worried that Takarabe was no match for Wakatsuki, consulted Fleet Admiral Tōgō and decided to send as "the highest naval adviser" Admiral Abo Kiyokazu—Katō's close friend since his boyhood, a Naval Academy classmate, a member of the Supreme Military Council, and a leader of "the command group."[34] A hard-liner representing views of the Naval General Staff, Abo became Katō's foremost spokesman at London. The second-ranking naval member, Rear Admiral Yamamoto Isoroku, also a hawk, could be counted on to take a strong stand.

Katō took care to include, among younger naval members, Captain Nakamura Kamesaburō, Chief of the Operations Section, a hard-liner. Such a lineup tended to isolate Vice Admiral Sakonji Seizō, Chief Naval Adviser, whose duty was to assist Takarabe. Former head of the Naval Affairs Bureau, Sakonji belonged to the administrative group and generally favored naval limitation.

How did the American government size up the Japanese delegation? Stimson had asked the embassy in Tokyo to prepare "biographical sketches" of the Japanese representatives. Wakatsuki was said to reflect "the desire of the Japanese government to select a man of equivalent standing with statesmen who might be appointed by other nations." The selection of Navy Minister Takarabe was "due more to the Japanese system of Government than to technical qualification." Fair enough, but the report overrated him as a decision maker when it explained, "As the final decision in the questions arising at the Conference would come before Admiral Takarabe as the Minister of Marine, it will be advantageous to have him present." Admiral Abo was overestimated, too, as "one of the big men in the Japanese Navy, professionally and politically . . . he was very influential in governmental and political circles behind the scenes." Rear Admiral Yamamoto was fondly described as having "a wide acquaintance among foreign naval officers; is well known in Washington; is a good mixer; speaks excellent English; and is rated as a smart, capable naval officer."[35]

THE AMERICAN DELEGATION

The American delegation was very distinguished. In fact, Stimson wrote in his memoirs that the American delegation was "as strong as any sent by the United States to an international conference in his lifetime." The choice of Stimson as its head ensured that the delegation would not suffer from a lack of prestige, as it had at the Geneva Conference. Delegates included two well-known and respected senators: David A. Reed of Pennsylvania, an influential Republican and Chairman of the Senate Naval Appropriations Committee, and Joseph T. Robinson of Arkansas, a leading member of the Democratic Party.[36]

Having learned a lesson from the Geneva Conference, President Herbert Hoover and Secretary Stimson excluded naval officers from the delegates and allowed them to serve only in an advisory capacity. The American delegates minimized the influence of the General Board by choosing Admiral William V. Pratt, Chief of Naval Operations, to head the naval advisers.[37] Pratt had been an admirer of Katō Tomosaburō at the Washington Conference, a friend of the Japanese navy, and a consistent supporter of naval limitation. He trusted Japan and believed that most political-economic problems could be solved peacefully. President Hoover hoped Pratt would counterbalance Rear Admiral Hilary P. Jones. An "old sea dog," Jones had provoked the Japanese delegates at both the Washington and Geneva Conferences with his extremely hard-line remarks. To the relief of the Japanese delegates, Jones had to leave London because of illness.[38]

At the outset, the Japanese and American delegations agreed that the conference should not be left to naval experts but would be "better done" by "responsible representatives of the government." A major difference was that whereas the Japanese delegation was rife with internal dissent, the American delegation, as Stimson reported to President Hoover, was "a harmonious and unanimous body with every man working hard and loyally."[39]

THE POLICY-MAKING STRUCTURE IN JAPAN

During Takarabe's absence, Prime Minister Hamaguchi assumed the titular portfolio of navy minister, but he left Vice Minister Yamanashi to assume the duty of controlling the navy and cooperating with the government. Having graduated from the Naval Academy second in his class, Yamanashi was a superb administrator. Wakatsuki called him "a man of sharp brain and strong sense of responsibility." (After the conference the Superintendent-General of the Tokyo Metropolitan Police told Yamanashi, "You were in such physical danger [of assassination] that I feared for the worst. You are indeed lucky to have stayed alive!")[40] Yamanashi was assisted by Rear Admiral Hori Teikichi, head of the Naval Affairs Bureau. Reputed to be the best brain ever to graduate from the Naval Academy, he was known for his judgment, broad outlook, and flexibility. Yamanashi and Hori, who had closely assisted Katō Tomosaburō at the Washington Conference, adhered to his philosophy of naval limitation.[41]

These moderate leaders, however, were no match for Chief of the Naval General Staff Katō Kanji, a full admiral. (Yamanashi was a vice admiral, having graduated from the Naval Academy seven years after Katō.) In 1930 the leadership of the Naval General Staff consisted of men who prided themselves on being "sea warriors." As the members of the "command group," they had built their careers as line or staff officers. Neither Katō Kanji nor Suetsugu, vice chief of the Naval General Staff, had held Navy Ministry posts to speak of. In contrast, key policy-making posts in the Navy Ministry went to an elite corps, an "administrative group" that excelled in politico-administrative ability. Yamanashi and Hori had had no important tours of duty in the fleet. This accentuated differences in outlook between the two groups. After the London Conference, the former was to be called the fleet faction and the latter the treaty faction.

With regard to policy concerning naval armaments, the unwritten tradition of the navy held that it was the responsibility and within the jurisdiction of the government (the Navy Ministry) to decide on the size of armaments while considering the views of the Naval General Staff. But there was no stipulation on measures to be taken if the two branches could not agree. (Katō Tomosaburō had foreseen this while attending the Washington Conference.) In the absence of a clear guideline, bureaucratic politics came to the fore as each player defined his own role in terms of his sectional interests.

As navy vice minister, Yamanashi took a flexible position: "Armament plans, drafted by the Naval General Staff from strategic-operational viewpoints, are not absolute; they must be agreed upon between the Navy Ministry and the Naval General Staff on the basis of a broad outlook that takes all factors into consideration." Hori went further and claimed that decisions on armaments involved budgetary (political) matters; hence they must be handled by the government (Navy Ministry).[42] On the other hand, Katō Kanji insisted that the chief of the Naval General Staff, who was in charge of strategic plans, must decide on arms limitation. He and his subordinates adamantly insisted that they were performing their duty in absolutely insisting on the 70 percent ratio.[43]

Taking an uncompromising stand on the Three Basic Principles, Naval General Staff leaders mobilized public opinion, burning bridges behind them. Katō Kanji recalled that at the time of the Washington Conference, he was handicapped by the lack of public support at home, and he was determined never to let that happen again. His vociferous public campaign on the Three Basic Principles in the press, business circles, and political and right-wing organizations embarrassed Wakatsuki, who felt that his hands were tied.[44] American Ambassador William R. Castle Jr. observed, "A large portion of [the Japanese] people have been taught to look upon this ratio [70 percent] as essential to national safety; that being so, they feel that they cannot surrender." He accurately reported, "The ratio has become a political doctrine of major importance. The fact that the United States refused to consider this ratio is taken as an indication that we foresee the possibility of war."[45]

Following the precedent of the Washington Conference, the navy had unthinkingly appointed Navy Minister Takarabe as the naval delegate. Yet Takarabe never came close to having Katō Tomosaburō's command and control over the naval establishment. Takarabe's lack of leadership confused the Japanese delegation, baffled the naval authorities in Tokyo, and resulted in poor coordination with Tokyo. Chief delegate Wakatsuki despaired of working with Takarabe and sent top-secret telegrams, without Takarabe's knowledge, to Hamaguchi and Shidehara, bitterly complaining about Takarabe's behavior. Wakatsuki's acts of nonconfidence in the navy were reciprocated by Takarabe and his naval advisers, who through chief naval adviser Sakonji directly wired the naval authorities in Tokyo without informing Wakatsuki.[46]

In addition to the navy's formal channel of communication—Navy Minister Takarabe (usually drafted by Sakonji) and Vice Minister Yamanashi—a tangle of irregular lines extended from London to Tokyo. When Admiral Abo, the highest naval adviser, sent his confidential telegrams to Katō Kanji, Chief Naval Adviser Sakonji personally ciphered his telegrams in order to prevent a leak. (In one of them Abo urged that special watch be kept over Wakatsuki, who was all too ready to succumb to "Anglo-American coercion.") In the next echelon, Sakonji was sending secret dispatches to Vice Minister Yamanashi and Naval Affairs Chief Hori. Yamamoto sometimes cabled Hori directly.[47] This jumble of cables from London confused Tokyo and bespoke the weak leadership of Takarabe.

THE RIFT AMONG THE JAPANESE DELEGATES

On 21 January 1930, the opening ceremony of the conference was held in the presence of King George V in the Royal Gallery of the House of Lords—a magnificent place decorated with statues of English monarchs and murals of scenes such as the death of Nelson. No better hall could have been chosen to lend formality to the occasion. Succeeding meetings took place in St. James's Palace, where the gilded portraits of English nobility looked down on the delegates.

Japanese-American differences, never resolved in the preliminary negotiations, soon resulted in a deadlock. Shortly after the conference opened, the civilian delegates, Wakatsuki and Matsudaira, came to a gloomy conclusion. Already on 25 January they decided it was not to Japan's advantage "to insist on its stated position to the last extremity." They proposed sending a telegram apprising the government of the impasse and asking it to "give the most careful consideration to the poblem." What they meant was that Tokyo should reconsider the Three Basic Principles. Takarabe and his naval advisers objected to Wakatsuki's draft telegram as "premature," so it was shelved.[48] The incident bespeaks the rift developing between Takarabe and the civilian delegates. On 20 February, when the conference seemed to founder on Japanese-American differences, Wakatsuki sent a confidential message to Shidehara without consulting Takarabe. He warned that there was no prospect of having Japan's demands accepted, but the "breakup of the conference would place Japan in an extremely difficult position internationally." In Tokyo, Prime Minister Hamaguchi and Foreign Minister Shidehara had to contend with Katō Kanji and the Naval General Staff, so they directed Wakatsuki to follow "the logical step of first consulting with Navy Minister Takarabe and jointly working out some appropriate measures."[49]

For Wakatsuki, however, "consultation" with Takarabe had become impossible. The civilian and naval delegates had become locked in irreconcilable differences. When the Japanese-American negotiations reached a critical point, Wakatsuki complained to Shidehara about Takarabe's intransigence, "Although I have urged delegate Takarabe to rise resolutely to the occasion as would befit a statesman and take broad-minded measures to save the situation, he disagrees with me in every instance and has instead aligned himself with Admiral Abo and other naval advisers. . . . To my great distress, it has proved beyond my power to persuade him despite my repeated efforts."[50]

In sending these dispatches Wakatsuki resorted to the most confidential telegraphic channel to circumvent Takarabe and the naval members of the delegation: he used a diplomatic pipeline, whose codes could be handled personally only by the chief of the mission, his co-delegate (and ambassador) Matsudaira. This attempt to bypass naval members failed, because even Matsudaira's "top-secret, personal" telegrams were "mere child's play" in the hands of the navy's cryptographic experts. The upshot was that it enraged the naval representatives.

On 17 February Wakatsuki significantly stated to the American and British delegates, "Japan's 70 percent demand is its national conviction but it is not my personal view."[51] He was going to apprise his government of his "personal view." In a secret telegram of 20 February (with request to "please burn it upon reading"), he stated to Hamaguchi and Shidehara, "Both Britain and the United States are opposed to our demands. . . . If we continue to be unyielding, an agreement will become impossible, posing great difficulties for Japan's international position. There is perhaps a delegate who disagrees with me [meaning, Takarabe], but please pay utmost attention to telegrams I shall be sending you. If the government does not desire the breakup of the conference, please make that point clear to us in your return instruction. It is because of my anguish for the future of our Empire that I ask special consideration before the matter reaches extremity."[52]

Shidehara cabled back a secret telegram agreeing that the breakup of the conference because of Japan's intransigence "would have extremely grave consequences for the future of our Empire." "However, if we are immediately to draw up a concrete compromise plan in Tokyo, *there will be difficulties in reaching an agreement within the navy.* . . . It will be the natural order of things for you to first consult with Navy Minister Takarabe, together formulate an appropriate measure, and request the government's instructions. We earnestly hope that you will then seek Admiral Abo's assistance in finding ways to influence the navy from within."[53]

While Wakatsuki and Matsudaira were sending their telegrams without Takarabe's knowledge, Admiral Abo was sending his own confidential telegrams to Katō Kanji. Abo urged keeping watch over Wakatsuki and stated, "Under the present circumstances, there is little hope that we can carry out our Three Basic Principles. Therefore a good case can be made for breaking off [the negotiations] at the present time when there still remain such great discrepancies in the assertions of both parties." Yamamoto was also "pessimistic" and told Wakatsuki, "There must never be political retreat without reason."[54]

THE REED-MATSUDAIRA COMPROMISE

On 5 February, the United States presented a tentative plan that provided for Japanese naval strength of 60 percent for both heavy cruisers and overall tonnage. With Japan insisting on 70 percent, the clash at the Washington Conference seemed to be repeating itself. Wakatsuki repeatedly argued that obviously the Japanese navy could not possibly attack the United States with a 70 percent strength, whereas the U.S. Navy could attack Japan with this ratio. If Japan was allowed merely 60 percent, an American attack would be much easier. Japan was seeking only regional security, whereas the United States was planning a transpacific offensive.[55] This line of argument never convinced the Americans. In late February negotiations reached a complete standstill.[56]

To find a way out of the impasse, the delegates turned to high-level political discussions. On 25 February, Matsudaira and the American delegate Reed entered into private, informal "free talking" to find a breakthrough. (While Matsudaira had no expertise in naval affairs, Reed was chairman of the Senate Naval Appropriation Committee.) Although the talks were not to be binding on either party, progress was slow and Reed complained to Stimson, "The negotiations with the Japanese are very tedious, as the Japanese, evidently in an endeavor to satisfy internal dissensions in their delegation, are bringing to us recurrent propositions which they know we will refuse." In light of the "free and nonbinding nature" of the talks, the Japanese civilian delegates decided not to report on them to Tokyo or consult with the naval members of the delegation. Success, they felt, required absolute secrecy.[57]

Meanwhile the naval leaders in Tokyo, although apprehensive about the course the Reed-Matsudaira talks were taking, refrained from expressing their wishes lest their intervention should obstruct the diplomatic talks in London. But Head of the Naval Affairs Bureau Hori cabled Sakonji, "The navy has throughout placed full confidence in your negotiations in London, trusting that, when necessary, you will as a matter of course send us necessary information."[58] It was extremely important, Hori said, to avoid poor coordination between Tokyo and its delegates in London, as had happened at the Geneva Conference in 1927. However, unknown to the navy, the Reed-Matsudaira talks had come to a head.

The two men at long last reached the "final" plan that came to be known as the "Reed-Matsudaira compromise."[59] It gave Japan an overall ratio of 69.75 percent. As for heavy cruisers, it provided for eighteen ships for the United States and twelve ships for Japan. This gave Japan a 60.2 percent ratio, but in the hope of satisfying the Japanese, the United States accepted a complicated arrangement whereby it would not launch the last three of its eighteen heavy cruisers until 1933, 1934, and 1935. (They would not be completed until 1936, 1937, and 1938.) Consequently, Japan would retain the ratios of 72.2 percent (1935), 67.8 percent (1936), 63.8 percent (1937), and 62 percent (1938). Thus Japan would possess a de facto 70 percent ratio until the next conference, which would be held in 1935. However, Japan, already in possession of eight heavy cruisers and four near completion, could not build a single ship, whereas the United States was free to build fourteen ships between 1930 and 1936. As for submarines, there would be parity in total tonnage, set at 52,700 tons. This meant that Japan could not construct a single new submarine to replace outdated ships, which meant that their existing tonnage of 78,000 would be reduced to 52,700 tons in 1936. (See Table 2.) Reed categorically stated that further compromise would be absolutely impossible.[60]

Next the head delegates of the three powers had to review this compromise. On 11 March, when Stimson had a bad cold, Wakatsuki had a heart-to-heart talk with Ramsay MacDonald, Britain's head delegate. Wakatsuki said, "In accepting [the Reed-Matsudaira compromise], I shall become the sole target of censure from the Japanese people, and there is no telling what will happen to my life and honor. . . . If we can come to a settlement, I don't care what happens to my life and honor."[61] Deeply moved, MacDonald shook hands with Wakatsuki without saying a word and hastened to Stimson, conveying to him the burden of his conversation with Wakatsuki. On the following day, 12 March, Wakatsuki met with Stimson to confirm the Reed-Matsudaira compromise.

Wakatsuki was satisfied with the compromise. He believed that it met Japan's demand for an overall cruiser ratio of 70 percent. Regarding submarine strength, the United States agreed to parity with Japan, which Wakatsuki thought was "a great concession" on America's part. "I had carried through the purport of the government's instructions, so I felt I could now sign the treaty."[62]

To Japan's naval advisers, however, the compromise came as "a bolt from the blue." Wakatsuki had assured them that any formula to come out of the informal talks with Reed would be merely a "private plan" with no binding force. Wakatsuki had promised that he would decide on a compromise formula "only after consulting with the naval advisors." However, the Japanese-American negotiations had forced the civilian delegates to commit themselves to a compromise plan that was purely civilian in origin and unacceptable to the naval members of the delegation.[63]

Despite the commotion among the naval advisers, Wakatsuki drafted a telegram to Tokyo on 13 March, stating there was "no prospect of obtaining more favorable terms" and pleading with the government to "make the final determination" on the basis of the compromise. That night, at 9 PM, four delegates met in Wakatsuki's suite in Grosvenor House to discuss the draft telegram. Takarabe was not happy about it at all. Expecting Katō Kanji's opposition as well as objections from naval subordinates in London, he demurred, saying the plan would not be acceptable to the Naval General Staff.[64] The meeting lasted four hours, and finally Takarabe reluctantly agreed to join the civilian delegates in sending a joint telegram to Tokyo. Satō Naotake, secretary-general of the delegation, was called in and ordered to cable it at once. Satō recalled in his memoirs that Takarabe seemed reluctant, and he sensed "difficulties." Takarabe detained Satō and asked him to show the draft telegram to Admiral Abo. Satō wrote in his memoirs that "I went at once to Admiral Abo's room and showed him the telegram. Admiral Abo agonizingly said that he would have to resign from the Supreme Military Council if this telegram were sent as it was."[65] Thereupon Saitō Hiroshi, head of the diplomatic section of the delegation, slightly revised the draft telegram to make it more acceptable to Takarabe and Abo.

This telegram was sent on the afternoon of 14 March. It advised the government to accept the Reed-Matsudaira compromise. "If we continue haggling *as we have been doing*, there is no prospect *for the moment* of making Japan's position more advantageous." (Italicized portions were revisions Saitō had made to appease Takarabe.) On the following day another telegram signed by all four delegates was sent to Tokyo. It contained an explicit warning: "Unless a new situation arises, it will be difficult to obtain further compromise." Depending on Japan's attitude, the conference might break up. The delegates asked the government to send them the final instruction directing them to accept the Reed-Matsudaira compromise.[66] Simultaneously Matsudaira sent Shidehara a supplemental secret telegram: "Now the time has come when we must finally make up our minds. The only thing left for us to do is to conclude the conference on the basis of the Japanese-American compromise. Although I had wished to spell out more clearly that we have no other option, it was necessary to word it in such a brief way because there was one delegate who did not want to have the full particulars explained."[67] The "one delegate who did not want to have the full particulars explained" was, of course, Takarabe. A full explanation would have committed Takarabe to the Reed-Matsudaira compromise, but he wanted to leave room for further negotiations.

The delegates' telegram asking for the government's instructions was to be the final one, but differences remained between Wakatsuki and Takarabe. Takarabe wavered and had only reluctantly consented, and his uncertainties would come back to vex the civilian delegates. On 16 March Chief Naval Adviser Sakonji, presumably on Takarabe's behalf, cabled to the navy vice minister and vice chief of the Naval General Staff a confidential telegram (without the knowledge of the civilian delegates) in which Sakonji stressed that "[as to the Reed-Matsudaira compromise] there is hardly room for consideration."[68]

Uppermost in Wakatsuki's mind was the importance of avoiding a clash with the Anglo-American powers and preventing an arms race. On this stand he said he staked not only "his position as chief delegate but his life itself." He declared to the naval aides, "No matter what instructions I receive from Tokyo, I am determined to stick to my convictions. If the Reed-Matsudaira compromise is disapproved by the government, there is no choice but to resign as a delegate."[69]

However, the Reed-Matsudaira compromise, purely civilian in origin, failed to comply with the terms stipulated in the Three Basic Principles. Wakatsuki honestly believed that this compromise was not only acceptable but advantageous to Japan, but in the eyes of its naval experts his arguments were "amateurish." Chief Naval Adviser Sakonji, though generally in favor of concluding a treaty, nevertheless felt compelled to oppose the compromise. On 16 March, he sent a confidential telegram to Yamanashi and Suetsugu on Takarabe's behalf (without informing the civilian delegates), stating that the compromise gave a mere token of an overall ratio of 70 percent while rejecting crucial demands on the heavy cruiser and the submarine. Yamamoto also wrote his friend Hori, Chief of the Naval Affairs Bureau, frankly expressing his opposition.[70] Under the compromise plan Japan was obliged to halt further construction of heavy cruisers until 1936, while the United States would be free to construct fifteen of them. The stipulation regarding submarines was more serious. Providing for only two-thirds of what

Japan demanded, the treaty force was not sufficient for Philippine operations. Because Japan would not be able to build a new submarine for the duration of the treaty, it would be difficult to maintain submarine technology. These were excruciating conditions for the navy, and the navy's morale was at stake.

Meanwhile the Reed-Matsudaira compromise had stirred up a hornet's nest among the naval members of the delegation. Admiral Abo flared up at Takarabe, accusing him of capitulating to the civilian delegate Wakatsuki. Sakonji criticized Wakatsuki's "failure to consult in good faith with the naval experts." The prudent course seemed to be for Wakatsuki to keep Abo, Sakonji, and Yamamoto informed about the Reed-Matsudaira talks. Naval historian Nomura writes, "Wakatsuki's decision making was too high-handed. It would have been better for subsequent developments if he had explained the decision to the leaders of the naval delegation." On the following night, 17 March, the naval members of the delegation pressured Takarabe, demanding that he annul the joint telegram to Tokyo he had signed urging compromise. Takarabe equivocated, however, saying he had to consider his position as a member of the Hamaguchi cabinet. Yamamoto, outraged by the compromise, told Takarabe to torpedo it.[71]

More agitated were younger staff officers such as Captain Nakamura, who directly appealed to Wakatsuki on 15 March and to Takarabe the following day, urging "a firm and resolute stand." Disappointed with Takarabe's equivocation, the younger officers turned to Yamamoto and demanded that to "overcome the present crisis," their strongly dissenting views be sent to the Naval General Staff. Their aim was to wrest "drastic" new instructions from the government that would turn the tables and reverse the "defeatist policy" of Wakatsuki. To mollify the young hawks, Yamamoto wired his friend Hori, Chief of the Naval Affairs Bureau, apprising him of their violent opposition.[72]

Sakonji, believing that acceptance of the compromise would result in a "national crisis," sent a confidential telegram on 16 March to the naval authorities in Tokyo, suggesting a final proposal that would come closer to the Three Basic Principles. "If a settlement cannot be reached on the basis of such a proposal," he advised, "the conference must adjourn." This telegram, presumably sent on behalf of Takarabe, contradicted the delegates' joint telegram of 14 March. Takarabe continued to vacillate and drafted a telegram reversing his earlier position and opposing the compromise, but Sakonji talked him into tabling it.[73] Sakonji's position was a delicate one; he drafted most of Takarabe's telegrams, but tried to restrain his chief from going to the extreme of breaking up the conference.

More unrestrained was the highest naval adviser, Abo. On 15 March he sent a strictly confidential telegram to Katō Kanji in which he urged that the government inform Takarabe of Japan's "final proposal" (incorporating some of the navy's wishes), which should be "presented [to the Anglo-American powers] with utmost determination." On 19 March Abo again cabled Katō that "Takarabe must oppose Wakatsuki to the bitter end." "In this case, an alarming situation will arise internally, so it is deemed most urgent that the government notify us [of] the final plan and guide the delegates with resolute determination."[74]

MOUNTING OPPOSITION IN THE NAVY

In Tokyo, the Reed-Matsudaira compromise had created consternation and indignation on the Naval General Staff. Katō Kanji fulminated against this proposal, which he intentionally misnamed "the American proposal." He blurted out, "It is a most high-handed proposal, offering us, as it were, only the crust of a pie without the filling." The Naval General Staff held that under the Reed-Matsudaira compromise, Japanese strategy would be jeopardized. Suetsugu especially warned about grave deficiencies in submarines to be deployed in the Philippine operations and also scouting in Hawaiian waters. This, Suetsugu said, would require "fundamental changes in Japan's operational plans."[75]

On the basis of such considerations, Katō on 17 March cabled Takarabe that "there is no room for considering [the] American proposal, which seemingly offers us concessions but in reality imposes U.S. demands on us." To exert pressure on Takarabe, he quoted at length what Fleet Admiral Tōgō had told him the previous day:

> Once we conclude the treaty, it will create an irreparable loss, just as the acceptance of the 60 percent ratio at the Washington Conference did. From the beginning we made a concession and offered 70 percent in the heavy cruiser, but the United States has not made the slightest concession. This being the case, there is no way but to break up the conference and come home. Even if we fail to obtain a treaty, it would not lead to great naval expansion, so there is no financial worry. Originally I wondered whether 70 percent was enough, but I agreed to it because I was assured . . . that the 70 percent was the absolute minimum below which we would not go. Since we have taken the position that our national defense cannot be assured with anything less, there is no use haggling over one or two percent. If they don't accept our demand, there is no way but to resolutely withdraw from the conference.[76]

Behind Tōgō was Imperial Prince Fushimi, who recalled that Takarabe had promised him twice, before departing for London, that he would "not retreat a single step from the Three Basic Principles." Prince Fushimi said that he was determined to appeal to the emperor to stand by these principles.[77] (As will be stated, the emperor supported the naval treaty.) Tōgō told Katō that a mere 60 percent for the 8-inch-gun cruiser simply would not do; Japan by all means must demand 70 percent, even risking the rupture of the conference. The government was hard put to cope with the extreme hard-line position of two of the navy's most influential leaders.

On the evening of 17 March the newspapers carried the full text of an unauthorized press statement from Vice Chief of the Naval General Staff Suetsugu. He declared that "America's final proposal" was "only a superficial concession." Fearing that the limit on submarine strength would nullify his attrition strategy, he said that "the navy cannot possibly accept this kind of proposal from the United States."[78] Suetsugu thus made public the Naval General Staff's opposition. He distorted the issue by calling the Reed-Matsudaira compromise "the American proposal" and giving the impression that the Naval General Staff's opposition represented the view of the entire navy. This was a serious breach of discipline.

On 19 March, Katō visited Prime Minister Hamaguchi at his official residence and harangued him for more than an hour, insisting that as the person charged with national defense and strategic planning, he "absolutely opposed" the compromise. The concession on heavy cruisers would cause "grave defects" for a fleet engagement with the U.S. Navy in the western Pacific, and shortage in submarine tonnage would severely hamper the attrition strategy. Suetsugu, "the father of the attrition strategy," was especially unsparing in his attack on the compromise on the submarine. The seriousness of Katō's opposition was relayed to Abo in London.[79]

Moderate leaders of the Navy Ministry such as Yamanashi and Hori, who worked hard to conclude the naval treaty, were not entirely satisfied with the Reed-Matsudaira compromise. On 22 and 25 March they came up with the navy's counterplan that partially incorporated the demands of the Naval General Staff; but they were prepared to forgo them when Prime Minister Hamaguchi proved firmly committed to the compromise.[80]

The view of the navy, both the Navy Ministry and the Naval General Staff alike, was that the Reed-Matsudaira compromise was unsatisfactory, resulting in deficiencies in naval defense. But navy ministry officials believed that, if proper measures were taken to make up for these deficiencies, strategic needs could be met. More important, Yamanashi and Hori took a "larger view" that transcended technical strategic considerations. In a dispatch of 22 March,

Yamanashi reminded Takarabe that "political and diplomatic imperatives" might override the demands of the navy. Their responsibility as ranking Navy Ministry officials was to weigh the diplomatic, political, and fiscal considerations that argued for a compromise settlement. Their views were shared by Admiral Taniguchi Naomi (Commander of the Kure Naval District), Vice Admiral Kobayashi Seizō (Head of the Naval Construction Department), and Vice Admiral Nomura Kichisaburō (Commander of the Yokosuka Naval District), who all believed that the 70 percent ratio was not an absolute demand. But they could not hope to restrain Katō Kanji.

Who could control Katō and Suetsugu, the latter being a string-puller behind Katō? Needing a mediator between the pro- and anti-treaty forces, ministry leaders turned to the naval elder Admiral Okada Keisuke. Having served as Combined Fleet commander (1924–26), and a member of the Supreme Military Council, he was the most senior officer, second only to Prince Fushimi. A fellow countryman hailing from the same province of Fukuii, Okada was regarded as the only person to whom Katō might listen. Okada, who fancied himself "a disciple of Katō Tomosaburō," used to say, "I have learned much from Admiral Katō about naval arms limitation. . . . He could fix the 10:10:6 ratio at the Washington Conference and yet no problem arose at home." In his memoirs Okada spelled out his philosophy of naval limitation:

> Generally speaking, there is no limit to naval armaments. No matter how much armaments are piled up, there never comes a point of saying, "That's enough, with that much we are safe." It is not a question of "We must not fight with Britain or America." . . . No matter how dogged our efforts, that sort of thing is impossible for a country like Japan whose national resources are inferior to those of major powers. If it were impossible, then it would be better to go easy.[81]

A man of common sense and great tact, Okada was ideally suited to be a mediator and troubleshooter. On 17 March he told Yamanashi, "If unavoidable, we will in the end have to swallow the whole proposal [the Reed-Matsudaira compromise] as it stands. We must not be responsible for breaking up the conference, but we should still try to push once or twice more to get what we want."[82] To appease the discontent among the hard-liners, Okada directed Yamanashi to obtain a promise from the government to enhance air power and other practical measures to make up for the deficiencies of the compromise formula. This was typical of Okada's style. As he recalled in his memoirs, "When I was running around as a mediator for the London Conference, my object was as much as possible to avoid a violent confrontation and gently ease everyone into an acceptable position. In dealing with the opponents of the treaty, I would sometimes adroitly carry things off by silently nodding as if I supported their ideas. With the pro-treaty people, I expressed opinions that smacked of the hardliners. In short, because they were all men of common sense, common sense was my *point d'appui.* In the most excited human being, there is some remnant of common sense."[83]

Okada also gave a revealing account of Katō and Suetsugu: "Katō Kanji and his group were very passionate in their opposition to the treaty. However, since there was only one honest course to take, it was easy for me to make my choice. Katō was a simple-hearted, rather nice fellow. Compared to him, the really sly fox was his scheming subordinate Suetsugu. In view of this, the only thing I could do was to take on Suetsugu as my opponent."[84]

Meanwhile in London, Takarabe was caught in the crossfire. He was aware of the violent opposition of Katō and Suetsugu, backed by Fleet Admiral Tōgō and Prince Fushimi. At the same time, Takarabe had to be mindful of his responsibility as a navy minister and a member of the Hamaguchi cabinet. On 22 March, Yamanashi cabled Takarabe, asking for his real views as a navy minister, not as a delegate. Yamanashi explained that because Katō was "absolutely opposed" to the Reed-Matsudaira compromise, it was "extremely difficult" to work out an agreement within the navy. In response, Sakonji cabled on behalf of Takarabe on 23 March that if the government decided to accept the Reed-Matsudaira compromise, "this would lead to the most serious disturbances" in the navy.[85]

On 26 March, Yamanashi received a long-awaited telegram from Takarabe, stating that if Japan was willing to risk the rupture of the conference, there was still room for negotiating better terms: "Let us express our determination to withdraw [from the conference] and say that we wish to wait patiently until the time is ripe. If they [the Anglo-American powers] show they are sincere in their wish to conclude a new agreement, we will confront them with our final proposal. . . . We will determine our course of action on the basis of their reaction to our terms. If we handle it this way, we surely will not have very much to fear from the breakdown of the conference." In short, Japan must show "the determination to withdraw" from the conference and see whether the United States and Britain would accept Japan's "final proposal." Even if this plan did not work out, Japan would not have much to fear. This telegram contradicted, in fact repudiated, the joint telegram of 14 March that Takarabe himself had signed. Commenting on this telegram, Prime Minister Hamaguchi said to Harada, "What he says doesn't seem to make sense. I think it's very odd."[86]

On the same day, 26 March, Wakatsuki also sent a long telegram to Shidehara. He refuted Takarabe's suggestion that if Japan gave one more push, the Anglo-American powers would make concessions. "If we are to make a new proposal with a view to improving our position, we must be prepared to withdraw from the conference in case it is not acceded to. If they [the Anglo-American powers] do not accept our demand, the prestige of our Empire will fall to the ground, and this is what I fear most." Japan could not risk breaking up the conference.[87] The two totally irreconcilable telegrams from Takarabe and Wakatsuki bewildered Tokyo. The modicum of harmony that had remained between the navy and the government, as well as between the Navy Ministry and the Naval General Staff, was shattered.

THE GOVERNMENT'S FINAL INSTRUCTION

Prime Minister Hamaguchi and Foreign Minister Shidehara were convinced that "if the Anglo-Japanese-American harmony collapses, stability of [the] international political situation will be jeopardized" and that it would be extremely dangerous to be optimistic about a naval race with the United States, "given its peculiar national character." At a meeting with naval leaders on 25 March, Prime Minister Hamaguchi stated that the government had decided not to risk breaking up the conference and starting a naval race. This resolve was unshakable, he said: "Though I lose the prime ministership, though I lose my life itself, this decision is unshakable." On 27 March he had an audience with the emperor, who told him "to make every effort to conclude speedily [the London Treaty] in the interest of world peace." These words had an electrifying effect on Hamaguchi. As far as the navy was concerned, this was the first instance of the emperor wielding his influence for peace, a stance he would maintain until late 1941. On the same day, 27 March, Hamaguchi called Katō, Okada, and Yamanashi to his official residence and alluded to the imperial wish. He explained that improving relations with the Anglo-American powers far outweighed any conceivable losses incurred from accepting the Reed-Matsudaira compromise.[88]

In his determination to conclude the treaty, Hamaguchi was supported by Prince Saionji Kinmochi and other influential court officials, such as Lord Privy

Seal Makino Nobuaki and Grand Chamberlain (Admiral) Suzuki. Saionji's view was essentially a restatement of Katō Tomosaburō's philosophy of naval limitation:

> A nation begins to have strength with real staying power only when its armaments are kept within the bounds permitted by its finances. . . . If Japan now steps forward and by accepting a 60 percent ratio leads this conference to a successful agreement, then the powers will recognize, especially in view of the present circumstances, that Japan is sincerely working to further international peace. If Japan takes the lead in making this conference a success, our future international position will be raised even higher. To march out in front chanting, "We have 70 percent come what may," will not get us what we want. . . . What profit is there in completely estranging ourselves from them [the United States and Britain]?[89]

Admiral Suzuki, who had served as Combined Fleet commander (1924) and Chief of the Naval General Staff (1925–29), told Harada, "I completely agree with Prince Saionji. If I were not a grand chamberlain, I would go and persuade Katō myself. I greatly regret the way he appeals to the public about the 70 percent and then arouses public opinion to carry through his own demand. Only a poor admiral would demand that he must have a 70 percent ratio or he cannot assure national defense. The Chief of the Naval General Staff must work with whatever strength is allotted to him, be it 60 or even 50 percent." "It was very odd," Suzuki continued, "for him [Katō] to say it must be 70 percent or nothing. It is completely wrong to say that young officers would, unlike olden days, not listen to anything below the 70 percent. It is up to the chief of the Naval General Staff to properly guide young officers. Katō, I am afraid, is too emotional."[90]

Prime Minister Hamaguchi's view, as related by the pro-treaty Admiral Kobayashi Seizō, was that "the question of whether to conclude the treaty or not is a question for the government to decide," not the chief of the Naval General Staff.[91] Hamaguchi and Shidehara were all the more anxious to conclude the treaty without further delay because the American ambassador Castle had told them that Stimson intended to immediately conclude an Anglo-American treaty in case Japan rejected the compromise. Already two weeks had passed since the Reed-Matsudaira compromise had been reached. Indeed Stimson had cabled Washington on 21 March, "Should Tokyo repudiate this agreement [the Reed-Matsudaira compromise] we would have difficulty in continuing to negotiate with a delegation which is without power and which its Government does not support. If the proposal is repudiated by Tokyo or a so-called counterproposal is sent we will immediately commence preparations of a two-power agreement with Great Britain."[92]

Late March was a crucial and incredibly tense period in Tokyo; confrontational meetings took place between the government and naval leaders. Records of these meetings show that on a few occasions Katō Kanji, whether under Okada's influence or not, implicitly acquiesced to the Reed-Matsudaira compromise in return for supplementary naval measures to compensate for deficiencies under the treaty. Subsequently, however, Katō claimed that as chief of the Naval General Staff, he absolutely opposed the compromise plan.[93] He argued that a decision on naval armaments was a matter on which the naval high command alone could advise the emperor.

What are the facts? At the 27 March meeting of naval leaders (Katō Kanji, Okada, Suetsugu, Yamanashi, and Hori), Katō and Suetsugu apparently agreed to accept the government's decision even if it was contrary to the navy's views. They acknowledged that the right to decide on the size of naval armaments lay with the government. This notwithstanding, Katō wrote on 31 March, "It looks as if the government is going to ignore the views of the Naval General Staff." He said with a tragic air that he would have to commit *hara-kiri* because he had not carried his point. Not taking him seriously, Okada sarcastically observed, "Those who go around publicizing about committing suicide seldom do."[93]

At 8:45 on the morning of 1 April, before the government's draft of the final instruction—acceptance of the treaty along the lines of the Reed-Matsudaira compromise—was presented to the cabinet, Hamaguchi met with Okada, Katō, and Yamanashi to obtain the navy's consent. Hamaguchi firmly stated that "from the military, diplomatic, and financial angles" he had decided to conclude the treaty. He stated in part, "If Japan should depart from cooperation with Britain and the United States, place itself in isolation, and by its own actions worsen international relations, Japan would find itself in an unspeakable predicament in international and other respects." Hamaguchi cautioned against the difficulties, antipathies, and obstructions that Japan would encounter from the Anglo-American powers in dealing with the China issue. His most compelling reason for concluding the treaty was, of course, the financial considerations. If the conference collapsed, the United States would pursue its building plan and start a naval race that would ruin Japan's national finance.[94]

Okada then spoke for the navy, saying that "if the cabinet should adopt the draft instructions, the navy will do everything in its power to devise a means of adjusting to the decision." During this meeting, Katō merely said that from a strategic and operational viewpoint, there were difficulties. But he did *not* say he opposed the final instruction outright, nor did he deny that what Okada had said represented the official naval position. On the contrary, Katō gave the impression of passive consent to the draft instructions.[95]

Upon hearing of the outcome of this meeting, Prince Fushimi relented and said that once the government had made its decision, there was no way left but to accept it. When Okada visited Fleet Admiral Tōgō, the latter said in a similar vein that he was no longer in a position to object and that the navy must strive to recover internal unity and devote itself to drills with renewed morale.

Meanwhile in London, Takarabe continued to vacillate. Even as the government's "final instructions" were being cabled, Vice Minister Yamanashi was deeply worried whether Takarabe would follow the instructions, so he sent him a most extraordinary cable urging "utmost prudence" and "circumspection":

> The government believes disruption of the conference by Japan would profoundly affect Japan's future. . . . It is feared that in the event you should take action at odds with Wakatsuki, it will divide our delegation in London to the detriment of its influence abroad. At home such actions will cause grave political difficulties, driving the navy into a most inimical and self-damaging position. Furthermore, such a situation will bring about most serious consequences for the future of our Empire. I earnestly beg you to act from the standpoint of the overall interest of the nation. I implore you to prudently bear with these difficulties and to fulfill your duty as a delegate. I truly fear that what I said above oversteps the bounds of my position. . . . I have been so bold as to forget the respect which is due you, and I have revealed my inmost thoughts.[96]

Okada, to whom Yamanashi showed his draft telegram, told him to delete the last three lines and add, "Admiral Okada is of the same opinion."

Yamanashi's warning against rash action betrayed his fear that at the last moment Takarabe might be swayed by hard-line naval advisers who demanded "one final thrust" to wrench concessions. The telegram from Yamanashi finally ended Takarabe's oscillation. In his reply to Yamanashi he promised, "I will not err with respect to the great work of the nation through reckless insistence on my own narrow views. I will refrain from behavior that may create problems for the future." In his diary Takarabe wrote that he was "overwhelmed with shame."[97] He had at long last come around to accepting the treaty.

Tokyo's instructions, which arrived in London on 1 April, produced an uproar among Japan's naval representatives, especially among the younger staff officers. Informed of the government's decision to accept the Reed-Matsudaira compromise, they were moved to tears. They denounced Wakatsuki and plotted to storm Takarabe's hotel suite. On their behalf Yamamoto went to Takarabe's room to deliver their overheated views. However, Yamamoto himself was not immune to the uproar. He felt that the government's decision would "be a great shock to the entire navy and adversely affect its morale." That night the naval aides gathered in Yamamoto's room and had an all-night session vehemently denouncing the compromise "as if they were mad men." Indeed, such was their excitement that they forgot themselves and punched a civilian member of the delegation. When Kaya, a ministry of finance representative, stressed the fiscal need for naval limitation, Yamamoto shouted, "Say another word, Kaya, and you will get a smack in the face!" When Yamamoto addressed Wakatsuki, "he almost seemed intent to do him in," in the words of one witness.[98]

The following day Yamamoto admonished his subordinates "not to commit a breach of service discipline," but he himself contradicted his own order and in fire-eating words challenged Takarabe, demanding that he take responsibility by resigning immediately: "The last and the only way left for the navy minister to preserve honor after this defeat at the conference is to resign in protest as befits the occasion and to prove to the Japanese people that 'the navy has not betrayed their trust.'" On a later occasion Yamamoto warned that surrender to the American position would "greatly shock our entire navy, destroy its morale, and bring about some untoward incident, which would have grave consequences on Japan's domestic and external policies."[99] He risked his own position when he so violently challenged Takarabe.

In Tokyo, a depressed Katō Kanji wrote in his diary, "I have been agonizing days and nights; there are moments when I think of committing suicide. Yet I must pluck up my courage." In fact, some right-wing elements exhorted Katō to commit *hara-kiri* or resign.[100] On 2 April, Katō went to the palace and submitted his memorial to the throne, stating that the "American plan" would create serious operational deficiencies. The rupture between the Naval General Staff and the Navy Ministry was now complete.

AMERICAN PERCEPTIONS

Was the London naval treaty another American "imposition" of an inferior ratio on Japan, as many of its navy men believed? American naval officers did not think so. On the contrary, they generally believed that Japan had obtained concessions that "made it practically impossible for the United States to support its policies in the Far East." Benefits accruing to Japan from the Washington treaty had now been "tilted farther to her advantage" at the London Conference. The U.S. Navy considered the London treaty ratio an important setback to its policy of insistence on 10:7 ratio for all warships.[101] Admiral Jones, the foremost hawk, objected that in light of American insular possessions in the Pacific, Japan's naval strength of 60 percent in real terms corresponded to more than 100 percent, so the London treaty meant "great disadvantages for the United States."[102] The General Board held that at the London Conference, Japan had obtained "indisputable naval supremacy in the western Pacific" and "absolute dictation in the affairs of the Far East." Resentful because the United States had not obtained an ironclad 10:6 ratio, the board stated that Japan had been allowed to secure naval hegemony in the western Pacific, at least until the next naval conference.[103]

On the other hand, America's foreign policy leaders disavowed convictions held by navy men that the next war would come over the China issue. Secretary of State Stimson never took seriously the admirals' talk about war with Japan. He called it "a fantastic fear," because he understood that no force lay behind the Open Door policy. "I cannot imagine," he said, "Congress declaring war on Japan because of anything Japan might do in China." On 25 January 1930 Ambassador Castle cabled Washington advising that "Japan be made to understand that we have no plans in regard to China which might conceivably lead to war."[104]

No such assurances were made to Japan, however. The problem was that American navy men were singing a different tune, and Japanese admirals were nervously listening to them. As Castle reported, the Japanese navy, public, and mass media "believe that we are building our navy with the thought in mind that we shall have to fight Japan on account of China."[105] The U.S. government complacently expected that the London naval treaty would bring about a rapprochement with Japan based on cooperation with its moderate leaders. Aware of the struggle between the pro-treaty and anti-treaty forces in Japan, Stimson wanted to aid the pro-treaty elements. He wrote to President Hoover on 17 February, "The Japanese Delegation is hampered by political conditions at home of a very serious character. They have unwisely made a public issue of the 10–7 ratio. . . . I feel it would be unwise to do anything which would weaken Wakatsuki's independent power in the meanwhile."[106]

Stimson believed he was making substantial concessions to Japan, with an eye to supporting the moderate-liberal forces represented by Hamaguchi, Wakatsuki, and Shidehara—men he hoped would contain Japan's rabid navalists. At a meeting of the Big Three in London, Stimson had said he regarded Japan as "a great stabilizing force. Japan presented a great advantage to America in her present position as an effective and stabilizing force in the Far East."[106] Senator Reed went even further: "The United States fully understands that Japan, in possession of certain naval strength, is the protector of peace in the Far East, just as the United States plays the same role in the Western Hemisphere."[107]

Addressing the House Committee on Naval Affairs, Admiral Pratt stated, "[The treaty] has been the most potent factor in eliminating friction between ourselves and Japan that it has been possible to devise. Instead of an atmosphere of distrust there has been substituted an atmosphere of confidence. . . . It may be said, with assurance, that in the course of a few years the mistrust, lack of confidence and suspicion . . . will be partially allayed through the medium of treaties for limitation of competitive armaments."[108]

Neither Stimson, Hoover, Reed, nor even Admiral Pratt fathomed the depth of the resentment most Japanese navy men felt or the seriousness of the dissension that was wracking the country. Stimson wrote in his memoirs that "the essential difficulty was one of Japanese pride, which had been seriously offended by the Washington ratio of ten-ten-six," but the domestic turbulence caused by the London Conference went much deeper than mere wounded pride.[109] The American delegates forgot about Japan's troubles once they put their signatures on the London naval treaty. To them the controversy over the "right of supreme command" must have seemed a tempest in a teacup. Stimson and company did not realize that the aftermath of the London treaty weakened Japan's moderate elements as well as the Washington system, exactly the opposite of what they had expected.

DOMESTIC ATTACKS ON THE LONDON TREATY

On 22 April 1930, the London naval treaty was signed at the Court of St. James's. Incorporating the Reed-Matsudaira compromise, the agreement provided in principle for a 60.2 percent ratio in the heavy cruiser category, but in practice it allowed Japan a 70 percent ratio until 1936. The treaty was stipulated to end on 31 December 1936. The next naval conference was to be held in 1935.

After the treaty was duly signed, Wakatsuki invited his colleagues and all members of the delegation, some seventy of them, to a dinner at Grosvenor House to thank them for their efforts. When the dinner was over, anti-treaty junior officers went up to Wakatsuki's head table to loudly vent their rage; some were so excited as to have nosebleeds, and others were drunk and began tussling. Alarmed, the civilian delegates urged him to retire to his room. But he remained and heard out the infuriated officers until they called it a night. If he left, Wakatsuki knew that those officers would think the chief delegate had ran away.[110]

In Japan, public reception of the London treaty was overwhelmingly favorable. When Wakatsuki and Takarabe arrived at the Tokyo Station on June 19, they were greeted by an unprecedented welcome with deafening shouts of "*Banzai!*" Rear Admiral Yamamoto, who had aligned with the hard-liners in London, was so moved by this enthusiastic reception that he began to reconsider his stand on naval limitation. Soon he switched to the support of naval limitation.

The "right of supreme command" controversy arose suddenly on 21 April when the 58th Diet session opened. The opposition party, the Seiyūkai, fired the first shot on the question of the "right of the supreme command" as the means of overthrowing the government. Sensational newspaper write-ups followed. Katō almost impulsively joined the controversy. The Naval General Staff became greatly agitated. Katō told Okada that "the worst things are happening. We cannot control our unruly naval subordinates." Some seventy retired admirals and vice admirals banded together to support Katō. Young officers in the Naval General Staff and the fleets would not allow their leaders to retreat from the Three Basic Principles; if compromise was to be ratified, they demanded that the chief of the Naval General Staff kill himself. Right-wing organizations joined the unrest. Overnight the "right of supreme command" question became the gravest political problem that shook the nation. The domestic backdrop of this controversy was party corruption and a serious economic depression; its international background was an impasse in Shidehara's diplomacy in Manchuria. The resulting agitation implanted a deep sense of crisis among military and naval men.

The right of supreme command is said to have been a cancer embedded in the Meiji Constitution. Without going into the details of this constitutional controversy, suffice it to note, on the basis of historian Kobayashi Tatsuo's detailed study, how differences arose between the Navy Ministry and the Naval General Staff.[111] The issue revolved around Article 12 of the Constitution, which stipulated the organization and peacetime standing of the military forces as an imperial prerogative. Article 12 became a point of contention between those responsible for state affairs (the Navy Ministry and the government) and the high command (the Naval General Staff). Regarding the London treaty, the orthodox constitutional interpretation held that the decision on the size of armaments rested with the Navy Ministry.

The Naval General Staff opposed this position; it held that any decision over military organization under Article 12 rested with the high command. It claimed that the consent of the Naval General Staff was required for the government's final instruction to London but that it had been disregarded, thus infringing on the "right of supreme command." By this time Katō had shifted the ground of his attack from "the deficiencies of naval strength" to the infringement of the right of the supreme command. On 3 May he said to Harada,

"When the government disregarded the Naval General Staff, it in effect disregarded the emperor's prerogative to command the military forces. I'll be damned if this is the way national defense is going to be decided!"[112] Of Katō's behavior Prince Saionji said, "Something must be done to maintain military discipline." On 10 June Katō presented his resignation directly to the emperor, claiming that His Majesty's right of supreme command had been infringed on. By this Katō virtually called the government a traitor. Prince Fushimi and Fleet Admiral Tōgō, the latter instigated by Vice Admiral Ogasawara Naganari, changed their minds again and rejoined Katō in attacking the treaty. But, as stated, no evidence supports Katō's argument. At the 1 April meeting Katō did not unequivocally oppose the government's final instruction to London; he only alluded to purely military-technical difficulties. Whatever Katō's real motives, the controversy over the right of supreme command had tragic consequences.

In opposing the treaty to the bitter end, neither Tōgō nor Prince Fushimi knew that the emperor had been supporting the treaty. Almost every day Katō Kanji went to see Tōgō and incited the aged fleet admiral to maintain dogged opposition to the treaty, which now posed the greatest political obstacle to its ratification. The fleet admiral declared that the government that had inhibited the navy should be overthrown as soon as possible to be replaced by a "clean government."[113]

The naval elder Okada dreaded the political consequences if the ratification of the naval treaty were aborted by Tōgō, the demigod of the Imperial Navy and "the Nelson of Japan." The only solution, suggested by another naval elder, Yamamoto Gonbei, was direct imperial intervention. Makino Nobuaki, Lord Keeper of the Privy Seal, appealed to the emperor. So on 15 July 1930 Hirohito solemnly told Grand Chamberlain (Admiral) Suzuki that Fleet Admiral Tōgō "must take a long view," adding that he, the emperor, did not approve of Tōgō's behavior. In these words the emperor expressed strong support of the treaty.[114] At long last on 1 October, the Privy Council ratified the London treaty.

On 14 November, Prime Minister Hamaguchi was shot at Tokyo Station by a fanatical ultranationalist youth, Sagōya Tomeo, who was disgruntled with the London treaty and stirred by the fleet faction's agitation. The prime minister died of the wound in August 1931. This was the first of several political assassinations that shackled the Japanese government during the 1930s. It is no accident that in the 26 February 1936 mutiny, the three naval elders—Admirals Suzuki Kantarō, Okada Keisuke, and Saitō Makoto, all moderate leaders who supported the London treaty—were assaulted. These developments undermined the premise of the Washington system—the continued ascendancy of the moderate leaders who were committed to parliamentary rule at home and to cooperation with the Anglo-American powers abroad.

PRELUDE TO TRAGEDY

Steering the London naval treaty to signature and ratification seemed a victory for the Navy Ministry group (notably Yamanashi, Hori, and Okada) and a defeat for the Naval General Staff group (Katō Kanji, Suetsugu, and their subordinates). Katō resigned as chief of the Naval General Staff, but under normal circumstances his behavior would have warranted forced retirement. Instead, Takarabe helped him to be appointed a member of the Supreme Military Council. As for Suetsugu, Prime Minister Hamaguchi resented him so much that he wanted to have him dismissed. For his insubordination on 17 March (making an intentionally misleading statement to the press without the permission of his superior), Suetsugu presented to Katō Kanji a "written apology," which read more like a vindication. Not surprisingly, Katō Kanji did not chastise Suetsugu, who was allowed to remain.[115] If Katō Tomosaburō had been in charge, both men would have been summarily ousted. In the navy ministry, Yamanashi was transferred to head the Sasebo Naval District and Hori to command the Third Squadron—definitely demotions.

Ironically, the outcome of the navy's strife was to enhance the power of the anti-treaty fleet faction and weaken the influence of the treaty faction. The violent split between these two groups plagued the navy in subsequent years. It became so acute that, as one officer recalled, "In the Navy Ministry they derided the Naval General Staff as crazy, and in the Naval General Staff they denounced the Navy Ministry as traitorous."[116]

The London treaty was sabotaged by the anti-treaty forces, and was destined to be short-lived. The navy held that the treaty, "seriously jeopardizing national defense, must not be allowed to last long." On 22 July, when the new chief of the Naval General Staff, Taniguchi Naomi, presented a memorial to the emperor, Hirohito surmised the navy's intent and tried to obtain an assurance that the navy "would not bind Japan's position at the next naval conference of 1935." This caveat notwithstanding, the Supreme Military Council stated in its official reply to the throne on 23 July, "It will be most disadvantageous from the viewpoint of national defense to be compromised by this treaty. We must complete our naval defense immediately upon expiration of this treaty by whatever means is deemed best." In other words, the navy opposed a continuation of the existing London treaty beyond its expiration in 1935.[117] Suetsugu wrote Katō,

"As things stand now, there is no way left but to force our way to the abrogation of the fatal treaty." Katō vented his indignation: "It is as if Japan were bound hand and foot and thrown into jail by the Anglo-American powers!"[118]

When one traces the origins of the collision course of the 1930s, the opposition building after the Washington Conference loomed large. In 1933 Prime Minister Saitō Makoto stated succinctly, "The present commotions have their roots in Admiral Katō Kanji's antipathy toward [the policy of] Adm. Katō Tomosaburō, the chief delegate at Washington."[119] No Japanese leader was better qualified to make this assessment. Heralded as "a new order of sea power," the Washington and London treaties—or Japan's response to them—were signposts on the Japanese navy's road to Pearl Harbor.

PART FOUR

JAPAN

ISOLATED

CHAPTER SEVEN

MEN, ORGANIZATION, AND STRATEGIC VISIONS, 1931–41

Anatomy of the Naval Establishment

I n the 1930s the Japanese naval establishment underwent momentous transformations that go far to explain its road to Pearl Harbor. The process may be studied as a breakdown, under mounting challenges from within, of its tradition of reason, moderation, and unity.

Several factors had defined the Japanese naval tradition. Originally patterned after the British model and subsequently influenced by the American strategic doctrine based on Alfred T. Mahan's sea power theory, the Japanese navy long retained traces of an "Anglo-American" orientation. Its officers prided themselves on their cosmopolitan and modern outlook, fostered by tours of duty at sea and abroad, that distinguished them from the more parochial army officers. Life on board ship tended to put a premium on the technological and professional aspects of seamanship.

The traditional navy was a relatively well-ordered and unified organization. While operational and tactical problems fell within the jurisdiction of the chief of the Naval General Staff, policy-making functions lay with the navy minister. Through clear lines of authority the navy minister controlled the naval establishment in peacetime, an arrangement that ensured internal harmony and a fraternal spirit among officers and men.

All this changed in the turbulent, crisis-ridden thirties. Beginning with the domestic crisis engendered by the London Naval Conference of 1930, the decade witnessed dissensions within the navy and the usurping of the navy minister's authority by high-command and middle-echelon officers (captains or commanders holding section-chief rank). As in other branches of the Japanese government, in the navy the policy-making process became decentralized.

The navy became increasingly influenced by anti-American, anti-British, and pro-German elements, especially in the middle echelons. The navy's policy became dominated by an emotional mode of thinking and myopic strategic preoccupations.

By the mid-1930s the "moderate" leadership holding on to the legacy of Katō Tomosaburō had been decidedly reduced to a minority. Perhaps the most significant change during the 1930s was the self-inflicted deterioration of naval leadership that failed to prevent the war with the United States in 1941.

The naval historian Robert G. Albion, in *Makers of Naval Strategy*, distinguished between the internal and external policies of the navy. Internal policy revolved around what the navy should *be*—that is, how large the navy should be and what types and quantities of weapons it ought to have. Internal policy also dealt with the navy's organization, structure, and personnel administration.[1] External policy dealt with what the navy should *do*. It pertained to what role the navy ought to play in foreign policy. Operational matters were subsumed under external policy. In the context of Japanese naval history, external policy included most importantly national policies that the navy pressed on the government.

This chapter analyzes the internal policy of the Japanese navy during 1930–41 by examining (1) the various groupings of elite naval officers and (2) the institutional framework for naval decision making. While the topic does not strictly pertain to "internal" policy, I will also discuss (3) the conflicting images, values, and strategic visions that conditioned the navy's attitudes and policies toward the United States.

Traditionally, gunnery officers were the elite of the Japanese navy, and despite the growing importance of aviation during the 1930s, few flying officers occupied sufficiently senior positions to influence naval policy. The navy's mainstream was officers who built their careers on battleships. Institutionally, the elite officer corps consisted of top-ranking graduates of the Naval Academy in Etajima, the Japanese Annapolis. Class standing at the academy virtually determined promotion.[2] Admiral Inoue Shigeyoshi, who graduated second in his class, testified that a student's record at the academy had influence comparable to twenty-five years of service after graduation.[3] After attaining lieutenancies, ambitious officers usually applied for the Naval Staff College, the counterpart of the Naval War College in Newport; about 16 percent of applicants were admitted. (For the period under consideration, only two admirals had not graduated from the Naval Staff College—Katō Kanji and Nomura Kichisaburō.) But graduates of the Naval Staff College did not enjoy anything like the privileged position of their army counterparts.

Salient characteristics of the navy's educational system must be noted here. Admiral Inoue, who graduated from the Naval Academy in 1909, reminisced that although rigorous discipline was the order of the day, "there was time for poetry and dreaming, too."[4] Starting around World War I, the academy increasingly emphasized rigorous training, regimentation, and memory work at the expense of originality, individuality, and creativity. Rear Admiral Takagi Sōkichi, who graduated in 1915, remembered his education at the Naval Academy as "Spartan and thrashing." The unimaginative emphasis on cramming and rote memory ended any original thinking. Rear Admiral Tomioka, who graduated in 1917, recalls that the Naval Academy was regimented and standardized. "It was a forcefully disciplined life with no leeway whatsoever."[5]

The Naval Staff College, though designed to train high-ranking commanders, functioned as a nursery for staff officers. Its curriculum emphasized narrowly strategic and tactical subjects to the neglect of a comprehensive "science of war." Ōi Atsushi, a student at the Naval Staff College in 1934–36, had understood strategy as a comprehensive study of the role of the military in relation to political, economical, and diplomatic factors, but the strategy lectures he attended hardly differed from lectures on tactics. Student officers were schooled in the tradition of Mahan. Taking a leaf from Mahan's *Influence*, their manual, the *Kaisen yōmurei*, (Naval Battle Instructions) held that "war once declared must be waged offensively, aggressively."[6] Day in and day out they conducted war games against the American fleet that culminated in a decisive Mahanian engagement in the manner of Tsushima. In commencement exercises officers conducted war games in front of the emperor, simulating a magnificent main-fleet battle based on the principle of "big battleships and big guns." Mesmerized by Mahan's strategic doctrines, officers developed an obsession with the decisive fleet battle that would annihilate the enemy armada at one stroke. Their bible was the aforementioned Naval Battle Instructions, initially developed by Lieutenant Commander Akiyama Saneyuki at the Naval Staff College and sanctioned in 1910. Reflecting Mahan's doctrine, it stated, "The battleship squadron is the main fleet, whose aim is to attack the enemy's main fleet." "The key to successful naval operations is initiative and concentration." This manual, though revised five times, essentially remained intact until the mid-1930s. The result was unfortunate.[6] After the Pacific War, Rear Admiral Nakazawa Tasuku, head of the Operations Section in 1939–40 and the Personnel Bureau in 1942, testified that "Japan lost the war because the navy was dominated by the top graduates of the Navy Staff College who blindly followed its instructions and were void of originality."[7]

The navy's system of personnel policy, based on class standing at the Naval Academy and "semi-automatic promotion," tended to accentuate bureaucratization of the navy. Seniority rewarded mediocrity over brilliance and often placed and kept in positions of importance older officers left behind in the march of technological progress and strategic innovation. As they became bureaucratized, their perspectives became narrow and preoccupied with promotion. Those with individual, untraditional, or unorthodox views, and a tendency to be outspoken, were shunned. The leadership of Japanese admirals steadily deteriorated after the days of Katō Tomosaburō. As the naval intellectual Rear Admiral Takagi Sōkichi wrote, outstanding leaders became few and far between, supplanted by "institutionalized authority" resting on organization.[8] A related problem was the aging of the admirals.[9] (Rear admirals should ideally be forty years old and full admirals fifty; this approximately coincided with the ages of those who commanded the battle of Tsushima. In 1941 flag officers were from five to eight years older than the ideal ages.)

Another feature of the navy's personnel policy was rapid turnover and constant reshuffling of officers, especially abler ones, which was bound to preclude consistent, well-thought-out policies. This was particularly the case with the so-called super-express group, who frequently rotated among posts in the Operations Division of the Naval General Staff and command positions in the Combined Fleet.[10]

THE TREATY FACTION VERSUS THE FLEET FACTION

The most apparent grouping of naval officers from 1930 to 1941 was along functional or organizational lines—the "administrative group" in the Navy Ministry and the "command group" in the Naval General Staff.[11] Officers were generally classed in these groups according to their relative length of service in each branch in the early stages of their careers. Important posts in the Naval General Staff— heads of the Operations Division or Section—required extensive previous experience as staff officers. (The outspoken Admiral Inoue called it "an incestuous relationship.") Appointments to these "command" posts tended to be separate from "administrative" positions. For example, Admiral Suetsugu, who together with Katō Kanji was a leader of the "command group," was a gunnery officer (later, submarine commander) in the fleet and never served in the Navy Ministry except for a brief stint as head of the Education Bureau. Admiral Yamamoto, though rich in fleet, aviation, and administrative experiences, never served on the Naval General Staff. A few admirals, such as Toyoda Soemu, urged more interchange between the two branches of the service, warning that officers would become one-sided in outlook. Rear Admiral Nakazawa, head of the Personnel Bureau, also pointed out that the skewed personnel policy made mutual understanding between the two branches difficult and precluded full cooperation between the Naval Ministry and the Naval General Staff. But their advice seems to have had little effect.[12]

Traditionally, key policy-making posts in the Navy Ministry, especially the Naval Affairs Bureau, went to brilliant officers, top graduates of the Naval Academy who excelled in politico-administrative ability. Pivotal positions in the Naval General Staff were occupied by "sea officers," often dubbed "sea warriors" ("old sea dogs" in Anglo-American parlance). As early as 1922 Captain J. P. R. Marriott, British attaché in Tokyo, had observed, "There is no question about it but that the higher ranks in the Imperial Japanese Navy are of two distinct types: (1) the Sea Officer; (2) the bureaucrat. . . . It is quite a common saying when one enquires the ability of a post-Captain in high position to be informed that he is a bad Captain of ship but very good in the office."[13] Until the late 1920s the "administrative group" represented the elite establishment in the Navy Ministry. The smoldering discontent of the "command group" at suffering from what it regarded as an inferior position finally erupted during and after the London Naval Conference.

As already noted, differences between the two groups in their attitudes toward the United States were brought out in full relief by the issue of naval limitation. The navy's factionalism during the 1930s was defined in terms of antithetical stands on the Washington and London treaties. Their supporters were labeled the treaty faction and their opponents the fleet faction. Most of the supporters of the Washington and London naval treaties—heirs to Katō Tomosaburō's legacy—were systematically "purged" in 1933–34 by Navy Minister Ōsumi Mineo, who was backed by the anti-treaty group, including especially Katō Kanji. Even after he had resigned as chief of the Naval General Staff in the bitter aftermath of the London Conference, Katō remained politically influential as a vocal member of the Supreme Military Council and the leader of the fleet faction. The navy was now under the control of the fleet faction. In February 1932, Katō pressured the navy minister to appoint his protégé Takahashi Sankichi vice chief of the Naval General Staff, in which capacity he virtually controlled the naval high command. In November 1933, Suetsugu was appointed Combined Fleet commander, and the following year he was succeeded by Takahashi. Admiral Ōsumi Mineo (Navy Minister in 1931–32) may also be regarded as a kindred spirit.

But Katō and Suetsugu wielded their greatest influence on the spirited younger officers of the line and the Naval General Staff. Some had fallen under Katō's sway as students when he was vice principal of the Naval Academy (1911–13), president of the Gunnery School (1916–18), and president of the Naval Staff College (1920–21). One graduate of the staff college could never forget how Katō, on his return from Washington, addressed student officers on the American "imposition" of the 60 percent ratio, tears rolling down his cheeks. Young officers acclaimed him to the point of idolization when he boasted about the invincible navy. Similarly, Suetsugu was greeted with cheers by young officers when appointed commander in chief of the Combined Fleet.[14] With the exception of Yamamoto Isoroku, Suetsugu was the most popular admiral to command the Combined Fleet.

THE RISE OF THE GERMAN FACTION

A new division of naval officers arose in the mid-1930s based on differences in foreign policy: an American (or Anglo-American) faction and a German (later, Axis) faction. This division was largely based on officers' experiences abroad as language officers, assistant attachés, and attachés. Traditionally the navy had sent promising young officers—top graduates of the Naval Academy—to the attaché's office in Washington and the ablest naval constructors to Greenwich, England, to train at the Royal Naval College for three years. But in the course of the 1930s, Germany became the preferred nation. This shift can be traced to the years immediately after World War I, when many officers resented what they saw as Britain's sudden abandonment of the Anglo-Japanese Alliance at the Washington Conference after exploiting Japan during the war as a "watchdog of the British Empire." (During World War I the Japanese navy, upon British request, had expelled German submarines from the South Pacific.) Young officers, susceptible to such resentment, had risen to captains or commanders by the outbreak of World War II. Britain ceased to extend privileges and assistance to the Japanese navy after the termination of the Yamamoto-Fisher agreement that accompanied the Anglo-Japanese Alliance, and after 1923 the Royal Naval College in Greenwich refused to accept Japanese naval architects. Consequently, Berlin became a much sought-after post for technical personnel. Japan increasingly turned to Germany for technical and scientific cooperation and assistance.

In 1919 the navy sent to Europe and the United States an investigative mission, headed by Rear Admiral Katō Kanji. While in Germany, Grand Admiral Alfred von Tirpitz arranged for Katō's party to visit ports and inspect state-of-the-art naval technology. Impressed with Germany's technology, especially in submarine and optical equipment, Katō submitted a report upon his return stressing that the navy would gain much by introducing German weaponry.[15]

An episode during this tour characteristically showed Katō overstepping his authority, almost ruining his career. On his own initiative he clandestinely concluded with German Chief of the Naval Command Admiral Adolph von Trotha what amounted to a secret German-Japanese submarine agreement. It stipulated that (1) Germany would hand over all its submarine plans to the Japanese navy; (2) Germany would place two of its submarine officers on reserve and send them to Japan; and (3) Japan would transfer all its technical improvements back to the German navy when Germany was allowed to possess a navy again. Germany, which had been forbidden by the Versailles Peace Treaty to have submarines, wanted to use Japan to maintain and develop its submarine technology. Navy Minister Katō Tomosaburō was afraid that such an agreement violated the Versailles treaty and, that, if disclosed, would antagonize the United States, Britain, and France, so he peremptorily ordered Kanji to cancel the agreement. To take responsibility for his unauthorized action, Kanji submitted his tentative resignation, and some in the Navy Ministry demanded that he be placed on the reserve list, but somehow he survived. Whereas Katō Kanji was preoccupied with technical-military advantages, Katō Tomosaburō was guided by a broad international viewpoint.[16]

In 1919 Japan received as war prizes seven German submarines, five of which were of the latest design, and they contributed much to submarine technology in Japan. In 1924–25 the navy invited to Japan German engineers who had designed U-boats during World War I. After 1934, when Japan issued a note to nullify the Washington treaty, Germany became an increasingly attractive source of naval technology. During the mid-1930s German-Japanese naval technical exchange became a part of the navy's efforts to counter Anglo-American power.[17]

During the latter half of the 1920s the Japanese navy sent more naval architects to Germany than to Britain or the United States. After 1936, the year the Anti-Comintern Pact was concluded between Japan and Germany, naval officers stationed in Berlin as attachés, assistant attachés, and members of the attaché office outnumbered those in Washington or London. Upon their return these officers formed the nucleus of the pro-German, anti-American faction in the Navy Ministry and the Naval General Staff.[18] In March 1940, German naval attaché Paul Wenneker reported from Tokyo: "For some time opinion of the Navy officer corps up to the rank of captain has been practically 100% pro-German. . . . The spirit of the junior officers would sweep away on the tide."[19] A likable and sociable man, Wenneker made close friendships with many middle-ranking officers, especially those who had served in Berlin. In July 1940, he wrote in his diary, "Reception for 140 Japanese officers. . . . A very interesting evening, as was evidenced by the large number of younger officers. Bearing in mind that in Japan much of the pressure comes from below, it is of the utmost importance to influence this circle."[20] The observation was quite astute. Ambassador Eugen Ott did his best to undermine the Japanese navy's "overestimation" of Anglo-American sea power.

With their enthusiasm for Nazi Germany, the German faction stood out in contrast to the older generation that had served in Berlin. Admiral Yonai Mitsumasa had spent two and a half years in Germany after World War I but became convinced of the danger of aligning with Germany, a conviction reinforced by his study of *Mein Kampf*. When younger officers took *Mein Kampf* as an oracle, Yonai cautioned that Hitler despised the Japanese as an inferior and unimaginative race—an unflattering depiction that had been carefully deleted from the Japanese translation.[21] Admiral Inoue, who was stationed in Europe from 1918 to 1921, also said that Japan must never line up with Germany, because that country had no hesitation in breaking treaties.[22]

In 1936 Commander Ishikawa Shingo, Katō Kanji's disciple and a leading member of the anti-American faction, took a ten-month fact-finding tour of Europe, Asia, and the United States. In Germany he was briefed by the assistant attaché, Commander Kami Shigenori, who was strongly impressed by Hitler's success in the Rhineland Crisis, and became a fanatic German admirer. Ishikawa came to believe that "Germany would rise in arms around 1940 and this would be Japan's golden opportunity to break through the encirclement around it."[23] By 1940 the German faction had come to occupy some of the navy's key middle-echelon posts (section chiefs) that provided a driving force in naval policy.

The German faction was lucky to have an old Germanophile as chief of the Naval General Staff during 1933–41: Fleet Admiral Prince Fushimi Hiroyasu, a cousin of Emperor Hirohito and the oldest officer on active duty. He had spent his impressionable years from ages sixteen to twenty-one in Germany, graduating from the naval academy and naval staff college in Kiel. He had served for many years as a sea officer in the fleets.[24] At the time of the London Naval Conference, he had supported Katō Kanji in his opposition to the treaty. (Katō was close to Prince Fushimi, having been an "official companion" in their Naval Academy days.) His appointment as chief of the Naval General Staff had been engineered by Fleet Admiral Tōgō, Vice Admiral Ogasawara, and Katō Kanji. During his incumbency for eight crucial years, Fushimi tended to side with the fleet faction and hard-liners. He presided over the Naval General Staff at such critical junctures as the Tripartite Pact in September 1940, the advance to southern Indochina in July 1941, and the fateful decision for war in late fall of 1941. Some officers of the moderate persuasion secretly called him "the cancer of the navy."

The antagonisms between these overlapping groups—the "administrative group" versus the "command group," the treaty faction versus the fleet faction, and the Anglo-American faction versus the German faction—were deep-rooted. Admirals Yonai and Suetsugu, leaders of the opposing groups, reportedly refused even to speak to each other.

THE ASCENDANCY OF THE NAVAL GENERAL STAFF

The upshot of the London treaty was a divided navy. According to an estimate by the naval intellectual Rear Admiral Takagi Sōkichi, the navy's political influence in national affairs, which normally amounted at most to one-third that of the army, was reduced to a fourth or a fifth.[25] Yet from this weakened position, the navy contended with the army to increase its share of the budget and war matériel. After the mid-1930s, Japan's national policy was increasingly influenced by army-navy rivalry.

The navy's division after the London Conference gave the Katō-Suetsugu group a chance to expand its influence, with the backing of disgruntled senior officers. Behind Katō were Fleet Admiral Tōgō—the naval demigod—and his minion, Vice Admiral Ogasawara (Ret.). Both had strenuously opposed the treaty. In January 1933 the fleet faction was strengthened when Admiral Ōsumi, a hardliner and opponent of naval limitation, was appointed navy minister with the backing of Tōgō, Ogasawara, and Katō Kanji. The first step to strengthen the fleet faction was to install imperial Prince Fushimi, the only remaining fleet admiral after Tōgō died, as chief of the Naval General Staff in February 1932. Already at the time of the London Naval Conference, Prince Fushimi had sided with the fleet faction. Admiral Okada, a senior naval leader of moderate persuasion, and Prince Saionji worried that Prince Fushimi might become a "robot" of his subordinates.[26] They also feared that his words might be regarded as reflecting the emperor's wishes. During his long and undistinguished tenure as chief of the Naval General Staff, February 1932 to April 1941, his vice chiefs invoked the august name of the prince to press the navy minister into acquiescing in the demands of the Naval General Staff. Further, as a member of the imperial family, Fushimi was not to be held accountable for any error or misjudgment. Because nobody could restrain him, he tended to be dogmatic, which only impeded the navy's policy making. As relations with the United States deteriorated, he displeased the

emperor with his hard-line recommendations. In October 1941, Fushimi presented "extremely belligerent arguments" about policy toward the United States,
profoundly disappointing the emperor.[27] In April 1941, Navy Minister Oikawa
Koshirō told Vice Admiral Inoue, head of the Naval Aviation Department, that
the ailing Fushimi wished to retire and asked his opinion. Inoue supported his
retirement. As he explained, a prince of the blood was simply not brought up to
assume such a position at such a critical time. But even after he retired in April
1941, Fushimi retained the right to have his say in the appointment of top leaders,
especially navy ministers.[28]

A second important move to strengthen the fleet faction was to restructure
the Naval General Staff after the manner of the army. Traditionally, the power
of the chief of the Naval General Staff had been subordinate to that of the Navy
Minister. Even regarding high-command matters (operations), the chief had
customarily sought the consent of the minister before making a presentation to
the throne. This tradition of the Navy Ministry's primacy over the Naval
General Staff had prevailed until the London Naval Conference.[29]

As already noted, Rear Admiral Satō Tetsutarō, Vice Chief of the Naval General
Staff, attempted in 1915 to enhance the authority of the chief of the Naval
General Staff and angered Navy Minister Katō Tomosaburō, who demoted him.
Again in 1922, Katō Kanji, then vice chief and absolutely opposed to a system of
civilian navy ministers, planned to revise the regulations of the Naval General
Staff to expand its authority. He ordered his protégé, Captain Takahashi, a leader
of the fleet faction, to draft a plan, but he did not dare present it as long as Katō
Tomosaburō was alive. The plan was revived when Takahashi became vice
chief of the Naval General Staff in February 1932. Fushimi ordered Takahashi
to revise the Naval General Staff regulations to enlarge its power. Disgruntled
with the Washington and London treaties, Prince Fushimi believed these treaties
were a result of the weak-kneed policy of Navy Minister Katō Tomosaburō and
his successors. The only way to rectify the deplorable situation, Prince Fushimi
believed, was to strengthen the Naval General Staff.

This time, circumstances were far more favorable. The London treaty controversy had given rise to a demand, inside and outside the navy, to establish
the right of the supreme command. The 15 May (1932) Incident, in which a
group of young naval officers played a leading role in the assassination of Prime
Minister Inukai Tsuyoshi, had an electrifying effect upon the navy, dramatizing
the need to placate young malcontents. A revision of the Naval General Staff
regulations would help appease hot-blooded young officers.[30] Japan's external situation also favored the revision. In a postwar reminiscence, Takahashi admitted

that one of his aims was to be prepared for war with the United States; he feared that the Shanghai Incident of 1932 might cause a Japanese-American war.

The main aim of strengthening the Naval General Staff was to transfer jurisdiction over the size of armaments from the Navy Ministry to the Naval General Staff. Already on 23 January 1933, Navy Minister Ōsumi Mineo and Prince Fushimi had met with Army Minister Araki Sadao and Chief of the Army General Staff Prince Kan'in and signed a secret document titled "Decision on the Size of Armaments." It stated that the size of armaments was "an absolute condition for national defense and strategy" and therefore a decision on it must be made by the chiefs of the Navy and Army General Staffs.[31]

Acting on Prince Fushimi's orders, Takahashi, a foremost leader of the fleet faction and generally regarded Katō Kanji's successor, presented to the Navy Ministry the demands, designed to "reduce the navy minister's authority to a minimum" (Inoue's words). The Naval General Staff demanded sole jurisdiction not only over command matters but the size of armaments, education and the training of the fleets, even personnel policy.[32] The Navy Ministry tried to oppose this. Captain Inoue, who as Chief of the First Section of the Naval Affairs Bureau negotiated with the Naval General Staff's representative, stoutly resisted. He later wrote that the Naval General Staff's demand was "a most outrageous act, tantamount to raising a standard of revolt against the navy minister." Inoue held that the problem of armaments, involving budget, must remain under the jurisdiction of the Navy Ministry. He felt that expansion of the authority of the Naval General Staff would only increase the danger of war.[33]

With Inoue refusing to budge, the negotiations were taken over by Terashima Ken, head of the Naval Affairs Bureau, and Shimada Shigejirō, head of the Operations Division. The matter had come to look like a feud between the fleet faction and the treaty faction. When a deadlock again ensued, Vice Chief Takahashi played his trump card with Navy Minister Ōsumi: he threatened that unless the demands of the Naval General Staff were met, Fushimi would resign. Katō Kanji also put pressure on Ōsumi.[34] When Fushimi himself confronted Ōsumi, the navy minister hastily complied. He was already inclined to side with the hardliners in the Naval General Staff. This was not the last time Prince Fushimi abused his status as a member of the imperial family to impose his and the naval high command's will that ran contrary to the emperor's wish. The Naval General Staff had its way even though naval elders—former Navy Minister Okada, Saitō Makoto (prime minister), and Suzuki Kantarō (grand chamberlain)—all opposed it. Okada said he had "never seen such an outrageous plan."[35]

The revised regulations of the Naval General Staff broke with the navy's tradition by establishing primacy over the Navy Ministry. With command over naval forces in peacetime transferred to the chief of the Naval General Staff, the regulations sharply reduced the navy minister's control over the naval establishment. Captain Iwamura Seiichi, Senior Adjutant to the Navy Minister, farsightedly confided to his friend Inoue that he feared the new regulations increased the danger of war by weakening the navy minister's ability to put "brakes" on the Naval General Staff.[36]

When the new regulations, after being sanctioned by the navy minister, came up for the emperor's approval in September 1933, they encountered unexpected opposition. The emperor sharply questioned Ōsumi, expressing fear that "a slight misapplication of the new regulations could cause excessive intervention by the Naval General Staff in budgetary and personnel matters that are under the government's jurisdiction." The emperor ordered Ōsumi to prepare a memorandum pledging that the Naval General Staff would not unduly intervene in government affairs. Only after Ōsumi submitted the required document four days later did Hirohito approve the proposed revision.[37] The London treaty would expire in 1935, and two years' notice of the nullification of the Washington treaty could be issued in 1934. The Naval General Staff now controlled the fate of the Washington and London system.

On 1 October 1933, the day the revision went into effect, Prince Fushimi addressed his assembled subordinates: "This revision is a great reform for the regeneration of the Imperial Navy." It proved to be, in the words of official naval historian Nomura Minoru, "an important milestone on the navy's road to the Pacific War."[38] Withdrawal from the Washington-London system in 1953–56, conclusion of the Tripartite Pact in 1940, and the determination to go to war—these were strongly supported by the Naval General Staff. During the crises of 1940–41, the Naval General Staff would take a more risk-taking stance than Naval Ministry leaders.

THE ŌSUMI PURGE

A third attempt to strengthen the fleet faction and to decimate the treaty faction was the so-called Ōsumi purge. During 1933–34 senior officers of the treaty faction who had supported the Washington and London treaties were systematically retired or placed on the reserve list. Navy Minister Ōsumi had the backing of Fleet Admiral Tōgō, Prince Fushimi, and Katō Kanji. Among the victims of the purge were some of the ablest officers known for their moderate views. Admiral Yamanashi Katsunoshin was fifty-six years old at the time of his forced retirement; of the vice admirals, Hori Teikichi was fifty-one, Sakonji Seizo fifty-five, and Terashima Ken fifty-two. (Normal retirement age for admirals was sixty-five, for vice admirals, sixty-two.)

The forced retirement of Hori was a great loss to the navy. Celebrated as "the finest brain ever produced by the Naval Academy," a greater brain than even Akiyama Saneyuki, he was a brilliant administrator.[39] A devoted disciple of Katō Tomosaburō, he carried the now-famous "Katō message" to Tokyo at the time of the Washington Conference. Hori had also attended the Geneva Conference and played a crucial role in concluding the London treaty as head of the Naval Affairs Bureau. Yamamoto Isoroku, then attending the preliminary naval talks in London, thought the loss of his friend and Naval Academy classmate was more costly to the Japanese navy than, say, a division of cruisers.[40] From London, where he was Japan's delegate at the preliminary naval talks of 1934, Yamamoto wrote Hori about his purge: "It will be in vain to attempt to save the navy. Perhaps there is no way left but to rebuild the navy after it has wrought its own ruin by such an outrage."[41]

The consequences of the Ōsumi purge cannot be overemphasized. It decimated the navy's finest leadership and weakened the moderate forces that might have exercised rational restraint over the Kato-Suetsugu group and, later, their fire-eating disciples in the middle echelons. Admiral Shimada Shigetarō, Navy Minister at the time of the Pearl Harbor attack, later reflected, "Had Hori been navy minister before the outbreak of the war, he would have coped with the situation more aptly."[42] In a similar vein, Inoue said that if Hori and Yamanashi had stayed in the navy, the history of Japan would have been quite different. Such lamentations bespeak the dearth of leadership that crippled the navy in 1940–41. Captain Takagi Sōkichi said he could now count only four first-rate admirals—Yonai Mitsumasa, Yamamoto Isoroku, Inoue Shigeyoshi, and Koga Mine'ichi—who "miraculously" escaped the purge; their "good fortune" was not being involved in naval limitation.

With revision of the Naval General Staff regulations, the "command group," which for years had chafed under the control of the navy minister and the "administrative group" now would have its day. One indication of the interest that the Naval General Staff had begun to take in "war guidance"—national defense policy and war preparations—was the creation of a post designated as the war guidance officer. Under direct control of the head of the Operations Division and holding section chief rank, the war guidance officer was to push for a hard-line policy toward the United States in 1940–41.

Within the Navy Ministry the locus of political functions was the Naval Affairs Bureau; its chief joined the vice minister in assisting the navy minister. The official directly in charge of state policy matters was the chief of its First Section, but he was handicapped by a vastly understaffed office. In 1936 the Japanese navy confronted a crisis following the nullification of the Washington treaty and withdrawal from the 1935 London Conference. Expansion into Southeast Asia was alluring. To bolster the navy's policy-making functions, lead national policy in the critical years ahead, and better cope with the army and its much larger staff, the navy in the spring of 1936 created three ad hoc committees for naval policy (the First Committee), organizational restructuring (the Second Committee), and the naval budget (the Third Committee). Because these committees were mainly staffed with key section chiefs (and also some bureau and division heads) of the Navy Ministry and the Naval General Staff, they enhanced the influence of middle-echelon officers on the making of national policy.[43]

Of the committees set up in 1936, the most important was the First Committee, charged with formulating "the Empire's national policy and concrete naval policy and its implementation in light of changes in the international situation, especially after the expiration of the naval treaties."[44] The results of its investigation and recommendations filtered into deliberations in the upper echelons that culminated in the now-famous "Fundamentals of National Policy" approved by the Five Ministers Conference on 7 August 1936, which for the first time incorporated the navy's policy "to advance to the South Seas."

ISHIKAWA AND THE FIRST COMMITTEE

On the Second Committee's recommendation, the Naval Affairs Bureau was restructured in November 1940. This organizational reshuffle was aimed at enhancing the navy's ability to cope with the United States, especially in the aftermath of the Tripartite Pact in September 1940. The chief of the First Section of this bureau was in charge of state policy matters and naval armaments, but his office was understaffed. The navy needed to raise its voice to vie with the army in national and defense policy. It therefore decided to divide its Naval Affairs Bureau and create a Naval Ordnance Bureau, to which many of its tasks were transferred. This new bureau, headed by Rear Admiral Hoshina Zenshirō, was in charge of fleet mobilization, munitions, and ships.

At the same time, the navy created the Second Section of the Naval Affairs Bureau, to which its First Section relinquished jurisdiction over political, diplomatic, and defense policy. Underlying this reshuffling was the navy's conviction that "to tide over the unprecedented national crisis attendant to the Tripartite Pact," it must now abandon the navy's traditional stance of nonintervention in politics and "resolutely venture into the hub of state activities." The Second Section was to be "a powerful organ of policy guidance" and its main task was to "strengthen the Imperial Navy's influence in national affairs from the broad viewpoint of war guidance."[45] By the very nature of its assigned task—to negotiate with the army to counter its demands as well as to make war plans—the Second Section assumed an extremely bellicose posture toward the United States and Great Britain.

The chief of the Second Section from November 1940 to June 1942 was Captain Ishikawa Shingo, regarded as "the direct heir to the Katō-Suetsugu line" and the foremost leader of the fleet faction. In 1931 he published, under the pseudonym Ōya Hayato, a book titled *Nihon no kiki* (Japan's Crisis) in which he frankly set forth his ideas.[46] He wrote, "American ambition in the Far East had revealed its caustic nature as early as Commodore Perry's arrival in Uraga in 1853. . . . When John Hay devised the Open Door policy, America fired the first gun of the war of invasion upon China." After listing America's ambitious designs that led to the Washington and London Conferences, Ishikawa declared that "all this is a systematic program formulated by the United States for the invasion of China and Manchuria." After describing America's Far Eastern policy in lurid colors, he appealed for "a grand national strife to secure our right of existence." This book was essentially a tract to justify occupation of Manchuria and inner Mongolia. That an active officer would write such a book even under an assumed name was irregular to say the least.

A resourceful and hyperactive man with a lust for power and a touch of fanaticism, Ishikawa was the most influential and most hawkish of the middle-echelon officers during the crisis of 1940–41. The Personnel Bureau had misgivings about his appointment because of his reputation for overpowering his seniors by "pressure from below [*gekokujō*]." Such reservation not withstanding, he was appointed thanks to the recommendation of Rear Admiral Oka Takazumi, Chief of the Naval Affairs Bureau, with whom he had been on close terms, and the intervention of Navy Minister Oikawa Koshirō himself. That an officer of such a description was appointed to an important new position showed how far the navy had departed from its customary personnel policy.

At the forefront of hard-liners, Ishikawa took a belligerent position toward the United States. In 1936 he had predicted that "Germany would rise in arms around 1940 and this would be Japan's golden opportunity to break through the encirclement around it."[47] Styling himself "the most politically minded officer in the navy," he maintained extensive contacts not only with radical army officers but political, bureaucratic, and right-wing circles—Foreign Minister Matsuoka Yōsuke and Prime Minister Konoe among them. General Hasunuma Shigeru, grand military chamberlain to the Emperor, told the newly appointed Navy Minister Shimada Shigetarō in October 1941, "In June both the army and the navy were opposed to war, but they changed their policy overnight because of the opposition of a certain section chief in the Navy Ministry" and decided to advance into southern Indochina. Hasunuma added that the emperor "expressed deep apprehension about the state of Japanese-American relations." That section chief was Captain Ishikawa.[48] Later in 1943, when commanding an air squadron at the Kendari base in the Celebes, Ishikawa boasted to his staff, "I am telling you, it was I who brought Japan to war." Admiral Yamamoto bitterly remarked that the navy was "overindulgent and spoiled Ishikawa."[49]

Another institutional factor that added to the influence of middle-echelon officers was the establishment in late 1940 of the new First Committee (not to be confused with the First Committee of 1936). As its senior member, Ishikawa dominated this committee. A controversy exists over the role this committee played in the coming of the war. Official naval historians of the War History Department of the Defense Agency, notably Nomura Minoru, minimize the influence of this committee in the navy's policy making. He regards this committee merely as Ishikawa's niche for his warlike assertions, or, more succinctly, "a synonym for Captain Ishikawa."[50] On the other hand, Tsunoda Jun, author of the final volume of *The Road to the Pacific War*, emphasizes the role played by the First Committee.[51]

Examination of the existing documentary evidence points to the importance of this committee. Like the Second Section of the Naval Affairs Bureau, the First Committee was created because the navy realized that "as the result of concluding the Tripartite Pact, Japan had established a national policy of opposing Britain and the United States." For this purpose the First Committee became "the nerve center" and "the pivotal organ" for establishing "a maritime national defense state." Aiming to complete armaments for total war, the committee was to press for a naval buildup, conduct strategic planning, and guide naval defense policy. Its tasks were to create a consensus of views about these matters among the key section chiefs, draft policy recommendations, and submit them to its superiors.[52]

The First Committee sought dynamic "collective leadership" on the middle-echelon level. The central figure was, of course, Ishikawa. Other members were

Captain Tomioka Sadatoshi, chief of the Operations Section; Captain Ōno Takeji, war guidance officer of the Naval General Staff; and Captain Takada Toshitane, chief of the First Section of the Naval Affairs Bureau. There were three "secretaries" or associate members: Commanders Shiba Katsuo (the First Section of the Naval Affairs Bureau) and Fujii Shigeru (the Second Section of the Naval General Staff), and Onoda Sutejirō (war guidance officer). In their mid-forties, they were the crème de la crème of officers of their generation; five of them had graduated at the top of the Naval Staff College or received imperial awards. The First Committee was "a powerful task force that cut across the naval establishment," but because it lacked a chairman, its locus of responsibility was unclear, and no member could restrain Ishikawa. Admiral Inoue, a moderate senior leader, was sharply critical of the First Committee for these reasons. He also severely criticized allowing members of Naval General Staff to participate in policy planning on the same footing as Navy Ministry representatives.[53]

These energetic middle-echelon officers tended to view Japanese-American relations from the strategic perspective of war planning and preparations. None of the committee's members except Fujii had any firsthand knowledge of the United States. Shiba, Kami, and Takada had returned from Germany. But their preoccupation with war preparations was not necessarily an excessively warlike stance, especially at a time of mounting tension with the United States. They may be said to have been attending to their duties. The First Committee simply formulated and recommended policies; it never became involved with decision making. The problem was that its bellicose recommendations met with little opposition from superiors. Because the navy's ranking officials failed to control subordinates, policy making came, as one of its members admitted, to "revolve around the First Committee."[54] When important policy papers circulated, he recalls, "superiors asked whether they had been cleared by the First Committee and if so, almost automatically approved them." As will be seen later, the committee's crucial document of 5 June 1941, arguing for an advance into southern Indochina and demanding "the determination to go to war" bore the seals of Chief of the Naval Affairs Bureau Oka, Navy Vice Minister Sawamoto Yorio, and Navy Minister Oikawa. The views of these supremely self-confident middle-echelon officers, whether voiced collectively or individually, carried more weight because the Ōsumi purge had decimated the navy's upper-echelon leadership. After the war, Admiral Inoue went as far as to say that ranking leaders were "merely robots who were overruled by their subordinates."

THE KATO-SUETSUGU GROUP
AND THEIR STRATEGIC THOUGHT

The idea of the inevitability of war with the United States that pervaded the thinking of the middle-echelon officers in 1941 can best be understood by turning again to Admiral Katō Kanji and the negation of the Washington treaty system that he personified. At the center of Katō Kanji's doctrine lay the Mahanian dictum that "the rise and fall of sea power determines the destiny of nations." Katō maintained that the "irresistible lure of the Pacific" spelled a showdown between Japan and the United States in which each side would vie with the other for domination in China. Echoing neo-Mahanian economic determinism, Katō asserted that as the foremost "capitalistic-imperialistic nation," the United States would find the outlet for its productive and expansive energies where it would meet the least resistance—the Pacific Ocean. Naval limitation was a humanitarian veil to hide America's desire for domination over East Asia, and the Washington and London Conferences were steps in this direction. The Washington treaty system was an instrument for perpetuating America's naval supremacy and preserving the status quo in East Asia.[55]

These ideas, of course, were not original with or even peculiar to Katō, but the way in which he related them to his Weltanschauung brought out ideological strains that were alien to the Japanese naval tradition. According to his reading of history, the westward advance of American civilization, with poisonous effects on Japan, was the culmination of four centuries of expansion of "materialistic Western civilization" since the battle of Lepanto in 1571, from its Mediterranean origins to the Atlantic, then across the American continent, finally to the Pacific. In this framework his anti-Americanism merged into a revulsion against Westernism, capitalism, and materialism——"isms" he identified externally with the Washington treaty system and domestically with the established political and social order. His doctrine came to be associated with an ultraright "spiritualism" or "Japanism." His speeches during the 1920s and the first half of the 1930s abounded in semimystical exhortations of the "unparalleled *Yamato* spirit," "*bushido*" (the way of the warrior), and "Japan's great mission to purify world thought."

Katō combined his Mahanian navalism with Japan's continental expansionism in China. The navy shielded Japan's continental program, protecting its oceanic flank and preventing intervention by the U.S. Navy. This nicely served the bureaucratic need for increased naval appropriations.

Like Katō, Suetsugu, in a manner reminiscent of Mahan in another context, argued that the United States, the center of Western material civilization, and Japan, the champion of Eastern spiritual civilization, were bound to be pitted against each other. He agreed with Katō in his denunciation of the status quo. "The status quo is a stock phrase of 'have-powers' like Britain and the United States already occupying advantageous positions, and Japan must destroy it. To solve its population problem Japan must expand in China—a policy which has led to economic warfare with the United States."[56] Behind Japanese-American antagonism was China's anti-Japanese attitude, instigated and aided by Americans. Japan's China policy boiled down to relations with the United States. In a June 1934 memorandum to Katō Kanji, Suetsugu wrote that issues of naval limitation and the Manchurian venture were "the two sides of the same coin." "The formidable presence of the Imperial Navy controlling the western Pacific" enabled Japan to defy America and its intimidation while the army was free to conquer Manchuria.[57]

Commander Ishikawa, Katō's disciple, similarly combined his anti-Western, ultranationalist spiritualism with revulsion against the Washington and London system. In a memorandum addressed to Katō in October 1934, he wrote that after World War I the Japanese people were inundated with Western liberal ideas that threatened to undermine the Japanese spirit. Japan seemed on the verge of national ruin as a result of the Washington and London Conferences when the Manchurian Incident broke out, reawakening the Japanese people.[58]

From a strategic viewpoint, the spiritualism that characterized Katō, Suetsugu, and Ishikawa may be regarded as psychological compensation for the inferior fleet ratio of 60 percent "imposed" upon Japan at the Washington Conference. To prevail, Japan would have to pit quality against quantity. In Katō's words, Japan must mobilize its "willpower" against America's physical superiority, "turning an impossibility into a possibility." After the Washington Conference, Katō ordered the Combined Fleet to engage in relentless drills and maneuvers "more heroic than under actual battle conditions." Its target, of course, was the United States. These drills "went beyond all rational bounds," in the words of the naval historian Ikeda Kiyoshi, and resulted, as already noted, in a double-collision accident off Mihogaseki in 1927. In time such spiritualistic obsession bred a mental habit of slighting the material basis of national power, so crucial to total war.

The navy's answer to its dilemma—confronting the U.S. fleet with a 60 percent battleship ratio—was a submarine strategy that offset the deficiencies of the Washington treaty ratio in capital ships. The submarine was "the weapon of the weak party." In the attrition strategy that preceded interceptive operations, the submarine's mission was to whittle down the enemy's fleet on its transpacific passage and join fleet operations in the decisive battle. Developed by Admiral Suetsugu when he was commander of the First and Second Submarine

Divisions in 1923–25, this doctrine "aimed at transforming the submarine from a weapon of passive, short-range defense to one of long range, active offense," as succinctly summarized by Evans and Peattie.[59] Suetsugu perfected this submarine strategy after he became commander in chief of the Combined Fleet in 1933. This attrition strategy was restated in the operational plan of 1936, the oldest existing plan, as follows: "At the opening of hostilities a portion of the submarine force of the Combined Fleet must speedily proceed to Hawaii and the Pacific Coast area of the United States, serve as an outpost of our entire operations and scout the movements of the enemy's main fleet, and seize an opportunity to operate in conjunction with the Combined Fleet."[60] Use of the submarine against the battleship was a unique feature of Japanese strategy. Other powers used the submarine for commerce raiding, but the Japanese navy paid scant attention to it because it banked on battleship encounter and also because of the Mahanian slightening of convoy operation.[61]

After 1924 Japan built large, high-speed fleet submarines with a large cruising radius—cruise submarines. From 1928 it led the world in construction of 1,800-ton submarines with a surface speed of 20 knots (8 knots submerged) and a radius of 10,000 miles (later extended to 20,000 miles). Between 1931 and 1934 the navy acquired eight 2,200-ton fleet submarines with a surface speed of 23 knots. Because the fastest American battleships had a maximum speed of 20 knots, Japan's cruiser submarines were believed capable of scouting and attacking the American fleet. Admiral Suetsugu declared that "The decisive battle would entirely depend on our attrition [submarine] strategy."

Japan's submarine drills were so rigorous that they simulated combat conditions. Overconfident about its own spiritualism, the navy underestimated American submarines. Assuming that the Americans by their national character were unsuited to submarine duty, naval planners saw two weeks as the limit of endurance for American crews. As Admiral Toyoda Soemu wrote after the war, there was a saying in the navy: "Because Americans are spoiled by their luxurious life, they could hardly withstand long-term operations in the cramped and hot quarters of the submarine." In a similar vein Admiral Yamamoto Eisuke wrote, "Americans are accustomed to a comfortable life, so they cannot endure the dangers and severity of drills aboard the submarine. When their submarine is berthed in Tsintao, its officers live in the Grand Hotel with their families and commute to their ships."[62] Hollywood had its influence on such imagery.

It is interesting to contrast Japanese confidence with American submariners' confidence. Commander Holloway H. Frost, a brilliant planner, stated that the submarine was a weapon "peculiarly fit for use by Americans, because

Americans are possessed of all the requisite qualities to handle them—alacrity, decisiveness, initiative, etc."[63] As it turned out, in the Pacific War, the American navy used the submarine to devastating effect, playing havoc with Japan's marine transportation and cutting its sea communications. (Sixty-three percent of Japanese merchantmen were destroyed by American submarines, which was one of the greatest causes of Japan's defeat. In contrast, Japanese submarines were a great disappointment: they could not sink even a single American battleship.)

Despite advances in weaponry and technological breakthroughs, the basic premise of the decisive fleet engagement remained intact during the 1930s. The anticipated theater moved eastward as ranges of ships and planes increased. In 1934 it lay in the vicinity of the Bonins and Marianas; in 1936 it moved west of the Marianas; and in 1940 it advanced to the line of the East Carolines and Marshalls.[63] Embodying the "principle of big battleships and big guns" and deriving perceived lessons from Tsushima and Jutland, Japan's interceptive operations hardened into a dogma that continued to govern strategic thinking until 1941. Building programs, fleet formation, war games and maneuvers, and education were all based on this premise. Flying units were never meant for more than an auxiliary role in the fleet engagement; at most, aircraft would provide cover for battleships.

In the 1930s the strategy of interceptive operations continued to raise questions that had disturbed some Japanese naval planners earlier. Would the U.S. Navy speedily throw its main fleet into a decisive engagement in the western Pacific? Or would it refrain from dashing westward until it had built up overwhelming superiority and logistic support? The questions had been raised in the 1920s, but they had now become more urgent. If the conflict turned into a protracted war, Japan would be at a mounting disadvantage in confronting America's industrial superiority. During the 1930s, America's shipbuilding capacity was estimated to be three to four times, possibly ten times, that of Japan; aircraft productivity six times; and steel productivity ten times. Japan would not be able to defeat such a formidable enemy by victory in one decisive battle or two.

Strangely, such a prospect did not receive attention until hostilities loomed. The General Plan for Strategy, revised in 1936, emphasized the importance of quick encounter, quick showdown, and taking the initiative and the offensive."[64] The annual operational plan (*Nendo sakusen keikaku*) of the same year, the oldest existing plan, provided for three stages of operations: (1) annihilate America's Asiatic Fleet in Far Eastern waters and capture and occupy the Philippines and Guam; (2) thereby compel the American fleet to advance to the western Pacific; and (3) seek a decisive battle on the Bonins-Marianas line, destroying the enemy fleet.[65] The subsequent phase of a protracted war was dismissed with an almost nonchalant statement that "such expedient measures as the occasion demands shall be taken." Although the revised National Defense Policy of 1936 stated that "future wars are likely to be protracted ones and we must be determined and prepared for this," there was no sign that Japanese naval planners seriously considered the realities of total war. The annual operational plan of 1941 remained essentially the same: "First annihilate the enemy fleet [the Asiatic Fleet] in the Far East and control the Far Eastern seas, then in cooperation with the army capture the enemy bases and occupy Guam and other enemy air bases. As to the main fleet of the United States, scout it and attack in the Hawaii area or enemy homeland, and when it stages transpacific passage, gradually reduce it on its passage, intercepting and annihilating it."[66] This operational plan could hardly be called a war plan. Year after year the navy tirelessly repeated this formula of a limited war. It certainly was no recipe for total war.

Katō, Suetsugu, and their heirs based their strategy on *their* perceived lessons of World War I, the importance of "quick encounter, quick showdown." (No decisive Mahanian engagement took place in World War I.) To prevail, Japan must seek a decisive engagement early in the war. However, even if a decisive fleet engagement materialized, within seventy-five days as was widely anticipated, the chance of victory remained moot. Naval planners in the mid-thirties expected that a devastating victory in a decisive fleet engagement would damage U.S. battleships enough to cripple America's will to keep fighting. The Mahanian fixation with the decisive battle caused the mainstream of the Japanese navy to forget Mahan's real teaching, namely that the decisive battle was a means to securing command of the sea and that it alone could ensure victory. Above all, the fixation with the decisive battle blinded the conservative majority of Japanese officers to the extent to which technological innovations, especially in air power, had transformed conventional warfare.

YAMAMOTO—"THE FATHER OF JAPANESE NAVAL AVIATION"

In contrast to the mainstream and their obsession with a main-fleet encounter stood Admiral Yamamoto Isoroku and Rear Admiral Inoue Shigeyoshi, who had readjusted their strategic thinking to the air age. Yamamoto's perceptions of the United States were radically different from those of the Katō-Suetsugu group. His views were informed by a realism derived from firsthand experience in the United States. Yamamoto never served on the Naval General Staff, so he was completely free of the "big battleships, big guns" ideology. In advocating the primacy of naval aviation, he was a heretic. His study and investigation in America went very far to mold his strategic vision.

During 1919–21 he was registered at Harvard, taking an English course for foreign students and auditing courses in American history and politics. In 1923–24 he accompanied Admiral Ide Kenji on his fact-finding tour of the United States, and in 1925–27 he served as naval attaché in Washington. His observations and experiences in the United States became the foundations of his strategic thinking. He devoted his full energy to the oil question, inspecting major oil fields and refineries, perusing all available literature on oil, and scanning some forty newspapers daily.

On the basis of his firsthand experience, Yamamoto warned against dismissing the American people as "weak-willed and spoiled by material luxuries"; on the contrary, they were infused with "a fierce fighting spirit and an adventurous temperament." He cited the exploits of Admiral David G. Farragut of "Damn the torpedoes!" fame, the blockading of Santiago, and the advance through a minefield in Manila Bay during the Spanish-American War. Contrasting the *Yamato* spirit with the Yankee spirit, he pointed out that while the former often degenerated into daredevilry, the latter was grounded on a rational and technological mindset, a case in point being Charles A. Lindbergh's recent transatlantic solo flight. Like Admiral Katō Tomosaburō at the Washington Conference, Yamamoto was deeply impressed with America's industrial might and resources. "Anyone who has seen the auto factories in Detroit and the oil fields in Texas," he used to say, "knows that Japan lacks the national power for a naval race with America." With such a country, a naval race, not to mention total war, was out of the question. As for the Washington treaty, he declared that "the 10:10:6 ratio works just fine for us; it is a treaty to restrict the *other* parties [the United States and Britain]."[67] Although Yamamoto had taken a hawkish position at the London Conference, he supported naval limitation after returning from that gathering.

Yamamoto has been rightly called the father of Japanese naval aviation. He had specialized in gunnery, like so many officers, but after the Washington Conference he saw that the future of naval armaments lay in aviation and in 1924 asked to be appointed executive officer of the new air-training base at Kasumigaura (the Japanese Pensacola), forty miles northeast of Tokyo. Kasumigaura became a base transformed, with a high level of training and a strong sense of mission. Thus began his lifelong identification with naval aviation, although he never learned to fly. In 1928–29 he commanded the carrier *Akagi*, one of the earliest and largest Japanese carriers, later lost at the Battle of Midway. About this time Yamamoto predicted that in the near future air power would become the mainstay of the navy. While in America he had likely fallen under the influence of *Winged Defense* (1924) by Brigadier General William (Billy) Mitchell, a fanatical advocate of air power. Upon his return from the London Conference in 1930, he requested appointment as chief of the Technical Division of the Naval Aviation Department. The navy was trying to offset the deficiencies of the treaty navy by enhancing its air power. Yamamoto trained carrier fliers for offensive operations. In 1933–34 he commanded the First Aircraft Carrier Division. During these years he seized the opportunity to make the fleet air arm an efficient part of the navy and won a huge following among fliers. Promoted to vice admiral in 1935, he became head of the Naval Aviation Department, and in the ensuing three years he laid the foundations to make Japanese naval aviation a first-rate force. He developed a generation of new carrier aircraft and issued an order to double aircraft procurement in two years. He saw to it that Japan's carrier-based aviators were the best trained in the world, averaging 700 hours in the air, compared to 305 for American carrier pilots in December 1941.[68]

Totally rejecting the doctrine of "big battleships and big guns," Yamamoto argued that however big the battleship might be, it was never unsinkable. In the future the striking power of aircraft would make it possible to destroy battleships before they fired a gun. Critical of "hardheaded gunners" (the Gun Club) and Suetsugu's attrition-interceptive strategy, he argued that a frontal engagement of battleships in the manner of a grand naval review was a thing of the past. Yet as late as 1936 he was admonishing naval aviation enthusiasts against calling the battleship a white elephant because the battleship was still regarded as the mainstay of the major powers and as such had "intangible political effects internationally as the symbol of naval power."[69] And he had enough political sense not to aggressively demand naval aviation for fear of creating friction.

INOUE, RADICAL ADVOCATE OF AIR POWER

While Yamamoto was still a transitional figure in this sense, Vice Admiral Inoue, head of the Naval Aviation Department from October 1940 to August 1941, was a zealous advocate of air power. Since the mid-1930s he had taken an interest in air power, and by 1937 he had concluded that Japan had no chance of winning a naval race with the United States. Building battleships would also be a waste of money, because decisive fleet engagement would never take place and aircraft would decide the issue of war. He proclaimed as early as 1937, "The days of the battleship are gone; it has been replaced by the aircraft." In 1940 he asked to be transferred from chief of staff of the China Area Fleet to the head of the Naval Aviation Department. Iconoclastic and outspoken, he envisioned nothing short of conversion of the navy into an air force.[70] In January 1941 he submitted to Navy Minister Oikawa a tightly and brilliantly argued long memorandum. It deviated so sharply from the prevailing view that he was aware he was risking his position, even his life. In this memorandum he pointed out how anachronistic Japan's armaments had been rendered by the "great revolution" in weapons technology. He derided the navy's fixation with fleet ratios—"ratio neurosis" he scathingly called it—and pointed out that the battleship was no match for aircraft. There would never be a "quick encounter, quick showdown" involving a decisive fleet engagement. "Who commands the air commands the sea" was his dictum. American admirals would not be "so foolhardy or reckless" as to mount offensive operations in the western Pacific as long as Japan controlled the air. And mastery of the air required adequately fortified air bases on the mandated islands in Micronesia. These were "unsinkable aircraft carriers." War with the United States would revolve around protracted air and amphibious contests for those islands. Unless Japan's armament plan was drastically changed, the nation was sure to lose the war, followed by American occupation of the entire country, including Tokyo, and a lack of daily necessities brought about by an American naval blockade. The forecast was remarkably prescient about the island-hopping campaign of the Pacific War.[71]

No less prophetic, Inoue urged the importance of convoy escorts to protect ocean transport from American submarine attacks so that resources from the southern region could be shipped to Japan. The Japanese navy did not fully recognize the importance of protecting sea communications, because it never had been threatened by submarines in the Russo-Japanese War, World War I, or the China War.[72]

In conclusion, he urged armament plans based on redefinition of the nature, form, and objectives of a war with the United States. He liked to recall that his drastic proposal fell like "a one-ton bomb on top naval leaders," but in reality it did not make any dent on the conservative mainstream, which was committed to the doctrines of "big battleships and big guns." His proposal came too late to have any effect, and Inoue regretted that he had not submitted his memorandum a few years earlier.[73] Japan's admirals were too-faithful students of Mahan to put faith in any weapon except the battleship. Construction of the superbattleship *Yamato*, to be completed on the eve of the Pacific War, reinforced this mindset.

While they did not always possess the broad outlook of men such as Yamamoto and Inoue, Japanese naval aviators had become convinced that the battleship was superfluous and must give way to aircraft. In April 1936, when Lieutenant Commander Genda Minoru, "a Japanese Billy Mitchell," was a student officer in the Naval Staff College, he was assigned a paper on armaments against the United States. He wrote, "The main strength of a decisive battle should be air arms, while battleships will be put out of commission and tied up." His proposal was sheer heresy and his "mental sanity questioned." But Genda was not alone in claiming the primacy of air power.[74] Some in aviation circles had adopted the concept of an air offensive against the United States. As early as 1936 the Naval Staff College produced a "Study of Strategy and Tactics in Operations against the United States." It contained this striking passage: "In the event that the enemy's main fleet units, particularly his aircraft carriers, are at anchor at Pearl Harbor prior to hostilities, sudden and unexpected attacks should be launched on those forces by carrier aircraft and flying boats."[75] In July 1937 the Naval Aviation Department declared that "a navy without strong air power is impotent." It asserted, "The creation of powerful land-based air power is the absolute precondition and the ratio of fleet strength would hardly come into the picture." The study suggested *reduction* of the fleet, on the grounds that a large part of its tasks could be performed by air power with greater effect and less cost.[76] But the aviation-oriented strategy failed to make headway because there were still too few flying officers of seniority occupying key positions.

Considering that in both the United States and Britain the battleship was regarded as the monarch of the sea and the index of naval power, and that in both countries the naval air arm during the 1930s remained an auxiliary service, the aviation-centered Yamamoto-Inoue group must be credited with unusual foresight. But it was a minority, its ideas too advanced to find acceptance by the Naval General Staff and the fleet commanders, which remained committed to the Mahanian decisive battle, a concept validated by Tsushima and seemingly confirmed by Jutland. In April 1941, Yamamoto asked the Naval General Staff to reconsider building a third superbattleship of the *Yamato* class (two were already being built under the Third Replenishment Program of 1937), but the head of the Operations Division would not listen. The outspoken Inoue became an embarrassment to the devotees of mammoth battleships, and Oikawa and Nagano sent him to Truck as commander in chief of the Fourth Fleet, whose mission was to defend the mandated islands, a definite demotion. Having built careers on battleships and gunnery, the mainstream—the Gun Club—remained committed to those weapons. The furthest the Japanese navy would go was a main-fleet encounter, with coverage by fighter planes.

CHAPTER EIGHT

ABROGATION OF THE WASHINGTON TREATY AND AFTER

The Manchurian Crisis and the Japanese Navy

The central concern of the Japanese navy during the first half of the 1930s was how to remove the "fetters" of the "humiliating treaties" of Washington and London. The memory of naval conferences had so conditioned Japanese navy men that disarmament and naval limitation conjured up a sense of American oppression. The widely accepted view held that at the Washington Conference, the United States had imposed an inferior ratio and obstructed Japan's expansion on the Asian continent and that at the London Conference, the United States and Britain had "ganged up" on Japan to repress its rightful demands.[1]

Japanese admirals were nervously listening to what their American counterparts were publicly saying: that if the naval ratio with Japan was 60 percent, the U.S. Fleet could advance to Japan's home waters and bring the nation to its knees. Admiral Mark Bristol (member of the General Board and former commander of the Asiatic Fleet) was generally of this opinion. Admiral Montgomery M. Taylor (head of the War Plans Division) stated that a 10:6 ratio would give America a "sporting chance." The most extreme claim was, as usual, made by the hawkish Admiral Hilary P. Jones (Ret.), who asserted that in the event of war, the United States would have to advance to Japan's home waters, and the 10:6 ratio together with Pacific nonfortification actually gave Japan a ratio of more than 10:10.[2] American admirals seemed to take it for granted that they would resort to force against Japan to defend the Open Door in China. (The policy of the U.S. government was not to fight with Japan over China.)

By the spring of 1934 the Japanese navy had concluded that its strategic situation had become unbearable. Advances in weaponry, especially aviation, and reinforcement of bases in Hawaii and Singapore had made it more difficult for Japan to conduct its attrition-interceptive operations. The strategic distances of the Pacific Ocean had been reduced by increases in cruising radius (which had doubled since 1922), speed, and firepower of ships and by advances in naval aviation. This, Japanese admirals were concerned, facilitated America's transpacific operations.[3] The strategic situation thus had altogether changed from the days of the Washington Conference. The Washington-London treaty system seemed less tenable than ever.

Tracing the Japanese navy's decision to abrogate the Washington treaty must begin in 1930. Efforts to offset the deficiencies of Japan's treaty navy had begun early, even before the Privy Council ratified the London treaty on 1 October 1930. As a quid pro quo for accepting the treaty's compromise formula, naval officials had won the government's consent to practical measures designed to minimize the "shortcomings" in naval defense. Naval aviation received special emphasis.[4] On 23 July 1930 the Supreme Military Council presented its official reply to the throne, in which it stated that upon expiration of the London treaty at the end of 1936, "the Empire must complete its naval defense by whatever means it deems best."[5] No one objected, which meant that the treaty would not be renewed in its existing form.

In early October 1930, soon after ratification of the London treaty, Navy Minister Abo Kiyokazu began to press for approval of the navy's supplemental budget plan. Behind Abo were Fleet Admiral Tōgō, Katō Kanji, and Suetsugu, who threatened to overthrow the government if their demand was not met. After wrangling with the Finance Ministry, Prince Fushimi pressured Finance Minister Inoue Junnosuke, who conceded budgetary support for the "first supplemental building program" to span the years 1931–36.[6] Under this program Japan proceeded to enhance its navy. The United States did not start building to treaty limits until the end of 1933, and by this time Japan was building close to the 70 percent ratio.[7] However, the Manchurian Incident of 1931 had so aggravated relations with the United States that the navy rapidly concluded that Japan's security required removal of all restrictions and attainment of parity with the United States.

Deterioration of Japanese-American relations following the Manchurian Incident constituted the background of the navy's hardening attitude. To restrain Japan, Secretary of State Stimson persuaded President Hoover in May 1932 to allow the Scouting Force, traditionally a part of the Atlantic Fleet, to remain on the Pacific Coast with the rest of the fleet after the 1933 annual maneuvers.[8] It was meant to be a "forceful bluff," but the Japanese navy took it very seriously.

The outbreak of fighting in Shanghai provoked by the Japanese navy in January 1932 further aggravated relations. Many naval leaders feared that war with the United States was imminent. (The American navy also feared war with Japan.

Secretary of the Navy Charles Francis Adams told Admiral Zachary Taylor, "It wouldn't have taken much hard luck or much hasty judgment to have developed a war between Japan and ourselves.")[9] The Japanese navy, left out of the Manchurian Incident, regarded the Shanghai Incident as a godsend, an opportunity to demonstrate its raison d'être and enhance its armaments in competition with the army. The navy hastily organized the Third Fleet and sent it to the vicinity of Shanghai. On 28 February 1932, Katō Kanji wrote in his diary, "I am most worried about increasing deterioration of our external relations, especially with the United States. Pessimistic telegrams have arrived from Captain Shimomura Shōsuke [the naval attaché in Washington]. . . . We are in the last five minutes [before war with the United States?]."[10] Katō was referring to a series of alarmist reports Shimomura had been sending that pointed to the danger of a Japanese-American clash.[11] His report noted "considerable war preparations on the part of the United States." In May Shimomura cabled that the American purpose in leaving its Scouting Force in the Pacific was to restrain Japan by taking an offensive posture in the Pacific. Joined by the Scout Force, the fifteen battleships of the Battle Force already in the Pacific impressed the Japanese naval men as a demonstration against Japan's China policy.

Commander Ishikawa Shingo—the foremost disciple of Katō Kanji, the leading member of the fleet faction, and a Naval General Staff officer in charge of armaments—clamored for a buildup of armaments against the United States. There was no foreseeing, he said, what would happen to Japanese-American relations. He described the navy's predicament in a memorandum as follows: "Depending on the development of our continental policy, there is no telling what will befall our relations with the Anglo-American powers, especially the United States. As far as the navy is concerned, there are grave defects in our fleet's preparedness. . . . If the Anglo-American powers should powerfully intervene and if we have to undergo the humiliation of another Triple Intervention [of 1895], the entire responsibility will fall on the navy."[12]

Taniguchi Naomi, an able admiral of moderate persuasion who had succeeded Katō Kanji as chief of the Naval General Staff, was victimized for having opposed the Manchurian Incident and for having warned that it might trigger a war with the United States, a war that Japan could not win. To prepare for such a war, he warned, Japan would have to put three and a half billion yen into naval armaments, clearly beyond Japan's capability. When Fleet Admiral Tōgō heard about Taniguchi's remarks, he mercilessly rebuked him: "Doesn't the Naval General Staff submit to the emperor its annual operational plans? If we cannot fight the United States, then we have been telling lies to His Majesty.

I myself report to His Majesty every year that annual plans are adequate [for national defense]. If we say we cannot fight, that means I too have been lying to the emperor."[13]

Luckless Taniguchi was forced to resign. (This episode haunted Oikawa Koshirō for years, and in 1940 when he was navy minister he refused to say, as Taniguchi did, that the navy could not fight the United States. A clear statement to this effect would have made a difference between peace and war.)

While the navy on the whole was negative or at best neutral about the Manchurian Incident, the fleet faction led by Katō and Suetsugu positively identified itself with the army's Manchurian venture. They linked the naval issue with the China question, arguing that in order to conquer Manchuria, Japan must possess a sufficiently powerful navy; conversely, naval limitation hindered Japan's China policy.[14]

THE NAVY'S SEARCH FOR PARITY

A deepening sense of isolation in the aftermath of Japan's withdrawal from the League of Nations in March 1933, the crisis in relations with the United States, fear of American (or Anglo-American) intervention in the Far East, and uneasiness about the incipient U.S. naval buildup under President Franklin D. Roosevelt—all these factors combined to convince Japanese navy men that the Washington and London treaties had become outmoded and disadvantageous. From his first days in office, Roosevelt had backed a naval buildup as contributing to national recovery and making the United States the naval equal of Japan. Recent developments in air power were a new factor that made Japan's defense more vulnerable.[15] The navy believed that technological advances facilitated the American fleet's transpacific passage and conversely made Japan's attrition-interceptive strategy more difficult to implement.

Japan had traditionally contended that it needed a 70 percent ratio to have a fifty-fifty or slightly better chance in a main-fleet engagement in the western Pacific, but this ratio no longer seemed adequate, given the drastic reduction in the strategic distances of the Pacific. Japan's naval planners rapidly concluded that the nation must abrogate the "unequal" treaties and demand parity at the forthcoming preliminary London talks, scheduled to open in October 1934 to lay the groundwork for the naval conference in 1935.[16]

Taking stock of Japanese sensitivities, Ambassador Joseph C. Grew wrote in his diary on 23 January 1934, "Whatever may happen with regard to the

Naval Conference in 1935 . . . it will inevitably subject Japan's relations with the United States, and perhaps Great Britain in less degree, to a more or less serious strain, with loud and angry vituperations against us for keeping Japan an 'inferior nation.'"[17]

An early and vociferous advocate of parity in the middle echelon was Commander Ishikawa Shingo. Like Katō Kanji, he fervently believed in the equality of the right of defense among sovereign nations. Characteristically, his claim bordered on irrationalism. He held that the parity question had "already ceased to be a matter of mathematical theory, so it is impossible even to explain it or have it understood."[18] On 21 October he submitted to Katō a long memorandum in which he argued that the United States would not refrain from using arms to enforce the Open Door policy. He declared that the success of the Manchurian venture would depend on naval parity. In fact, Japan must be "prepared for war if it could not attain the parity at the forthcoming naval conference." To Ishikawa, the parity demand and the Manchurian venture were two sides of the same coin. He wrote, "The next naval conference is not only a meeting to discuss naval strength but will be an open forum for the United States, Britain, and China to censure Japan's program in China. In short, the next naval conference is a crucial gathering to decide whether our Manchurian policy is going to be a success or failure, and the conference will mark the initial stage of international struggle in the Pacific."[19]

In a similar vein Admiral Suetsugu argued that the Manchurian question was inseparable from the problem of naval defense. Was it not, he demanded, the presence of the Imperial Navy that enabled Japan to defy the League of Nations and ward off American intimidation?[20] As Ishikawa asserted, "It is obvious that our Empire must choose between the two options: one is to give up without a fight at the next naval conference, thus abandoning our national policy and accepting the fate of self-ruin; the other option is to find a way out of a great difficulty by risking war. Therefore, as long as the United States does not scuttle its traditional Far Eastern policy, naval limitation is deemed impossible."[21] Like Katō and Suetsugu, Ishikawa assumed that the United States would fight a war to support the Open Door in China, and that this was why the American navy demanded preservation of the 10:6 ratio. At the coming conference, the United States would reject any Japanese proposal, parity or not, that would jeopardize America's chance of victory. In insisting on parity, Ishikawa argued, Japan was only demanding "the right of a sovereign nation to equality in armament." This was identical to the view Katō had held since the Washington Conference.[22]

Meanwhile the navy representative Rear Admiral Yoshida Zengo, chief of the Naval Affairs Bureau, had been negotiating with his Foreign Ministry counterpart, Tōgō Shigenori, chief of the Europe-America Bureau. Tōgō, a strong advocate of Japanese-American détente and a supporter of naval limitation, strenuously opposed the navy's parity demand, saying it would lead to a naval race and end in a Japanese-American war. Yoshida countered that if the two nations were to fight, treaties that limited Japan's naval buildup would be disadvantageous.[23] Failing to reach agreement at the bureau chief level, the negotiations were moved to the vice minister level, then ministerial, and finally to the cabinet meeting.

At the Five Ministers Conference (an inner cabinet consisting of the prime minister, foreign minister, service ministers, and finance minister) held on 16 October 1933, Navy Minister Ōsumi declared, parroting Katō, that parity was an absolute demand, based on "the right of national survival and equal right of armaments." To complete sufficient armaments to "resolutely repel" American intervention in the Far East, Japan must abrogate the Washington treaty. He concluded that "it could not be helped" if Japan's demand was rejected and no new treaty concluded. He succeeded in having his statement confirmed in a Navy–Foreign Ministry memorandum.[24]

ABROGATION OF THE WASHINGTON TREATY

At the meeting of Supreme Military Councilors and fleet commanders on 8 June 1934, Ōsumi stated again that parity was "absolutely required for the protection of the nation's right to survive," adding that if "the right of equality of armament" was denied, the London talks would break up.[25] Katō next spoke up, denouncing the inferior ratio, particularly its pernicious effect on the navy's morale. He declared, "The success or failure of the parity demand would have grave effects on the control of naval subordinates and the morale of officers and men, and it will determine the fate of Japan's policy toward China and Manchuria. Therefore, parity is an absolute demand. The navy as a whole has burned its bridges behind this demand." He argued that the root of all evil was the Washington treaty, which—by assigning the 60 percent ratio—deprived Japan of the right to decide on necessary naval armament. "If only the 'cancer' of the Washington treaty could be excised, the morale and self-confidence of our navy would be so bolstered that we could count on certain victory over any hypothetical enemy, no matter how overwhelming the physical odds against us."[26] This sweeping assertion, disregarding Japan's limits of national power, typified the irrational, all-or-nothing psychology that was spreading in naval circles.

The Ōsumi purge had ousted most leaders of the treaty faction who possessed a broad international outlook. No counterforce remained to restrain the intransigents of the Katō-Suetsugu group. Headed by Suetsugu, Combined Fleet commander, naval spokesmen became so shrill in inflammatory talk of "the coming crisis of 1935–36" (when the Washington and London treaties could be terminated) that Foreign Vice Minister Shigemitsu Mamoru feared in all seriousness that the navy wanted to "fight the United States around 1936."[27]

The initiative in restraining the navy came from the army ministry leaders, sensitive that budget appropriations for war against the Soviet Union might be diverted to a naval race with the United States. The navy's intransigence worried the army, which opposed further aggravation of relations with the United States because that would give precedence to naval armaments. For example, Captain Suzuki Teiichi of the Army Staff College told Harada Kumao, Prince Saionji's secretary, that he wanted a member of the treaty faction chosen as the delegate to the coming London talks, but few members of the treaty faction remained. Army Minister Araki Sadao even worried that "a race with the United States would become unmanageable, and I think it would eventually lead to war with the United States."[28] In army-navy meetings beginning in the spring of 1934, army representatives tried to iron out differences, but could not shake the navy's determination to withdraw from the treaties. By early summer the navy ministry was openly demanding nothing less than parity—"equality with the United States, a ratio of 10:10"—although it admitted that there was not the slightest chance that this demand would be accepted at the preliminary London talks.[29]

On 20 July, Army Minister Hayashi Senjūrō urged Ōsumi to reconsider the policy that, he said, was bound to break up the negotiations. The navy minister refused. In reply to the objection that the announcement of abrogation of the Washington treaty would provoke an Anglo-American front at the London talks, Ōsumi retorted: Would not the United States team up with Britain in any event? Had it not been its practice to browbeat Japan with the specter of a naval arms race? Ōsumi, once enraged at the "high-handedness" of the Washington Conference, harbored deep distrust of the United States and was prepared to force a showdown. By this time, he declared, the navy had reached "a determined consensus that the breakdown of [the coming London talks] could not be helped."[30]

A few officers, such as Captain Iwashita Yasutarō, chief of the Operations Section, and Commander Nakazawa Tasuku of the same section, felt that a treaty should be concluded if necessary with an 80 percent ratio, the strength Japan supposedly possessed, but this position was taboo in the navy. Katō and

Suetsugu, who got wind of this, absolutely opposed any inferior ratio, saying it would end in a repetition of the London Conference fiasco.[31]

On 8 July 1934, Okada Keisuke, former Navy Minister, received an imperial mandate to form a new cabinet. He was chosen because, as the naval elder who had worked so hard for the London treaty, he was deemed best qualified to restrain the Katō-Suetsugu group, control the navy, and obtain a new treaty. Faithful to Katō Tomosaburō's philosophy of naval limitation, Okada contended, "Japan is a poor country and is hardly in a position to compete with the United States in a naval race. . . . The problems of national defense are best solved by means of diplomacy. So, we must conclude a new naval treaty and I am determined to do so by every means. The emperor desires Japan to follow a righteous path and insofar as possible avoid a naval race and conflict with other powers."[32]

Navy Minister Ōsumi was utterly opposed. He protested that he had agreed to remain in the Okada ministry on the condition that the new cabinet approve "the naval view" he had presented to the previous cabinet demanding abrogation of the Washington treaty. On 13 July 1934, shortly after Okada assumed office, Ōsumi threatened to resign unless the navy's demands were accepted. The navy's demands for parity, Ōsumi darkly intimated, had been presented to the emperor by Prince Fushimi, chief of the Naval General Staff, and had won His Majesty's approval. Ōsumi was abusing Prince Fushimi's position as a member of the imperial family—this time to intimidate the prime minister.[33] Indeed, on 12 July Prince Fushimi met with the emperor and submitted a sealed letter containing the "determination" of the navy, drafted by his vice chief: "There is no other choice but to discard the existing ratio system and vigorously pursue a policy of equality; otherwise, the navy *will not be able to control its officers.*" But the emperor had rejected the document, commenting with unusual severity that he would not tolerate any such behavior on the part of the chief of the Naval General Staff, who constitutionally was not in a position of responsibility. Hirohito harshly scolded Prince Fushimi, twenty-six years his senior. He held that not even a member of the imperial family should appeal to him privately concerning naval limitation, which fell under jurisdiction of the government.[34] In fact, the emperor was so angered that he said he did not want see Prince Fushimi anymore.

At the Five Ministers Conferences of 14 and 24 July, held to discuss Ōsumi's demand, Prime Minister Okada said it was important to proceed with the London talks without having arrived at a decision on parity. Okada wanted to reach an agreement at the coming talks; at the least, he suggested, Japan might agree to achieve parity over a period of time, say, eight years. He maintained that a notice to abrogate the Washington treaty must be delayed at least until the London talks. Okada had the support of the army, foreign, and finance ministers; uppermost in their minds were the financial consequences of a naval race when Japan was suffering from the Great Depression. Although Japan might be able to hold out for a few years, they knew, it would sooner or later face bankruptcy. They also argued against presenting demands at the London talks that had no prospect of being accepted, which would result only in causing the Anglo-American powers to bring about "grave consequences" on Japan's China policy. These arguments failed to move Ōsumi, who repeated that "naval subordinates could hardly be persuaded."[35] This was a confession of helplessness on the part of the navy minister, who had lost control of his subordinates. (This happened again and again during the critical period 1940–41.) Okada considered replacing Ōsumi with a moderate admiral, Kobayashi Seizō, who had experience in naval limitation, especially at the Geneva Naval Conference, but Okada found it "too dangerous" in light of the Katō-Suetsugu group's heightened activities.[36]

KATŌ-SUETSUGU MANEUVERS

Ōsumi threatened that "officers in the fleets can hardly be pacified by anything less than parity." This was an allusion to Katō Kanji's backstage activities. He had summoned Captains Nagumo Chūichi and Machida Shin'ichirō of the Combined Fleet, telling them that the Washington treaty must be abrogated at once and that they should sign a manifest demanding an end to the treaty. This memorandum was submitted by Chief of the Naval General Staff Suetsugu to Prince Fushimi and Ōsumi. Fushimi wondered about the origin of the message and had the matter investigated. It soon turned out that Katō Kanji had instigated the whole matter. Katō overdid himself: he gratuitously proposed to the assembled commanders that he was best qualified, as the next prime minister, to carry out the parity demand. Katō's blatantly political and self-serving activities offended Prince Fushimi, whose confidence in him began to wane. The emperor, who heard about Katō's political maneuver, came to greatly distrust him. Hirohito, with his Anglo-American orientation and desire for international cooperation, particularly came down on Katō's hard-line ultranationalism.[37]

Suetsugu, Combined Fleet commander, had been making a public clamor. On 25 August he spoke at the Great Asian League (*Dai Ajia kyōkai*). He demanded parity and immediate abrogation of the Washington treaty, threatening that if this demand was not met, he would resign. If its demand was not accepted, Japan would not shrink from breaking up the conference. On 15 October 1934 he addressed a large audience in the Osaka Central Civic Auditorium on "the present state of emergency and the national defense problem," appealing for "abolition" of the discriminatory ratio system and the establishment of the right of parity. He caused a commotion by stating that with the present ratio he could not take responsibility for national defense. In other words, Suetsugu would threaten resignation, and the total collapse of naval discipline would follow.[38] On 24 October the emperor told Prince Fushimi to restrain Suetsugu from making sensational agitations.[39]

Meanwhile, Katō inflamed hawks in the fleets and then threatened the government that unless it obtained parity, the navy would "no longer be able to control its officers."[40] And Suetsugu threatened the government that any compromise in the parity demand "would inevitably rekindle commotions over the London treaty, enrage both the navy and the public opinion, and give rise to some untoward incident far surpassing the 15 May incident."[41] As commander in chief of the Combined Fleet, Suetsugu was in direct control over younger officers and was in a position to incite them to such an incident.

Prince Saionji had considered asking the emperor to warn Prince Fushimi or issue an order to restrain the navy from making an "unreasonable" demand. Vulnerable to such pressures, Ōsumi became frantic. Any attempt to "suppress the prevailing wish of the navy," he told Harada, Saionji's secretary, would end up in "utter disaster." Recalling the crisis after the London Conference of 1930, court circles opposed any such intervention by the emperor.[42] Such apprehensions notwithstanding, the emperor subtly made his wish known to the departing delegates. Hirohito wanted Rear Admiral Yamamoto Isoroku and Ambassador Matsudaira, the delegates to the naval talks in London, to exert themselves for the success of the conference. The emperor actually felt that an 80 percent ratio would suffice and that parity should be achieved over several years. On 8 September, Hirohito asked Prince Fushimi the reasons for demanding parity but could not obtain a satisfactory answer. Three days later the emperor asked Ōsumi about the danger of starting a naval race. When Ōsumi replied that there would be no such danger, the emperor considered this assurance so important that he made his aide-de-camp record Ōsumi's reply as the "evidence" for future reference.[43]

Okada persisted in his efforts to contain the navy, but finally on 7 September 1934 he admitted defeat, and the cabinet decided to issue before the end of the year the two-year notice required for abrogation of the Washington treaty. Because the navy remained intransigent, there was no other way to avoid a domestic crisis.

A navy ministry memorandum, written about this time, stated, "If by any chance the coming naval conference should recognize the traditional discriminatory ratios, our Empire will forever be ordered around by the Anglo-American powers, and it is obvious that our Empire will go to ruin. This is the reason why the coming conference has far greater consequences to our Empire than the Washington and London naval conferences."[44]

Public opinion in 1934 was different from that at the time of the London Conference. Japan's position had deteriorated after it withdrew from the League of Nations in 1933. Japanese admirals claimed that the United States and Britain were reinforcing their bases at Hawaii and Singapore, which they said threatened Japan (although, in reality, there was no matériel strengthening of the Hawaiian base). At home, party government had been replaced by what the American journalist Hugh Byas called "government by assassination."

Within the navy, the Ōsumi purge had made such a sweep of the treaty faction that few voices of caution remained. Makino Nobuaki, Lord Keeper of the Privy Seal, noted the baleful effect of interference in national policy by navy officers, deploring that the upper echelons could not control them.[45] The emperor worried that the navy was "jeopardizing vital diplomatic issues *for the sake of placating subordinate officers.*" On 8 July Hirohito had asked Ōsumi, "Are you in control of your naval subordinates? I hear there are some moves of *gekokujō* [pressuring from below]." The emperor's wish to restrain the navy was futile. He told Okada that at the least he wanted the Washington treaty abrogated in such a way that it would not provoke the Anglo-American powers; "Japan must not be the villain in the piece."[46]

Above all, the nightmarish memory of the 15 May 1932 assassination immobilized government leaders. They were haunted by fear that another fight over naval limitation would rekindle violence that would surpass early assassination incidents. Jingoists and right-wing malcontents might incite young naval officers to destroy the political and social order. Suetsugu had been warning that such would be the consequences of retreat from parity.[47] His and Katō's connections with ultra-right-wing forces lent color to such a threat. The finance ministry, hypersensitive to the economic consequences of a naval race, nevertheless felt compelled to remind ruling circles of the importance of handling the navy with kid gloves; it was important to assure the navy that the government would rather break up the London talks than go against the navy's wishes.[48] Even moderate admirals of the treaty faction, such as Kobayashi Seizō and Nomura Kichisaburō, admitted that emotions in the navy had been allowed to go too far for the government to control, much less reverse.[49] Okada consulted with the two admirals about what to do when Ōsumi staked his position to carry through the parity demand. He even considered replacing Ōsumi with Kobayashi as navy minister as the only way to control the navy.[49] Yet Okada refrained from such a radical solution. For the navy as a whole, it was all-important to give notice of abrogation by the end of 1934 so that Japan could attend the Second London Conference in 1935 "with a clean slate."

The navy had browbeaten the government into turning against cooperation with the Anglo-American powers within the framework of the Washington treaty system. In a private letter of 25 December 1934, Katō Kanji wrote, "We have finally been freed from the fetters [of the Washington treaty] after thirteen years; I don't know how to express my deep emotions."[50] Four days later, when Ambassador Saitō Hiroshi handed the notice of abrogation of the Washington treaty to Secretary of State Cordell Hull, Katō, dressed in his full navy uniform, made a joyful trip to the grave of Fleet Admiral Tōgō in the Tama cemetery to report the good news. He visited Vice Admiral Ogasawara and, finding him absent, left a card on which he scribbled, "At long last the notice of the abrogation has been delivered and it signals the dawn of the regeneration of the Imperial Navy."[51]

How could the navy expect to attain its goal of security by withdrawing from the Washington-London system? How could parity serve Japan's security? The emperor asked Prince Fushimi about the self-defeating nature of the demand: Would it not result only in wrecking the naval conference and starting a new arms race? In that case, would Japan not be outbuilt by the United States? Prince Fushimi and Ōsumi repeated the navy's stock answer: there was nothing to fear from an arms race because it would entail no substantial increase in naval expenditure. The emperor was not satisfied with Prince Fushimi's reply. The Naval General Staff contended that unfettered naval construction would actually be *more economical*, because Japan would be able to concentrate on ship categories "best suited to its peculiar requirements." The emperor remained unconvinced.[52] The key to this question was the superbattleship of the *Yamato* class, which will be discussed presently.

THE LONDON NAVAL TALKS OF 1934

The choice of delegates to the preliminary London talks to set the stage for the Second London Conference posed a problem. Bitterly recalling the fiasco of the civilian-dominated London Conference of 1930, the government was intent on appointing a naval officer as the principal delegate, but senior officers who had experience with naval conferences—such as Yamanashi, Hori, and Saionji—had already been eliminated by the Ōsumi purge. The choice for principal naval delegate was Rear Admiral Yamamoto. He had been a hawk at the 1930 London Conference, but since then had moved closer to the treaty faction, presumably under the influence of his best friend, Hori Teikichi. Through Hori, Yamamoto maintained a connection with whatever remained of the treaty faction. Seeing through the unrealistic nature of the parity demand, he hesitated before accepting the mission. Katō Kanji was critical of Yamamoto's appointment: "He [Yamamoto] was not trusted to achieve a great thing."[53]

The government's instructions to Yamamoto stiffly stated, "The Imperial Government can hardly condone conclusion of an agreement upholding limitations that are to our disadvantage . . . or to the detriment of our Empire's national defense." Yamamoto was to demand "a common upper limit" that must be set as low as possible.[54] Renewal of the naval treaties in any form was out of the question. His hands thus tied, Yamamoto was critical about his instructions. Before his departure for London, he told Captain Inoue Shigeyoshi, "I have yet to receive satisfactory explanations from my superiors [about the parity demand], so it will be all the more difficult to persuade the American and British delegates."[55] Inoue agreed with him that "limitation of capital ships to 10:6 by the Washington treaty was actually [to the] great advantage of Japan."[56]

Two matters needed to be cleared before the coming London talks. First, the Japanese delegates were to do their best to separate the naval issue from political questions in the Far East and prevent the latter from being discussed. This point was particularly emphasized by Captain Ishikawa, among others. There would be no repetition of the Washington Conference. The discussion of the China question would merely mean the reenactment of Japan's bitter experience at Geneva (the League of Nations) regarding the Manchurian Incident. No challenge to Japan's position in the Far East must be allowed.[57] As it turned out, at the London naval talks Japan's demand to exclude political questions was accepted without much hesitation by the American and British delegates.

Second, the Japanese navy decided to withdraw from Article XIX of the Five-Power Treaty relating to Pacific nonfortification. This was an important problem, far more so than was realized at the time. Recall that at the Washington Conference, Japan had accepted the 10:6 ratio in return for the status quo regarding fortifications in the Philippines and Guam. The provision was manifestly to Japan's advantage, but the navy now considered that this advantage had all but disappeared because of what it perceived as reinforcement of the Hawaiian base, as well as technological advances in ships and aviation. The increase in cruising radius, which had doubled since the Washington Conference, greatly facilitated a direct American attack on Japan, rendering fortifications in the Philippines "irrelevant."[57] Japan also needed to free itself from the limitations placed on fortifications in the Bonins, Taiwan, and the Kuriles, because they were essential for defense of the homeland.

More realistically, the army emphasized the strategic advantages of restrictions on the Philippines and Guam. The navy's traditional attrition strategy, the army reminded the navy representatives, was to intercept the enemy fleet far from Japan's homeland, and advances in air power would reduce the need for fortifications on Japan's nearby islands. The army warned that if Japan was surrounded by reinforced bases in the Philippines, Guam, and the Aleutian Islands, the United States would be able to command the sea in the western Pacific.[59]

Disregarding these cogent arguments, the navy concluded that the gains from parity would offset the loss of the nonfortification agreement. The American navy, of course, did not object, in fact welcomed Japan's abandonment of nonfortification because it felt that this agreement had merely abetted Japanese aggression in the western Pacific and East Asia. That the Japanese navy gravely miscalculated would become clear in late 1940 and early 1941 when the United States rapidly built up air power in the Philippines, posing a threat to Japan.

The Japanese government had been fully warned about the "firm attitude of the United States regarding naval limitation." Consul-General Horinouchi Kensuke cabled from New York that if the London talks broke down, the United States would not desist from a naval race backed by its "vast resources and financial power." Under the National Industrial Recovery Act of June 1933, President Roosevelt had resumed building ships and would step up construction if the forthcoming talks failed.[60]

The preliminary London talks opened on 24 October 1934, at the Court of St. James's. This was the first time Yamamoto appeared prominently in the American public eye. His biographical sketch in the Office of Naval Intelligence described him as "exceptionally able, forceful, and a man of quick thinking."

In accordance with his instructions, Yamamoto stated that the increased cruising radius of ships, more than doubled since the Washington Conference, and enhanced speed, gun power, and scouting capability, gave strategic advantage to the attacking fleet over the defending one. (The American fleet no longer needed to be refueled in the mid-Pacific, which made Japan's attrition strategy more difficult.)[61] These new factors, Yamamoto argued, necessitated parity for Japan in all warship types, including battleships and aircraft carriers.

He soon realized that the demand for parity was futile. President Roosevelt knew a great deal about the Japanese navy from his experience in World War I as assistant secretary of the navy, which inclined him to distrust Japan's intentions in East Asia. He saw little reason to appease Japan and was eager to keep the Washington and London treaties in effect.[62] Congress had passed the Vinson-Trammel Act in March, authorizing the president to build to treaty limits, and this gave Roosevelt confidence. He felt that accepting Japan's demands would be tantamount to condoning its violation of the Open Door and the Nine-Power Treaty.[63] He told British Ambassador Ronald Lindsey that if Japan insisted on parity and denounced the treaties, he would ask Congress for $500 million for naval purposes, adding that he would have no difficulties in getting it. He said that the Japanese "were pushing a very long distance program of imperial expansion in Asia."[64]

The General Board of the U.S. Navy held that Japan was seeking "an indisputable naval supremacy in the western Pacific and absolute dictatorship in Far Eastern affairs." In a 1934 report the board warned that Japan was seeking territorial expansion and commercial and political domination of the Far East. The U.S. Navy was determined to uphold the treaty system in East Asia. Admiral William H. Standley, Chief of Naval Operations and an American delegate, explained, "If we desire to give adequate support to the policies which we have been following in the past, such as the Open Door, the Nine-Power Treaty, the Kellogg-Briand Pact, etc., then we must possess adequate naval force." In order to deter further aggression by Japan, the United States would need to maintain naval strength.[65] In response to Hull, Standley stated that the treaty ratios "must be maintained at all costs. . . . Without [them], we could exercise no strength in the Far East."[66]

While the American civilian delegates did not agree that the Open Door required naval support, they insisted on upholding the Washington-London treaty system. They believed, too facilely, that if the United States reaffirmed its commitment to this system and pressed for renewal of the treaties, Japan would have little choice but to accept it. The General Board understood that if talks failed because of Japan's intransigence, the United States with its superior resources could easily stand a race with Japan. The chairman of the American delegation, Norman H. Davis, frankly warned Yamamoto that if Japan tried to disturb the existing relative strength, "the USA and Great Britain will outbuild her whatever she does."[67]

Faced with this firm Anglo-American front, Yamamoto asked his superiors in Tokyo to reconsider their inflexible position on parity, but was roundly scolded. Although his hands were tied, he did his best to reach a modicum of understanding with the Anglo-American powers.[68] He argued that even if the Japanese navy was equal in size to the American navy, it could not possibly launch an offensive against the U.S. mainland.

While Yamamoto focused on Japan's perceived security needs, the American delegate insisted on preserving the Washington treaty system. Davis charged that Japan's demand was "destroying the collective system we had set up for promoting peace and cooperation in the Far East" in accord with the principles established by the Washington treaties. The issue was "much greater than a mere technical question and they were most eager not to destroy any part of the world's peace machinery." Secretary Hull agreed that to yield to Japan not only would jeopardize security in the Pacific but meant "demolishing the entire system of interlocking agreements negotiated at the Washington Conference," especially the Nine-Power Treaty relating to China.[69] To Hull, of course, these treaties were sacred. Such last-minute reaffirmations of the Washington system could not shake the conviction of Japan's navy men that the system posed a threat to Japan's security. There was no way to break the deadlock.

American delegates were personally sympathetic toward Yamamoto's plight. Norman Davis had concluded that "one of our difficulties here was the limited authority enjoyed by Admiral Yamamoto." Admiral Standley told the British delegation that "he thought Admiral Yamamoto had seen things in a rather different light [from his government]." He had several conversations with Yamamoto and found him very human: Yamamoto was bound by his instructions, so was not a free agent. He seemed to "be really anxious to reach some form of understanding, but the Japanese government was committed to a policy of denunciation [of the Washington treaty]."[70]

On 11 December Yamamoto cabled Tokyo a carefully worded warning: "I endeavored to sacrifice myself to the principle of parity, anticipating inevitable rupture of the talks. It goes without saying that this policy would have a grave consequence upon our foreign relations."[71] On 28 March 1935 he visited the British naval attaché to say that "he had completed his report to the government and was going away for a holiday 'as he was very tired because there were too many diehards in the Japanese navy.'"[72] A sympathetic Davis noted that "Yamamoto had been deeply impressed by the impact of meeting face to face with the two greatest Naval Powers and he would return to Tokyo either to convert his government to a more reasonable stand or to lose his head."[73]

Upon returning to Tokyo, Yamamoto subtly registered his disagreement with his superiors when he reported to the throne: "There was no appearance whatsoever of any two powers combining to oppress the third [Japan] at these talks." By this he meant that there was no Anglo-American collusion or oppression.

But Navy Minister Ōsumi paid no attention to what he had to say.[74] In private Yamamoto remarked, "It's very regrettable that the Washington and London treaties should have to be done away with." "I greatly regret their abrogation; the ratio of 10:10:6 is just fine with us because they are treaties that limit the other parties [the Anglo-American powers]."[75] He ruminated that "we must come to an agreement on naval limitation with the Anglo-American powers for the sake of both world peace and Japan's existence," but "diehards" torpedoed his mission. On this point Ambassador Grew shrewdly observed, "Younger Japanese officers have freely spoken of eventual war with the United States as a foregone conclusion on the ground that Japan has certain definite policies in China which the United States will oppose and the result will be inevitable conflict. One of the officers who so expressed himself is an aide to Admiral Kato Kanji."[76]

SECOND LONDON NAVAL CONFERENCE, 1935–36

As the principal delegate of the Second London Conference, which opened its sessions on 9 December 1935, the navy chose the blunt and forceful Nagano Osami, a protégé of Katō and a member of the fleet faction. Yamamoto was asked to join the delegation but he firmly declined. By this time the notice of abrogation of the Five-Power Treaty was a fact. Japan's policy at the Second London Conference was spelled out as follows: "If by any chance the Anglo-American powers should try to impose a discriminatory ratio on us as happened in past naval conferences, it is clear that Japan will follow the course of fall and decline. Thus the present conference has far graver impacts on our Empire than the Washington and London Conferences had."[77]

Nagano was bound by government instructions to the common upper limit worked out at a cabinet meeting on 4 November. Parity was absolutely necessary, they stated, for the Imperial Navy to control the western Pacific, protect vital sea communications, and secure Japan's position as a stabilizing power in East Asia.[78] Nagano argued that in demanding parity, Japan was merely seeking security: he considered parity or the common upper limit to be "the essential preliminary to attaining a state of non-menace and non-aggression." The American delegates used the same arguments they had repeated time and again in the preparatory talks: "The Washington treaty gave equal security and . . . Admiral Katō [Tomosaburō] had at that time [the Washington Conference] said that he did not want equality with the U.S.A. An attack on Japan with the existing ratio was not a possibility. On the other hand, the U.S.A. had the Philippines and Alaska to protect . . . and the Japanese proposal would make it impossible for the U.S.A. to defend these places if Japan attacked them."[79]

Admiral Standley said that if the United States granted parity to Japan, its navy would have absolute superiority in the Philippine and Alaskan waters, and many Americans were suspicious of Japanese plans to attack the Philippines.[80] Nagano retorted that under the Washington Conference ratio, the U.S. Navy had the capability to operate in Far Eastern waters and that the Philippines as a base of operations could menace Japan. Norman Davis replied that the United States was not trying to deprive Japan of anything. Nagano still insisted that Japan merely wanted to remove a "grave threat" against Japan's homeland. Thus the two sides talked at cross purposes. With Nagano showing no willingness to come to any agreement, the conference ended in failure. He seemed eager to return home, and on 15 January 1936, the delegation walked out of the Second London Conference. This was "a proper death knell to a noble experiment in naval limitation," wrote Admiral James O. Richardson.[81]

Lieutenant Commander Prince Takamatsu, the emperor's younger brother, who was then studying at the Naval Staff College, observed critically in his diary, "Even before he left Japan, the Japanese naval delegate had no intention of con- cluding an agreement and he is preoccupied with finding an excuse for the fail- ure of the conference. Japan must be criticized for lack of sincerity, for it showed no desire for the success of the conference and willingness to compromise. In my way of thinking, such withdrawal [from the Second London Conference] brings national disgrace upon Japan, for it shows to the entire world the lack of discipline in the navy."[82] Whatever the case, the Japanese demand for parity destroyed the whole idea of naval limitation. And some Japanese naval officers retroactively felt that it was a proximate cause of the Pacific War.

Japan's diplomats were painfully aware that withdrawal from the Second London Conference meant denunciation of the Washington system, the cooperative framework in the Pacific and East Asia. Isolation was the price Japan had to pay. As Foreign Vice Minister Shigemitsu Mamoru observed, "[Japan] had cast aside the last defense that shielded its international status." "Isolation begat anxiety, and anxiety begat feelings of inferiority and rest- lessness. And this led to a sense of crisis and a demand for further arms expansion."[83]

The Vinson-Trammell Act, passed by Congress in March 1934, authorized construction of 102 ships and 1,184 planes during an eight-year period, provid- ing for a "treaty navy" that would build up to the limits allowed by the Washington and London treaties. The Naval General Staff, seeing in the Vinson Plan a means of putting pressure on Japan, warned that Japan faced a crisis following its withdrawal from the Washington-London treaties.[84]

TOWARD RESUMPTION OF A NAVAL RACE

In response to the Vinson-Trammell Act, the Japanese navy announced in March 1934 a "second supplemental building program" for 1934–37. It projected forty-eight ships, the maximum allowed under the London treaty. It augmented air power by eight squadrons. By the end of 1935 Japan had exceeded the quotas set by the Washington and London treaties. Its ratio compared to the United States at the end of that year was to be 80 percent, because the United States did not build up to the treaty limits.

Japan now braced itself for an arms race. Admiral Suetsugu offered this assurance in a public lecture: "A naval race will easily occur; even if it should occur, there is nothing to fear."[85] A pamphlet issued by the Publicity Bureau of the Navy Ministry in 1934 stated, "In the course of history there have been countries which were ruined by defeat in war, but there has never been a single country that was ruined by excessive expenditures on armaments." This passage was lifted from Satō Tetsutarō's *Teikoku kokubō shiron* (1908), a classic manifesto of navalism. In the memorandum to the emperor drafted by the high command in May 1935, chief of the Naval staff, Prince Fushimi stated that after the demise of the Washington and London treaties, Japan would be able to maintain a naval strength of 70 to 80 percent of the American fleet for ten years."[86] The Japanese navy was confident that the United States would not embark on a naval race, counting on American economic troubles and lack of willpower. Subsequent developments showed how badly the navy miscalculated. It would confront one crisis after another in a desperate attempt to cope with the arms race.

The Naval General Staff claimed that naval building, unhampered by the Washington and London treaties, would be more economical than maintaining the treaty navy. The key to this position, of course, was the plan, ready in October 1934, to build a superbattleship displacing 50,000 tons, mounting nine 20-inch guns, and having a top speed of more than 30 knots. The *Yamato* class, as it emerged in the 1937 plan, actually provided for two 64,000-ton mammoth battleships mounting nine 18-inch guns each, with a top speed of 27 knots. These were to be the world's largest battleships ever built or to be built. Overwhelming in firepower, armor, cruising range, and speed, the *Yamato* was meant to be the decisive weapon in a main-fleet engagement. Its huge guns had a greater range than those of the enemy, and naval leaders expected that it could destroy enemy battleships before they even reached the area of decisive battle. Its planning was completed while the naval treaties were still in effect; the *Yamato*'s keel was laid in November 1936 as soon as Japan withdrew from the treaties. In order to keep the ship's construction a strict military secret, the navy built high fences around the dock and allowed each construction worker to see only a small section of the ship.

The navy counted on getting a jump of at least five years on the U.S. Navy. Even if the latter should attempt to catch up, the resulting ships would be too large to pass through the Panama Canal. (Faithful to Mahan's dictum on concentration, American battleships were designed to be capable of navigating the canal. As a result, the largest ships the United States launched after the demise of the Washington treaty were of the 45,000-ton *Iowa* class.)

Commander Ishikawa, one of the early enthusiasts for the plan, wanted five *Yamato*-class ships mounting 20-inch guns (even larger than those actually used for the *Yamato*). In a letter to Katō he calculated that they would "at one bound raise our ship strength from the present ratio of 60 percent of U.S. strength to absolute superiority."[87] Here was an expression of what Admiral Inoue called "ratio neurosis." Despite technical innovations, the *Yamato* plan rested on—in fact, only improved on—the conventional concept of "big battleships and big guns."[88] In contrast with the high expectations of the Japanese navy, it is ironic that the *Yamato* class served only as sacrificial bait for American planes toward the end of the Pacific War.

From the moment of the *Yamato* class's inception, air power advocates attacked the plan as anachronistic. Yamamoto, then head of the Naval Aviation Department, derided the chief naval architect Rear Admiral Fukuda Keiji of the Naval Construction Department: "I don't like to be a wet blanket, and I know you're going all out at your job, but I am afraid you'll be out of work before long. From now on, aircraft are going to be the most important thing in the navy."[89] Captain Ōnishi Takijirō, Head of the Education Division of the Naval Aviation Department, went to the Naval General Staff and protested against the construction of superbattleships, claiming that for the cost of one *Yamato*, the navy could produce one thousand top-of-the-line fighter planes.[90] But the demands of the air enthusiasts went unheeded.

THE BEGINNING OF SOUTHERN EXPANSION

After the expiration of the Washington and London treaties, the Japanese became haunted by a sense of crisis concerning the United States. The goal of naval security that the navy had sought by withdrawing from the Washington-London treaty system seemed further away. The navy's search for a rationale for fleet expansion led to the formulation of the southward advance as a fundamental national policy. At this stage the navy's southern strategy—"defend the north and expand to the south"—was essentially a budgetary strategy to contend with the army, which advocated preparations against the Soviet Union—"defend the south and expand to the north."

An economic reason also lay behind the navy's southern strategy. As long as Japan could obtain such resources as petroleum, rubber, and scarce metals through trade with the United States and the western colonial powers in Southeast Asia, the navy did not need to intervene. However, as relations with the United States deteriorated, the navy became increasingly concerned with the possible short-age of petroleum for its fleets and naval aviation. To research the oil question, the navy had established in July 1935 the Committee to Investigate Southern Policy, with Vice Chief of the Naval General Staff Shimada Shigejirō as chairman.[91] For the first time the navy began to systematically investigate petroleum resources in Southeast Asia, especially in the Dutch East Indies, to prepare for a Japanese-American conflict. Commander Nakazawa Tasuku, a member of this investiga-tive committee, stated that any advance to the East Indies might very well result in a clash with the Anglo-American powers.[92]

In March 1936 the navy created three committees "to study and formulate naval policy." Their aim was "to prepare naval armaments that will give confi-dence in national defense in view of the fact that at the end of this year [1936] naval treaties will expire."[93] The most important among them was the First Committee, whose task was to study and formulate "a firm and concrete policy of southward expansion." For this purpose it was necessary to build up naval power. This committee was dominated by Captain Nakahara Yoshimasa of the Naval General Staff, "the King of the South Seas." The First Committee worked out the southern policy that was incorporated in the paper "Principles of National Policy," adopted in April 1936. It stated that Japan, in expanding into the South Seas, must "as a matter of course anticipate obstruction by the United States, Britain, and the Netherlands." Japan must provide for the worst eventuality by preparing for "resorting to armed force." This paper included for the first time Britain and the Netherlands as possible enemies, but the United States remained the target. "The navy's armaments must be placed in full readiness to cope with the traditional Far Eastern policy of the United States."[94] Clearly, in reformulating national policy during 1936, the navy had begun to seize the initiative from the army.

The next important document, the "Fundamental of National Policy," approved on 7 August 1936 by the Five Ministers' Conference—the prime minis-ter, the foreign minister, finance minister, and the navy and army ministers—was more belligerent toward the United States. In preparing this document, the navy seized the initiative for "expansion of naval armaments."[95] As far as the navy was concerned, the real object of the southward advance was to build up armaments against the United States. The army was equally adamant in its demand for preparation against the Soviet Union. The deadlock could not be broken by interservice negotiations, and the outcome was a bureaucratic compromise that would increasingly characterize army-navy talks. The result was the now-famous "Fundamentals of National Policy" which registered claims of both services, expansion toward both south and north.[95] As Foreign Minister Hirota Kōki recollected, the real aim of the "Fundamentals of National Policy" was to justify fleet expansion after the Washington and London treaties expired.[96] This paper stressed the need to "strengthen naval armaments in order to secure command of the western Pacific against the United States Navy." Armed with this provision, Navy Minister Nagano obtained an appropriation for a Third Replenishment Program.

The navy's characteristic mode of policy making stood out. Instead of formulating strategic and armament plans based on national policy, it worked backward: the navy started with its organizational interests—preparations against a hypothetical enemy and budgetary support—and calculated backward to define national policy. A typical product of interservice compromise, the policy decision of 1936 failed to establish any strategic priorities or coordinate military with foreign policy.

In 1936 the navy took the initiative to revise the Imperial National Defense Policy, last revised in 1923. The international situation had changed with the repudiation of the naval treaties in 1935 and 1936, which isolated Japan. The army-navy deliberations again resulted in compromise. The navy tried to restrain the army's clamoring for preparations against the Soviet Union, while demanding southward expansion and naval buildup that would allow it to seize command of the sea in the western Pacific. The new National Defense Policy could not fix strategic priorities between the United States and the Soviet Union, so both appeared as Japan's hypothetical enemies. What interested the navy most was natural resources, especially oil in Southeast Asia. And advance into the Dutch East Indies presupposed hostilities with the United States and Britain.[97]

The strategic plan that accompanied the Imperial National Defense Policy of 1936 was essentially a rehash of the 1923 version, reiterating a "quick encounter, quick showdown." At the same time, the policy emphasized that "because great fear exists that future war will be a prolonged one, we must have determination and preparation to endure it."[98] As in the 1923 strategic plan, the exigencies of total war never filtered down to the level of annual operational plans.

In the mid-1930s, Japan's leading advocates of an aggressive southern policy were Captain Nakahara and Commander Ishikawa. Ishikawa had recently returned from a tour of Southeast Asia and presented a report to Navy Minister Nagano. Ishikawa had become convinced that to the south of Japan, an "Anglo-American-Chinese-Dutch encirclement" was in the making. In particular, he stressed economic, military, and political "oppression" by the United States. Japan would have to face "either escaping from death by resorting to war or succumbing without a fight." He counted on Germany's rise in arms around 1940 and predicted that it would be Japan's golden opportunity to break through this ABCD encirclement. Anticipating such an eventuality, Ishikawa urged that in view of the rapid buildup of American sea and air power, Japan should prepare sufficient armaments to ensure victory in war with the United States.[100] In 1936 such an encirclement existed only in Ishikawa's fertile imagination, but it was self-fulfilling, for in June 1941 he and his colleagues called for an armed southward advance and expressed their "determination" to go to war with the United States to break through the anti-Japanese encirclement.

STEPPING STONES TO SOUTHERN REGIONS

With the "Fundamentals of National Policy," southern advance entered a new stage. After 1936 the governing factor, as envisioned by men such as Nakahara and Ishikawa, became the need to obtain advance bases in the South China Sea. In September 1936 a perfect pretext for acquiring such a territory seemed to be presented by an incident in Pakhoi, on the south-central Chinese coast bordering the Gulf of Tonkin, that involved the murder of a Japanese national. A plan drafted by Captain Nakahara and approved by Rear Admiral Kondō Nobutake, Vice Chief of the Naval General Staff, foresaw occupation of the Chinese island of Hainan, about the size of Taiwan, lying off northern French Indochina and rich in iron ores. It would be ideal as a springboard for reaching the Philippines, Malaya, and the Dutch East Indies. Kondō anticipated that occupation of Hainan would bring confrontation with the United States and Britain. The Naval General Staff went so far as to draft a plan for preparatory fleet mobilization against not only China but also the Anglo-American powers.[101] The Operations Division saw the possibility of war with these powers. Although this coercive, even belligerent, measure advocated by the Naval General Staff did not materialize because of opposition of Navy Ministry leaders, reaction to the Pakhoi incident foreshadowed the expansionist course the navy demanded once the China War broke out in July 1937.[102]

During the China War the navy was apprehensive lest the army claim the navy's share of budget appropriations. The navy remained a censorial bystander watching the army's "positive policy," as long as hostilities were confined to north China, but began to outdo the army once fighting spread to central and south China, the navy's traditional "sphere of defense." On 11 July 1937, four days after the Marco Polo Bridge Incident, the Naval General Staff wrung from the reluctant navy minister an agreement to send marines to Shanghai and Tsingtao to protect Japanese residents. Navy Minister Yonai Mitsumasa opposed the expedition for fear of provoking the United States and Britain, but on 12 August he yielded to the Naval General Staff. At the same time the navy decided to step up its armament plans with a view to repulse "interference by the Anglo-American powers."[103]

The China War had revived the navy's hope of acquiring Hainan. Again, views of the Naval General Staff prevailed. Despite the initial opposition by Navy Minister Yonai and his vice minister Yamamoto, in February 1939 the navy occupied Hainan, the farthest southern point of penetration up to that time. The Naval Affairs Bureau cautioned that occupation "would greatly provoke Britain, the United States, and France and that these powers would cooperate to bring pressure to bear on Japan."[104] Captain Kusaka Ryūnosuke, chief of the Operations Section, justified occupation as a foothold for future expansion to the south.[105] Naval leaders in Tokyo generally held that "Tonkin operations were to prepare for future war with the Anglo-American powers."[106] As anticipated, this step provoked the United States. A month later the navy annexed the Spratley Islands, a group in the South China Sea, between Indochina and the Philippines, previously claimed by France. The Spratleys in Japan's hand could threaten the Dutch East Indies and French Indochina as well as the Philippines. The United States issued a warning. On 15 April 1939 President Roosevelt ordered the U.S. fleet to shorten its sojourn in the Atlantic and steam to its regular station in the Pacific.

One reason why the moderate naval leaders, from Yonai on down, did not more actively restrain the southward drive was that seizure of these islands accorded with the policy of southward expansion the navy had been planning since 1936 and provided a rationale for an increase in naval armaments. Besides, these moderate leaders had their hands full trying to block a military alliance with Germany. As Admiral Inoue later testified, "A large part of our time and energy was spent, not in positive and constructive endeavors, but in negative efforts at naysaying."[107]

Southward expansion would enter a new stage with the outbreak of World War II in August 1939, followed by Germany's conquest of the Netherlands and France in the spring of 1940. Japan's attempt to take advantage of the European war would result in armed southward advance and a military alliance with Germany, to deter the United States. The navy knew that this would bring Japan a step closer to war with the United States.

CHAPTER NINE

THE JAPANESE NAVY AND THE TRIPARTITE PACT

The Yonai-Yamamoto-Inoue Triumvirate

Yonai Mitsumasa was chosen navy minister in February 1937 because he was regarded as the best qualified to restore control and order within the navy, which had been allowed to all but disintegrate during the terms of Ōsumi and Nagano. Yonai and his vice minister Yamamoto Isoroku had been particularly critical of the blatantly political activities of Katō Kanji and Suetsugu concerning parity as jeopardizing the navy's service discipline. In fact, back in 1934, when Yonai was commander of the Sasebo Naval District, he had harshly upbraided Katō, two years his senior, for having "instigated" younger officers to the 15 May 1932 assassination of Prime Minister Inukai.[1]

Yonai had built his career in the fleets, in naval districts, and as an instructor of gunnery schools, and he had served briefly as commander in chief of the Combined Fleet before he became navy minister. He had no previous experience in the navy ministry, but he proved a powerful leader. Particularly mindful of controlling younger malcontents, he forbade subordinates to meddle in politics and was determined to assume full responsibility for handling the question of an alliance with Nazi Germany. He would strictly adhere to Katō Tomosaburō's legacy of cooperation with the Anglo-American powers. He had the full support of Yamamoto and Inoue Shigeyoshi, Head of the Naval Affairs Bureau. For Yamamoto, whose political shrewdness made him Yonai's right-hand man, here was an opportunity to rebuild the navy along orthodox lines. Yonai and Yamamoto were prepared to dismiss followers of Katō Kanji and Suetsugu if they stood in their way. They maintained that without discipline and control, the navy would "degenerate into an armed mob."[2] They adopted a strict top-down system of policy making. "Orders must naturally come," Yamamoto said, "from the top to the bureau chiefs [and through them to the section chiefs] and the subordinates are to devise merely means of implementing these policies."[3]

By all accounts Yonai was one of the strongest leaders ever to preside over the navy ministry. Admiral Okada described him as "clearheaded and quite interested in politics despite his bland look. His point of view was quite similar to mine."⁴ He was taciturn, but when occasion called for it, he did not mince words. He held a broad view on international affairs and understood that Japan's interests lay in cooperation with the Anglo-American maritime powers. He had the loyal support of his vice minister Yamamoto, who thereby became a target of assassination by radical young army officers; armed military police had to guard his official residence.⁵ A charismatic and dynamic leader, Yamamoto possessed administrative talents and understood politics. Possessed of a "razor sharp" analytical mind, he never compromised his principles.

Yonai and Yamamoto were ably assisted by Inoue, a brilliant man of iron will who styled himself a "radical liberalist"—a rare bird in the navy. A rationalist through and through, he refused to yield on matters of principle. One critical subordinate later commented, "Inoue was a great man but was not good at persuading those who opposed his view. Perhaps he would have succeeded as a philosopher."⁶ Enomoto Jōji, who as a senior councilor of the navy ministry (with the rank of vice admiral) had his office between Yonai's and Yamamoto's, knew them well and described them in a nutshell: "Yonai was a man of few words but resolute action. Yamamoto was a man of hidden passion, and Inoue was a man of sharp intellect." In the words of Rear Admiral Takagi Sōkichi, this trio had "miraculously" survived the Ōsumi purge because they were not involved in naval limitation.⁷

In August 1938 the navy took up the question of a military alliance with Germany proposed by Joachim von Ribbentrop, the Nazi Party's foreign minister. Germany's objective was to use the Japanese navy to deter American intervention in the European war against Germany. Any German alliance would be an ill-fated match between sea power and land power, and no faithful disciples of Mahan would condone such a marriage of convenience. Yonai, Yamamoto, and Inoue opposed the alliance because of the risk of alienating, even fighting, the United States.

But the Yonai-Yamamoto-Inoue trio was from the beginning a minority within the navy. They were outnumbered by the pro-German faction and also had to contend with army supporters of an alliance with Germany. Among the middle-echelon pro-German forces were Captain Oka Takazumi, chief of the First Section of the Naval Affairs Bureau; Commander Shiba Katsuo of the same section; Commander Kami Shigenori of the Operations Section; Commander Fujii Shigeru of the Second Section; and Yokoi Tadao, war guidance officer.

Kami, Shiba, and Yokoi were Nazi sympathizers, having returned from the
attaché's office in Berlin. Their views were revealed in a remark made in the summer of 1938 by Rear Admiral Inagaki Ayao of the Naval Aviation Department to
German naval attaché Paul W. Wenneker: "For different reasons, Germany and
Japan have the same interest in 'smashing' England. Both countries need a few
more years before they are sufficiently armed for this."[8] Such an anti-British
sentiment would soon be imbued with an anti-American view. In July 1939 Vice
Admiral Kondō Nobutake, who had been stationed in Germany in 1935–37 and
would soon be vice chief of the Naval General Staff, told Wenneker that he "did
not believe that it will come to a war with England and America. Even if it should,
it is manifest that the one opponent worthy of attention, America, can do practically nothing to get the better of Japan militarily."[9]

Wenneker was active among middle-echelon officers. On 1 June 1939,
Ambassador Eugen Ott reported that Japan's "middle-ranking officers are increasingly taking our side." He tried to use the influence of Admiral Richard Foerster,
former Commander in Chief of the German fleet, who was visiting Japan, "to
undermine their assessment of the Anglo-American fleet." Ott reported to the
foreign ministry, "Admiral Foerster has applied himself with great skill and
obvious success to the task of strengthening the self-confidence of the leaders
of the Japanese Navy in their attitude toward the British and American fleets."[10]
Foreign Minister Arita Hachirō told Harada Kumao, secretary to Prince
Saionji, that "a careful watch must be kept on Wenneker because there are considerable pro-German elements in Japan." Yonai was also concerned about
Wenneker's effort to wean Japanese officers from "overestimation of the Anglo-
American naval position."[11] Neither American Ambassador Grew nor his naval
attaché cultivated special relations with pro-American officers, singly or as a group.

HOLDING THE LINE

One way for the Yonai-Yamamoto-Inoue triumvirate to control subordinates
was to keep them ignorant of policy deliberations at higher levels. After Yonai
returned to the navy ministry from the Five Ministers Conferences, he talked
only to Yamamoto and Inoue, sometimes joined by Vice Chief of the Naval
General Staff Koga Mine'ichi. This approach had the drawback of causing
resentment among section chiefs, who were mortified because their counterparts
in the army seemed apprised of matters discussed at the Five Ministers Conference.
As an "absolutely confidential memo" written by Captain Oka Takazumi stated,
"Because middle-echelon officers are kept utterly in the dark about the intentions

of their superiors, they are unable to decide how to act." If they continued to be ignored, Oka warned, "the dissatisfactions of the lower echelons would finally come to explode." Lack of communication between the upper and middle echelons hampered and misled the latter in their efforts toward policy coordination with army representatives. Admiral Nomura Kichisaburō, though opposed to a German alliance, felt it necessary to advise Yamamoto to "ventilate" communication with the navy's middle echelons.[12] A sympathetic official biographer of Inoue admits that perhaps Inoue did not fathom the depth of his subordinates' feelings; "he needed to take a step or two forward to reach their hearts."[13]

The navy's middle-echelon officials had assumed that Navy Minister Yonai approved of a pact against not only the Soviet Union but also Britain and France. Support for a German alliance drew strength from anti-British feelings permeating naval circles, especially among middle-rank officers. An idea of the hostility felt toward Britain can be gleaned from a memorandum drafted by the Naval General Staff in September 1938. This memorandum revived the image of Britain as a haughty, selfish ingrate that had exploited Japan during World War I but then had abandoned the Anglo-Japanese Alliance and joined the United States in imposing the 60 percent ratio on Japan at the Washington Conference.[14] In another memorandum, Captain Oka asserted that the China war had resolved itself into "diplomatic warfare" with Britain in which Japan's hand would be strengthened by alliance with Germany. The anti-British feelings of middle-echelon officials were based on a sense of international isolation that expressed itself in the charge that Britain had been mobilizing other nations to "form an encirclement of Japan."[15] An alliance with Germany, they felt, would go far to end Japan's isolation as well as terminate the China War successfully.

Oka was certain that America would never align itself with Britain. Leaders in Washington, he asserted, had learned from World War I, which cost the United States $25 billion, only to result in bickering over payment of Allied war debts. "It is only by maintaining its neutrality," he declared, "that the United States can hold the 'casting vote' in the world and fish in troubled waters."[16] Oka revealed the navy's inner motive for an anti-British alliance when he argued that if the pact was against the Soviet Union, it could not be "used for the pursuit of national policy (*expanding into the South Seas, etc.*)."[17] An anti-Russian alliance would concede the army's priority in armaments, whereas a broader pact against Britain would accord with the navy's policy of southern advance and help win priority for preparations against the Anglo-American powers. Bureaucratic politics constituted a factor in the navy's stand. Advocacy of a German alliance found a candid, if inverted, expression in a memorandum that Captain Takagi Sōkichi, Chief of the Research Section of the ministry, presented to Harada Kumao, Prince Saionji's secretary, on 25 January 1939:

> We have established Britain and America as the targets of our fleet expansion programs, and we have not hesitated to demand naval appropriations amounting to a billion and a half yen. By completely discarding this stand and agreeing to confine our target to the Soviet Union alone, we would not only expose contradictions and inconsistencies in our naval policy, but also cause the army to misunderstand us and draw the erroneous conclusion that the navy, though ready to use Britain and America as a "pretext" for obtaining a large budget, does not really intend to take on these powers. The army will then dogmatically conclude that the navy will follow the army in going to war with the Soviet Union.

Captain Takagi put it more bluntly when he wrote on another occasion, "If we say we shall absolutely never fight the United States, the army will grasp Japan's total national strength and financial power for its own purposes."[18]

In mid-December 1938 the navy's middle-echelon officers found themselves in an awkward position against their counterparts in the army when they learned that Navy Minister Yonai had all along opposed an alliance against Britain, France, and the United States.[19] Yonai's objection was straightforward. An alliance against Britain would "most likely cause the United States to join hands with Britain and together they would apply crushing economic pressures, and Japan would be dragged into war with the Anglo-American powers."[20] Japan's military obligations in such a war would have to be shored up by the navy alone. At the Five Ministers Conference of 8 August 1939, Yonai flatly declared, "There would be absolutely no chance of Japan's winning a war of this nature—the Japanese navy is simply not made to fight against the United States and Britain, to begin with. As for the German and Italian navies, they would be of no help at all."[21]

Earlier, at the Five Ministers Conference of 7 May, Yonai had warned that even if not engaging in hostilities with the United States, by joining camp with Germany, Japan would face an absolute stoppage of trade with the United States. Yonai had taken seriously the "moral embargo" of July 1938 whereby the U.S. government persuaded aircraft manufacturers not to sell planes to Japan—a harbinger of increasing economic pressure. On 21 August, Yonai told Army Minister Itagaki Seishirō that if the army desired an alliance against Britain, he was prepared to block it, even by risking his position.[22]

Another factor that underlay Yonai's opposition to a German alliance was the wish of the emperor. Vice Admiral Hirata Noboru, naval assistant to Hirohito, conveyed to Yonai the emperor's opposition to the pact. The emperor appreciated the navy's opposition to a German alliance and told Hirata that Japan was "saved by the navy."[23]

Yamamoto's reasons for opposing an Axis alliance were clear-cut: "To side with Germany, which is aiming at a new world order, will inevitably embroil Japan in a war to overthrow the old Anglo-American order, but given the existing state of naval armaments, especially in naval aviation, there is no chance of winning a war with the United States for some time to come." To fight the United States, he said, one must be prepared to fight the whole world. As Yamamoto and Yonai told Harada on 1 July 1939, "The problem of the Tripartite Pact is one over which our national fate is at stake."[24]

In similar vein Inoue cautioned that the economy was almost entirely dependent on the Anglo-American powers, and the navy needed steel and oil from America. War with Britain would mean war with the United States. From Germany, Japan could expect virtually no military aid, except perhaps a few U-boats.[25] When Hitler invited the pro-German Admiral Ōsumi Mineo to attend the Nazi Party rally in July 1939, Inoue warned, "You must realize that there is a great danger that a German alliance might turn the United States and Britain into Japan's enemies, so please don't be taken in by Hitler's offer of any such alliance." In a speech at Yūshūkai, the association of naval officers, he stated that "a Tripartite Pact would spell national ruin for Japan."[26]

Faithful to Katō Tomosaburō's legacy, Yonai, Yamamoto, and Inoue held to the naval orthodoxy: the Japanese fleet was an instrument of deterrence, not of war with the United States. Their efforts not to provoke the United States had been apparent during the crisis over the *Panay* in December 1937, when a U.S. gunboat on the Yangtze near Nanking was sunk by Japanese naval aircraft. Yamamoto hastened to the U.S. Embassy—some said in tears— to offer not only sincere regrets but also unusually detailed explanations and a large indemnity of $2.2 million (equivalent to the cost of two hundred fighter planes). He was moved by a desire to continue commercial relations with the United States. President Roosevelt, who had even considered the possibility of naval action or economic sanctions, abandoned such measures for fear of war. After Japan had apologized and offered to pay for damages, he closed the case.[27]

Symbolic of Yonai's and Yamamoto's posture toward the United States was the hospitality extended to the officers and the crew of the USS *Astoria*, the ship that brought home in April 1939 the ashes of the late Ambassador Saitō Hiroshi. During a dinner in honor of Captain Richmond Kelly Turner, Yonai whispered to a pleased Ambassador Grew that "the element in Japan which desires Fascism for Japan and the consequent linking up with Germany and Italy had been 'suppressed.'" He stated that the navy had not changed by one iota its policy of never fighting the United States. As for naval arms limitation, he regretted that it was not feasible at the moment. "But navies are 'dangerous toys,' the progressive increase in naval armaments could only lead to bankruptcy or a general explosion, and some day an agreement must be reached. There must be disarmament." Grew wrote in his diary, "This was one of the most important and significant conversations that we have had, and I regard it as marking a new trend, indeed a milestone, in Japanese-American relations, for Yonai can be trusted."[28]

Yonai's view of national defense was in the tradition of Katō Tomosaburō: "National defense was not the monopoly of the military." Considering the limit of Japan's national strength and the international situation, Japan's armaments must be held to the minimum necessary. The nation would be ruined if all its might was concentrated in armaments and other matters are neglected. Yonai opposed a military alliance that would play havoc with a rational armament plan.[29]

In the course of seventy-eight sessions of the Five Ministers Conference, Yonai fought with Army Minister Itagaki Seishirō. Yamamoto supported Yonai at the risk of assassination, while Inoue took the brunt of the dissident subordinates' contentions. But their efforts were destined to be no more than a holding action. They had never managed to persuade their subordinates and, by ignoring the convictions of middle-echelon officers, alienated them. Captain Takagi feared that "if a clash should ever occur between the higher and lower echelons, discontent within the navy will cause such an explosion that it will have wide ramifications."[30]

The Yonai-Yamamoto-Inoue leadership was highly personal, resting on force of character. Therein lay its weakness. Control over pro-German elements began to falter as soon as the leaders left their posts after the cabinet of Hiranuma Kiichirō fell in the bewildering aftermath of the Nazi-Soviet Pact on 23 August 1939. Yonai left active duty and was appointed prime minister; Yamamoto was appointed commander of the Combined Fleet; and Inoue became chief of staff of the China-Area Fleet. The leadership of this celebrated trio was similar to that of Katō Tomosaburō in that both used a highly personal style that ignored subordinates' opposition and both collapsed with the departure of the leaders from policy-making positions.

Doubt remains as to how much Yonai and his associates were aware of their precarious position. When Yamamoto recommended his mild-mannered Naval Academy classmate Yoshida Zengo as navy minister and the soft-spoken

Sumiyama Tokutarō as vice minister, he said, "No matter who becomes navy minister or vice minister, it is absolutely impossible for the navy ever to be taken in by any such scheme as an offensive-defensive Axis alliance." On another occasion he said, "Even if I get killed [by an assassin], the navy's thinking will never change. The new navy minister will say the same thing. The navy's position will not change in the least even if it has five or ten new vice ministers."[31]

The navy needed forceful leaders who could be counted on to continue the policy of Yonai, Yamamoto, and Inoue. The succeeding minister, Yoshida, who had the trust of Yonai and Yamamoto, was an able administrator, moderate in his views, and opposed to a Tripartite Pact and armed southern expansion. Like Yonai, he held that Japan as a maritime nation heavily depended economically on the Anglo-American powers, which Japan was incapable of fighting. But as Admiral Inoue remarked, Yoshida "was not cut out to be a great leader, for he was conscientious to a fault about petty details and too modest about boldly asserting leadership." He would have difficulty controlling his subordinates.[32] Wenneker observed in his diary, "It appears that as a result of a dearth of outstanding figures in the navy, no one more suitable could be found."[33] Vice Minister Sumiyama, a graduate of Gakushūin (Peers' School), was so gentle he was dubbed "the principal of the Gakushūin *Girls* School." He was not suited to be vice minister and could not support Yoshida. Could it be that Yamamoto had been overconfident about the navy's tradition and control that were being challenged?

Later, when Yonai learned of the conclusion of the Tripartite Pact, he remarked, "Our opposition to the alliance was like desperately paddling against the rapids only a few hundred yards upstream from Niagara Falls." Asked whether he would have opposed the pact had he remained in office, he replied, "Of course, but we would have been assassinated."[34] Yonai had Yamamoto appointed Combined Fleet commander because Yonai feared for Yamamoto's life if he remained in Tokyo.

MOUNTING PRESSURES FOR THE PACT

The contest over a Tripartite Pact entered a new level with outbreak of the war in Europe in September 1939. That had immediate repercussions on the navy's attitude toward Britain and the United States. On 22 October, middle-echelon officers presented to the new Navy Minister, Yoshida Zengo, a paper titled "Outline of Policy toward America," indicating that their attitude was hardening. In view of the inseparable connection between Britain and the United States, the paper stated, "A program of preparedness must be stepped up to guard against a sudden unpredictable turn in American policy."[35] This stiffening of attitude had been prompted when Washington gave notice to terminate the 1911 Japanese-American Treaty of Commerce and Navigation, to take effect in six months.

In May–June 1940, the German conquest of Denmark, Norway, the Netherlands, Belgium, and France so dazzled naval officials that they clamored for a so-called southward advance. Britain's ability to defend the empire and indeed its existence seemed in doubt. "Don't miss the bus" became the catchphrase. Few asked whether the bus was a safe one or where it was going. Hitler's rapid Blitzkrieg intensified Japanese admiration for Germany and disdain for the Anglo-American powers. Those who urged a cautious policy toward the United States were branded cowards or weaklings. The fervor for an alliance with Germany and an advance southward was revived. Navy Minister Yoshida resisted, seeing that this course was fraught with danger of war with the United States.

Middle-echelon officers tended to believe that Germany would soon invade the British Isles. Among them were Captain Ōno Takeji (war guidance officer), Commander Kami (Operations Division), and Commander Shiba (Naval Affairs Bureau). Yoshida saw that Britain retained command of the sea and that German air superiority was not sufficient to defeat England. Nor did Germany possess enough submarines to blockade the British Isles. He estimated that the European war was bound to be protracted, in which case the United States would sooner or later intervene, forcing German defeat. Japan must not be misled by the tide of war that favored Germany. Opposed to a war with the United States, Yoshida resisted a German military alliance.[36]

German naval attaché Wenneker noted in his diary, "Junior staff officers had no sympathy for his [Yoshida's] lukewarm leadership."[37] Pro-German forces, no longer limited to middle-rank officers, came out into the open, working with army supporters of the pact. To keep a close watch over subordinates, Yoshida with his usual meticulousness personally checked all important policy papers, even those bearing the signatures of the vice minister and bureau chiefs. But he had no support from his vice minister Sumiyama nor the new head of the Naval Affairs Bureau, Abe Katsuo; the latter had visited Berlin and returned pro-German. In the Naval General Staff, Prince Fushimi, an old Germanophile, threw his weight to the side of the German alliance, and Vice Chief Kondō, who had studied in Germany, was also pro-German.

That the policy of a Tripartite Pact and southward expansion were two sides of the same coin was revealed in a document drafted in the Foreign Ministry and discussed by the representatives of the navy and the army on 12 July. "Under the changing international situation," Japan's aim was "to speedily establish a close cooperative relationship among Japan, Germany, and Italy, striving to establish the New Order in East Asia, and strengthen ties with Germany and Italy, struggling to create a new order in Europe." In other words, Japan was to make Germany and Italy recognize that "French Indochina and Dutch East Indies, etc." were Japan's Lebensraum, while recognizing Germany's leadership in Europe and Africa. Japan and Germany would cooperate to restrain the United States from interfering in areas other than the Americas.[38]

On 30 July 1940 middle-echelon naval officials adopted a policy paper that stated, "The Empire must in principle consent if Germany and Italy propose an anti-British military cooperation." A week later these officials approved a document drafted by Foreign Minister Matsuoka that stated, "If Germany and Italy propose military cooperation against Britain, the Empire will in principle be ready to consent." And they redoubled their effort for a military alliance directed against Britain and the United States.[39]

YOSHIDA AS "THE LAST FORTRESS"

On 19 July 1940, three days before Konoe Fumimaro's new cabinet was formed, he called Yoshida, General Tōjō Hideki, and Matsuoka (who would become navy, army, and foreign ministers) to a conference at Konoe's villa in the Tokyo suburb of Ogikubo. Among the policies to be pursued by the new cabinet, they discussed (1) "the strengthening of the Japanese-German-Italian axis"; (2) "positive measures to include the British, French, Dutch, and Portuguese colonies in the New Order of East Asia"; and (3) "the question of a Tripartite Pact." The meeting reached an agreement: "While Japan will try to avoid unnecessary clash with the United States, Japan is firmly resolved to resist any armed intervention by that power in our establishment of the New Order in East Asia." This agreement again made it clear that the Tripartite Pact was treated as inseparable from southward advance. However, the 27 July meeting of the Liaison Conference could agree only on "strengthening political ties with Germany and Italy." Yoshida persisted in resisting a military alliance.[40]

At the meeting of naval leaders held in early August at his official residence, Yoshida again cautioned against being blinded by Germany's victory, reiterating that an alliance with Germany would bring war with the United States. That meeting concluded that in the event of war, the Japanese navy would be able to hold its own for only a year, but the U.S. Navy would resort to a protracted war. Yoshida was absolutely opposed to risking such a war by concluding a German alliance. Because of his opposition, the Tripartite Pact made no headway.

On 12 August a disgruntled army staff officer scrawled in the Confidential War Journal, "I hear the matter is still under consideration by the navy minister. Ugh!"[41]

Pressure mounted when Matsuoka placed the United States next to Britain as a target of alliance. His plan stated, "In the event of either contracting party entering into a state of war with the United States, the other contracting party will assist that power *by all possible means.*" The background of Matsuoka's hardening posture toward the United States was America's mounting economic pressure on Japan. On 25 July, Washington announced that it would include scrap iron and oil among items under federal license. On 31 July, it placed an embargo on aviation gasoline. Washington had warned Tokyo not to move troops into northern Indochina. In response, Matsuoka redrafted the alliance proposal, strengthening its anti-American provisions. While Matsuoka and the army talked about a *military* alliance, Yoshida persevered in strengthening merely a *political* alliance.[42]

Isolated and overtaxed beyond endurance, Yoshida had been confiding to his wife, "There is nobody reliable to assist me, yet the situation is momentous, and if we make one false step, it can very well lead to war."[43] He continued to resist pressure from naval subordinates as well as from the foreign and army ministers. As late as 27 August he reaffirmed his position at a conference of naval leaders.

In holding out against the pact, Yoshida was indeed the "Last Fortress," to borrow the title of a biography of Yoshida by Captain Sanematsu Yuzuru. On 30 August Yoshida remarked, "As things stand, Japan will be facing national ruin."[44] On 3 September, Captain Ishikawa went to see Yoshida and demanded that he make up his mind on the Tripartite Pact, warning him that he could not refuse the pact without fighting the army. The harassed Yoshida murmured, "But we are not prepared for war with the United States." Ishikawa pressed hard for an answer, saying it was entirely up to Yoshida. For a mere section chief to put direct pressure on a navy minister on a matter of high policy was highly irregular.[45] That night the navy minister suffered a physical and nervous collapse; hospitalized, he submitted his resignation. This was followed by a reshuffling of the navy ministry, causing a vacuum in the navy's top leadership.

THE NAVY CONSENTS TO THE PACT

Prince Fushimi recommended Oikawa Koshirō as succeeding navy minister and Toyoda Teijirō as vice minister. Oikawa was chosen for his ability to work with the army. These appointments tipped the balance in favor of the Tripartite Pact. Oikawa, reputedly a great authority on Sinology, was by nature a man of few words who expressed opinions rather than conviction and avoided infighting. After the war Admiral Inoue criticized the appointment of the "unprincipled and incompetent" Oikawa.[46] All too anxious to avoid fighting with the army, he put up little resistance to pressures for the Tripartite Pact. The emperor, who had known Oikawa since his military assistant days (1915–22), worried about his appointment, wondering whether he could be a strong leader. Vice Minister Toyoda Teijirō, who was said to be a slick operator and "political schemer" (in Oikawa's words), to a large extent took over the negotiations of the Tripartite Pact.

On 7 September, Matsuoka began secret negotiations with the recently arrived Heinrich Stahmer, personal emissary of German Foreign Minister Ribbentrop. The resulting Tripartite Pact, signed in Berlin on 27 September 1940, recognized Japan's sphere of influence in Asia in return for recognition of German and Italian interests in Europe. Each party pledged to assist the other if attacked by "a power at present not involved in the European War or in the Chinese-Japanese War."[47] At the navy's insistence Oikawa demanded and obtained a secret protocol stating that Japan retained the right to determine the time and circumstances for fulfilling its obligation to go to war. With this as the sole condition, which relieved Japan from any obligation of automatically going to war, Oikawa consented to the pact. Speaking for the navy at the Liaison Conference of 14 September, he demanded that "the government, particularly the army, give special consideration to the completion of the navy's preparations." He thus coupled his consent to the pact with a request for additional naval armaments. At the same Liaison Conference, Vice Chief of the Naval General Staff Kondō discussed the strategic outlook of a Japanese-American war: "The navy has not yet completed its war preparations vis-à-vis the United States. They will be complete next April and Japan will stand a fair chance of winning on the basis of 'quick encounter, quick showdown.' But if the United States should turn the war into a protracted struggle, it will become very difficult for Japan. On the other hand, the United States is rapidly building ships and, in the future, discrepancies in the naval ratios will widen and Japan will not be able to catch up. In this sense, today is the most advantageous moment for starting a war."[48]

At the Imperial Conference of 19 September, it was not Navy Minister Oikawa but Prince Fushimi, Chief of the Naval General Staff, who stated that the navy consented to the Tripartite Pact. Nobody present questioned whether it was proper for the chief of the Naval General Staff to speak out for the conclusion of an alliance treaty. Prince Fushimi reiterated that as a war with the United States would be a protracted one, it was important for the navy to obtain more war matériel, especially oil.[49]

Why did the navy, which had blocked the alliance for more than two years, so quickly reversed its position? Controversy exists on this point. According to an explanation offered by Vice Minister Toyoda, the consideration was "political." The navy feared that a clash with the army might precipitate a domestic crisis, possibly an army coup. Oikawa said that he feared that the Navy Ministry would be held responsible if the Konoe cabinet fell and a domestic upheaval ensued. However, there is no evidence that the army plotted a coup.

Prime Minister Konoe, who had hoped that the navy would say it could not take on the United States, could not understand why the navy consented to the Tripartite Pact. When he later asked, Toyoda answered, "The navy is at heart opposed to the Tripartite Pact. However, the navy cannot persist any further in its opposition in the face of the domestic political situation. So the navy is forced to consent. Although the navy does so for political reasons, from a military viewpoint the navy is not confident about fighting a war with the United States." A confounded Konoe retorted, "We politicians can take care of domestic politics; you in the navy must consider the matter from a strictly military standpoint. And if you are not confident [about fighting with the United States], you should have opposed the Tripartite Pact to the last. This is the only way to be loyal to the country."[50]

Because war with the United States would be first and foremost the navy's war, Oikawa's duty as navy minister was to advise political leaders about the navy's capability. If he had had the courage to say, as Yonai did in 1939, that the navy could not fight the United States, in all likelihood the Tripartite Pact would have been aborted.

Equally important were pressures from subordinates. The majority of naval opinion from the bureau and division chiefs had tilted toward the Tripartite Pact. Oikawa, a yes-man, was by temperament susceptible to pressure from below.[51] He avoided the categorical statement that the navy could not fight the United States, because he feared that such a confession of weakness would jeopardize the navy's morale and call into question its raison d'être. Oikawa also said he recalled how harshly Fleet Admiral Tōgō had reprimanded Chief of the Naval General Staff Taniguchi for having said at the time of the Manchurian Incident that the navy could not fight the United States.[52]

The navy's desire for a larger share of appropriations and war matériel was an important, perhaps the most important, factor. It had been anxious to reverse the priority given the army since the outbreak of the China war. This would be served by an alliance against the Anglo-American powers. Toyoda later stated that war with the United States must be avoided but "preparations, with emphasis on planes, must be made just in case of war with the United States and naval armaments must be increasingly built up."

With this in mind, Oikawa coupled his consent to the Tripartite Pact with a demand for increased naval preparations, arguing that its conclusion necessitated rapid preparatory fleet mobilization."[53] Rear Admiral Ugaki Matome, chief of the Operations Division, who opposed the Tripartite Pact from the operational viewpoint, later wrote that completion of the navy's war preparations was "the hidden purpose behind the conclusion of the [Tripartite] Pact."[54]

Years later Toyoda corroborated this statement: "The navy accepted the Tripartite Pact, but it desired so far as possible to avoid war with the United States and to reserve Japan's freedom of action should hostilities break out between Germany and the United States. As regards the United States, however, we had to be adequately prepared to meet the worst contingency. We therefore demanded completion of naval armaments."[55] This ambivalence, dictated by bureaucratic considerations—a desire to avoid war coupled with a demand for war matériel—proved to be the undoing of the Japanese navy, as we shall see. The emperor was much worried about the Tripartite Pact. After the interim cabinet meeting of 16 September, Hirohito, with a grievous tone of voice, asked, "Will the navy be able to hold its own in a war with the United States?"

Yamamoto Isoroku, Combined Fleet Commander, was enraged by the Tripartite Pact, which he was sure would bring war with the United States. On 15 September, he attended a conference of high-level leaders convened by Navy Minister Oikawa to obtain approval of the pact. Yamamoto attacked it, stressing the serious shortage of war matériel in the event of war. He recalled that when he was navy vice minister a year before, 80 percent of matériel was supplied from areas under the control of America and Britain. Signing the Tripartite Pact would mean losing those supplies. "I want you to tell us quite clearly what changes have been made in the materials mobilization program in order to make up for the deficiencies."[56]

Yamamoto had come to the meeting with charts depicting the strength of Japan and the United States—ships and strategic matériel (oil, coal, aluminum, copper). To his chagrin, Oikawa silenced him, turning to Admiral Ōsumi Mineo, the most senior and pro-German member of the Supreme Military Council, to close the meeting by stating that those present were in complete agreement with the navy minister. Upon his return to the fleet, Yamamoto unburdened himself to his chief of staff, Rear Admiral Fukudome Shigeru: "A year ago the navy authorities did not consent to the conclusion of the Tripartite Pact because this alliance was bound to lead to war with the United States and in that event there was no chance of victory, given the existing state of naval armaments. . . . The only chance of success lies in the augmentation of our air power, but it takes years. It is only a year since that time and it is hardly likely that sufficient armaments for war with America have been built."[57] If Yamamoto had stayed in Tokyo as navy minister or vice minister, there is no doubt that he would have risked his position, even his life, to oppose the Tripartite Pact. He reluctantly accepted the pact because he respected the naval tradition that the navy minister was the sole authority to participate in politics, a tradition he himself had attempted to rebuild as vice minister.

On 14 October, Yamamoto told Harada that the Tripartite Pact spelled war with the United States. No doubt he would die aboard his flagship, *Nagato*, and Konoe would be "torn into pieces by the revengeful Japanese people."[58] The emperor was worried about the Tripartite Pact. On 20 September he told Konoe, "I understand under the present circumstances the Japanese-German military pact cannot be helped. But what about the navy when it comes to fighting a war with America? I heard that in war games held at the Naval Staff College, Japan is always the loser in any war with America." He continued, "I am extremely worried about the present situation. If Japan should lose the war, what would be the consequences? In the worst case, will you, prime minister, share my travails with you?" In these plaintive words, the emperor made clear his opposition to any course leading to war with the United States. Hearing these words, Konoe was moved to tears.[59]

THE UNITED STATES AND THE TRIPARTITE PACT

How did the navy anticipate the American reaction to the Tripartite Pact? The Japanese navy saw its impact in terms of America's stepped-up economic "oppression" and further aggravation of relations with the United States. The purpose of these oppressions would be to stifle Japan's activities.[60] On 28 September 1940, the Intelligence Division estimated that the United States would be "greatly shocked" by the conclusion of the Tripartite Pact and would tighten its economic "oppression." (On 26 September, President Roosevelt had placed the export of all grades of scrap iron under government control.) Another report prepared by the Intelligence Division warned that American "oppression" would force Japan to launch a southward advance, thus causing war. "Under the banner of defending democracy," the United States would conclude an Anglo-American agreement to defend Britain's Pacific possessions and the Dutch East Indies, and would reinforce bases in the Philippines and Guam. "It is all-important to complete Japan's naval preparations in order to contain American activities in the Pacific and the Far East." Japan also had to cope with a defense agreement among the United States, Australia, New Zealand, and Canada.[61]

The navy's decision to conclude the Tripartite Pact was based on faulty intelligence on the military situation in Europe. From early summer into the fall of 1940, naval planners, especially in the Naval General Staff, tended to draw an optimistic picture of German victory, believing that German air strength ensured the outcome of a cross-channel operation. The report submitted on 7 September 1940 by the Intelligence Division, headed by Captain Oka, stated that the Battle of Britain was shaking the morale of the English people; "There is every indication that Germany will stage an invasion of Britain."[62] On the basis of such an estimate, the navy came to look on the pact as an instrument to restrain the United States from going to war with Germany and interfering with Japan's southward advance at least until the end of 1940, by which time Britain would have been disposed of and the war in Europe concluded. Of course, Hitler had issued an order on 14 September 1940 indefinitely postponing the invasion.

The navy did not entirely lack realistic estimates. In September 1940 Commander Ōi Atsushi, a member of the Research Section of the Navy Ministry, cautioned his superiors that even if German forces invaded the British Isles, Britain would not easily surrender. And Lieutenant Commander Genda Minoru, who returned to Tokyo in October 1940 after a tour as assistant attaché in London, reported that despite German air strength, the Battle of Britain was developing in Britain's favor. Genda did not think that John Bull would easily succumb.[63]

In retrospect, the navy obviously misconceived the Tripartite Pact from the beginning. The Americans were surprised and shocked but not cowed; on the contrary, the pact provoked them as nothing else could. However, military advisers to President Roosevelt opposed drastic retaliation, which was likely to provoke an unwanted conflict in the Far East. Admiral Harold R. Stark, Chief of Naval Operations, recognized that the United States was not yet prepared for hostilities in the Pacific. Secretary of State Hull also dissuaded the president from declaring an oil embargo for fear that it would drive Japan to the East Indies. Hull cautioned the president that the alliance meant that Germany and Japan might quickly make a move that would force the United States into war.[64]

This official policy of nonconfrontation and nonprovocation of Japan did not hide the fact that Roosevelt, Hull, and the members of the cabinet "burned with resentment at Japanese attempts to intimidate the United States." On 5 October Secretary of the Navy Frank Knox in an address stated that the pact was aimed directly at the United States and the American way of life was threatened as never before.[65] On 12 October Roosevelt made a ringing declaration that "no combination of dictator countries of Europe and Asia will stop the help we are giving to almost the last free people now fighting to hold them at bay." In his Fireside Chat a week later, the president said that the so-called new order in Europe and Asia was nothing but an "unholy alliance" that would enslave mankind.

As the Japanese anticipated, Washington, in response to the Tripartite Pact, began to retaliate by curtailing trade with Japan and by the end of 1940 cut off all exports—iron ore, pig iron, steel, main articles made of steel—except oil. Already the United States was secretly engaged in joint strategic studies with Britain and other nations to form a common front against the Japan-Germany-Italy combination.

This sense of global crisis began to grip the United States. In Tokyo, Grew wrote, "It became evident that the Far Eastern problem had ceased to be even practically a separate question but had become an integral part of the world crisis created by Adolf Hitler's bid for world domination." Grew, once sympathetic to Japan, wrote, "Japan has associated herself with a team or system of predatory Powers. . . . It will be the better part of wisdom to regard her no longer as an individual nation, with whom our friendship has been traditional, but as part and parcel of that system which, if allowed to develop unchecked, will assuredly destroy everything that America stands for."[66] President Roosevelt cabled Grew that Japan was "openly and unashamedly one of the predatory nations and part of a system which aims to wreck about everything the United States stands for."[67] As Hull put it, "Germany and Japan . . . were returning the world to the Dark Ages." The American leaders were convinced that "the signing of the [Tripartite] agreement left no doubt that the world [was] confronted not with merely regional or local wars but with an organized and ruthless movement of conquest."[68] The Tripartite Pact meant that the U.S. Navy no longer had the luxury of thinking about a war on only one front.

Japanese naval leaders failed to realize that the Tripartite Pact had combined the European war with the Far Eastern conflict, creating a world crisis for the United States. On 21 January 1941, President Roosevelt cabled Grew, "We must recognize that our interests are menaced both in Europe and in the Far East. . . . Our strategy of self-defense must be a global strategy."[69] Admiral Pratt had warned his friend Admiral Nomura that Japan must never underestimate the power of ideology in American foreign policy. The Japanese navy failed to understand that the Americans were already in an undeclared war to save the Western "democracies" from the "totalitarian" Axis.[70] Preoccupied with the strategy of southward advance and anxious to obtain budgetary precedence over the army, the Japanese navy did not realize that the pact had quickened the pace of American foreign policy in a manner previously inconceivable.

America's hardening posture was made clear to the Japanese. Ambassador Horinouchi Kensuke reported to Tokyo that although "for the present, the United States will try to avoid war with Japan . . . it is endeavoring to restrain Japan through strengthening joint Anglo-American policy." American officials believed, he reported, that continued Japanese expansion in the south would result in a total embargo that pointed to an eventual war.[71]

The Intelligence Division reported on an increasing tendency for the United States to become "united" with Britain. "As Britain recedes, the United States will take its place, and this will bring about a serious situation that cannot be overlooked. It would threaten our national policy of establishing the Greater East Asia Co-Prosperity Sphere."[72]

The Japanese navy's realization that with the conclusion of the Tripartite Pact, Japanese-American relations had entered a new critical stage was reflected in an important organizational reshuffle that took place in late 1940, which resulted in the creation of the First Committee and the Second Section of the Naval Affairs Bureau. They were aimed at "establishing [a] national policy of countering Britain and the United States that resulted from the Tripartite Pact." Their purpose was to "reinforce the navy's national policy in accord with the new policy set by the Tripartite Pact." The navy would take the lead the nation as "a maritime self defense state." (See p. 235-36.) Lieutenant Commander Fujii Shigeru, an associate member of the First Committee, recorded that with the conclusion of the Tripartite Pact, Japan had embarked on the policy of "commencing hostile actions against the United States." He added, "The grave problem was how to persuade the government to provide armaments and matériel for the acceleration of the navy's war preparations."[73] The Tripartite Pact had thus become a bureaucratic weapon in the hands of the navy to obtain budget and materials to cope with the United States.[74]

During long debates over the conclusion of the Tripartite Pact, no one overtly pointed to the folly of Japan, a sea power, aligning with Germany, a land power. The pact was a great aberration from Mahan's teachings. Yonai, Yamamoto, and Inoue, who understood this, fought against the pact. The navy, which one would expect to hold on to Mahan's legacy, was absorbed in bureaucratic infighting with the army and lost sight of the danger of allying with Germany, with which the United States was already fighting an "undeclared war" in the Atlantic.

PART FIVE

PACIFIC

CONFRONTATION

CHAPTER TEN

THE SOUTHWARD ADVANCE AND THE AMERICAN EMBARGO

The Impact of the European War

The outbreak of the European war on 3 September 1939 markedly lessened the hold that the preoccupied Western powers maintained over colonial possessions in Southeast Asia. This presented a magnificent vista for Japan to expand southward. Suddenly it seemed possible to conquer the Dutch East Indies, French Indochina, British Malaya, and Singapore. The navy's program shifted to a frankly opportunistic policy of taking advantage of the European war.

On the day Britain declared war on Germany, Captain Nakahara Yoshimasa, the foremost proponent of a southward advance ("the King of the South Seas"), wrote in his diary, "The important thing is to take this opportunity to reorient Japan as a sea power and concentrate its efforts on naval expansion." This was a restatement of the Mahanian sea power doctrine as applied to Southeast Asia. Nakahara asserted that Japan "must take advantage of the opportunity provided by the European war to quickly resort to the force of arms and control Southeast Asia." To attain this objective, he said, the Japanese navy should not flinch from fighting Britain and the United States.[1] In an expansive moment, Captain Nakahara wrote, "Under present circumstances, Japan must advance east of the Dutch East Indies to Malaya (naturally Australia would come under our control) and to the British possessions in the South Seas. For this purpose, an arms buildup program must be promoted."[2]

He thus linked his vision of southward expansion to the navy's call for fleet expansion. This accorded with the navy's demand for primacy in defense spending. But his program of armed southward advance was too extreme to be acceptable to leaders of the navy, who feared that it would bring war with the United States.

The navy's actual policy, set in October 1939, was based on the premise that Japan must not become embroiled in the European war. It gave priority to settlement of the China war, emphasizing that Japan must aim to make third parties stop assisting the Chinese Nationalists. This policy of noninvolvement in the European war was endorsed by the foreign, army, and navy ministries in late 1939. They rejected the radical view held by middle-echelon officers such as Nakahara that "the South Seas regions must become a part of our Empire's self-sufficient economic sphere."[3]

The navy had stiffened its attitude toward the United States after July 1939, when Washington presented the notice of abrogating the 1911 Treaty of Commerce and Navigation, to take effect in six months. This was in response to Japan's proclamation of "the New Order in East Asia" on 3 November 1938, directly contradicting America's Open Door policy in China and nullifying the Washington treaty system. Termination of the commercial treaty would remove the legal obstacle to commercial restriction; the United States would soon be free to impose economic sanctions. Navy leaders regarded abrogation seriously in light of Japan's dependence for petroleum and strategic materials. In 1939 Japan imported 90 percent of its oil from the United States. The commercial treaty expired on 26 January 1940, after which Japan was kept in a state of uncertainty.[4] As Secretary of State Hull later recollected, "I was careful to give them no enlightenment. I felt that our best tactic was to keep them guessing, which might bring them to a sense of the position in which their flagrant disregard of our rights and interests in China was placing them."[5] The Cabinet Planning Board complained that it became difficult to draft material mobilization plans.[6] The United States had embarked on a policy of economic deterrence, but Japan's reaction was to look south, especially toward the East Indies and Indochina, to free itself from dependence on the Anglo-American powers. Ambassador Grew warned President Roosevelt that this "sword of Damocles" might prompt Japan to strike south.[7]

Many members of the Roosevelt administration realized that economic sanctions, to be effective, must include an oil embargo, but it would be met by Japan's "forcibly taking over" the East Indies.[8] The East Indies, of course, was important to the United States because it supplied 90 percent of the nation's rubber and tin. The Roosevelt administration's search for a way to deter Japan by pressing it economically continued until late 1941.

On 20 October 1939 the Naval Affairs Bureau drafted a paper on policy toward the United States. It stated, "To cope with America's economic oppression, the supply of resources must be switched to countries other than the United States. Armaments should be stepped up to provide against any contingency in light of quick turns of American diplomacy, as shown by its notice to terminate the Treaty of Commerce."[9] It meant that southern policy would soon be activated.

The German blitzkrieg during May and June 1940 and the fall of the Netherlands and France brought a reversal of the policy of noninvolvement in Europe. German successes so dazzled Japanese officials as to generate clamors for the southern advance. As early as April 1940 a conference of section chiefs had declared that now was "the best chance to occupy the Dutch East Indies," and in June French Indochina seemed a "ripe persimmon." Shortly after the German conquest of France, middle-echelon officers urged that "the Empire must take advantage of the war to attack Southeast Asia."[10]

The Roosevelt administration was not prepared to condone Japan's southward drive, and decided to back up words with naval pressure. In April 1940 the president deployed the Pacific Fleet to Pearl Harbor, two thousand miles closer to Japan. As Admiral Harold R. Stark, Chief of Naval Operations, explained, the fleet was in Hawaii "because of the deterrent effect on the Japs going into the East Indies." Pacific Fleet Commander James O. Richardson had strenuously objected to the decision to retain the fleet at Pearl Harbor after its annual maneuvers, instead of returning it to southern California. He protested that the fleet in Hawaii was undermanned and unprepared for any offensive operation across the Pacific, but Roosevelt rejected his protest.[11]

Japanese admirals took very seriously the offensive capability of the Pacific Fleet at Pearl Harbor. They feared that the fleet in Hawaii would undermine their strategy. War games had convinced them that the Pacific Fleet could attack the flank of the Japanese fleet moving southward. Admiral Yamamoto called the Pacific Fleet in the Hawaiian base a "dagger pointed at Japan's heart." Admiral Fukudome Shigeru, head of the Operations Division, explained the strategic threat posed by the Pacific Fleet: "Now, with the U.S. Fleet already advanced to its Hawaiian base, it could readily move to the western Pacific, thus creating a definite threat to Japan. As long as it remained at its Hawaiian base, it concocted a strategic situation incomparably more tense and threatening to Japan than had existed when it was based on the Pacific coast."[12]

YOSHIDA OPPOSES THE SOUTHERN ADVANCE

Since his appointment in August 1939, Navy Minister Yoshida Zengo had been resisting pressure for the southward advance by the middle echelons. He was more convinced of the need for caution because a large-scale map maneuver conducted during 15–21 May 1940 demonstrated that a surprise attack on the Dutch East Indies would lead to simultaneous war with the United States, the Netherlands, and Britain. Conducted in the presence of leading members of the Naval General Staff and the Navy Ministry, the maneuver showed that only at the initial stage of hostilities could Japan hold its own; within a year and a half its fleet would be reduced to 50 percent of that of the United States. A "quick encounter, quick showdown" and the main-fleet engagement that provided the only chance for success were unlikely to occur. As the map maneuver of May 1940 had demonstrated, Japan had no chance of victory unless it could seize oil fields in the East Indies within four months after opening hostilities. The discrepancy between Japanese and American war materials turned out to be much more glaring than previously estimated. Japan would have no chance for success if the war turned into a protracted conflict.[13] The findings of this map exercise, on the largest scale prior to Pearl Harbor, strongly affected naval leaders. Yoshida's comments went straight to the point: "Even if we occupy the East Indies, it will be difficult to control sea routes to transport oil resources to Japan. If so, would it not be pointless to occupy the East Indies?"

In response, Rear Admiral Ugaki Matome, chief of the Operations Division, pointed out that because the navy's preoccupation was with a main-fleet engagement, protection of sea communications was secondary. This, he explained, was dictated by Japan's limited economic capacity. Therefore almost all of the warships, aircraft, weapons, and personnel had to be devoted to the Combined Fleet. Convoy escorts would have to be hastily assembled once war became imminent.[14] The navy's neglect of convoy protection, which was, in Mahanian tradition, focused on a big battleship encounter, continued until the Pearl Harbor attack and beyond, causing heavy casualties.

On 2 August, Yoshida assembled naval leaders at his official residence and discussed measures to be taken if the United States imposed an embargo. As stated, President Roosevelt had announced on 26 July that the United States would place all exports of aviation fuel and high-grade scrap and steel under federal license. The Japanese navy considered such a restriction, somewhat exaggeratedly, "a matter of life and death for our Empire." Vice Admiral Toyoda Soemu, head of the Naval Construction Department, stated that in the event of an embargo, vital war matériel could hold out only for a year. Hearing out the discussions, Yoshida spoke: "The Imperial Navy can fight the United States only for one year, but the United States will resort to a protracted war. To fight such a war is reckless in the extreme. Is ours not a shaky navy?"[15] Yoshida thus opposed any policy that involved risking war with the United States. Skeptical about Germany's victory, he rejected an armed advance into Indochina; he was sure that it would bring a total embargo. He also warned naval leaders never to be dragged by the army or to be swayed by their section chiefs and their subordinates.[16]

But Germany's conquests in the west had mesmerized middle-echelon officers, and Yoshida faced increasing difficulty containing their clamor for southward advance.[17] Japan's southward advance and the conclusion of a military alliance with Germany became the cornerstones of policy advocated by middle-echelon officers. In early September Navy Minster Yoshida, who almost single-handedly had been opposing the tide, suffered a physical and nervous collapse, followed by hospitalization and resignation.

OPPORTUNISTIC SOUTHERN POLICY

France had fallen on 18 June, and in early July 1940 the German invasion of the British Isles seemed imminent, promising the collapse of the British Empire. The rising tide of southward expansion found expression in a policy paper drafted on 3 July by a handful of the army's middle-rank staff. The army handed its draft to its navy counterparts for coordination on the following day. The document revealed their impatience to take advantage of the European war and resort to "use of force" against French Indochina and, depending on the circumstances, against the Dutch East Indies also. Opportunity for such military advance would arise when the British were defeated or when the United States entered the European war, with little strength to spare in the Pacific.[18] The explanatory memorandum that accompanied the army draft shows the full extent of the Greater East Asian Co-Prosperity Sphere, Japan's Lebensraum: "It is the mission of our Empire to free ourselves from dependence on Britain and the United States . . . and to establish a sphere of self-sufficiency, centering on the Japan-Manchuria-China core, and including South Sea areas east of India and north of Australia and New Zealand. Today the whole world is in the midst of great historic transformations, and such opportunity to act will never return. . . . Japan must anticipate use of force for a thoroughgoing solution of the southern problem."[19]

Navy representatives were pleasantly surprised by the army's swing to a policy of "defend the north and advance to the south," the navy's traditional policy. But the navy pointed out that the army draft's weakness was that it "did not consider relations with the United States seriously enough." The army had assumed that in moving southward, Japan would clash with Britain only, but the navy emphasized the "inseparability" of Britain and the United States, warning that such a clash would bring war with the United States as well.[20]

Yoshida was surprised by the slipshod nature of the army draft and directed his division and bureau chiefs to revise it. The differences between the navy and the army were never resolved, but without much deliberation or revision, the Liaison Conference of 27 July approved this document as a fundamental national policy bearing the ponderous title "Outline of the Main Principles for Coping with the Changing World Situation."[21] Given the portentous nature of the decision, it should have been discussed at the Imperial Conference. Yet the adoption of the "Main Principles" signaled the government's commitment to southward advance, a military alliance with Germany, and the navy's full-scale preparations against the United States.

In a significant passage the "Main Principles" stated, "In resorting to use of force, utmost efforts will be made to limit the enemy to Britain, but hostilities against the United States might become unavoidable, so sufficient preparations must be made."[22] Two days later, on 29 July, a worried emperor summoned the chiefs and vice chiefs of the Naval and Army General Staffs to ask about the new national policy. Though no record of his remarks has survived, it is known that he asked whether the navy had confidence in a victory like that of the Battle of the Sea of Japan. He was also apprehensive about an armed southern advance.[23] Indeed, until 1 December 1941, the emperor was to make clear his desire for peace. He repeatedly expressed his worries and dissatisfactions through exhortations, warnings, queries, and even scolding. As a constitutional monarch, however, he chose not to reject the unanimous decisions of the Liaison Conferences.

What attracts attention in the formulation of the "Main Principles" for our purpose is the navy's emphasis on the prospect of war with the United States. The navy's memorandum, prepared for discussion with army representatives, stressed that "since war with the United States may become unavoidable, suffi-cient preparations must be made for this eventuality." How serious was the navy's talk of war with the United States? The available documentation shows that naval leaders wanted to avoid an armed southern advance that would bring war with the United States. Their primary concern was rapid fleet expansion. Faced with America's naval buildup, the navy feared that Japan would be forced to "succumb without putting up a fight."[24]

But in demanding a larger share of budget and matériel, the navy was in a bind in relation to the army. The navy had a chance in a quick and short war, but it had no confidence in an attritional war, which was most likely to ensue. But the navy would not come right out and say this, especially when demanding budget allocations. Bureaucratic factors go far to explain the navy's stand. As Commander Kawai Iwao of the Operations Section testified, "If we say the navy is not con-fident, then the army would take away the navy's share of matériel and try to cut down the naval budget. This was the navy's weakness until the very end. . . . Inwardly we felt we could not fight with the Anglo-American powers, but we could not unequivocally say so. We have called ourselves an invincible navy and we have been telling the army that we could take on the United States. . . . So, we could not say we lacked confidence now. We were afraid that the army would say, 'If the navy can't fight, give us your matériel and budget.'"[25]

This dilemma (if we can call it that) was to immobilize the navy leaders' efforts to avoid war. (We have already seen how interservice bureaucratic considerations immobilized the navy's opposition to the Tripartite Pact.) To put it simply, the navy was using a huge budget to build ships and produce airplanes, while saying Japan must avoid war with the United States. This was a reasonable position, but once army-navy rivalry was injected, a bitter bureaucratic conflict emerged. The army would say that the navy, having used up its huge budget, was hardly in a position to say it could not fight the United States. If the navy could not fight, the army would say, why not give the entire naval budget to the army, so that the army could combine both budgets and complete armaments against the Soviet Union?[26] Until the late fall of 1941, this interservice contention bred mutual suspicion bordering on a feud.

Behind the emphasis on the need for naval preparations lay frantic efforts to cope with the escalating naval race with the United States. The navy urgently sought precedence over the army in budget and matériel allocations. In interservice negotiation Vice Chief of the Naval General Staff Kondō infuriated the army by demanding the army's share of war matériel so that the navy could complete war preparations.[27] As usual, the army suspected that the navy was using "danger of war with the United States" as a lever for appropriations.

The background of the navy's preoccupation with arms buildup was the huge building programs the United States had announced in the wake of German conquest in Europe. In June 1940, Congress passed the third Vinson Act, followed in July by the Stark Plan. In just two months Congress had provided astronomical funds to America's gigantic building programs, which came as a shock to the Japanese navy. Caught in the ever-escalating arms race and seeking to establish precedence over the army, the navy desperately needed a rationale. Viewed in this context, the navy's belligerent stance toward the United States, as expressed in the "Main Principles," was more budget- and matériel-minded than war-minded. In fact, the navy's demand for a larger share of steel in the revised materials mobilization plan was to result in an increase of 283,000 tons, which reversed the army-navy precedence.[28]

THE ESCALATING NAVAL RACE

Back in May 1935, Prince Fushimi, chief of the Naval General Staff, had reported to the throne that the navy was confident that, after the demise of the Washington and London treaties, Japan would be able to maintain a naval strength of 70 to 80 percent of the American fleet for ten years.[29] Within a few years this prospect had vanished.

In 1937, Japan embarked on the Third Replenishment Program, a large-scale plan that provided for sixty-six ships, including two *Yamato*-class super-battleships and two carriers. This was Japan's first replenishment program after the Washington-London treaties expired. To cope with the new crisis occasioned by the China war, the U.S. Congress passed in May 1938 the second Vinson Bill, authorizing an increase of 20 percent—sixty-nine ships and a buildup to eighteen battleships. This marked the first time the American fleet went above the limits set by the Washington and London treaties. It was four times the size of Japan's Third Replenishment Program, and the navy feared that the American plan, when completed, would reduce Japan's strength to 50 percent. It would, the navy feared, "overpower Japan by force of arms and depriving Japan of all its special position in China."[30] To counter the second Vinson Plan, Japan launched its Fourth Replenishment Program in 1939, a year earlier than planned. This program was larger than the third plan—eighty ships, including two more *Yamato*-class battleships, and doubled air power in five years.

Then in June 1940, Congress, threatened with the German conquest of Britain and Japan's imminent advance southward, announced the third Vinson Plan, an 11 percent increase of naval strength in a two-year period—twenty ships, including three carriers and fifteen hundred aircraft. It was followed on 19 July by the Stark Plan, the so-called Two-Ocean Navy, which enabled the U.S. Navy to conduct simultaneous operations in both the Atlantic and Pacific. It provided for expanding the American fleet by 70 percent and fifteen hundred aircraft. The American plans amounted to more than 2 million tons, four times Japan's Third and Fourth Replenishment Programs put together (560,000 tons) and four times Japan's projected air power.

The announcement of the "astronomical" Two-Ocean Navy plan came as a great shock to the Japanese navy. Recognizing that industrial inferiority precluded quantitative competition, the navy tried to counter the American plans qualitatively by placing a special emphasis on the *Yamato*-class superbattleship. The Naval General Staff agonized as it began preparing the Fifth Replenishment Program, which was ready in rough form in January 1941. It called for twice the ships and aircraft provided for by the Fourth Replenishment Program, and included three more superbattleships mounting 20-inch (instead of 18-inch) guns.[31]

The shipbuilding capacity of the United States was estimated to be three times that of Japan, perhaps five to six times if the mass-production systems were applied to fleet expansion. According to the Naval General Staff's estimate, Japan's capital ship ratio compared to the United States would reduce to about 50 percent in 1943, and to 30 percent or less by 1944. As for aircraft, American productive capacity would be more than ten times that of Japan. At the end of 1941, Japan's naval strength would reach a peak of 70 percent of the U.S. Navy's, but the United States would be building three times as many ships as Japan. The navy insisted that only by obtaining primacy in naval armaments could it confront the U.S. Navy. Naval planners declared that only by striking the United States in 1941 would Japan have a chance in a war.

THE LOGIC OF MUTUAL ESCALATION

By this time the Japanese navy feared that the United States might impose an oil embargo. Indeed, the hawks in the Roosevelt administration (Henry L. Stimson, Harold Ickes, and Henry Morgenthau) had been urging a total oil embargo. The American navy was split on the oil embargo, but senior admirals feared that an oil embargo would goad Japan into attacking the Dutch East Indies and that this would bring war. Admiral Stark, Chief of Naval Operations, strongly opposed any diversion from Europe, asking for "no open rupture" with Japan "particularly at this time." In the end, on 26 July 1940, Washington settled on a compromise that placed scrap iron and oil under license; on 31 July it prohibited export of aviation-grade gasoline and lubricating oil. Roosevelt hoped that Japan would be deterred by a firm, though not crushing, show of American will.[32] But this did not have much deterrent effect on Japan, which could purchase all other petroleum products in the United States. But a total oil embargo would be an entirely different matter.

A significant paper prepared by the Naval General Staff on 1 August stated that Japan would go to war if the United States threatened Japan's "existence" by imposing a total embargo or "apply, singly or in cooperation with Britain, such pressures as would threaten Japan's existence." The new policy was part of a broader scenario presented in the Operations Division's paper "A Study on Policy toward Indochina," which postulated that a chain reaction would be set in motion by advance into Indochina. This document contained a peculiar style of circular reasoning: (1) To strengthen Japan's strategic position in the event of war with the United States, Japan would march into Indochina, both northern and southern, for raw materials and strategic advantages; (2) the United States would retaliate by imposing a total trade embargo on Japan; (3) the oil embargo, a matter of life or death to Japan, would in turn compel Japan to seize the East Indies to secure oil resources; and (4) this step would involve a "determination to initiate hostilities" against the United States.[33] A paper prepared by Naval General Staff officials on 28 August again spelled out this vicious cycle theory: "If the United States resorts to total embargo, Japan will have to strike to obtain the necessities for the Empire and if the United States and Britain, jointly or singly, should oppress Japan and alter the status quo in the Pacific to endanger the Empire's national defense, the Empire cannot help but resort to force in the south."[34] Not until the spring of 1941, however, did this scenario begin to be activated and the demand for advance into southern Indochina prevail. Meanwhile Japan advanced into northern Indochina.

THE ADVANCE TO NORTHERN INDOCHINA

Northern Indochina was strategically important to Japan, because one of the most practicable supply routes into southern China to aid the Chiang regime originated in Tonkin and because this region was the gateway to Southeast Asia. The objective in negotiations with the French authorities in Indochina was passage of Japanese troops and use of air bases. Indochinese authorities refused to accept the demands, but the fall of France in June 1940 undermined them. On 22 September, Japanese troops began entering northern Indochina. Japan did not expect a peaceful intervention to bring American embargo. However, whether peaceful or not, the entry of troops into a foreign territory was a grave matter and the United States saw it as a prelude to further advance into Southeast Asia.

Japan's entrance into northern Indochina, followed by the Tripartite Pact with Germany and Italy on 26 September, surprised the United States, but it adhered to the policy of nonappeasement and nonprovocation. Although hawks in the Roosevelt administration renewed their quest for drastic economic sanctions, Roosevelt and his advisers kept to a Europe-first policy. As stated, Admiral Stark was convinced that Japan, if denied oil, would seize the East Indies. Roosevelt, therefore, responded on 26 September with an embargo limited to iron and scrap metal. He hoped Japan would be deterred by the show of American will; but Japan's middle-echelon planners instead pressed for a further southward drive.[35]

After forces went into northern Indochina, navy planners weighed the pros and cons of an advance into southern Indochina also. They held that occupation or military use of Saigon and Cam Ranh Bay would enhance Japan's position for operations against the United States. On the other hand, they feared the "greater risk" of an American embargo, "a matter of life and death for our Empire." While the navy was not prepared to take this risk, it secretly instituted on 15 November a preparatory fleet mobilization, a step toward converting the navy to wartime footing. This was a departure from Navy Minister Yonai's policy of eschewing any measures that anticipated and prepared for hostilities.[36]

THE RISE OF HARD-LINERS

As a result of an informal agreement by which the navy consented to the Tripartite Pact in return for priority in war matériel, it gained precedence over the army in mobilization plans. The navy could now be more confident of its preparedness. But instead of calming the clamor for a belligerent policy that was motivated by demand for naval budget, the progress in the navy's preparations ironically encouraged bellicose middle-echelon officers to advocate war. In October 1940, Vice Admiral Inoue, who had been transferred from chief of staff of the Third (China) Fleet to head the Naval Aviation Department, was surprised to see how much the Anglo-American powers were held in contempt.[37] That same month Commander Kami Shigenori of the Operations Section in charge of war preparations and operational plans told his army counterpart that by mid-April 1941—when Japan would attain a peak ratio of 75 percent of U.S. fleet strength—southern operations must be conducted, which meant war with the Anglo-American powers; "*otherwise it would be difficult to control young officers.*"[38] Here was an undisguised expression of the "ratio neurosis" that Inoue had derided. Of course, the 70 or 75 percent ratio, obtained when hostilities began, would become meaningless once the war began, because the United States, mobilizing its gigantic strength, would greatly outbuild the Japanese navy. However, fixation with ratio was by no means confined to the middle echelons. Vice Chief of the Naval General Staff Kondō Nobutake had been arguing that because the navy's preparations would be complete by April 1941, it would be to Japan's advantage to strike at its peak level of 70 percent. Japan's relative strength would never be better than in 1941, and the superbattleship *Yamato* and its sister ship *Musashi* would soon follow. Kondō argued on 14 September 1940, when he consented to the Tripartite Pact, "We stand a chance of success in a quick and decisive war" if hostilities commenced in 1941. In a protracted war, however, he feared that the United States "would rapidly outbuild Japan and the disparity between naval ratios will progressively widen so that Japan will not be able to cope with it."[39]

From his flagship, *Nagato*, Combined Fleet Commander Admiral Yamamoto tried to restrain such war talk. He warned that shortage of matériel precluded war. On 26–28 November he conducted a war game in the presence of leaders of the Naval General Staff, the Combined Fleet, and the Naval Staff College. In this war game he tried to demonstrate how grave the deficiencies in Japan's matériel and preparations were. He also warned that section chiefs and their subordinates had been bragging that the time had come to strike in the south. And in a letter of 10 December to Admiral Shimada Shigetarō, his Naval Academy classmate, he warned, "The probability is great that the launching of our operation against the Netherlands Indies will bring an early commencement of war with America, and since Britain and Holland will side with America, our operation against the Netherlands is almost certain to develop into a war with America, Britain, and the Netherlands. Consequently we should not launch the southern operation."[40]

Yamamoto's apprehension did not reach middle-echelon officers. From late 1940 onward the navy, prompted by middle-echelon officers like Captain Ishikawa and Commander Fujii, began to seize the initiative by drafting programs for southward advance. They were fatalistic about the coming of the war with the United States.[41]

When the border dispute between Thailand and French Indochina broke out in January 1941, the navy prepared to use force if necessary to press Indochina into accepting Japan's terms. On 24 January the emperor summoned the chiefs of the Army and Navy General Staffs and warned them about the "grave consequences" of provoking the Anglo-American powers, which had "very strong influence in Thailand." When this border dispute escalated into a clash in February, the Japanese government, fearing Thailand might seek British protection, intervened. Tokyo decided to take coercive actions—the army by reinforcing troops in northern Indochina and the navy by maneuvering in Indochinese waters. The navy's clamor for air bases and harbor installations in Indochina had become so shrill that it not only deeply worried the emperor but also provoked the United States and surprised even the Army General Staff.[42] "As long as the mutual provocation is allowed to go unchecked," Commander Fujii became convinced, "a Japanese-American war will become inevitable." On 11 February Fujii wrote, "Establishment of a self-existent and self-sufficient sphere is our strategic imperative, and building of military bases [in Southeast Asia] is a self-defensive measure." If the United States imposed a total embargo or stepped up its military pressure on Japan, this would threaten Japan's "self-existence" and "self-defense," and it would have to resort to "armed southern drive and war with the United States." (As Admiral Inoue later pointed out, "self-existence" and "self-defense" were much abused slogans whose meanings were never made clear, but they were used as if they were self-evident.) A memorandum that Captain Ōno Takeji, war guidance officer, handed to his army counterpart took it for granted that "an armed advance southward spells war with the United States."[43]

The belligerent attitude of these middle echelons alarmed Admiral Yamamoto. On 15 February 1941 from the Nagato he wrote a message to be delivered to Navy Minister Oikawa: "As to our military demands [on Indochina and Thailand], no one will doubt that these steps constitute advances in our military position against the Anglo-American powers. . . . In the final analysis, the new policy contains the dangerous probability that events will develop into a war against the United States and Great Britain. . . . Judging from the fact that the United States is no longer merely posturing, if we decide to apply military pressure in French Indochina, we may suddenly find ourselves in a critical situation."[44]

In late March 1941 the navy restated its position on war. "Japan must resort to force," it held, "when the United States, alone or in cooperation with Britain and the Netherlands, imposes total embargo," thus threatening Japan's "self-existence and self-defense." On 17 April, the Naval General Staff elaborated this point in an important policy paper, "The Outline of Policy toward the South," that Japan must resort to force "for the sake of self-existence and self defense when the United States alone or in cooperation with Britain, the Netherlands, and China, etc. should tighten their encirclement of Japan, thus creating a intolerable situation for Japan."[45]

Interservice negotiations in March convinced the army representative that the navy had abandoned its opportunistic policy of taking advantage of the European war to advance southward (as spelled out in the "Main Principles"). Hitler, having failed to win the Battle of Britain, seemed to have given up invasion of the British Isles, at least for the moment. The navy appeared to have retreated from the "Main Principles," which was based on a German victory. However, the navy had actually taken a step closer to war when it decided it must fight with the United States in the event of total embargo. The navy thus reaffirmed its logic of mutual escalation first formulated on 1 August 1940 by the Operations Section: advancing to south Indochina would provoke total embargo, which in turn would force Japan to "determine" to go to war with the United States. The navy's southern policy, then, hinged on whether the United States would resort to a total embargo.

Meanwhile, the navy's upper-echelon leaders, hoping to avoid war, rejected this logic of mutual escalation. On 20 March the navy representative restated to his army counterpart that the navy was "not prepared to resort to force against the United States, but war preparations are necessary and the navy will demand priority in matériel and budget."[46] Again the navy's stance was "war preparations without war determination." The Confidential War Journal of the army's War Guidance Office scathingly noted, "If the navy is advocating war with the United States for the sake of expanding its own armaments, are they not traitors to the country?"[46] But just then, in April 1941, the navy's middle-echelon officers were stepping up their pressure for "war determination." Fujii, who had returned from his tour of Europe as Matsuoka's attendant, stated, "Is it not our mission to move with irresistible force, resolutely undertake war with America, eradicate all the damages wrought by the Anglo-American powers, and save our next generation from the bitter experience we have suffered?"[47]

THE FIRST COMMITTEE URGES DETERMINATION FOR WAR

In retrospect, the replacement in April 1941 of the ailing Prince Fushimi with Nagano Osami as chief of the Naval General Staff was a milestone on the navy's road to Pearl Harbor. Prince Fushimi had nominated Nagano. Nagano came to head the Naval General Staff just when middle echelons began to take the initiative. By this time Nagano had fatalistically concluded that war was inevitable and that no efforts could prevent it. In fact, of all the ranking naval officers he became the strongest and earliest war advocate. Nicknamed "Elephant" or "Big Gun" for his physique and for his once having been a pugnacious Combined Fleet commander, he had visibly slowed down at age sixty-one.

As a young man Nagano was a fine figure, having graduated at the top of his class at the Naval Academy and serving as language officer at Harvard (1913–15) and as attaché in Washington (1920–23), but his understanding of America had long since faded and in 1941 he became the leading war advocate. A full admiral since March 1934, he had held a string of important posts—president of the Naval Academy, vice chief of the Naval General Staff, navy minister, and Combined Fleet commander—but he was miscast as the chief of the Naval General Staff at this critical point. Apparently the only reason he was appointed was that he was the oldest admiral on the active list. By this time, instead of controlling his subordinates, he left the field to aggressive middle-echelon officers, to whose pressure he was more than amenable. An impulsive man, he tended to make abrupt bellicose statements at meetings that stunned his colleagues. He lacked the moral courage to lead; instead, he swallowed the recommendations of such fireeaters as Ishikawa and the members of the First Committee. He was aware that he did not have the emperor's trust, yet he remained in his post. Admiral Kobayashi Seizō (Ret.), who kept an anxious eye on him, attributed the hardening of Nagano's attitude in the early summer of 1941 to deteriorating health and the influence of aggressive middle-echelon officers.[48] His vice chief, the pliant Kondō, who had also been calling for hostilities, could hardly be expected to restrain Nagano. The succeeding vice chief, Itō Seiichi, a good public-relations type, was opposed to war but did not forcefully speak out.

In the navy ministry, Oikawa, though opposed to war, lacked conviction and willpower. In the Liaison Conference he was strangely silent while Nagano spoke about the strategy of the coming war. Upon Oikawa's appointment as navy minister, the emperor had expressed doubts about his leadership qualities. As navy minister Oikawa was a disaster. He had never served in the navy ministry before and did not understand politics. He was notorious for his willingness to please everybody all the time. His vice minister, Sawamoto Yorio, was a moderate and opposed to war, but he served mainly as a good bureaucrat and did not have much influence on his chief. And the head of the Naval Affairs Bureau, Oka, a cautious and apt player of naval politics, served mainly as a mediator between Oikawa and Nagano. Neither Sawamoto nor Oka was a strong character who could effectively control bellicose subordinates.

In a desperate effort to stem the drift, Combined Fleet Commander Yamamoto Isoroku urged Navy Minister Oikawa to buttress the navy's leadership by appointing Admiral Yonai as chief of the Naval General Staff, Admiral Yoshida or Rear Admiral Koga Mineichi as vice chief, and Vice Admiral Inoue as vice navy minister. Not surprisingly, Oikawa ignored this appeal, losing the last chance to rebuild a leadership that could be relied on to avert war.[49]

The middle-echelon "nucleus group," now asserting a sort of collective leadership through the First Committee and composed of leading hawks of sectionchief rank, became the locus of the navy's policy making. (See pp. 235–36.) As these middle-echelon officers grew more vociferous, narrow strategic requirements dominated the making of national policy. Their demands for war preparations would eventually drive the ranking naval leaders into an impasse, forcing their determination for war.

By April 1941, preparatory fleet mobilization had made satisfactory progress and planners counted on soon attaining a peak ratio of 70 percent in relation to the United States. Now was the time, they argued, to start a war. The section chiefs conference had come out in favor of opening hostilities. Captain Tomioka Sadatoshi, Chief of the Operations Section, told Chief of the Operations Division Fukudome, "The prospect of winning is good enough: let's make up our minds to join battle now." Captain Ishikawa was heard to say, "Now is the time to strike; we won't be defeated."[50]

Occupation of strategic areas in the south was considered essential in preparing for war. In late April the head of the Intelligence Division, Rear Admiral Maeda Minoru, was secretly dispatched to Indochina and Thailand to estimate the consequences of an advance into southern Indochina. He reported, "Britain will not repulse our move by force of arms because of the insufficient state of its armaments in Singapore. Nor would America rise in opposition—although it *might conceivably resort to an oil embargo.* If we are to march into south Indochina, the sooner the better."[51] He urged that Japan advance into southern Indochina in preparation for war with the United States. On 5 June he reported to Prime Minister Konoe, "The navy deems it quite safe to move into southern Indochina." Maeda regarded it as preemptive occupation of strategic points before the United States could militarily move in. This head of the Intelligence Division, a disciple of Katō Kanji, had scant knowledge of America, having made only cursory stops in passing. Yet, he styled himself a "leading war advocate." Captain Ishikawa was of the same mind. Ever since 1936, Ishikawa had been predicting that Nazi Germany would rise up in arms around 1940, which would be a golden opportunity for Japan to break through the "ABCD encirclement." He said war would become "inevitable" in October or November 1941.

On 5 June the First Committee produced a notable policy paper titled "The Attitude to Be Adopted by the Imperial Navy under the Present Circumstances," drafted by Commander Fujii under Captain Ishikawa's direction.[52] Pervading this document was the fatalistic belief that war with the United States was "unavoidable." The authors displayed confidence gained by the progress in the navy's preparatory mobilization program. They demanded an end to the nagging uncertainty and the vacillation of superiors, which had made it impossible to push war preparations to the final stage. They feared that, as long as war or peace hung in the balance, Japan would lose the opportunity to strike. The navy held "the key to the issue of war or peace," and the time had come when naval leaders must decide on war with the United States and seize "by armed force"

Indochina, the East Indies, and Thailand regardless of the outcome of the Hull-Nomura negotiations in Washington.

The First Committee justified these moves as "preemptive" actions against the Anglo-American "military offensive." It maintained that inasmuch as the United States was reinforcing the Philippines, aiding Chinese aviation, preparing joint strategies with Britain, and consolidating its strategic, political, and economic position in Southeast Asia, Japan found itself forestalled on all fronts unless it moved quickly into southern Indochina. The committee members feared that the United States and Britain might "establish military positions in Thailand, French Indochina, and South China." Their paper made much of the "ABCD encirclement" that forced Japan to strike southward.[53] There was, of course, no evidence that such an "encirclement" ever existed. But the notion of being oppressed cast a spell on middle-echelon planners, who argued for breaking through for the sake of "self-existence and self-defense." It never occurred to them that if Japan had not advanced southward in the first place, there would have been no such "encirclement."

One genuine threat was the rapid buildup of American air power in the Philippines. The navy had not foreseen such a buildup in the Philippines at the time of the Second London Conference in 1935 when it unthinkingly abandoned the Pacific nonfortification provision of the Washington Five-Power Treaty. Now Secretary of War Stimson saw that B-17 long-range heavy bombers (Flying Fortresses) in the Philippines would serve not only as a deterrent against Japanese aggression but also in the strategic air offensive against Japan.[54] Gradually the United States was coming to view the Philippines as a strategic asset rather than a liability, which they long had been.

The mood surrounding the 5 June document of the First Committee was expressed by Captain Nakahara, the leading advocate of the southward drive: "Our Empire is encircled by the enemies and the advance into Indochina is the first step in our efforts to find a way out of the fatal situation."[55] Similarly Fujii, who drafted the report of the First Committee, wrote in his diary, "If the United States and Great Britain stand in the way of Japan's southward advance, we must strike them." He was satisfied that the committee's report "seems to have a great impact on the top leadership from the navy minister on down and had considerable effect in crystallizing their determination for war." He further wrote, "Around this time my efforts to persuade my superiors succeeded and both the Navy Minister and the chief of the Naval General Staff have become extremely belligerent. They are now determined not to flinch from war with the United States and Britain."[56]

That the report of the First Committee had an impact on Oikawa is doubtful, but it certainly impressed Nagano, who used to say that he "trusted the middle-rank officers most because they are in the know." His remarks at the Liaison Conferences of 11 and 12 June reflected the report of the First Committee: "We must build bases in French Indochina and Thailand in order to launch military operations. We must resolutely attack anyone who tries to stop us. We must resort to force if necessary." Again: "If the Anglo-American powers should take countermeasures and threaten our self-existence, we must risk war with them."[57] His clamor for an advance to southern Indochina seemed more vociferous than even the army's posture.

Throughout these meetings Navy Minister Oikawa remained silent. Captain Ishikawa's diary conveys the sense of mounting impatience among middle-echelon officers: "Our Empire is under siege by enemies, and by resorting to war we will be taking a desperate action to break through and seek our survival. And this step must be taken just as soon as possible because of accelerated Anglo-American military and economic oppression of Japan, the dwindling of our fighting capability (especially with regard to the stockpile of matériel), and considerations of the morale of the Japanese people."[58]

THE GERMAN-SOVIET WAR AND JAPAN

On 22 June Hitler invaded the Soviet Union, a total surprise to the Japanese. The army advocated an immediate attack on Russia, but the navy opposed deviating from its southward advance. Washington was aware of differences. Following Japan's internal division through the Magic intercepts (intercepted and deciphered Japanese diplomatic messages), President Roosevelt wrote Harold Ickes on 24 June:

> I think it will interest you to know that the Japs are having a real dragdown and knockout fight among themselves . . . trying to decide which way they are going to jump—attack Russia, attack the South Seas (thus throwing their lot definitely with Germany), or whether they will sit on the fence and be more friendly with us. No one knows what the decision will be but, as you know, it is terribly important for the control of the Atlantic for us to help keep peace in the Pacific. I simply have not got enough Navy to go round—and every little episode in the Pacific means fewer ships in the Atlantic.[59]

On 23 June, middle-echelon officers such as Commanders Fujii and Onoda Satejirō decided that "to remove every obstacle to our drive southward, we must first obtain military bases in French Indochina." At this meeting Nagano abruptly called for war with the United States and Britain. Fujii then drafted a paper stating that Japan "must advance to the important southern area and lay the foundations for its self-existence and self-defense." For this purpose Japan "would not flinch from war with the Anglo-American powers." Despite this belligerent statement, the army representatives still did not believe the navy had come around to "determination" for war and, as usual, regarded the navy's posture as "a means of winning naval arms expansion and budgetary appropriation."[60]

The German-Soviet war had intensified Japanese expansionism and opportunism, and as President Roosevelt predicted, it accentuated army-navy differences over northern or southern advance. At the same time it strengthened the relative position of the United States. Whichever direction Japan moved, historian Waldo H. Heinrichs wrote, "Japan must be boxed in, contained, immobilized." And the strongest weapon for deterrence was economic embargo.[61] The Japanese leaders, engrossed in their dispute about a northern or southern march, failed to see America's incipient hardening of attitude toward Japan.

At the crucial Imperial Conference of 2 July, leaders formally decided that "war preparations against Great Britain and the United States [must] be stepped up." Japan would advance into the southern region to preempt its position in French Indochina and Thailand, and "our Empire will not desist from war with the Anglo-American powers." This was an irrevocable decision on the highest level of the government. Nagano added that "in view of the still greater tightening of Anglo-American oppression of Japan, we must be resolved not to flinch from a war with Britain and the United States in order to break through their oppression."[62] This was the first time that the top naval leader *officially* stated that Japan must not flinch from war with the Anglo-American powers. This significant phrase was included at the navy's insistence, but the army considered—and rightly so—that it was really aimed at obtaining a larger naval budget and more matériel. In the words of Captain Ōno Takeji, the navy's war guidance officer, this stipulation merely gave the navy "grounds for expediting preparations for the Anglo-American powers."[63]

Navy Vice Minister Sawamoto, startled by the bellicose statements of the navy at the 2 July conference, questioned Navy Minister Oikawa about his real intention. Oikawa minimized its importance, explaining, "I want to avoid war [with the United States], but the army demands attacking both north and south, so we could not restrain the army with anything less [than strong demand for southward advance]." Captain Ōno later stated that if the army entered war with the Soviet Union, it would take both budget and matériel, so the navy must show that it was prepared to advance southward in order to augment its armaments. "It did not mean that we were really thinking of starting a war."[75] The ministry's ranking leaders were not ready for war with the United States, but felt obliged to forcefully clamor for southward expansion in order to prevent the army from attacking the Soviet Union. As historian Hatano Sumio remarks, marching to southern French Indochina was no longer an external question but had become a domestic question of army-navy contention. No wonder the navy was not sufficiently concerned with how the United States would respond.[64]

Again, the navy's bureaucratic concern for budget and matériel was the real but hidden motive of its belligerent stance. The navy felt that in order to contain the army, it had no choice but to advance southward at the risk of war. But navy ministry leaders were not actually thinking of starting a war.[65] Lacking objective assessment of the international situation and a realistic estimate of the chance of victory, the navy was absorbed in "contention, rivalry, and negotiations with the army."[66] Not surprisingly, the Liaison Conference and army-navy meetings failed thoroughly to discuss whether advancing into southern Indochina would trigger a total American embargo. As for the stipulation that Japan would not "desist from war with the Anglo-American powers," which had been inserted at the navy's request, army representatives, as usual, did not believe this indicated the navy's determination for war. They saw the navy's belligerent posture merely as a means of acquiring budget and matériel.[67]

FATAL DECISION: ADVANCE IN SOUTHERN INDOCHINA

At the Liaison Conference of 21 July, Nagano said he had decided on war and argued for prompt commencement of hostilities: "Although there is now a chance of achieving victory, the chance will diminish as time goes by. . . . The United States will probably prolong the [Hull-Nomura] negotiations until it has completed its naval preparations. . . . Accordingly, with the passage of time, the Empire will be put up with a mounting disadvantage. Moreover, if we occupy the Philippines, it will be easier, from the navy's point of view, to carry on the war."[68]

This was the first time Nagano stated so starkly and boldly an offensive plan against the United States. Nagano's belligerent statement was based on the First Committee's 5 June report. Vice Chief Kondō was equally bellicose: "If we don't start war now, we shall be 'gradually pauperized,' until finally we don't have the slightest chance of success. The strength of air power in the Philippines is about a third that of Japan now and we must strike before it becomes one half that of Japan. If they further reinforce their buildup, we won't be able to cope with it. So we must promptly reach our determination [for war]." Navy Vice Minister

Sawamoto felt that talk of striking the Philippines was ill advised, because it gave the wrong impression to the army, namely that the navy had completed its armament and did not need further funding.[69]

During all this time Navy Minister Oikawa still hoped that war could somehow be avoided, but he remained passive and silent in meetings. Although the feeling in the Naval General Staff had turned to war, leaders of the ministry, though acquiescing in the southward drive, hoped it could be accomplished without triggering war. Chief of the Naval Affairs Bureau Oka, taking pains to mediate between Oikawa and Nagano, recalled, "We did not think America would impose a total embargo, *although we did recognize the risk.* But when the ABCD encirclement threatened Japan, there was no other alternative but to accede to the demands of the high command."[70] Oka implied that ministry leaders could not resist the demands of the Naval General Staff.

Whatever the thoughts of Oikawa, there is little doubt that Nagano and some of his subordinates knew they were taking a very serious risk of American reprisal in the form of total embargo when they decided to send forty thousand troops into southern Indochina on 28 and 29 July. As he put his stamp of approval on the drive into southern Indochina, Nagano was heard muttering, "This means war with America." Captain Ishikawa had foreseen that a total embargo would spell war with the United States. Captain Tomioka, chief of the Operations Section, considered the chance of an embargo "fifty-fifty." Commander Onoda, liaison officer between the Naval General Staff and the Navy Ministry, believed that "with the move into Indochina Japan crossed the Great Divide. After this event there was no turning back." Oka recollected, "The response of the Anglo-American powers will become serious, but I did not anticipate [that the Americans would] go as far as a total embargo."[71]

Oikawa made up his mind to advance to southern Indochina after he received Rear Admiral Maeda's report and an assurance from Captain Chūdō, chairman of the Indochina Expeditionary Committee, that "the advance into southern Indochina would not lead to war with the Anglo-American powers." In a similar vein, Fukudome, chief of the Operations Division, later recalled that he did not even dream that advancing into southern Indochina would bring war with the United States.[72] Even if the ranking ministry leaders feared such an outcome, they lacked the grit to oppose it, instead drifting with the current. Rear Admiral Oka, head of the Naval Affairs Bureau, felt it was "a dangerous situation, but I did not feel that the United States would go to the extent of imposing a total embargo, but it could not be helped."[73] These naval officials simply ignored telegrams from Ambassador Nomura Kichisaburō in Washington, who repeatedly warned that a drive to southern Indochina would bring an American embargo.

Ishikawa and Maeda, who had accepted that war with America would take place in the fall of 1941, would not be surprised by an embargo. Committed to the logic of mutual escalation, they took it for granted that the advance to southern Indochina would result in a total embargo, forcing Japan to commence hostilities.

Just as with the conclusion of the Tripartite Pact, the leaders of the fleets and those in charge of armaments were completely left out of the decision for southward advance; upon being informed of the decision, they were furious. On 3 July, an incensed Inoue, head of the Aviation Department, denounced the top leaders for their failure to consult him. "You cannot make such a decision unless you are determined to fight the United States, but our aircraft production is making very slow progress. I cannot take responsibility if hostilities are opened." Yamamoto curtly questioned Oikawa, "Do we have sufficient planes to fight the United States?"[74] But they were not in central decision-making positions and their objections were futile.

By this time Nagano had given up any hope for Ambassador Nomura's negotiations in Washington. On 24 July, Nagano met with Admiral Kobayashi Seizō (Ret.), former leader of the treaty faction and ex-governor general of Taiwan, to discuss a letter from Nomura dated 20 June in which Nomura emphasized the risk of southward advance. Nagano told Kobayashi that the situation had drastically changed during the past month and that he had decided that "there was no way but to fight." He said he had reliable information that the United States had decided on war. "The United States is greatly reinforcing its armaments surrounding Japan and completing an ABCD encirclement. With the completion of this iron chain strangulating our neck the United States would doubtless tell us, 'Listen to what we say, or we will tighten our squeeze.' Having reached this impasse, there is no way but to stand up resolutely and cut through the iron chain. Compromise settlement through diplomatic negotiations is something we can hardly accept."[75]

In marching into southern Indochina, Japan had taken a fateful step. Thenceforth it was in a position to threaten the East Indies, the Philippines, and Malaya. On 29 July, Nagano was again reported to have muttered, "This means war." When Nagano had an audience and stated that he was doubtful of the outcome of a war with the United States, the emperor sharply scolded him for planning for a "desperate war."[76] Ever since he had opposed the Tripartite Pact, he had been warning and restraining the military.[77]

Before we proceed with America's stringent reaction to Japan's advance to southern Indochina, we will pause here to examine the desperate efforts of Admiral Nomura Kichisaburō, Ambassador to Washington, to prevent the advance to southern Indochina, which he knew to be a step destined to bring war.

NAVY DIPLOMAT NOMURA'S PEACE EFFORTS

Nomura had been called out of retirement at age sixty-four to be ambassador to Washington. The Foreign Ministry was having difficulty filling the vacancy in the embassy, and he was the "last trump card" of the navy's upper echelons opposed to war. His career seemed ideally suited to this mission. Having graduated from the Naval Academy in 1898 second in his class, he served from 1914 to 1918 as attaché in Washington, where he met Franklin D. Roosevelt, then Assistant Secretary of the Navy.[77] The Office of Naval Intelligence remembered Nomura's attaché days: "He is frank, honest, broad-minded, levelheaded and outspoken. As the result of the courtesies shown him during his three years as Naval Attaché in Washington he feels most friendly and grateful toward Americans in general, but particularly toward Naval Officers."[78] It was, however, when he served as senior aide to Admiral Katō Tomosaburō at the Washington Conference that Nomura's perspective on international affairs and friendly sentiment toward America were forged. His friend Admiral William T. Pratt wrote, "I have felt that he imbibed many of his liberal tendencies from sitting at the feet of Baron Kato."[79]

As Katō's self-conscious successor, Nomura had defended the Washington treaty system during the 1920s. During the Shanghai Incident of 1932 he was commander of the Third Fleet and displayed diplomatic acumen in soothing an explosive situation. His image of Americans was encapsulated in the following words: "I can say this from my experiences during World War I when I was naval attaché in Washington. When confronted with peril, Americans will accomplish things that are of totally different scale from what we Japanese are accustomed to. They are a people with formidable potential power and flexibility materially and spiritually."[80] In February 1939 he had received a letter from Admiral Pratt, his old friend, reminding him that although the Americans were often called materialists, they harbored an ideology that must never be underestimated.[81] Nomura was one of the few Japanese naval leaders who understood the ideological factor in American foreign policy. As ambassador, he warned his government: "The majority of Americans, above all the president, see the present world war as a struggle between the 'democratic' and 'totalitarian' camps . . . and will aid Britain, the stronghold of the democracies, to the hilt."[82]

When approached about ambassadorship by Foreign Minister Matsuoka in late August 1940, Nomura hesitated, saying that Matsuoka's pro-Axis policy was incompatible with improvement of relations with the United States. Naval leaders urged him to accept. Before he did so, he met with Prime Minister Konoe and warned that if Japan advanced southward, the United States would retaliate with an oil embargo, which would force Japan to advance into the East Indies, and a Japanese-American war would ensue. (This circular reasoning rings a familiar bell; it was the scenario of mutual escalation written by the hard-line elements of the Naval General Staff to prepare for the coming war. Nomura emphasized the same logic in order to prevent southern advance and war with the United States.) Nomura said that the chance of the southward advance bringing war with the United States would be fifty-fifty. The United States would not oblige Japan by forcing a decisive fleet encounter early in the war, and Japan could not wage a protracted war, he repeatedly warned.[83]

Arriving on 11 February 1941, Nomura was received cordially by President Roosevelt as an old friend, who remarked that he proposed to call him "Admiral" rather than "Ambassador." Secretary of State Hull had this impression of Nomura: "He was tall, robust, in fine health, with an open face, differing considerably in physique from the average Japanese." Hull credited Nomura with "having been honestly sincere in trying to avoid war."[84] However, Nomura faced a Sisyphean task in mediating between Foreign Minister Matsuoka, who took a bellicose stand backed by the Tripartite Pact, and Secretary Hull, who lectured on international morality.

The middle echelons tried to sabotage Nomura's peace efforts. On 16 April, Nomura cabled Tokyo the Japanese-American Draft Understanding, worked out by private individuals (the so-called John Doe Associates) as a basis of Japanese-American negotiation. Two days later Captain Yokoyama Ichirō, naval attaché, cabled Navy Minister Oikawa and the Chief of the Naval General Staff Nagano, advising that they immediately instruct Nomura to commence negotiations on the basis of this draft. A copy of Nomura's telegram was forwarded to the Naval Affairs Bureau, where it was subverted by Commander Shiba, backed by Captains Ishikawa and Onoda. Shiba opposed any compromise with the United States, because it would jeopardize the plan for southern advance. Upon consultation with Captains Onoda and Ishikawa, both leading hawks, Shiba drafted a telegram to Yokoyama, urging him to prevent Ambassador Nomura from entering negotiations. Acting Navy Vice Minister Inoue Shigeyoshi, who was all for the negotiations, found out about Shiba's maneuver, reprimanded him in front of Oikawa, and so completely rewrote the telegram that in the end it was never sent. Commander Onoda and Captain Ōno, the war guidance officer, who were convinced that war was inevitable, believed that the draft understanding was political intrigue on the part of the U.S. government that had no hope of success. This episode shows that middle-echelon naval officers did not hesitate to subvert Nomura's peace efforts.[85]

In his telegram of 15 April, Nomura urged against any armed advance southward, warning that the United States was "beginning to think seriously about a Japanese-American war." The United States was preparing itself for a protracted war, mobilizing its national strength. He feared for the future of the Imperial Navy, which in the event of war "single-handedly would have to fight the combined navies of the United States and Britain." On 8 May he cabled, "The United States is taking measures to strengthen its force in the Pacific in the event that it fights Japan and Germany." On 3 July, Nomura warned Tokyo, "If the government is determined to advance south by force of arms, there will be no room whatsoever for adjusting Japanese-American relations." He also warned Tokyo about a chain reaction: If economic relations ruptured, Japan would undertake the southern advance, and this would inevitably bring war with the United States and Britain. Again, he alerted to the danger that an advance to southern Indochina would without fail bring a total trade embargo.[86]

On 10 July, a desperate Nomura, resorting to a back-channel communication through his attaché, Yokoyama, sent an important telegram to Oikawa and Nagano. Reminding them that the navy had implored him to go to Washington, he wrote that he had accepted the mission convinced that "Japanese-American relations were the navy's responsibility." The hard-liners in the United States were advocating stepped-up economic pressure. He chided the two men: "In the end Japan would have to fight the United States, Britain, the Soviet Union, China, and the Dutch East Indies—all of them simultaneously." Japan, Nomura asserted, was "truly at a crossroad now." On 15 July, Nomura received a reply from Oikawa and Nagano. Their references to "the Empire's demand to secure freedom to control Greater East Asia" and the claim to "self-existence and self-defense" pointed to a southward advance.[87] This was not the navy Nomura knew.

On 2 July the Imperial Conference's fateful decision to advance into southern Indochina was relayed. On the following day Nomura scolded his government, "If you are determined to use force to advance southward, I believe there is no room whatsoever for adjusting Japanese-American relations." On 23 July he again warned that Japan's southern advance would "lead to the rupture of diplomatic relations."[88] Perhaps recalling Katō Tomosaburō's statesmanship at the time of the Washington Conference, Nomura urged taking "a large view": "It looks as if Japan is unwittingly plunging single-handedly into a war against Britain and the U.S. It is my earnest desire that you exercise the utmost prudence and cope with the situation for the sake of a far-sighted state policy, by politically taking a long view of the whole situation, even though quick decision may be necessary from a military viewpoint."[89] The naval leaders did not heed Nomura's plea. His usefulness as ambassador, to all intents and purposes, was over.

AMERICA'S TOTAL EMBARGO

The United States had been carefully following Japan's decision to advance into southern Indochina. On 2 July, Washington received a Magic intercept that revealed the decision of the Imperial Conference of that day: "Preparations for southward advance shall be reinforced and the policy already decided upon with reference to French Indochina and Thailand shall be executed." Deciphered Magic telegrams were incorrectly rendered in Washington as implying Japan's preparation for attack on the Dutch East Indies also. (At this time Japan was not planning an attack on the East Indies, and this misperception might have strengthened the hands of the hawks in the Roosevelt administration.)[90]

On 18 July, after Tokyo had demanded the Vichy regime's acquiescence, President Roosevelt worked out a program of sanctions. The debate within the administration boiled down to whether an oil embargo would provoke attack on Dutch and British possessions. Leaders again decided to avoid war with Japan because the United States was already fighting an undeclared war with Germany in the Atlantic. Consulted by Roosevelt, Stark turned to Rear Admiral Richmond Kelly Turner, head of the War Plans Division, who recommended against a total oil embargo: "It is generally believed that shutting off the American supply of petroleum will lead to an invasion of the Netherlands East Indies . . . and possibly would involve the United States in early war in the Pacific."[91] In short, the navy was not ready for war with Japan. Admiral Husband E. Kimmel's Pacific Fleet was substantially inferior to Yamamoto's Combined Fleet.

On July 24, the Vichy regime acceded to Japan's demands. A day later Roosevelt signed an executive order freezing Japanese assets in America. Britain followed on 26 July and the Netherlands on 27 July. Japan confronted a global embargo. Japanese-American trade came to a complete standstill. Full economic warfare was on.

An oil embargo was quite a different matter. Mindful of the U.S. Navy's warning, Roosevelt gave his cabinet "quite a lecture" against it. As Ickes recorded in his diary, the president "was still unwilling to draw the noose tight. He thought that it might be better to slip the noose around Japan's neck and give it a jerk now and then."[92] The de facto oil embargo that went into effect on 1 August was, according to one American authority, more "the result of a bureaucratic reflex rather than the product of a carefully deliberated policy decision."[93]

After Roosevelt left to meet with Prime Minister Churchill off Argentia, Newfoundland, the hawks, headed by Assistant Secretary of State Dean Acheson, made sure that no license was granted for the export of oil to Japan. When Roosevelt returned, the noose around Japan's neck had been pulled so tight that he could not loosen it. Once this *unintended* act of provocation was taken, any retreat from what had been believed, in Japan and the United States, to be an oil embargo would look like a sign of weakness.

Tokyo's response was quick. Already, on 24 July—a day *before* the United States announced the freezing of assets—Nagano was heard to say that there was "no choice left but to fight in order to break the iron fetters strangling Japan."[94] And starting on 1 August, as the de facto oil embargo took effect, the oil gauge and the clock stood side by side. Grew wrote in his diary, "The vicious circle of reprisals and counter reprisals is on. Unless radical surprises occur in the world, it is difficult to see how the momentum of the down-grade movement can be arrested, or how far it will go. The obvious conclusion is eventual war." Yet American officials who engineered the oil embargo thought only in terms of deterring Japan from a drive to the East Indies and were heedless of the fact that they had forced Japan's back to the wall until it felt compelled to strike.

Washington hoped that if the matter could be strung out until Hitler was destroyed, changes in the international situation might force Japan to shift to a nonwar policy. Acheson and other hawks such as Stanley K. Hornbeck of the State Department had fallen into a rationalist fallacy when they argued that "no rational Japanese could believe that an attack on us could result in anything but disaster for his country."[95] Men like Nagano and the fire-eating middle echelons were not "rational," according to Hornbeck's definition.

The Japanese navy reached the point of no return when Japanese forces marched into south Indochina. Yet the decision had been made without thorough consideration of its consequences. There is no evidence that the Liaison Conference weighed its risks and ramifications. More difficult to account for is that some members of the First Committee were "stunned" by the severity of the American reprisal. Summoned by an urgent nighttime call, the only thing these members could say was "Oh, no!" As Captain Ōno, war guidance officer, remembered, he and his colleagues had underestimated the risk of an oil embargo because they had not expected Washington to take such a drastic measure. The American leaders must surely realize, he reasoned, that Japan would be compelled to attack, and that the United States was hardly ready to face a two-ocean war.[96] Ōno had paid scant attention to repeated warnings from Captain Yokoyama, attaché in Washington, and Ambassador Nomura, who had cabled that the United States, while pursuing a Europe-first strategy, was girding itself for a two-ocean war and might "very well impose an all-out embargo."[97] When the American embargo did finally materialize, Nagano and naval planners took it as proof that the United States had opted for war with Japan. In fact, they regarded the American oil embargo as substantially constituting an act of belligerence, and they redoubled their efforts to obtain "war determination."

As American historian Robert Butow remarked, the oil embargo seemed to the Japanese to be the "final, major link in a chain of encirclement" by the ABCD powers.[98] The logical escalation pointing to war, foreseen by the Operations Section a year before, had now become reality, driving Japan to war.

DECISION FOR WAR

"Gradual Pauperization"

In the end Japan's advance into southern Indochina and the strident American response precipitated the navy's determination to go to war. Yet it is difficult to pinpoint exactly when this determination was reached. What is certain is that middle-echelon officers came to the determination before ranking leaders did and that the Naval General Staff reached the decision before the Navy Ministry did. Lacking leadership and a sense of direction in the top echelon and racked with confusion and dissension in all ranks, the navy drifted or tottered into war determination. Preoccupied with bureaucratic and sectional interests and fearful of a preemptive American strike, naval officials failed to foresee the consequences of the southward advance. Whatever the reasons for miscalculation, by the end of July 1941 it was too late for Navy Minister Oikawa and ranking ministry officials to stop the drift. They had long since abdicated leadership, and in any event they hardly had the moral courage to oppose Chief of the Naval General Staff Nagano, who pressed for a quick decision. At cabinet meetings Oikawa maintained silence even on matters pertaining to the navy.

Shortly after the de facto oil embargo took effect on 1 August 1941, the Navy Ministry made a fresh assessment of the supply of and demand for petroleum. If the embargo continued, the consumption of petroleum would far exceed supply in the first year of war. Oil reserves would be exhausted in the middle of the second year.[1] With the lifeblood of the fleet being drained at the rate of 12,000 tons per day, time was running out. "Battleships without oil cannot move." Japan was like a fish in a pond from which the water was being drained.[2] Unless Japan could break this impasse by diplomacy, and quickly, it would have to fight.[3] But the navy was far from the decision to open hostilities. The army's war guidance officer was poetically inspired to write in the Confidential War Journal:

No new developments
Days of agonies and ruminations continue
One day's delay means waste of so much oil
One day's delay means sacrifice of so much blood
Yet they say we must avoid a hundred years' war with America![4]

From Nagano down, the naval high command felt that their country had been strangled by the embargo and was compelled to strike. To be sure, they had only their own miscalculation to blame for their predicament, but the miscalculation was mutual. America's total embargo, meant as a deterrent to keep Japan from advancing to the East Indies, goaded its navy to "war determination." Japan by its own logic was now faced with the necessity to decide to go to war.

From the foregoing, the navy might be expected to reach war determination immediately, but the facts were more entangled. For one thing, the emperor made clear his opposition to war. On 30 July, Nagano and Sugiyama, Army Chief of Staff, had an audience with the emperor. Nagano reported that in the event of war, "oil would be exhausted within a year or two, so Japan had no choice but strike south now." A shocked Hirohito demanded whether a victory like Tsushima was unlikely, to which Nagano replied that he was not confident that Japan could win at all. After Nagano left, Hirohito told his Grand Military Chamberlain Hasunuma Shigeru, "It is dangerous in the extreme to make war out of desperation."[5] He told Hasunuma how aggrieved he was by Nagano's belligerency. He wondered about the mentality of the chief of the Naval General Staff, who argued that war must be commenced even though there was little chance of success. This and other earlier statements by Hirohito would belie the contention of some "revisionist" historians that the emperor played an active role throughout in deciding on war with the United States.[6]

The fact that Nagano had lost the emperor's confidence should have been a sufficient reason for resignation in itself, but the fawning Oikawa did not have the courage to dismiss Nagano. In fact, Nagano had grown so belligerent that such moderate elders as Admirals Yonai, Okada, and Kobayashi believed that he must be relieved of his position. About this time Admiral Kobayashi noted that Nagano looked "like a sick man" and wondered whether he was in a condition to tackle the problem of peace or war.

On 7 August the emperor, concerned about the ascendancy of the hawks within the navy, asked Oikawa, "How about the control of naval subordinates?" He knew through Hasunuma that there were hard-liners among the section chiefs in the Navy Ministry and the Naval General Staff. Oikawa replied that the navy vice minister and the head of the Naval Affairs Bureau held their subordinates under control.[7]

The emperor's apprehension did not reach the middle echelons. At the 29 July meeting between army and navy planners, Commander Fujii said that the navy's middle-echelon officers had decided on war. The naval representatives had confidence in the first stage of operations involving attacks on the Philippines, the Dutch East Indies, and Malaya. Japan stood a fair chance of success in the decisive battle with the U.S. fleet, but they admitted that there was no sure means of forcing such an encounter. Fearing that a protracted war would result, the planners urged that the sooner Japan opened hostilities, the better. At this point Captain Ōno Takeji, the navy's war guidance officer, interjected, "We must come to a determination to strike south in early August." He added that, faced with the depletion of oil, "the navy's top leaders will determine for war soon."[8]

Reflecting such a sentiment, the First Committee, composed of middle-echelon fire-eaters, had been urging speedy completion of war preparations, insisting that Japan must "plunge into war." It drafted a policy paper to this effect, but the head of the Naval Affairs Bureau, Oka, opposed it, so on 3 August the committee drafted an alternative, toned-down paper. It stated that preparations for war must parallel diplomacy and that if by mid-October diplomacy did not succeed, hostilities must begin.[9] The oil embargo had set a time limit. Planners were convinced that the United States was deliberately prolonging the Hull-Nomura negotiations to gain time. The clock on the wall ticked away; Japan was being "gradually pauperized."

On 15 August the Naval General Staff drafted a plan for accelerating preparations, and the Combined Fleet demanded completion of war preparations by 25 October. The navy was to implement by the end of August the second stage of the preparatory fleet mobilization, converting the entire navy to a wartime footing. Specifically, this meant preparing ammunitions and other war materials and mobilizing necessary personnel. The operation would be completed in mid-October. (The first stage of preparatory fleet mobilization had been instituted in August 1940.) In other words, as the army suspected, the navy was trying to complete preparations for war without having arrived at "war determination."[10] Captain Nakazawa Tasuku, chief of the Operations Section, demanded that the army revise the materials mobilization program to give priority to the navy.[11] An incensed army staff officer wrote in the Confidential War Journal, "Is the navy determined for war? Is it trying to push forward its thoroughgoing operational preparations without having arrived at war determination? The navy is utterly incomprehensible."[12] The army's distrust of the navy continued until late November 1941.

Nagano had been urging that "if we are going to war, we must do so quickly." On 16 August navy officials presented to the army-navy conference of bureau and division chiefs a draft of national policy: (1) "To proceed with both war preparations and diplomacy in parallel until late October; (2) if diplomatic settlement cannot be reached by mid-October, resort must be made to armed force." This draft policy was based on the aforementioned paper prepared by the First Committee.[13] At interservice meetings the army took exception to the navy's accelerating war preparations *without* having reached "war determination." For the navy, the former meant assembling and preparing its fleets, aircraft, and matériel at advanced bases; it was easy to withdraw them if a diplomatic settlement was reached. So the navy could proceed with war preparations without having reached "war determination." For the army, however, preparation meant mobilization and movement of 4 million troops southward, which would be practically impossible to withdraw. Hence preparations required "war determination."[14] Interservice distrust, even feuding, largely stemmed from the different nature of mobilization between the two services.

At the Liaison Conference of 3 September, Nagano restated his position: "When there is no hope for diplomatic settlement and when war becomes unavoidable, we must make a prompt determination [for war]." Regarding the strategic outlook, he explained that there was "a chance of victory now," but it would diminish with the passage of time. If the enemy opted for a quick and short war, Japan could stage a decisive fleet engagement. But the United States would in all likelihood turn the war into a protracted conflict, in which case Japan would be threatened with a shortage of matériel. Therefore it was vitally important to acquire "an impregnable position in the south" to obtain resources. And he hoped that Japan could take advantage of "changes in international situation," by which he meant German victory. In short, the only way to prevail was a "quick opening of hostilities and seizing the initiative."[15]

In early September Fukudome, head of the Operations Division, circulated among the ranking naval leaders a paper urging a speedy decision to go to war; otherwise Japan would miss the moment to strike. He listed the reasons as follows: The monsoon season would set in from December until the following March, making landing operations difficult. The Pacific Fleet in Hawaii and air power in the Philippines were steadily being augmented, posing a threat to Japan. The United States would accelerate shipbuilding and production of other weapons so that within one year, American strength would more than double that of Japan. And, finally, Japan's oil storage would last only for a year and a half. To most of those who saw this paper, determination to commence hostilities seemed compelling.[16]

With respect to the date for opening hostilities, Chief of the Army General Staff Sugiyama Hajime proposed the first ten days of October. Navy Minister Oikawa tried to tone down this provision, and in the end they agreed on the following phraseology: "In the event that *there is no prospect* of our demands being met by the first ten days in October through diplomatic negotiations, we will immediately decide to commence hostilities with the United States (Britain, and the Netherlands)." Oikawa's wording in italics ensured that the government would not be automatically be forced to decide on war even if negotiations did not succeed by early October.[17] The army's war guidance officer complained that Oikawa's revision "actually guts the document."[18]

The Imperial Conference of 6 September was a milestone on the road to the Pacific War. It stipulated, "Our Empire, for the purposes of self-defense and self-preservation, will complete preparations for war, with the last ten days of October as a tentative deadline, resolved to go to war with the United States, Great Britain, and the Netherlands if necessary." When Oikawa stated that war preparations and diplomatic effort had equal weight, the emperor pointedly asked, "Will it not impede diplomatic negotiations if we accelerate war preparations at the same time?"[19] Like the decision of the Imperial Conference of 2 July, this decision "to be resolved to go to war" did not mean real "war determination" on the part of the ranking naval leaders.

NAGANO'S OPERATIONAL PLANS

At the historic Imperial Conference of 6 September, Nagano gave the fullest exposition of Japan's operational plans. He warned that oil and other strategic materials were dwindling daily; if Japan let too many days go by, the navy would become immobilized. "The United States is accelerating with unusual speed its military buildup in the Far East. By the latter half of 1942 it will become impossible to cope with it." As for Japan's chance, Nagano stated that if the United States opted for a war of "quick encounter, quick showdown" and sent its principal naval units to Far Eastern waters, there was hope for destroying them. However, Nagano admitted, even this would not terminate the war; the United States would wage a protracted war. The first requirement for fighting such a war was to occupy, at the outset, Southeast Asia to obtain materials.[20]

Commenting on Nagano's war plan, the naval elder Okada wrote in his memoirs, "Something was the matter with Chief of Naval General Staff Nagano. He was scolded by the emperor for saying that Japan must go to war although we will be the loser."[21] The emperor had censured Nagano's strategy on 31 July as "a desperate plan" and wondered how Japan could start a war with so little chance of success.[22] By "chance" Nagano meant only in the initial stage of war.

Suffering from what Admiral Inoue had called the "ratio neurosis," he based his hope on the current fleet strength of 70 percent of the U.S. fleet. If Japan were to fight, it must do so while it retained this ratio. Queried about Japan's prospect in a protracted war, Nagano equivocated: he could say "nothing for certain" beyond the first two years. Japan's fleet ratio compared to the United States in the latter half of 1943 would be reduced to less than 50 percent.[23] Nagano, however, contended that Japan would be able to overcome difficulties by establishing an "impregnable sphere" in the southern resource area. However, even if the southern area was captured and controlled, the problem remained of shipping materials to Japan under wartime conditions. In reality this plan was hardly feasible. Little had been accomplished in the way of fortifying the mandated islands in Micronesia, despite Vice Admiral Inoue's urgent request in January. Inoue, appointed commander of the Fourth Fleet in August 1941 and charged with defending the mandated islands, discovered that not even minimum fortifications had been built on these islands. Further, air power to defend the "southern impregnable sphere" was not provided in the Fourth Replenishment Program of 1939. The Fifth Replenishment Program, hurriedly drawn up in January 1941, involved a huge sum beyond the nation's capacity. Commander Miyo Kazunari, an aviation staff officer, testified that most Naval General Staff leaders, committed to the Mahanian strategy of a decisive battle, did not recognize the importance of air power.[24]

In addition, there was a shortage of ships to transport oil and other resources from Southeast Asia, and ships assigned for convoy escort were pitifully inadequate, despite Navy Minister Yoshida's emphasis on the importance of escorting in May 1940. Preoccupied with the decisive battleship engagement, the navy was indifferent to the protection of vital sea communications. The Japanese navy was also influenced by Mahan's dictum that commerce destruction was a secondary form of warfare. Prior to hostilities, not a single staff officer was in charge of convoy escort in either the Naval General Staff or the Combined Fleet. There was, then, little to support Nagano's operational plan. In short, the navy failed to face the reality of modern warfare. Further complicating Nagano's strategic calculations were the presence of the Pacific Fleet at Pearl Harbor that menaced the flank of Japan's southern operation. There was also the rapid buildup of American air power in the Philippines. Above all, he felt threatened by the depletion of oil, 400 tons per hour. The implication was that after the third year, Japan would lose the war.

Nagano's tortured arguments at the Imperial Conference of 6 September reveal that, driven to extremity, he abandoned strategic realism and rational calculation of Japan's chances, reverting to a brand of spiritualism that sounded like that of Admiral Katō Kanji. Nagano maintained that "since Japan is unavoid-ably facing national ruin whether it decides to fight the United States or submit to its demands, it must by all means choose to fight. Japan would rather go down fighting than ignobly surrender without a struggle because surrender would spell spiritual as well physical ruin for the nation and its destiny."[25]

In his audience with the emperor, Nagano used a morbid simile: a risky sur-gical operation. "Suppose there is a child suffering from appendicitis. Left unat-tended, he is sure to die, but with an operation he may have [a] 30 percent chance of survival. As a parent there is no alternative but to consent to a risky operation."[26] The emperor, not assured by this medical metaphor, ignored it and tried to receive commitment that "diplomacy be given precedence." To register his oppo-sition to war, Hirohito unexpectedly pulled a piece of paper out of the pocket of his robe and read a poem composed by his grandfather, Emperor Meiji:

> All the seas in every quarter are
> As brothers to one another,
> Why, then, do the winds and waves of strife rage
> So turbulently throughout the world.[27]

Hirohito said that he always reminded himself of "the peace-loving spirit" of his revered grandfather.

In a rapidly deteriorating crisis and under a merciless time limit, Nagano was driving himself to the brink, although he later said that he was driven by what he called Fate. As is often the case with decision making under stress, Nagano's statements were all-or-nothing, one-dimensional, and myopic. His "do or die," "now or never," "fight or surrender" dichotomies reflected an effort to escape from the predicament that the navy's earlier decisions had created. Nagano showed the symptoms of a defective decision maker in crisis: an incomplete sur-vey of the alternatives and a failure to fully examine the risks of his preferred choice. And it was often easier to decide on "a desperate gamble involving almost certain ruin" than to revise his skewed definition of the crisis he faced.[28]

The choice Japan faced was not as narrow as Nagano defined it, as shown when Navy Vice Minister Sawamoto, alarmed by Nagano's belligerency, con-sulted the naval elders (retired admirals). Yonai said, "There are many questions that are solved by the passage of time. Consider, for example, the European situation. Utmost care is needed not to enter war precipitously." He suggested that a third alternative always existed. Okada, former navy minister and then prime minister, said, "Domestic questions can be solved if we are determined to do so." He was referring to Nagano's exaggerated fear that if the navy opposed war, the army would stage a coup.

Whatever Nagano's psychology may have been, Combined Fleet Commander Yamamoto saw through the fatal flaws in Nagano's strategic plan, and on 29 September he sought a meeting with him but could not dissuade him from war. A recent war game had reconfirmed Yamamoto's belief that the war would turn into a protracted conflict in which Japan's chances would progressively diminish. "The Imperial Navy has never obtained a single great victory in repeated map maneuvers and if the situation continued it was feared that Japan would suffer from 'gradual pauperization,' so maneuvers were called off." Judging from recent American strategic thought, Yamamoto was convinced that the U.S. fleet was unlikely to engage the Japanese fleet in the western Pacific early in the war. Thus he ruled out the traditional strategy of interceptive operations.[29]

NO COMPROMISE WITH THE UNITED STATES

The talks in Washington had reached a deadlock, as Captain Yokoyama reported in an important dispatch in late September. The United States, recognizing that Japan was increasingly suffering from economic warfare, seemed intent on prolonging the Hull-Nomura negotiations, pending its arms buildup. If success of the negotiations was imperative for Japan, he urged, Japan must immediately withdraw its troops from China and Indochina.[30]

Even at this late hour the senior leaders of the navy ministry were willing to consider withdrawing from China "in principle" if it was required to save the Hull-Nomura negotiations in Washington and if Konoe took the initiative. On 4 October, Oikawa told Prime Minister Konoe, "In order to promptly adjust relations with the United States [so that Japan could get oil], Japan must be prepared to accept wholesale the American demand regarding troop withdrawal." Two days later, ranking naval leaders met in Oikawa's official residence, where Oikawa took up the matter of troop withdrawal from China. Most, including Oka and Yamamoto, agreed that "it will be absurd to involve the nation in a war with the United States solely over the issue of troop withdrawal." The China issue, of course, had been the chief bone of contention in the Hull-Nomura negotiations. Oikawa, addressing himself to Nagano, asked whether if worse came to worst, it would be all right to propose troop withdrawal even if it meant coming to blows with the army. Nagano loudly interjected, "Well, I doubt that!" Oikawa felt he was undercut. No official present—Vice Minister Sawamoto, Vice Chief of the Naval General Staff Itō Seiichi, or Chief of the Naval Affairs Bureau Oka—supported Oikawa. Thus disappeared a little ray of hope.

Nagano had already abandoned any hope for successful negotiations in Washington and wanted to avoid a clash with the army at a time when he was pushing for early commencement of war.[31]

At the Liaison Conference of 4 October, Nagano proclaimed, "This is no longer time for discussion. We want quick action [decision for war]." What he meant was that "prolongation of diplomatic negotiations will cause grave difficulties for our operations." If negotiations were dragged out and if he was asked to fight after the negotiations collapsed, he would be placed in a predicament, he explained.[32]

On 7 October, Nagano met with Oikawa and Chief of Army General Staff Sugiyama and said, "I think there is no prospect for diplomatic settlement. Since 15 October is the time limit for deciding for peace or war, we must not allow the negotiations to drag on; otherwise we shall miss the right moment for opening hostilities." Timing was of the essence. (Unknown to the Japanese, the Joint Board of the United States was telling President Roosevelt that by mid-December, air strength in the Philippines would become "a positive threat to any Japanese naval operations south of Formosa.") When Sugiyama said, "I understand the navy is not confident about war," Nagano replied, "That's not true. We have a chance of winning if we start war right now. But if you say too fastidious things like the navy minister, it may give rise to the contention that the navy's armaments are not necessary."[33] Nagano was again voicing fear that the army would say that a navy unable to fight the United States needed no more budget.

Pressure on Oikawa from middle-rank officers had stepped up. On the night of 10 October, a group of officers led by Captain Ishikawa and Commander Shiba Katsuo descended on Oikawa's official residence and demanded that "he make a decision on war or peace on his responsibility as a navy minister." About the same time, other officers of section-chief rank pressed Oikawa, "Are you really willing to take responsibility as navy minister?" Navy Vice Minister Sawamoto and Head of the Naval Affairs Bureau Oka, busy with maintaining communication between Nagano and Oikawa, could hardly control the fire-eating middle echelons.[34]

On 9 October, Prince Fushimi met with the emperor and said, "Since war with the United States is unavoidable, the sooner we open hostilities the better. Please convoke an Imperial Conference at once." This "extremely radical" view profoundly distressed the emperor, who replied, "This is not the time for war. We must do our best by means of diplomatic negotiations."[35]

OIKAWA EQUIVOCATES

On 1 October Oikawa met with Konoe and told him that if things were allowed to drift, resources would soon be exhausted. Negotiations in Washington must come to a prompt settlement. "For this purpose, we have to be determined to swallow the American proposal whole. If you are resolved to press forward in this course, the navy is prepared to support you to the hilt, and the army will follow suit."[36] Oikawa hinted that he would follow the prime minister's lead, but he never took the initiative to avoid war.

The last chance to register the navy's opposition to war was lost when, at the Five Ministers Conference of 12 October, Oikawa failed to state unequivocally and openly that the navy lacked confidence in regard to war with the United States. He merely stated that he would leave the decision of peace or war up to the prime minister; he felt it was a political question for political leaders (the government) to decide. The task of the military, he said, was that once war was decided on, to fight no matter how great the odds.[37] This was a fatuous argument, because a service minister was precisely the official to estimate the chances of victory. Oikawa evaded his professional responsibility as navy minister.

Controversy remains about Oikawa's position. He meant to say that as a service minister, he was not in a position to say whether there should be peace or war. He felt it was a political question for political leaders to decide. But he should have categorically stated that war with the United States would develop into a simultaneous war with the United States, Britain, the Netherlands, and China—a war that Japan was certain to lose. Recall that in 1939, then Navy Minister Yonai flatly stated that Japan stood no chance of winning against the Anglo-American powers.[38]

An explanation advanced by Oikawa's defenders is that if he had said that the navy could not fight, it would have brought an army-navy clash, the downfall of the Konoe cabinet, and domestic turmoil that would have forced Japan to enter war badly divided. But as Admiral Yamamoto observed, a domestic revolution would never cause national ruin, whereas a hopeless war could. Oikawa also said his mind was dominated by the memory of Fleet Admiral Tōgō's severe upbraiding of Chief of the Naval General Staff Taniguchi, who had said at the time of the Manchurian Incident that Japan could not fight the United States. Oikawa believed it a naval taboo to say the navy could not fight.[39]

One hidden reason for Oikawa's failure to clarify Japan's prospect in war was, as usual, bureaucratically inspired. As was later explained by Navy Vice Minister Sawamoto, the navy, "after so many years of clamoring about its 'invincible fleet,' was hardly in a position to say it could not take on the United States; it would have no ground to stand on in dealing with its officers as well as the army and the public." If the navy minister had said the navy could not fight, it would have lost its raison d'être and the fleet's morale would be destroyed. Furthermore, the navy would lose out in its scramble with the army for war matériel. Regarding the last point, Sawamoto added, "The army said there is no need to give war matériel to a navy that cannot fight." Later he wrote, "The navy had to defend itself from the army's accusation that 'a navy that cannot make war is worse than useless.'" This was the same logic behind Oikawa's consent to the Tripartite Pact.[40]

After the war began, Yamamoto lamented, "If I had been in charge as navy minister, I would have said frankly that there can be no final victory against the United States, I really would have." Later Admiral Toyoda Soemu, known for his opposition to the army, criticized the navy precisely on this account: "In such an abnormal situation, the problem of whether Japan could fight or not was not an issue for the navy alone; more importantly, it was a matter of national strength, and the navy was not responsible for national strength. Therefore, it would have been perfectly all right for the navy to say it could not fight a war practically against the entire world for any number of years. I simply could not understand the navy's logic." Toyoda also stated, "A Japanese-American war is primarily the navy's war. How could its highest authority, [the] navy minister, say that it would be all right to fight a war and equally all right not to fight a war? I cannot believe that the navy minister was aware of his grave responsibility."[41] The emperor was equally distressed. According to his Grand Military Chamberlain Hasunuma, "The emperor was anguished, for Navy Minister Oikawa never made the navy's position clear."

SHIMADA DECIDES ON WAR

Strategic imperatives and operational requirements now dominated national policy. On 18 October, Admiral Shimada Shigetarō was appointed navy minister with the backing of Prince Fushimi, who, as the only fleet admiral in the navy, exercised the right to nominate navy ministers. Shimada's familiarity to Prince Fushimi was well known: he had served under Prince Fushimi as the head of the Operations Division in 1933 when Prince Fushimi pushed for revision of the Naval General Staff regulations and as vice chief of the Naval General Staff in 1935–36 when Japan withdrew from the Washington and London treaties. The two men worked in tandem in reaching the "determination" to go to war.

Since the summer of 1941, naval elders had discussed installing Yamamoto as navy minister in the hope that he would prevent war. But the intriguing possibility never materialized, and Shimada, a protégé of Prince Fushimi, was appointed. Shimada belonged to the fleet faction and was a total misfit as navy minister. In the words of Commander Chihaya Masataka, "Admiral Shimada is a character of the so-called 'Oriental Hero Type, just rough-hewn,' lacking precision of thought and a clear-cut sense of responsibility."[42] He was a yes-man and always swam with the tide. He certainly was not the type to oppose Nagano. He lacked conviction and went to Fushimi when crucial matters came up.

Shimada had served only in command posts and had a distaste for politics. More important, Shimada had been away from Tokyo for four years as commander of the Second Fleet, the Kure Naval District, and the China-Area Fleet. Worse yet, he had not been briefed by Oikawa on the state of Japanese-American relations; he was simply told to look at documents in the office safe. Shimada was shocked to learn about the fatal decisions at the Imperial Conferences of 2 July and 6 September ("not to desist from war with the United States").

Yamamoto sent his Naval Academy classmate Shimada a desperate letter on 24 October: "Taking a large view of the matter, it goes without saying that we must avoid a Japanese-American war, if at all possible, and endure untold difficulties [for the sake of peace]. This requires extraordinary courage and exertion. Will Japan, having been cornered into the present impasse, be able to manage such a turnabout?"[43] The letter was wasted on Shimada; he simply did not have that kind of courage and perspicuity. About 20 October the emperor, through his Grand Military Chamberlain Hasunuma, let the new navy minister, Shimada, know that he had been greatly perturbed by Captain Ishikawa Shingo's role in reversing the peace policy.[44]

On 27 October, Prince Fushimi urged Shimada to decide on war: "Unless we speedily open hostilities, we shall lose the opportune moment to strike." Shimada was more responsive to Prince Fushimi's war advocacy than to the emperor's desire for peace. Shimada succumbed, and on 30 October he reached his decision to go to war, although he admitted that it had been barely ten days since he was appointed and that he had not had time to study the matter carefully. He told Sawamoto and Oka, "As it is, there is no telling when the United States will make a preemptive strike." The U.S. fleet would steam across the Pacific in full force as soon as Japan ran out of oil and its fleet was stranded. "Japan's operational plan will be completely nullified and our chance for victory will disappear." If the matter turned out this way, "I of course would commit *hara-kiri*, but no matter how many navy ministers committed *hara-kiri*, it would be no good." Sawamoto remonstrated that "in light of its national character and the need to obtain Congressional approval, the United States is unlikely to make a preemptive attack on Japan."[45] Shimada's distrust of the United States ran too deep to be assuaged by a reasoned argument.

How totally Shimada misread American strategy becomes clear when we turn to what was happening within the U.S. Navy. Admiral Stark, chief of naval operations, opposed early war and on 5 November he and General Marshall wrote President Roosevelt, "At the present time the United States Fleet in the Pacific is inferior to the Japanese Fleet and cannot undertake an unlimited strategic offensive in the Western Pacific. In order to be able to do so, it would have to be strengthened by withdrawing all naval vessels from the Atlantic. . . . War between the United States and Japan should be avoided while building up defensive forces in the Far East, until such time as Japan attacks or directly threatens territories whose security to the United States is of very great importance."[46] In other words, unless Japan directly attacked British, Dutch, or American territory, the United States would not fight. Adhering to the Europe-first strategy, President Roosevelt agreed that a Pacific war must be avoided.

Shimada's understanding of America's position can be gleaned from his remark that "America's economic sanctions already constitute an act of war, albeit without resort to arms." In his diary Shimada recorded reasons for his decision to go to war: "Under the present circumstances, no matter how hard I try to avoid war, it is impossible. Unless we determine for war, domestic conflict will be confounded with the result that we shall lose an opportune time to commence hostilities." Shimada also emphasized, "If the navy opposed the war at this late stage, there would be a real danger of a domestic clash and in that case we'll lose everything. . . . We [have] no choice but to agree [to commence hostilities] in order to avoid the worst situation of the army and the navy fighting with each other."[47] This day, 30 October, may be regarded as the day the navy finally decided on war.

When on 1 November Shimada expressed his "war determination" to Army Minister (concurrently Prime Minister) Tōjō Hideki and Army Chief of Staff Sugiyama, he coupled it with a request for an increased allotment of steel; the navy needed more steel to carry out the Fifth Replenishment Program. Even at this climactic moment the navy was preoccupied with a bureaucratic concern: a larger share of matériel. Sugiyama asked Shimada, "Will you decide for war, Shimada-san, if the navy gets the steel it demands?" The navy minister nodded in assent. As a result, in the materials mobilization plan for 1942, the navy was to receive 1,100,000 tons of steel, and the army 790,000 tons.[48] With scathing contempt an army staff officer wrote in the Confidential War Journal, "The navy has determined for war in return for 300,000 more tons of steel. How pathetic the navy is!"[49]

Now that Shimada had agreed to hostilities, other naval leaders followed suit. Nagano was satisfied. On 1 November he told Shimada, "Ever since January this year [when Japan intervened in the Thai-Indochina dispute] we have steadily moved in the direction of opening hostilities. And it is impossible to stop it now." At the Liaison Conference on the same day (the last Liaison Conference to meet, lasting seventeen hours), Nagano made a somber statement about Japan's strategic outlook: "In the third year of war . . . we shall have no margin left whatsoever in war matériel and industrial power. . . . So there is a rather great fear whether we can maintain war-making capacity."[50]

When Finance Minister Kaya Okinori asked Nagano whether he thought the U.S. fleet would really come out and attack Japan, he replied, "I think the chances are 50–50." When Foreign Minister Tōgō Shigenori took exception, Nagano replied, "There is a saying, 'Don't rely on what won't come,'" implying that the United States would launch a preventive attack on Japan. Kaya asked when Japan could go to war with a chance of winning, and Nagano thundered, "Now! The time for war will not come later!" He explained, "The United States is daily tightening its encirclement of Japan and increasing its aid to Chiang Kai-shek and the Soviet Union. Japan will dwindle away into nothing. The time to start war with the United States is today."[51]

At the Imperial Conference of 5 November, Nagano again stressed the advantage of quick attack. With regard to the Mahanian decisive battle, Nagano was optimistic, saying that Japan had ample chance for success, given its existing fleet ratio compared to the United States and geographic advantages. "Our fleet ratio is 75 percent but 40 percent of the American fleet is in the Atlantic Ocean, and 60 percent in the Pacific. The United States would need considerable time since it must withdraw ships from the Atlantic and come to attack us. . . . We are, therefore, confident of victory. We can destroy their fleet if they want a decisive battle." Nagano stated that in a war of attrition, which was more likely, Japan's position would become "extremely difficult," but he assured leaders that protecting Japan's sea communications would be possible. This underestimation of American submarines courted catastrophic losses in the Pacific War. Because American bases were distantly located, Nagano said, less than one-fourth of American submarines would reach the Japanese coast or the South China Sea.[52]

At this Imperial Conference leaders decided that if the negotiations in Washington did not succeed by the beginning of December, Japan would commence hostilities. As to the means of terminating the war in Japan's favor, Nagano foresaw three possibilities: (1) to establish an impregnable sphere in the southwest Pacific and, at an appropriate time, to annihilate the U.S. main fleet once it reached the western Pacific; (2) to use "positive measures" to bring about Chiang Kai-shek's surrender; and (3) to align with Germany, which hopefully would have invaded and defeated Britain. Japan expected that if these two allies were brought to their knees, the United States would lose its will to keep on fighting a costly war in the western Pacific. However, Nagano's scenario was based on highly wishful estimates and on factors that were beyond Japan's control.[53]

YAMAMOTO'S EFFORTS TO AVOID WAR

At age fifty-nine in 1941, Yamamoto was at the peak of his career as commander in chief of the Combined Fleet. No other Japanese officer was as well known by his American counterparts. Lieutenant Commander Edwin T. Layton, Admiral Richardson's intelligence officer who knew Yamamoto personally, considered him "a very thoroughly grounded and trained officer. . . . He possessed more brains than any other Japanese in High Command." Layton told Admiral Husband E. Kimmel, who replaced Richardson as the Pacific Fleet commander, that Yamamoto "could win at poker among good poker players. His mind was keen, alert, and that also from my personal observation and from general service reputation, he was an outstanding officer."[54]

Yamamoto spoke highly of Kimmel: "The American commander is no ordinary or average man. Such a relatively junior admiral would not have been given the important position of CinCPAC [Commander in Chief, Pacific Fleet] unless he were able, gallant, and brave. We can expect him to put up a courageous fight. Moreover he is said to be farsighted and cautious."[55]

In the Japanese navy Yamamoto was known for his razor-sharp intellect, flexible thinking, and broad perspective. (He graduated second in his class from the Naval Staff College.) His pronounced individuality was so rare among Japanese navy men that one former officer remarked that he was almost a "product of mutation." He was bold and original, never compromised his principles, farsighted, and known for charismatic leadership. By all accounts, he should have been in Tokyo as navy minister or chief of the Naval General Staff in the critical years 1940–41. We have already seen how persistently he opposed war. On 10 December 1940 he had written Shimada, "Looking at the circumstances under which the Tripartite Pact was signed and the way [the] subsequent materials mobilization program has been handled, the present government's way of doing things is putting the cart before the horse. It is too late now to be surprised, enraged, and distressed by America's economic oppression; it is like a schoolboy who lives for the moment and behaves thoughtlessly."[56] Even after the war started, he told Admiral Kobayashi Seizō, "Since we marched to [Southern] Indochina determined to fight a war with the United States, America's reprisal [embargo, etc.] was a matter of course." His consuming task was how to prevent war. "A war between Japan and the United States would be a major calamity for the world, and for Japan it would mean, after several years of [China] war already, acquiring yet another powerful enemy—an extremely perilous matter for the nation."[58] He wrote to Shimada on 24 October 1941 that war must be avoided, although it would take "extreme courage and power" to do so. For Japan, which had been driven to this present predicament, the only remaining way to turn the tide and avoid the war, Yamamoto suggested "with trepidation," was to seek the emperor's "sacred decision."[59] Yamamoto seemed to be asking his classmate Shimada whether he, now navy minister, could somehow tell the emperor that war must be avoided. But Shimada preferred to listen to Prince Fushimi's war advocacy.

Nor did Yamamoto hesitate to say, privately, that Japan would face defeat in any war with America. Already on 14 October 1940, he had told Harada Kumao, Prince Saionji's secretary, referring to the Tripartite Pact, "To fight the United States is like fighting the whole world. But it has been decided. So I will fight the best I can. Doubtless I shall die on board *Nagato* [his flagship]. Meanwhile Tokyo will be burnt to the ground three times. Konoe and others will be torn to pieces by the revengeful people, I [shouldn't] wonder."[60]

Admiral Inoue Shigeyoshi, an admirer of Yamamoto, faulted him on one score. Shortly after the Tripartite Pact in September 1940, Yamamoto urged Konoe to avoid war with the United States by all means. When Konoe questioned him about the navy's chances in such a war, Yamamoto said, "If we are ordered to do it, then I can raise havoc with them [the American navy] for the first six months or a year, but I have absolutely no confidence as to what would happen if it went on for two or three years." After the war Inoue took Yamamoto to task for this slip of the tongue: Yamamoto should have categorically stated that the navy could not take on the United States at all, as Yonai had said in 1939. "It should have been obvious," Inoue explained, "that such a talk with a man like Prince Konoe, who was innocent about military matters, would give him a vague but encouraging idea about Japan's fighting capability." Going further, Inoue believed that Yamamoto should have unequivocally opposed war, even by risking his position. But Yamamoto felt that any opposition to war must come from the navy minister or the chief of the Naval General Staff, and not the commander in chief of the Combined Fleet, whose duty was to fight when the decision was made.[61]

In late October and early November 1940, Yamamoto attempted to prevent war by bolstering the navy's top leadership. He told Navy Minister Oikawa, "Unlike pre–Tripartite Pact days, great determination is required today to make certain that we avoid the danger of going to war." He proposed a drastic reshuffling of the leadership: Yonai as chief of the Naval General Staff, Yoshida or Koga as vice chief, and Inoue as vice minister. "This aligning of like minds," Yamamoto was convinced, "could work together to achieve the difficult feat." He wrote, "This is a critical moment upon which the fate of the country depends. It is not because I fear the military might of the United States and Great Britain, but because there are no able men among the naval authorities in Tokyo." Unknown to Yamamoto at about this time, there was some talk among naval elders, retired admirals, about installing him as navy minister. Of course, it would have been impossible to remove him from the Combined Fleet, but if he had been appointed navy minister, he would have risked his life to prevent war with the United States.[62]

On 29 September 1941 Yamamoto sought a meeting with Nagano. He spoke bluntly, not as commander in chief of the Combined Fleet but "as an admiral and an objective observer":

> It is obvious that a Japanese-American war will become a protracted one. As long as tides of war are in our favor, the United States will never stop fighting. As a consequence, the war will continue for several years, during which matériel will be exhausted, vessels and arms will be damaged, and they can be replaced only with great difficulties. Ultimately we will not be able to contend with [the United States]. As the result of war the people's livelihood will become indigent . . . and it is not hard to imagine [that] the situation will become out of control. We must not start a war with so little a chance of success.[63]

Yamamoto urged that relations with the United States be "adjusted" even if it involved "compromise to some extent, especially regarding the Tripartite Pact." He was also in favor of withdrawing troops from China. Virtually until the last moment he hoped for a successful outcome of the Hull-Nomura negotiations. On 12 September 1941 he asked Prime Minister Konoe not to "show an antagonistic attitude [toward the United States] even if his proposed conference [with President Roosevelt] should fail to materialize, for there is no last word in diplomacy."[64] On 11 November he wrote Hori that "the last recourse is the emperor's sacred decision [to avoid war]." As late as 3 December he stopped at Navy Minister Shimada's official residence and said that "since Nomura is a remarkable man, he will somehow be able to successfully conclude the Japanese-American negotiations."[65]

That Yamamoto hoped against hope for their peaceful outcome, until the last minute, is clear from the fact that at the final briefing to commanders of the task force on 13 November at the Iwakuni airbase, he sternly admonished them to return, even after their takeoff, if the Hull-Nomura negotiations succeeded. Those who could not obey this order, he grimly enjoined, must submit their resignations immediately.[66]

YAMAMOTO AND THE PEARL HARBOR ATTACK PLAN

Yamamoto's inner feelings as he made ready for the Pearl Harbor attack were conveyed in a letter to his friend Hori Teikichi on 11 October 1941: "What a strange position I find myself in—having been assigned the mission diametrically opposed to my own personal opinion, with no choice but to push full speed in pursuance of that mission. Alas, is that fate?"[67] It was certainly a cruel irony that Yamamoto, who liked America and was liked by American naval officers more than any other Japanese admirals, would have to fight the United States against his will. Few men in Japan wanted to avoid war with America as fervently as he did, but no one was as daring as he in planning an attack on the United States. Yet he knew that "in the end we shall not be able to stand up to them."

Combined Fleet Commander Yamamoto, with his enormous prestige and aura, ordered full preparation of the fleets, while at the same time undertaking to overhaul what he saw as a hopelessly anachronistic strategy of the Naval General Staff. His was a gargantuan task: to overturn single-handedly the Mahanian concept of decisive engagement and fixation with the battleship, to which the navy had been committed for more than thirty years. As he told a few trusted subordinates, "The Naval General Staff is still devoted to the strategic thinking of the Meiji era [1868–1912]." War, to be successful, must be of short duration, before the United States would fully mobilize its war potential. "With the advent of aircraft, the battleship has become window dressing. The navy is still trying to win a war with America by means of a decisive fleet encounter, but there is no way." To oppose or criticize the conventional attritional-interceptive strategy was a strict heresy in the navy, and a lesser commander than Yamamoto would have been displaced; but Yamamoto enjoyed enormous prestige and numerous followers that the Naval General Staff could not ignore.

A large body of literature exists on the inception, planning, and execution of the Pearl Harbor attack, most notably the massive authoritative works of Gordon W. Prange, and there is no need for retelling this. It is sufficient for our purpose to bring out certain salient points of interpretation.

As early as 1928 Yamamoto, returning from the attaché's office in Washington, gave a lecture at the Torpedo School and said that air power would become the mainstay of the navy, and Japan, instead of conducting defensive operations, must resort to such offensive actions as attacking Pearl Harbor. But he did not give it serious thought. Yamamoto was not the originator of the Pearl Harbor idea; it was talked about considerably in the late 1930s. In 1936 the Naval Staff College worked out a study of a surprise attack by air. In March 1940 Yamamoto, impressed with an air squadron's torpedo exercise, murmured to his chief of staff Fukudome, "I wonder if an aerial attack cannot be made on Pearl Harbor?" This appears to be the first time that Yamamoto discussed a surprise air attack, but Fukudome believed this idea to be no more than a passing notion.[68]

On 26–28 November 1940, Yamamoto presided over a war game with leading members of the Naval General Staff and the fleets. It demonstrated that an attack on the Dutch East Indies would bring war with the United States, which would develop into a simultaneous war with Britain and the Netherlands as well. He stressed that unless Japan was determined and fully prepared for war with the United States, it must not undertake southern operations. If war was unavoidable, Japan must at the beginning attack the United States. By late November 1940 he seems to have reached the conclusion that Japan's only chance would be a surprise air attack on the fleet in Hawaii. In April 1940 President Roosevelt had deployed the Pacific Fleet to Pearl Harbor. That provided a good bait to Yamamoto.[69]

On 24 November, he wrote Oikawa presenting for the first time his idea of a Pearl Harbor attack. He explained that the navy had not achieved a single victory in war games simulating intercepted operations. From what he knew of Admiral Kimmel's character and the trend of American strategic thought, he doubted that the United States would obligingly throw its fleet into a great decisive engagement early in the war. Because a protracted war was out of the question, the only chance for Japan was by air attack at the outset of hostilities. "We should do our best to decide the fate of the war on the very first day."[70] As stated, Yamamoto strenuously opposed the war, but once the decision was made and he was ordered to fight, as commander in chief of the Combined Fleet he was duty bound to fight on his own terms, which was the Pearl Harbor attack.

On 7 January 1941 Yamamoto sent Oikawa a long memorandum elaborating his plan. He categorically declared, "I don't think that throughout the whole period of the anticipated war there will be such things as all of the Combined Fleet closing in on an enemy force, deploying, engaging in a gunnery and torpedo duel, and finally charging into the enemy force in as gallant a way as possible." Throwing overboard the conventional strategy, Yamamoto pressed for his plan.

"The most important thing for us to do at the outset of the war with the U.S., I firmly believe, is to fiercely attack and destroy the U.S. main fleet at the outset of the war, so that *the morale of the U.S. Navy and the American people goes down to such an extent that it cannot be recovered.*"[71] He repeated this idea in his letter to the new navy minister, Shimada, on 24 October 1941: "The only way for us is to give a powerful air force strike at the enemy's heart at the very beginning of the war and thus *deal a blow, material and morale, from which it will not be able to recover for some time.*"[72] Yamamoto feared that if the navy took the defensive wait-and-react strategy, the United States would conduct air raids on Tokyo and other big cities from its carriers, destroying Japanese morale.

What Yamamoto aimed at was the psychological shock as well as physical devastation of a Pearl Harbor attack. But if he had counted on shattering the American morale, he badly miscalculated American national character. What had become of his earlier warnings that the "Yankee spirit" should never be underestimated? For all his vaunted knowledge about America, how did he fail to see that a surprise attack would unite the American people, guaranteeing that they would turn their full fury against Japan, preventing anything like a negotiated peace? Did he not understand that a democracy fights in anger? Japanese historians have generally concluded that Yamamoto indeed shared with his countrymen a general underestimation of the American people. In reality, however, he seems to have been fully aware of the risk of provoking the American people. In the summer of 1941 he told Prime Minister Konoe, "There are some who say that if we give a terrible blow to the enemy at the outset of the war, warships cannot be replenished quickly, so Americans will raise their hands and surrender. But such a view totally ignores America's national wealth, industrial might, national character, etc. In addition, you have to guard against American air power. Even if we destroy their fleet and give a toast aboard our ship, enemy aircraft may attack Tokyo and you may get killed."[73]

It is possible that Yamamoto exaggerated the fragility of the American morale in order to sell his Pearl Harbor plan to the incredulous Naval General Staff. The latter was still wedded to the Mahanian concepts of a decisive fleet encounter. Yamamoto rejected as totally infeasible this Mahanian doctrine.

Yamamoto's proposed operation was a supreme gamble; he admitted that "this operation is so difficult and so dangerous that we must be prepared to risk complete annihilation of our fleet."[74] Yamamoto's operational plan states, "In the moon-lit night or the dawn, we throw our entire air strength, anticipating a total annihilation." He expressed his innermost feelings when he confessed to Shimada that the operation was "conceived in desperation."

The Naval General Staff, committed to the traditional strategy of interceptive operations plus the southern operation, vehemently opposed Yamamoto's
plan. It would divide the fleets. It wagered the entire first-line carrier striking
force on a single operation, one that might be futile if the Pacific Fleet was absent
from Pearl Harbor. Japan could not spare the ships from the all-important
southern operation that a Pearl Harbor attack would require. After the war, Rear
Admiral Tomioka, Chief of the Operations Section at that time, summarized
his reasons for objecting to Yamamoto's plan: "In the first place, the idea cut
across the grain of all our thinking and planning prior to that time. Secondly,
as everyone agreed, it was a plan of tremendous complexity. Thirdly, Japan's
fate so completely depended on her fleet that we could not bring ourselves to
accept the staggering losses we thought inherent in such an inadmissible risk.
Lastly, we considered the southern operation of such importance that we did
not want anything else to jeopardize its success."[75]

To the Naval General Staff the idea of surprise air attack was too risky, but
to Yamamoto the war with America was itself risky in the extreme:

> But even more risky and illogical, it seems to me, is the idea of going to war
> against America, Britain and China following four years of exhausting opera-
> tions in China . . . and having, moreover, to sustain ourselves unassisted for ten
> years or more in a protracted war over an area several times more vast than the
> European war theater. If, in the face of such odds, we decide to go to war—or,
> rather, are forced to do so by the trend of events—I, as the authority responsible
> for the fleet, can see little hope of success in any ordinary strategy.[76]

Bitter controversy developed between the Naval General Staff and Yamamoto's
Combined Fleet staff, but he doggedly persisted. On 19 October Nagano finally
gave in, not because he was persuaded but because Yamamoto threatened to
resign with his entire staff. Nagano had to consider Yamamoto's popularity and
prestige.[77] Leaders decided to launch the Pearl Harbor raid simultaneously with
attacks on the Philippines and Singapore. Nagano's assent to a Pearl Harbor
attack, however, did not preclude interceptive operations. In fact, as late as
15 November the Liaison Conference adopted a strategic plan that was approved
by Nagano. It reiterated the wait-and-react strategy: "Our Empire will promptly
conduct a war to overthrow American and British bases in East Asia and the
southwest Pacific, thus establishing a superior strategic position. At the same
time we shall endeavor to secure an important resource area and main lines of
sea communications so as to establish a long-term posture of self-sufficiency.
Every available means must be used *to lure the main force of the United States at
an appropriate time and annihilate it.*"[78]

This seemed to be a restatement of traditional interceptive operations. The Naval General Staff regarded the air attack on Hawaii as a subsidiary operation to delay transpacific advance of the U.S. fleet pending the establishment of the "impregnable southern sphere." The object of the Naval General Staff's strategy was to delay the advance of the U.S. fleet, allow Japan to complete occupation of the southern resource area, and prepare for interceptive operations. In such operations the battleship was regarded as the main prop and aircraft as merely an auxiliary weapon.

This strategy stood in sharp contrast to Yamamoto's Pearl Harbor plan to destroy the Pacific Fleet at the outset. To Yamamoto, the air attack was the major operation intended to bring about a short war, Japan's only hope. In conducting the Pearl Harbor attack, "we must be determined to settle the issue of war on the first day" even though this involved the risk of "the total annihilation" of Japan's air power.[79] The directive to the Combined Fleet that the Navy Department of the Imperial Headquarters handed to Yamamoto was contained in an imperial decree of 1 December 1941. It stated that the mission of the Imperial Navy was "to annihilate the enemy fleet in the Far East; to intercept and annihilate the enemy fleet when it advanced to Far Eastern waters; [and] to capture the main bases of the United States, Britain, and the Netherlands and occupy these areas in the south. "Pearl Harbor was conspicuous by its absence. The Naval General Staff put a premium on" establishing an impregnable area in the south and at the same time annihilating the enemy fleet and *in the end* destroying the enemy's fighting morale." This was at odds with Yamamoto's plan to destroy the American fleet *at the outset*. To him, the initial attack on Hawaii was the all-important task that would decide the issue of the war.[80]

If, indeed, the possibility of destroying American morale ever existed, such a possibility was shattered by the surprise attack on the morning of 7 December, which improvidently turned into a "sneak attack" on account of the incredible ineptitude of the Japanese Foreign Ministry and its embassy officials in Washington. The Pearl Harbor attack was phenomenally successful in its shock effect, but its impact was exactly the opposite of what the Japanese had counted on. As Prange observes, "The American people reeled with a mind-staggering mixture of surprise, awe, mystification, grief, humiliation, and, above all, cataclysmic fury."[81] "Remember Pearl Harbor" became the rallying cry, instantly uniting the American people and turning what Japan had conceived to be a limited war into an unlimited war, a fight to the finish.

In launching air attacks from carriers, leaders of the Japanese navy, even those who planned and commanded the Hawaiian operation, were unaware that it was revolutionizing naval warfare. Their Pearl Harbor plan had not been formulated in order to revolutionize the world's naval strategy; they had conducted the surprise attack for the sole purpose of damaging the Pacific Fleet in Pearl Harbor. But the attack showed beyond doubt that the prop of sea power was no longer the battleship; air power now occupied center stage. However, steeped in the Mahanian tradition of the primacy of the battleship and decisive fleet engagement, the Japanese navy failed to shift to the idea of air war. Rear Admiral Fukudome, chief of the Operations Division and a devotee of the principle of "big battleships and big guns," wrote after the war, "Having for many years been preoccupied with fleet drills centering on the battleship, I could not make a mental switch, and even after the great success of the task force in the Pearl Harbor attack, I believed that the task force should be assigned auxiliary operations and that the main prop of the decisive fleet encounter was the 'big battleships and big guns.'"[82]

Mahan observed in *Naval Strategy* that a lesson of war is to be found in the operational record of failure. The Japanese did not learn a lesson from their success at Pearl Harbor and the success was its own undoing—witness the Japanese defeat at the Battle of Midway in June 1942 when the Japanese navy still thought in terms of a fleet encounter centering on the battleship. It was not until 1944 that leaders decided to concentrate the navy's efforts on aircraft carriers. Ironically, the U.S. Navy quickly learned the "lesson of Pearl Harbor," and American admirals from Ernest J. King on down turned to air power to bring ultimate victory. The American carrier task force taking off from Marshalls, Truck, Marianas, the western Carolines, the Philippines, and Iwo Jima wrought devastation on Okinawa and finally Japan's mainland.

THE "HULL NOTE" AND THE DECLARATION OF WAR

In late November negotiations in Washington had come to a halt. On 26 November Secretary of State Hull handed to Ambassadors Nomura and Kurusu Saburō, the latter a professional diplomat who had arrived to assist Nomura, a stringent document that went beyond any statements in the long series of Japanese-American conversations. It contained a demand for full and unconditional troop withdrawal from China (presumably including Manchuria) and Indochina, repudiation of the Greater East Asia Co-Prosperity Sphere, reaffirmation of the Nine-Power Treaty, and nullification of the Tripartite Pact.[83] The Hull note (a term coined in Japan) was received with consternation in Tokyo. Japanese leaders agreed that accepting it would be tantamount to defeat, abandoning all of

Japan's hard-won gains since 1931. Shimada remembered, "The note was hardly acceptable to the Japanese government and Japanese people. . . . The hardening of anti-Japanese sentiment in the United States, acceleration of joint Anglo-American war preparations, and the reinforcement of U.S. armed forces in East Asia—given these facts we had to consider the danger of the United States taking positive [preemptive] operations. So we had no choice but to regard the Hull note as tantamount to an ultimatum." Rear Admiral Ugaki Matome wrote, "Not a single one of our claims had been accepted. The note incorporated the selfish demands of the United States and the wishful conditions [of China and Britain]. Having come to this impasse, what need is there for further consideration? There is no way left but to attack the United States." Navy men shared with army officers the feeling that the Hull note was "the grace of Heaven. It ensures war. A happy ending."[84]

Even after the Hull Note was received, a handful of naval elders voiced caution about commencing hostilities. On 29 November Okada gathered elder statesmen who belonged to the "peace faction," such as Admirals Yonai and Kobayashi. Okada's own view was, "Domestic problems [the army-navy conflict] can be settled if we resolutely deal with them, but if we fail in our external problems it would plague the nation for a hundred years." Yonai believed that "there are other important factors than that of 'gradual pauperization.' There are questions that only time can solve, such as the course of the European war, and great caution must be taken not to start hostilities precipitately." He warned about the danger of losing everything at once by trying to avoid "gradual pauperization."[85] On 26 November the worried emperor suggested to Prime Minister Tōjō that elder statesmen be allowed to attend the Imperial Conference because of the momentous issues involved. Because Tōjō objected on procedural grounds, naval elders gathered at the palace on 29 November, followed by a luncheon with the emperor. Yonai and Okada hoped there would be no war, although they pledged to support the government if war came. Yonai repeated that greatest care should be taken "not to lose everything all at once." Okada felt that oil was insufficient for war, as were tankers to carry resources from the south.[86] But these were voices in the wilderness, because elder statesmen had no power.

On the morning of 30 November Prince Takamatsu, the emperor's younger brother now assigned to the Operations Division, called on Hirohito and told him that the navy seemed to have its hands full and wanted, if at all possible, to avoid war. Takamatsu advised the emperor that because his decision would be irrevocable, he should immediately send for Shimada and Nagano to ascertain the real situation in the navy. The emperor asked the naval leaders whether the navy could proceed with protracted war. Nagano replied, "Commander in Chief Yamamoto has considerable confidence and is completely prepared for his operations." Shimada also stated, "We are confident that we are better prepared to fight now than we will ever be at any later date." The morale of the fleets was high, especially those participating in the Hawaii operation. These oblique answers seemed to satisfy Hirohito. He then ordered Prime Minister Tōjō to proceed with the operation as planned.[87] Prince Takamatsu's last-minute intervention collapsed in the face of Shimada's and Nagano's evasive replies. Whatever the emperor's inner doubt, the navy was to commence hostilities if diplomatic negotiations did not produce a result by midnight on the morning of 1 December.

On the afternoon of 1 December the Imperial Conference met in an atmosphere of crisis, desperation, and ritualistic formality. Apparently Hirohito's attitude had changed since 6 September, when he had urged that diplomacy take precedence over war preparations. Now he said nothing about diplomacy or peace or universal brotherhood. In his "monologue," recorded by an aide in 1946 and published in 1991, Hirohito stated, "Because I thought it would be futile to oppose [the war], I didn't utter a single word." Giving an ex post facto explanation, he said, "If I repressed war advocates, domestic opinion would have reached a boiling point accusing the government of surrendering to the United States without putting up a fight and this would have occasioned a coup d'etat."[88] When Prince Takamatsu still had doubts about war, the emperor replied that as a constitutional monarch he had to respect the unanimous view of the government and the high command. The emperor, who since 1930 had cautioned, warned, even scolded naval leaders in the interest of peace, kept silent at the climactic moment.

The imperial rescript of the declaration of war on 8 December (Japan time) stated that faced with America's embargo, Japan had resolutely arisen for "self-existence and self-defense."[89] This fulfilled the logic of armed escalation that had first been articulated by the Naval General Staff on 1 August 1940, elaborated in the 5 June 1941 report of the First Committee, and sanctioned at the Imperial Conferences of 2 July and 6 September. And the war was to be for "self-existence and self-defense," a vague slogan that had so often appeared in policy documents since 1940 but was never defined. And nothing was said about the establishment of the Great East Asian Co-Prosperity Sphere. This was to be a war without war aims.

On the night before embarking on the Pearl Harbor attack, Commander Fujita Kikuichi, a staff officer of the Eighth Squadron who joined the carrier task force, wrote in his diary, "We have endured British and American tyranny under the fetters of the Washington treaty and for twenty years have sharpened our swords to fight them against heavy odds."[90] On 8 December, Admiral Suetsugu, hearing the news of the successful attack, declared, "Ever since the 10:6 ratio was imposed by the Washington treaty, we have endured unspeakable drills for over twenty years, and today we must say these drills produced a wonderful result. Furthermore we may say that these drills and pent-up resentment exploded today to produce this success."[91] It is significant that these men went all the way back to the Washington Conference to identify the root cause of the war. Such a view recalls Admiral Katō Kanji's denunciation of the Washington treaty system. In fact, Suetsugu's first thought upon hearing about the Pearl Harbor success was of Katō Kanji and how it would please him in the grave. (Katō had died in 1939.)

I once wrote that the ghost of Katō Kanji hovered over Japanese naval leaders on their course to Pearl Harbor.[92] This does not mean Katō the individual but rather his legacy—negation of the Washington system, destruction of the Japanese naval tradition, decimation of Japan's finest naval leadership, supremacy of the Naval General Staff over the Navy Ministry, the obsession of a 70 percent ratio and inevitability of war with the United States, and reopening of the arms race. All these had their origins in decisions made under Katō's influence, by men such as Suetsugu, Prince Fushimi, Ōsumi, and Nagano. And their decisions were implemented by disciples of Katō Kanji and his spiritual heirs, foremost among them being Ishikawa Shingo.

I have written also that the ghost of Alfred T. Mahan hung over these leaders as they prepared for the Pearl Harbor attack.[93] For almost half a century Japanese naval leaders uncritically held to Mahan's theories as they understood them— preoccupation with the battleship, a decisive fleet encounter and annihilation of the enemy's armada, neglect of convoy escort, and, above all, a fatalistic belief in the coming of a Japanese-American war. These doctrines formed mirror images.[94] Another legacy of Mahan was the idea of an inevitable war over China trade, an idée fixe shared by both Japanese and American navy men. This obsession was derived from economic determinism underlying Mahan's philosophy of sea power. Equally disastrous was the Japanese navy's bureaucratic use or misuse of Mahan's sea power doctrine for budgetary precedence over the army. By the 1930s the perceived Mahanian doctrines had hardened into unquestioned dogmas—articles of faith—in the Imperial Japanese Navy.

CONCLUSION

"Limited War" Mentality

In an age of total war, the Japanese navy conceived of the coming conflict essentially in terms of a limited war. Unable to foresee the course of war beyond the initial two years, Japan could not visualize an unlimited war, a war to the finish, or a war that would end only with unconditional surrender. Chief of the Operations Section Tomioka Sadatoshi confessed in his memoirs that "before the opening of hostilities, I saw this as a limited war," a war that would be terminated with negotiated settlement. "Our plan, "Tomioka explained," was to cause the enemy a great damage and thus to win a balance of force in our favor and terminate hostilities on the basis of compromise settlement while Japan still had a margin of strength left."[1] The navy had no plans for a protracted war, and Japan's war leaders hoped that the defeat of American allies, especially Britain, would so damage America's morale that it would seek a compromise peace rather than continue to make sacrifices in the south Pacific.

The Japanese leaders failed to heed Carl von Clausewitz's dictum that "no one starts a war—or rather, no one in his senses ought to do so—without first being clear in his mind what he intends to achieve by that war and how he intends to conduct it." The Japanese navy had no war aims in Clausewitz's sense. To quote Tomioka again, who became head of the Operations Division in 1944, "We naval planners thought exclusively about self-existence and self-defense. The establishment of the Greater East Asian Co-Prosperity Sphere and the liberation of the Asian colonies were not on their mind." Shimada agreed, "We believed that the war was strictly for self-existence and self-defense. Such ideas as the New Order [of East Asia] emerged only after hostilities had commenced and operations progressed." He added that it was deemed unnecessary to discuss war aims in the Naval General Staff, because Japan planned to fight for survival, which was threatened by the oil embargo.[2] This stood in sharp contrast with the United States, which pursued universalistic war aims in the form of the Atlantic Charter of August 1941.

Rear Admiral Nakazawa Tasuku, who became Head of the Operations Division in 1943, later wrote that Japan actually had no comprehensive war plans, but only annual operational plans.[3] The navy's operational plans hardly constituted

287

a grand strategy. Only in March 1941 did the Naval General Staff draft in out-line form the strategy toward the United States and Britain. As for simultaneous operations against a coalition of enemies—the United States, Britain, and the Netherlands—the Operations Division began to draft its plan in June 1941. Completed in rough form in late August, this plan merely added to the con-ventional strategy of war against the United States the operations to seize the "southern resource area."[4]

Japan's war leaders tended to consider the war exclusively in military-strategic terms. They did not fully consider the vast differences in the sinews of national power. Their perception of the coming war might seem almost like a throwback to the pre–World War I age, lacking the understanding of total war that had informed Katō Tomosaburō at the Washington Conference. In 1941 navy men failed to give much thought to the interrelatedness that Katō had emphasized—the linkage of military-strategic, economic, technological, political, diplomatic and ideological factors. Only in August 1945, on the eve of Japan's surrender, did the Research Section of the Navy Ministry admit that the navy had failed to recognize the realities of total war and that the navy was so absorbed in strategic-military operations that it had neglected broader nonmilitary factors.

Total war presupposed total mobilization of national power. But Japan had no master plan based on a reliable estimate of national strength. To be sure, the government, with the backing of the high command, had established the Total War Research Institute in October 1940.[5] Its task was to assemble and analyze essential data for the making of national policy. However, this hastily assembled institute came too late and served merely for research and the training of young officials. It could not provide data for long-term comprehensive policy. Nor could accurate estimates on the nation's war resources be obtained from the Cabinet Planning Board. Its task was to draft annual materials mobi-lization programs, estimate supply and demand of a wide range of materials, and allocate them to the army and the navy. However, this board was racked by interservice rivalry. The two services were so suspicious of each other that they refused to share information on their oil holdings. As the result, the board did not possess even rough figures of the nation's oil stockpiles until late October 1941.[6] To make matters worse, Admiral Okada recalled, the president of the Cabinet Planning Board, Suzuki Teiichi, "told egregious lies," vastly underesti-mating shipping losses in the event of war. When Suzuki was questioned, it turned out that Japan did not have the resources to fight beyond the initial two years. The board often fabricated figures to suit the convenience of the high command.[7]

Within the navy ministry, mobilization and allocation of war matériel were handled by the War Mobilization Bureau, but its assessments were impaired by "pressures bordering on intimidation" from middle-echelon officers in charge of war planning. In late October, Rear Admiral Hoshina Zenshirō, Chief of the War Mobilization Bureau, stated at a bureau chiefs conference that it was impossible to build enough ships to fight a war with the United States, but Captain Ishikawa silenced him, saying, "Such an estimate makes it impossible to go to war!"[8] He pressured Hoshina, forcing him to reverse his estimate. When in October the chief of the Mobilization Section of the Naval General Staff, Captain Hashimoto Shōzō, expressed anxiety about an oil shortage, Ishikawa came up with his own estimate of oil stockpiles. He seemed oblivious to the fact that Japan's oil stocks would last through only the initial eighteen months of hostilities. About the same time, the chief of the Mobilization Section of the Navy Ministry, Captain Kurihara Etsuzō, stated that "the estimates of the Cabinet Planning Board, built on hypothetical figures, were concocted to make it appear that we can wage war." Captain Tomioka of the Operations Section called him to task for voicing a "counsel of defeatism" and told him it was his duty to devise ways of fighting with the limited resources at hand. When Miyo Kazunari, senior air staff, said that with the existing naval air strength he was not confident about war with the United States, Tomioka snapped, "It's not a matter of confidence; it's a matter of life and death."[9]

INTELLIGENCE ABOUT THE UNITED STATES

If the Japanese navy's estimates of its own national sources were faulty, its assessments of American resources were much more so. The Naval General Staff, especially its Operations Division, tended to underestimate American war potential while overestimating that of Germany.

It was not that naval planners lacked information about the United States. Reports from the attaché in Washington, Captain Yokoyama Ichirō, were of high caliber. While he was stationed in the United States as assistant attaché in 1931–33, he studied American history and naval limitation at Yale. When he was appointed attaché in Washington in October 1940, Yokoyama, a friendly, affable, and open-hearted officer, renewed and cultivated acquaintances among American officers. He especially maintained close contact with Rear Admiral Richmond Kelly Turner, Director of War Plans, with whom he had been on friendly terms ever since Turner's visit to Japan in 1939 as captain of the USS

Astoria. A worried Yokoyama asked Turner whether it was too late for the newly appointed ambassador, Admiral Nomura, to attempt a peaceful breakthrough. Turner replied that it was never too late, assuring him that the United States did not wish to fight Japan, and that he would do his very best to avoid war with the "heroic Japanese Navy." But because of his position as director of war plans, Turner said he must operate covertly to cooperate with Nomura. Until the virtual breakdown of the Hull-Nomura negotiations in October 1941, Turner and Yokoyama maintained contact.[10] Such a naval pipeline ensured that Yokoyama's cables to Tokyo were unusually reliable.

Yokoyama's mission was of special significance. Upon his appointment, Navy Minister Oikawa had told him, "You are not going to be the usual sort of naval attaché: instead of collecting naval intelligence, you must help Ambassador Nomura prevent war with the United States." Yokoyama was aware that American public opinion was united in their conviction that no appeasement was possible between democracies and totalitarian nations. If war was to be avoided, Japan would have to discard its aggressive policy. In early February 1941, Yokoyama reported that the United States, while trying to avoid war with Japan, would stiffen its economic oppression of Japan and was rapidly completing war preparations. To normalize relations with the United States, Yokoyama suggested to Tokyo that the Tripartite Pact be speedily abrogated. Taking a page from Mahan, Yokoyama argued that Japan, an oceanic power, should not be an ally of a continental power like Germany or expand in China, recommending that troops be withdrawn from China and Indochina. Instead he urged the Naval General Staff to pursue peaceful maritime expansion to ensure a supply of oil from the United States.[11]

In March 1941, Yokoyama had a "violent altercation" with Captain Yamaguchi Bunjirō, chief of the Fifth (America) Section of the Intelligence Division, then visiting Washington. Shocked to learn about the warlike stance of the Naval General Staff, Yokoyama urged caution and pointed to the industrial might of the United States, but his warnings went unheeded. On the eve of Japan's advance to southern Indochina, Yokoyama cabled Tokyo, "In case of advance to southern Indochina, the United States would without fail totally break off economic relations." On 23 September, Yokoyama warned that the United States might well decide to wage a two-ocean war. The navy authorities in Tokyo dismissed his messages.[12]

These policy recommendations were ignored in the Intelligence Division, which, looked like a stronghold of anti-American officers. Attaché reports from Washington were accumulated in the Fifth Section of the Intelligence

Division, but little effort was made to use such information for operational purposes. In drafting annual operational plans, the Operations Division did not turn to the Intelligence Division; it had its own channels, such as the scouting activities of the Combined Fleet and intercepted foreign communications.

The Intelligence Division did not enjoy anything like the privileged position of the U.S. Office of Naval Intelligence. For one thing, in 1941 its staff was much smaller: 230 for the Office of Naval Intelligence and a mere 79 for Japan's Intelligence Division.[13] Intelligence was one area that was most slighted in the Japanese navy. Members of the Intelligence Division derided themselves, calling their office "the dumping ground for third-rate officers." Neither the Naval Academy nor the Naval Staff College offered a modicum of training in intelligence. Intelligence officers were mostly recruited from language specialists or signal corpsmen, and with the exception of division chiefs, no one had any background in gunnery, torpedoes, navigation, or aviation. After 1936 the Intelligence Division was headed by pro-German, anti-American officers: Nomura Naokuni (1936–38), Abe Katsuo (1938–39), and Oka Takazumi (1939–40). Maeda Minoru (1940–42), a follower of Katō Kanji, was a self-styled "leading war advocate." As late as June 1941 Maeda seriously believed that Germany would land on the British Isles. Conversely, he greatly underestimated the United States. As Maeda recalled, "there was not a single voice of caution in the Intelligence Division; since April or May [1941] a warlike mood became dominant." It is also not surprising that Yokoyama's efforts to save Japanese-American relations were not taken seriously in the Intelligence Division.

Above all, what misled middle-echelon planners was their hubristic confidence that the navy was best informed about its "hypothetical enemy number one." The leading war advocate, Captain Ishikawa, boasted that on the basis of the intensive study he had made at the Naval Staff College, he was better versed in the history of American Far Eastern policy "than any specialist in the Foreign Ministry." In 1936 he had visited the United States on the last leg of a fact-finding tour of Southeast Asia (where he became alarmed at the "encirclement of Japan" led by the United States) and Europe (where he was impressed with Hitler and busied himself gathering data on Germany's strength). How much he learned in the United States may be gathered from a nonchalant statement in his memoirs: "I passed through America in a relaxed tourist mood, because the Japanese navy constantly received detailed information about that country."[14] Ishikawa seemed blind to America's industrial might, estimated to be tenfold that of Japan. As Admiral Inoue Shigeyoshi later remarked, the middle-echelon officers "neglected to inform themselves about the United States." None of the regular members of the First Committee had been stationed in Washington. Captain Hoshina Zenshirō, who taught American naval history at the Naval Staff College in 1934, was surprised by his students officers' lack of knowledge about and underestimation of the United States. In a similar vein Admirals Toyoda Soemu and Inoue criticized the navy's recklessness in "making operational plans without knowing sufficiently about the United States."[15]

The Japanese navy as a whole suffered from grievous misperceptions of American national character. Chihaya Masataka, a lieutenant commander at the time of the Pearl Harbor attack, later wrote, "We thought that we could easily tackle them [Americans]; a race so steeped in material comfort and absorbed in the pursuit of pleasure was spiritually degenerate." Rear Admiral Nakazawa, chief of the Operations Section in 1939–41, believed that the American people, "a composite nation of immigrants, lacked unity, could not withstand adversity and privations, and regarded war a form of sport, so that if we deal a severe blow at the outset of hostilities they would lose the will to fight."[16] Ambassador Grew, who knew the Japanese as well as any American, testified, "They regarded us as 'a decadent nation,'" in which "pacifism and isolationism practically ruled the policy of our Government."

"GROUPTHINK"

Regarding the psychological environment in which decisions leading to war were made, Operations Division Head Fukudome recalled, "When we [naval leaders] were discussing tête-à-tête, we were all for avoiding war, but when we held a conference the conclusion always moved step by step in the direction of war. It was really very strange." Again: "When we took our positions as individuals, we were all in favor of avoiding a Japanese-American war by all means, but each time we got together and conferred, things moved in the least desirable direction. I think the general trend of events simply lay beyond human control. You may call it Fate and I often discussed with Vice Chief of the Naval General Staff Itō and Chief of Naval Affairs Bureau Oka why people who are so opposed to war moved step by step to in the direction of starting a war each time we met in a conference."[17]

Drifting with the tide attested to the surrender of leadership. Nagano was one such fatalist: "As I see it, the truth of the matter was that it was the force of circumstances that gradually compelled us to a war determination." It is easier to make decisions in the face of great uncertainty if one is a fatalist. What characterized these men in the navy's high echelons were almost pathological lethargy, abandonment of independent thinking, and evasion of responsibility.

Decision-making excessively based on consensus building may be characterized as "groupthink." The psychologist Irvin L. Janis writes, "Doubts were entertained but never pressed, partly out of fear of being labeled 'soft' or undaring in the eyes of colleagues."[18] The historian Robert J. C. Butow's observation is perceptive: "Had anyone attempted to probe deeply, he would very likely have been told not to quibble. He might even have been thought a coward. Hence, as a general rule, no one said anything even when assailed by doubts."[19]

ARMY-NAVY RIVALRY AND BUREAUCRATIC POLITICS

Army-navy rivalry was an important factor in Japan's drift toward war. The First Committee and middle-echelon officers urged a "determination to go to war" so that the navy could complete its war preparations regardless of diplomatic negotiations in Washington. The more cautious leaders of the navy ministry tried to draw a line between "war preparations" and "war determination." For the army, however, the two words were synonymous: "preparations" involved mobilization of manpower, hundreds of thousands of troops, and concentration and deployment toward the south—a process that, once set in motion, could not easily be stopped, much less reversed. So the army could not complete "war preparations" unless "war determination" had been reached. On the other hand, the navy could proceed with "war preparations" without having reached "war determination." Ships and aircraft could be withdrawn to bases should a diplomatic settlement be reached. So the navy could respond flexibly to the problem of peace or war.[20] Fearing that the navy might pull out at the last minute, the army wanted to bind the navy to "war determination," but navy ministry leaders would not oblige as long as there was a ray of hope for diplomacy.

This organizational difference lay at the heart of the interservice distrust and feuding that accompanied formulation of national policy. Indeed, until late November 1941 the navy's advocacy of "war preparations without war determination" seemed to army planners a "political trick" to procure budget and war matériel at the army's expense. Disgusted army staff officers scrawled in the Confidential War Journal, "If the navy is advocating war with the United States in order to increase its armaments, is not the navy a traitor to the country?" (17 February); "The navy is as unprincipled as a woman!" (23 February); "The navy's whole attitude and preparations to date have been directed toward the single aim of expanding itself" (16 October); "Is the navy a warrior and samurai? At this critical moment that will decide the nation's fate, the navy is begging for matériel like a panhandler. Is it not the navy's usual trick to get matériel without determining for war?" (1 November).[21]

It was not just middle-echelon officers who were absorbed in the scramble for budget and materiel. Admiral Inoue, whose sound judgments we have noted throughout, was not immune to the bureaucratic game. He wrote, "The army is like a madman, almost pillaging domestic resources. . . . As far as materials are concerned, a state of anarchy prevails."[22]

Of course, army-navy differences could also be found in the United States—for example, over the defense of the Philippine base, the drafting of War Plan Orange, or, for that matter, the military force of other powers—but nowhere did interservice differences reach such intensity as in Japan. Army-navy conflict cancelled out well-thought-out strategy. Hara Shirō, a former officer of the Army General Staff, has cited four reasons for this: (1) the geopolitical situation of Japan as a sea power as well as a continental power; (2) the idea of parity between the army and the navy; (3) the inability of the emperor under the Meiji Constitution to directly intervene and dissolve army-navy differences; and (4) the existence of an organ for intragovernmental "coordination"—the Liaison Conference—which, on the contrary, tended to exacerbate interservice differences.[23]

Interservice infighting and the bureaucratic contention for a larger share of budget or war matériel accompanied formulation of any major national and defense policies. Here one glimpses the world of illogic reminiscent of *Catch-22*, Joseph Heller's novel about World War II. The navy could not say that it could not fight the United States lest the army say there was no need of budget and materiel for a navy that could not fight. But if the navy claimed that it was ready to fight the United States, the army would reply that the navy by its own admission did not need an increase. When Chief of the Naval General Staff Nagano stated at the Liaison Conference of 21 July 1941 that "if Japan struck now it could easily take the Philippines," Navy Vice Minister Sawamoto, who was a moderate, thought this was a very inopportune remark: "It can be interpreted to mean that the navy has already completed its preparations. Since the navy ministry is bent on increasing its naval budget by clamoring for completion of war preparations, Nagano's utterance was a most untoward one." Commander Fujii, a fire-eating extremist, also criticized Nagano's statement: "To say that we can strike now implies that the navy does not need further arms increase."[24]

The navy's preoccupations with budget and matériel could be found both in war advocates such as Commander Fujii and in moderate leaders such as Inoue and Sawamoto. The fundamental difficulty, as Inoue stated, was that "the army's armament against the Soviet Union is incompatible with the navy's armament aimed at Britain and the United States." The tragedy was that the navy lacked strong leaders who could transcend sectional and bureaucratic differences and declare, as Katō Tomosaburō had at the Washington Conference, that "national defense is not a monopoly of the military."

The Army General Staff's denunciation of the navy's "irresponsibility" was also inspired by bureaucratic interests, but it contained a grain of truth. The navy's all-too-frequent invocation of such slogans as "War with America" and "Our Enemy the United States" to fortify its claim to budgetary appropriations so vulgarized these terms that many of its officers—especially in the middle and lower echelons—had become numbed to their significance. In June 1936, when Navy Minister Nagano was pushing for the "Fundamentals of National Policy," he had the sense to say confidentially to Vice Admiral Sakonji Seizō, "It is for the sake of the morale and training of our forces [and, he might have added, for budgetary purposes] that we make an outward pretense of some day conducting operations against the United States and Britain. But in reality I wish to guide the navy toward friendly relations with these powers."[25] A former officer put in a nutshell the dilemma that faced naval leaders: "Although the navy demands priority to complete its armaments against the United States in order to prepare for the worst, it does not desire to go to war with that power. But we cannot say it is absolutely opposed to war with the U.S. either, for others [the army] will retort that in that case naval armaments against the United States are unnecessary."[26] Such an ambivalent policy went bankrupt as soon as it confronted a real crisis. Middle- and lower-echelon officers, trained to fight America as "*the* enemy," had become obsessed with the idea of war. In the end, concern for the "morale of our fleet" and "control over naval officers" became a matter of overriding importance that immobilized Navy Minister Oikawa and overcame his inner reservations about the Tripartite Pact and, finally, his opposition to going to war.

FAILURE OF NAVAL LEADERSHIP

We have traced the decline of peacetime leadership of the Imperial Japanese Navy starting with the death of Katō Tomosaburō in 1923 and the catastrophic effects of the Ōsumi purges of 1933–34, which decimated leaders of moderate persuasion. Admiral Shimada, navy minister at the time of the Pearl Harbor attack, said after the war, "If Hori Teikichi had been navy minister, the outcome would have been quite different." Shimada meant that perhaps the war could have been avoided.[27] Aside from the Yonai-Yamamoto-Inoue triumvirate that had successfully blocked the Tripartite Pact when they held office, few leaders during the 1930s could exert effective control over the unruly subordinates. After the war, Vice Admiral Sawamoto, navy vice minister (1941–44), wrote reflectively:

1. What prevailed was a competition of mediocrities; there was no outstanding leader of outstanding ability. Pressure from subordinates was the order of the day. Younger officers would not respect their seniors and this made the matter even more difficult.

2. Everybody wanted to evade responsibility and no one had the grit to sacrifice himself to do his duty.

3. The atmosphere was such that it put a premium on parochial and selfish concerns for either the army or the navy; considerations of the nation and the world were secondary.[28]

Admiral Inoue was even more outspoken in his attack on senior naval leaders: "In late 1940 and early 1941 the navy took the lead in intervention in Thailand and Indochina. As subordinates in the Navy Ministry and the Naval General Staff began preparations and mobilization, they were governed by the idea of inevitable war, whipping up a belligerent spirit in their speeches and actions. Senior leaders of the Navy Ministry and the Naval General Staff did not have the courage and resources to control their subordinates, thus creating one crisis after another."[29]

Generally in the decision-making process, the more serious the crisis the more limited the number of players, and top leaders take charge. Participation of subordinates—with attendant preoccupation with bureaucratic politics—is kept to a minimum. National interest and security become the overriding concern on the part of the central policy maker. The Cuban Missile Crisis of 1962 was a case in point. But Japan's decision to go to war with the United States constitutes a conspicuous exception to this generalization. Naval leaders failed in "crisis management," that is, the exercise of detailed control by top leadership. Externally, the navy failed to control the crisis with the United States and, internally, it failed to contain rivalry with the army as well as control the navy's own subordinates. In the navy of 1941 responsible, "centralized decision makers" hardly existed. To the extent they existed, they were under pressure from their unruly subordinates to open hostilities as soon as possible. Chief of the Naval General Staff Nagano was a case in point. He was pressured and influenced by fire-eating middle-echelon officers. Pleas for rational decision making to avoid war did come from men such as Yamamoto and Inoue, but they were not in central decision-making positions and could not yield much influence. Viewed from the standpoint of the decision-making process, therefore, the Japanese navy's road to Pearl Harbor can best be studied in terms of the failure—or absence—of leadership.

TABLES

	Total National Budget*	Naval Budget*	Percentage of Naval Budget
1917	780	119	15.2%
1918	902	185	20.5%
1919	1,064	250	23.4%
1920	1,505	399	26.5%
1921	1,591	502	31.6%
---------------------------------Washington Conference---------------------------------			
1922	1,501	397	26.5%
1923	1,389	279	20.0%
1924	1,785	282	15.8%
1925	1,580	227	14.4%
1926	1,666	240	14.4%
1927	1,759	256	14.6%
1928	1,857	271	14.6%
1929	1,774	269	15.2%
1930	1,828	278	15.2%
1931	1,498	212	14.1%
1932	2,091	315	15.0%
1933	2,321	404	17.4%
1934	2,224	489	22.0%
1935	2,215	530	23.9%
1936	2,418	583	24.1%

*Amounts in millions.

Source: Senshishitsu, *Kaigun gunsenbi*, 1:741–42.

TABLE 2.   The Reed-Matsudaira Compromise, 1930

Category	United States (tons)	Japan (tons)	Japan's Ratio
8-inch-gun cruiser	(18)* 180,000	(12) 108,400	60.2%
6-inch-gun cruiser	143,500	108,415	76%
Destroyer	150,000	97,500	65%
Submarine	52,700	52,700	100.00%
Total	526,200	367,050	69.75%

*Number of ships in parenthesis.

Source: TSM, 1:63.

TABLE 3.   Japan's Naval Strength Compared to That of the United States,
December 1941 (including outdated ships)*

	Ships		
Category	United States (tons)	Japan (tons)	Japan's Ratio
Battleship	(17) 534,300	(10) 301,400	56%
Carrier	(8) 162,600	(10) 152,970	94%
Heavy cruiser	(18) 171,200	(18) 158,800	93%
Light cruiser	(19) 157,775	(20) 98,855	62%
Destroyer	(172) 239,530	(112) 165,858	69%
Submarine	(111) 116,621	(65) 97,900	84%
Total	(345) 1,382,026	(235) 975,793	70.6%

*Number of ships in parenthesis.

Source: TSM, 7:323.

TABLE 4.   Japan's Naval Aircraft Strength Compared to That of the United
States, December 1941

	United States	Japan	Japan's Ratio
Total	5,500	3,300	60%
Selected	2,600*	1,669**	64%

*Number of aircraft operational for use against Japan.

**Number of aircraft belonging to the Combined Fleet.

Source: Hoshina, Daitōa Sensō, 60–61.

TABLE 5. Projected Ratios of Japanese Warships to
U.S. Warships, 1942–44

Year	Excluding Obsolete Ships	Including Obsolete Ships
1942	65%	76%
1943	50%	60%
1944	30%	30%

Source: TSM, 7:324.

TABLE 6. Japan's Projected Naval Aircraft Strength
Compared to That of the United States,
1942–44

Year	United States	Japan
1942	47,900	4,000
1943	85,000	8,000
1944	more than 100,000	12,000

Source: Ibid.

NOTES ON PRINCIPAL
SOURCES

The single most important source for this study is the official records pertaining to the naval conferences between the wars. These massive records, 259 volumes, were carefully preserved in their entirety by the late Enomoto Jūji, a specialist in international law and naval limitation who served as professor at the Naval Staff College and councilor to the Navy Ministry. As adviser to the Japanese delegations, he participated in all the naval conferences and kept the basic materials. The records include cables, instructions, and reports. Because of his efforts, these documents escaped destruction at the time of Japan's surrender. I was allowed to study Enomoto's papers at his home in 1975 and learned much from conversations with him. He was, so to speak, a "walking encyclopedia" on naval limitation. After his death in 1979, the bulk of his papers went to the library of the Institute of Defense Studies, Japanese Defense Agency, where they are in record group "Gunbi gunshuku" [Naval Armament and Limitation]. (However, some materials were retained by his surviving family. In my endnotes, this portion is indicated as the Enomoto Papers.)

Nicely complementing the Enomoto Papers is the equally valuable but much smaller collection of Vice Admiral Hori Teikichi, which I take credit for unearthing some twenty-six years ago. A consistent advocate of naval limitation, he attended the Washington and Geneva Conferences and was chief of the Naval Affairs Bureau at the time of the 1930 London Conference. The bulk of the Hori collection relates to the London Conference of 1930 but contains some important memoranda on the Washington Conference. The originals of the Hori Papers are deposited at the library of the National Maritime Self-Defense Staff College. (Access to the Hori Papers at the NMSDC is unduly restrictive; it is much easier to use them at JDA, which photocopied a large part of them.)

Among many source materials, printed or unpublished, the most interesting is the diary of Admiral Katō Kanji, the leading opponent of naval limitation from 1921 onward, recently published together with some of his papers. Rear Admiral Takagi Sōkichi, the navy's "political antenna" as chief of the Research Section during the latter half of the 1930s, has left a sizable manuscript collection, a portion of which has been published as *Nikki to jōhō* [Diary and Reports] (2 volumes). Unfortunately, some of the papers and diaries of important officers remain closed.

Sugiyama memo, notes by Chief of the Army General Staff Sugiyama Hajime, records the Imperial Headquarters–Government Liaison Conferences. They have been edited and translated by Ike Nobutaka as *Japan's Decision for War: Records of the 1941 Policy Conferences*.

Unlike in the United States and Britain, authors of official Japanese war history were former army and navy officers, to the exclusion of academic historians. The Japanese government never seems to have learned that military/naval history is too serious a business to be left to former officers. This notwithstanding, the official war history volumes listed in the bibliography are of high quality. Because of the virtual nonexistence of official naval records for 1936–41, I extensively used those volumes in lieu of primary sources, because they copiously cite from extensive interviews with surviving officers. In 1973–74 army historians published a five-volume account of the origins of "the Greater East Asian War." As if to reenact the prewar and wartime interservice differences, naval historians responded by publishing a two-volume study in 1979 that brought out the navy's view of the origins of the Pacific War. If this study seems to rely excessively on those volumes, I must say that I use them almost as primary sources. Also important, and perhaps more authoritative, are excellent volumes on the Combined Fleet by Nomura Minoru and on naval armament by Suekuni Masao.

The standard collaborative work on diplomatic and military/naval history in the 1930s remains the Japan's Road to the Pacific War series, selective translations under the general editorship of James William Morley. The relevant volumes for my purposes are *Japan Erupts, 1928–1932*, valuable for the London Conference; *Deterrent Diplomacy, 1935–1940*, for the Tripartite Pact; *The Fateful Choice, 1939–1941*, for the southward advance; and particularly *The Final Confrontation, 1941* (superbly translated by David Titus). Although their Japanese original, *Taiheiyō sensō e no michi* [The Road to the Pacific War], appeared in 1963, these volumes have not yet been superseded. *Bekkan shiryōhen* [Separate Volume on Documents] is the single most valuable collection of extant documents.

Memoirs by former naval officers must be read with care. It is ironic that officers of the vanquished navy have written far more extensively than their American counterparts. The tone of their works varies from self-justificatory, nostalgic, and tragic to censorious. Takagi Sōkichi has published half a dozen useful memoirs and histories. A series of naval biographies by the novelist Agawa Hiroyuki, himself a former naval officer, are both highly readable and well researched. Another former officer who turned naval historian par excellence is Nomura Minoru, whose official history, *Rengō kantai* [The Combined Fleet], and numerous other books set a standard for naval history. Among naval biographies, the one on Admiral Inoue Shigeyoshi is most rewarding.

With a few exceptions, no oral history project exists in Japan on the scale of the Columbia University project. Some records of interviews exist both at the War History Office of the Japanese Defense Agency and at the Office of War Crimes Materials at the Japanese Ministry of Justice.

The essential encyclopedia of naval (also army) history is Hata Ikuhiko, ed., *Nihon rikukaigun sōgō jiten,* which contains biographical sketches of all important officers, a directory of officers who held important posts, institutional changes, a list of graduates of the Naval Academy and the Naval Staff College, and other materials.

ABBREVIATIONS

CNO: Chief of Naval Operations

DL: Kokkai Toshoikan Kensei Shiryōshitsu (National Diet Library)

HMSO: Her Majesty's Stationery Office

JDA: Library, Institute of Defense Studies, Japanese Defense Agency

JMFA: Japanese Ministry of Foreign Affairs

JMJ: Archives of the Japanese Ministry of Justice, Senpan Shiryōshitsu (Office of War Crimes Materials)

LC: Library of Congress

NA: National Archives

NGS: Naval General Staff

NMSDC: National Maritime Self-Defense Staff College

NWC: Naval War College

ONI: Office of Naval Intelligence

PRO: Public Record Office

ABBREVIATED TITLES

DBFP: Documents on British Foreign Policy

DGFP: Documents on German Foreign Policy

FRUS: Foreign Relations of the United States

GS: Gendaishi shiryō

Harada-Saionji: Harada Kumao, *Saionjikō to seikyoku*

Inoue Shigeyoshi-S: Documents appended to this biography

Kaigunshō shiryō: Ōkubo Tatsumasa et al., eds., *Shōwa shakai keizai shiryō shūsei: Kaigunshō shiryō*

Kimitsu sensō nisshi: Daihon'ei Rikugunbu Sensō Shidō Han, ed., *Kimitsu sensō nisshi*

NGB: Nihon gaikō bunsho

Nihon kaigunshi: Kaigun Rekishi Hozonkai, ed., *Nihon kaigunshi*

Pearl Harbor Attack: U.S. Congress, *Hearings before the Joint Committee of Investigation*

Senshibu, *Kaigun kaisen keii:* Bōeichō Bōei Kenshūjo Senshibu, *Daihon'ei Kaigunbu Daitōa sensō kaisen keii*

Senshitsu, *Rikugun kaisen keii:* Bōeichō Bōei Kenshūjo Senshibu, *Daihon'ei Rikugunbu Daitōa sensō kaisen keii*

TSM: Taiheiyō sensō e no michi

TSM-S: Taiheiyō sensō e no michi: Bekkan shiryōhen (Supplementary Volume of Documents)

NOTES

CHAPTER ONE   MAHAN AND JAPANESE-AMERICAN
RELATIONS

1. Roosevelt, *Letters*, 1:221–22.

2. Mahan, *Influence of Sea Power upon History*; Karsten, "The Nature of 'Influence,'"
585–600.

3. Puleston, 145, 154–60.

4. Poultney Bigelow to Mahan, 12 April 1897, Mahan Papers.

5. Dingman, "Japan and Mahan," 50.

6. Oriental Association to Mahan, 1 April 1897, Mahan Papers.

7. Mahan, *From Sail to Steam*, 303.

8. In all, five of Mahan's books and an anthology have been translated into Japanese.

9. The translation of *The Interest of America in Sea Power* is Minakami Umehiko,
trans., *Taiheiyō kaiken ron*.

10. Seager, *Mahan*, 2–5.

11. Mahan, *From Sail to Steam*, xiv, 274.

12. Ibid., 198.

13. Mahan, *Letters*, 1:43–44.

14. Sir Rutherford Alcock, *The Capital of the Tycoon: Narratives of a Three Years'
Residence in Japan* (New York: Harper, 1863).

15. Mahan, *From Sail to Steam*, 243–47.

16. Ibid., 254.

17. Mahan, *Letters*, 1:140, 334–35, 337–38; Mahan, *From Sail to Steam*, 235–36.

18. Mahan, *From Sail to Steam*, 129, 135, 236, 247, 335.

19. Seager, *Mahan*, 119; Puleston, 48.

20. The U.S. Navy played a role in the modernization of the Imperial Japanese Navy,
having accepted seventeen Japanese students at Annapolis from 1869 to 1906.
Ellicott, 303–7.

21. Mahan, *Interest of America*, 10; Vincent Davis, 110; Baer, 1.

22. Mahan, *From Sail to Steam*, 324.

23. Mahan, *Influence*, 29–89; Seager, *Mahan*, 7.

24. Weigley, *American Way of War*, 176, 178.

25. Sprout and Sprout, *Rise of American Naval Power*, 3.

26. Ibid., v; Mahan, *Influence*, 287–88; Vincent Davis, 112.

27. Spector, *Eagle*, 43.

28. Baer, 16, 121; Crowl, 475.

29. Mahan, *Influence*, 28, 53.

30. Mahan, *Interest of America*, 6; Sumida, 27; Karsten, *Naval Aristocracy*, 226; Sprout and Sprout, *Rise of American Naval Power*, 219.

31. LaFeber, *New Empire*, 88–93; LaFeber, "Note on the 'Mercantilistic Imperialism.'"

32. Vincent Davis, 108.

33. Mahan, *Interest of America*, 7–8.

34. Ibid., 47, 49.

35. Seager, *Mahan*, 249.

36. Iriye, *Pacific Estrangement*, 49–50.

37. Mahan, *Interest of America*, 31–32; *Letters*, 2:92–93; Love, *History of the U.S. Navy*, 1:386; Iriye, *Pacific Estrangement*, 53–56.

38. Braisted, *The United States Navy in the Pacific, 1897–1909*, 12.

39. Mahan, *Letters*, 2:506.

40. Puleston, 182; Turk, 119.

41. Mahan, *Letters*, 2:538.

42. Cited in Pratt, *Expansionists of 1898*, 3; Iriye, *Pacific Estrangement*, 49–52; Livezey, 170.

43. Vlahos, "Naval War College," 24; Mahan, *Letters*, 2:506–7.

44. Mahan, *Interest of America*, 243, 259.

45. Ibid., 162, 235, 237, 251–52.

46. Mahan, *Letters*, 2:569, 619.

47. Ibid., 579–80.

48. Ibid., 579–80; Livezey, 4.

49. Mahan, *Letters*, 2:582–83.

50. Puleston, 1; Livezey, 176; Mahan, *Problem of Asia*, 63–67; Mahan, *Interest of America*, 236; Mahan, *Letters*, 2:658.

51. Mahan, *Problem of Asia*, 87–90, 154, 165, 167.

52. Vlahos, "Naval War College," 26, 63.

53. Mahan, *Problem of Asia*, 108.

54. Ibid., 101–2, 106–7, 110, 148–49, 151; Mahan, *Letters*, 2:707.

55. Mahan, *Letters*, 3:80.

56. Seager, *Mahan*, 472; Turk, 59, 89.

57. Mahan, "Some Reflections upon the Far Eastern War"; Mahan, "Retrospect upon the War between Japan and Russia"; Mahan, *Naval Strategy*, 422–23.

58. Mahan, *Letters*, 3:221–22; Ōmae, "Kyū Nihon kaigun," 13–14.

59. Vlahos, "Naval War College," 28.

60. Quoted in Love, *History of the U.S. Navy*, 1:440.

61. Mahan, *Letters*, 3:226; Mahan to Roosevelt, 2 December 1911, Roosevelt Papers; Seager, *Mahan*, 479.

62. Report from the United States, No. 86, No. 89, Taniguchi to Tōgō, 29 April 1907 (No. 11, secret), Papers of Saitō Makoto.

63. Mahan, *Letters*, 3:277–78; Levy, 281.

64. Yamamoto Eisuke, *Danshaku Ōsumi Mineo*, 382.

65. Mahan, *Letters*, 3:355.

66. Hattendorf, *Mahan on Naval Strategy*, 175; Mahan, *Letters*, 3:495–99.

67. Mahan, *Letters*, 3:500; Tokutomi Sohō, *Jimu ikkagen* [My Opinions on Current Affairs], Tokyo: Min'yūsha, 1913, 471–73; Kodera Kenkichi, *Dai-Ajia shugiron*, 421–23.

68. See Asada, *Ryō taisenkan*, 296–304; Neumann, "Franklin Delano Roosevelt," 713–19.

69. Turk, 93; Asada, "Jinshu to bunka," 297–300.

70. Mahan, *Letters*, 3:355–56.

71. Ibid., 3:380–83; Braisted, *The United States Navy in the Pacific, 1909–1922*, 33–35.

72. Mahan, *Letters*, 3:380, 389–93, 439, 480–83; Seager, *Mahan*, 482–88; Braisted, *The United States Navy in the Pacific, 1909–1922*, 32–35; Spector, *Professors of War*, 105; Miller, *War Plan Orange*, 29.

73. Evaluations of Mahan's proposal vary. William R. Braisted argues that Mahan's proposal was "brilliantly conceived" (*The United States Navy in the Pacific, 1909–1922*, 34). Mahan's biographer par excellence, Robert Seager, says Mahan's proposal was "realistic and incisive" (*Mahan*, 482). On the other hand, Edward S. Miller calls Mahan's proposal "sophomoric" (*War Plan Orange*, 334).

74. Mahan, *Letters*, 3:353.

75. Mahan, "The Open Door"; *Letters*, 3:353.

76. Neumann, "Franklin Delano Roosevelt"; Freidel, 46–47. After Roosevelt's death, Mrs. Roosevelt was asked which books her husband considered most influential in his own thinking. In reply she said he had always talked of Mahan's history as one of the books he found "most illuminating." Neumann, "Franklin Delano Roosevelt," 717, 719. Neumann, *America Encounters Japan*, 143.

77. Freidel, 1:234–35; Neumann, "Franklin Delano Roosevelt," 716–17.

78. Miller, *War Plan Orange*, 111.

79. Puleston, 304; Turk, 171; Lyle Evans Mahan, 91.

80. Turk, 4.

CHAPTER TWO   MAHAN'S INFLUENCE ON JAPANESE
SEA POWER

1. Mahan, *Interest of America*; Minakami Umehiko, trans., *Taiheiyō kaiken ron*, 8.

2. Quoted in Taylor, 115. What relevance does Mahan have in contemporary Japan? This question intrigued me when I edited and translated a Mahan anthology in 1977 as a volume in the Classics in American Culture series. I was pleasantly

surprised that my Mahan volume sold more than most other titles in the series. It was used as one of the textbooks at the National Maritime Self-Defense Staff College, the Japanese counterpart of Newport. As of November 2004, the book has gone into its sixth printing, selling four thousand copies.

3. Ogasawara, *Teikoku kaigun shiron*, I, preface, 193–1; *Nippon teikoku kaigun kaijō kenryokushi kōgi*, 9, 79, 85, 168, 214.

4. Spector, *Eagle*, 43.

5. Baer, 16, 475.

6. Ogasawara, *Teikoku kaigun shiron*, 193–1; Ogasawara, *Nippon teikoku kaijō kenryokushi kōgi*, 9, 79, 85, 168, 214.

7. Ibid., 431, 447, 463.

8. Akiyama Saneyuki Kai, 99; Peattie, "Akiyama Saneyuki," 61–69; Koyama, 253–56; Dingman, "Japan and Mahan," 49–66; *Yamanashi ihōroku*, 23–24.

9. Shimada Kinji, *Amerika ni okeru Akiyama*, passim.

10. Ibid., 3.

11. Ibid., 498–500.

12. Dingman, "Japan and Mahan," 58–59; Sakurai, 309; Akiyama Saneyuki Kai, 86–88; Kusumi, 352–58.

13. Quoted in Tomioka, *Kaisen*, 160–62.

14. Mizuno; Evans and Peattie, 73.

15. Yasui, 137; Sakurai, 307–9; Shimada Kinji, *Roshia senō zen'ya*, 2:714, 722, 764.

16. Senshishitsu, *Kaigun gunsenbi*, 1:125–29, 135–42.

17. Akiyama Saneyuki Kai, 309.

18. Quoted in Evans and Peattie, 84; *Yamanashi ihōroku*, 23; Sakurai, 236–37, 388.

19. Akiyama, *Kaigun ōyō senjutsu* (secret), JDA; Akiyama Saneyuki Kai, 300; Shimada Kinji, *Roshia senō zen'ya*, 2:893–95.

20. Kusumi, 354–56.

21. Higuchi, *Nihon kaigun kara mita Nitchū*, 17, 23–27, 37–38.

22. Higuchi, "Nihon kaigun no tairiku seisaku," 63–91; Sakurai, 254–56; Akiyama Saneyuki Kai, 256–62.

23. Higuchi, *Nihon kaigun kara mita Nitchū*, 23–26; Hirama, 174.

24. Murakami Teiichi, 287–88, 293–98.

25. Rivera, 97–98.

26. Tsunoda, *Manshū mondai*, 648–50.

27. Shinohara, 451.

28. Satō, *Teikoku kokubō shiron*, 78–79, 337, 456, 758, 831, 870, 877–78. See also Satō, *Teikoku kokubō shironshō*, passim; *Yamanashi ihōroku*, 23.

29. Evans and Peattie, 137.

30. Satō, *Teikoku kokubō shiron*, 70–71, 160, 718, 752, 758.

31. Ibid., 50, 752, 756–59.

32. Ibid., 160.

33. Mahan, *Interest of America,* 180.

34. Satō, *Teikoku kokubō shiron,* 748, 760.

35. Ibid., 28, 760, 814–15 (emphasis Satō's).

36. Satō, "Kokubō sakugi," 4; Satō, *Teikoku kokubō shironshō,* 509, 512–13; "Kokubō sūgi" [Commentaries on National Defense], 1914? in Saitō Papers, 37; Satō, "Kokubō sakugi," 21–24.

37. Satō, "Kokubō sakugi," 21–24. In January 1909, Navy Vice Minister Takarabe Takeshi wrote in his diary, "The American proposal concerning the Manchurian question is an extremely grave matter." Takarabe, 39.

38. Satō Tetsutarō et al., *Kokubō mondai no kenkyū* [A Study of the National Defense Problem] (1913), JDA; Satō, "Kokubō sakugi," 21; Saitō Seiji, "Kokubō hōshin daiichiji kaitei no haikei," 31–32; Kobayashi Michihiko, "Teikoku kokubō hōshin no dōyō," 60–61.

    Another interesting theme that appeared in this booklet was southward expansion: "The South Sea region is an area which Japan must regard most important from political, commercial, and colonial viewpoints. The Dutch East Indies is one of the areas which our Empire must regard as most important for our national expansion."

    The theme of a strong fleet to prevail in "trade conflict," the centerpiece of neo-Mahanian doctrine, was accepted and even improved on by the Japanese navy. Throughout the period treated in this study, American trade with China was insignificant in comparison with Japanese-American trade. It may be that navalists, both in the United States and Japan, perpetuated the myth of trade rivalry as a lever for fleet expansion.

39. Satō Tetsutarō, *Teikoku kokubō shironshō,* 509; Satō, "Kokubō sakugi," 25–26, 34.

40. Satō Tetsutarō, *Teikoku kokubō shiron,* 160, 338; Satō, *Teikoku kokubō shi ronshō,* 440.

41. *Gensui Katō Tomosaburō den,* 259; Asada, "Japanese Admirals," 145.

42. Ishikawa Yasushi, 337–39.

43. Ibid., 356, 358.

44. Satō Tetsutarō, *Teikoku kokubō shiron,* 144.

45. *Katō Kanji taishō den,* 233–47, 825–2.

46. Ibid., 521–23.

47. Ibid., 577–78.

48. Ibid., 823–34, 831; Katō Kanji's memo, "Gunshuki shoken" [My Views on Arms Limitation], January 1930, JDA; NGS memo, "American Armaments since the Washington Conference," 14 December 1929, submitted by Katō to Saitō Makoto, Saitō Papers.

49. Ibid.

50. Memo prepared for the 1935 conference of naval limitation, No. 1, Navy Ministry, JDA.

51. Mahan, *Beikoku kaigun senryaku,* 1–2.

52. Ibid.

53. Weigley, *American Way of War*, 286, 293, 311, 334.

54. W. H. Gardiner to William S. Sims, 17 July 1921, 27 September 1921, Gardiner Papers.

55. U.S. naval attache, Tokyo, "Some Observations on the Navy of Japan," received 25 February 1920, U.S. Navy Department Policies, "The Navy of Japan," RG 45, NA.

56. Louis Hacker, "The Incendiary Mahan: A Biography," *Scribner's Magazine* 64 (April 1934).

57. Nakahara Diary, 3, 29 December 1939, 15 January 1940, June 1940, JDA; Nakahara, "Dainiji sekai taisen," Vol. 1.

58. *Inoue Shigeyoshi-S*, 295.

59. John L. Gaddis, *Long Peace: Inquiries into the History of the Cold War* (Oxford and New York: Oxford University Press, 1987), 224.

CHAPTER THREE   FROM ENMITY TO DÉTENTE

1. The text of the Imperial National Defense Policy appears in Shimanuki, "Nichi-Ro sensō ikō ni okeru kokubō hōshin," 2–11. Drafted and decided on by the high command, it provided for defense policy in the narrow military sense of the word, not a comprehensive defense plan.

2. Senshishitsu, *Kaigun gunsenbi*, 1:225–26.

3. Itō Masanori, *Kasō tekkoku* [Hypothetical Enemy] (Tokyo: Sasaki Shuppanbu, 1926) is the best Japanese analysis of the idea of a hypothetical enemy. 1:246–48.

4. Nomura Minoru, "Tai-Bei-Ei kaisen," 26–27; Senshishitsu, *Rengō kantai*, :156–59; Nomura Minoru, *Taiheiyō sensō*, 287–89; Kobayashi Seizō, *Kaigun taishō Kobayashi Seizō oboegaki*, 2–22 (hereafter cited as *Kobayashi Seizō oboegaki*).

5. Quoted in Sprout and Sprout, *Toward a New Order*, 23.

6. Miller, *War Plan Orange*, 32; Itō Masanori, *Gunshuku*, 242–74; Pelz, 89–91.

7. Senshishitsu, *Kaigun gunsenbi*, 1:246–48.

8. The text of the General Plan for Strategy is printed in Senshishitsu, *Rengō kantai*, 1:119–120.

9. Senshishitsu, *Kaigun gunsenbi*, 1:246–48.

10. Senshishitsu, *Rengō kantai*, 1:132–35; Senshishitsu, *Kaigun gunsenbi*, 1:145–46; Senshishitsu, *Daihon'ei rikugunbu*, 1:223; Evans and Peattie, 189.

11. Senshishitsu, *Rengō kantai*, 1:132–35; Senshishitsu, *Kaigun gunsenbi*, 1:145–46.

12. Miller, *War Plan Orange*, 24–25; Love, *History of the U.S. Navy*, 1:448.

13. Tsunoda, *Manshū mondai*, 721–22; quoted in *Nihon kaigunshi*, 2:314.

14. Miller, *War Plan Orange*, 111.

15. File XSTP, 1895–1916, Old Naval War College Archives, record lot No. 1, Naval Historical Collection, NWC; ONI to CNO, General Board, 5 August 1918, GR 45, NA.

16. Portfolio No. 2, Asiatic Station, General Considerations and Data (confidential), February 1916, War Plans Division, Naval History Division; ONI to the General Board, Reg. 6347 c-10-a, WA 5, GR 45, NA; Hagan, *This People's Navy*, 254.

17. Braisted, *The United States Navy in the Pacific, 1909–1922,* 207–08.

18. Ibid, 208.

19. Takeshita Isamu, *Kaigun no gaikōkan,* 48 (italics added).

20. Naval General Staff Report No. 38, 1916, Saitō Papers.

21. Naval Staff College, *Dai-6 hen kimitsu hoshō* [Confidential Supplement, Vol. 6, to The Naval War History of World War I], n.d., JDA.

22. Kaigun Daijin Kanbō, *Kaigun gunbi enkaku,* 3–4.

23. Itō Masanori, *Dai kaigun,* 313.

24. Kobayashi Tatsuo, ed., *Suiusō nikki,* 299, 303.

25. Nomura Minoru, *Rekishi no naka no Nihon kaigun,* 35.

26. Takagi, *Shikan,* 64–66; Takagi, *Jidenteki Nihon kaigun,* 49. I could not find in the U.S. naval record a paper exactly corresponding to this document, but it does not differ in essential ways from Admiral Robert E. Coontz (CNO) to Secretary of State, 27 February 19, P.D. 198-2, RG 80, NA.

27. Braisted, *The United States Navy in the Pacific, 1909–1922,* 206–08.

28. Senshibu, *Rengō Kantai,* 1:168.

29. Braisted, *United States Navy in the Pacific, 1909–1922,* 472, 474–75.

30. Asada, "Japanese Admirals."

31. *TSM-S,* 3–7; Senshishitsu, *Kaigun gunsenbi,* 1:146; Saitō Seiji, "Kaigun ni okeru daiichiji sensō kenkyū," 16–32.

32. *Katō Kanji taishō den,* 756–57; Katō Kanji, "Gunshuku shoken," Saitō Papers; Kurono, 6.

33. Niimi, 216–17; Hirama, 276–77.

34. Yamanashi calculated that the maintenance cost alone of the eight-eight fleet, once it was completed, would be 600,000,000 yen. The government budget at that time was about 1,500,000,000 yen. *Yamanashi ihōroku,* 66; Yamanashi, *Katō Tomosaburō gensui,* 8.

35. Proceedings of the budget committee of the House of Councilors, 5 February 1919, 27.

36. Yamanashi, *Rekishi to meishō,* 151–52.

37. *Yamanashi ihōroku,* 66–67.

38. Braisted, *The United States Navy in the Pacific, 1909–1922,* 539–40.

39. Shidehara, *Gaikō 50-nen,* 59.

40. Sprout and Sprout, *Toward a New Order,* 102; Shidehara Heiwa Zaidan, *Shidehara Kijūrō,* 2.

41. Kennedy, 31.

42. Quoted in Love, *History of the U.S. Navy,* 1:526.

43. Albert P. Niblack to the General Board, 24 February 19, RG 45, WA-5, NA; Braisted, *The United States Navy in the Pacific, 1909–1922,* 546.

44. Theodore Roosevelt Jr. to Mrs. Roosevelt, 14 July 1921, Papers of Theodore Roosevelt Jr.

45. Report of the General Board on Limitation of Armament, memos for the use of the American delegation, No. 1 (GPO, 1921), 8–16, 24, copy in the Hughes Papers; Folder 139, Op-29, Folder No. 4, War Portfolio No. 2, Asiatic Station, January 1919; Folder 141, Op-29, Folder No. 6, War Portfolio No. 3, General Board No. 425, Strategic Survey of the Pacific, 26 April 1923; General Board and the Conference on the Limitation of Armament, 2:147; Director of War Plans C. S. Williams to chief of naval operations, 28 October 1921, 500.A41a/145; Report of the General Board, 8, 11, 14–16, 24; 500.A41a/121, NA; Wheeler, "The United States Navy and the Japanese 'Enemy,'" 63.

46. Frederick McCormick, *The Menace of Japan* (Boston: Little, Brown, 1917); Lothrop Stoddard, *The Rising Tide of Color against White World Supremacy* (New York: Scribner, 1919); Sidney Osborne, *The New Japanese Peril* (New York: Macmillan, 1921); Walter Pitkin, *Must We Fight Japan?* (New York: Century, 1921).

47. Baer, 121.

48. Katō Kanji, "Gunshuku shoken."

49. Kaigun Kokusai Renmei Kankei Jikō Kenkyūkai [Navy Ministry's Committee to Investigate League of Nations Matters], "Kafu kaigi gunbi seigen mondai ni kansuru kenkyū" [Studies on the Arms Limitation Question at the Washington Conference], 21 July 1921, Enomoto Papers.

50. Kaigun Kokusai Renmei Kankei Jikō Kenkyūkai, "Taiheiyō shotō no gunjiteki shisetsu teppai moshikuwa seigen ni kansuru kenkyū" [Study on Dismantlement or Restriction of Military Installations on Pacific Islands], JDA.

51. Hori, memo on the Washington Conference (secret), February 1946. Draft request for Navy Minister Katō's approval, August 1921 (never sanctioned), Hori Papers, NMSDC; instructions from Navy Minister Katō to Vice Admiral Katō Kanji, "Memo on Treatment of Naval Matters at the Washington Conference," 28 September 1921, Enomoto Papers.

52. The government's instructions appear in JMFA, *NGB: Washinton kaigi*, 1:181–87.

53. Shidehara, *Gaiko 50-nen*, 2.

54. Bull, 349–57; Goldman, passim.

55. Ian Nish observes that in the hasty preparations and hurried give-and-takes at the conference, the participating powers could not devise a "master plan," nor did they have much awareness that they were "devising a carefully balanced structure," Ian Nish, *Japanese Foreign Policy, 1869–1942: Kasumigaseki to Miyakezaka* (London: Routledge, 1977), 141–42. But Japan and the United States shared the view that as a result of the Washington Conference, there emerged a new international order of regional cooperation in the Pacific and East Asia encompassing both naval and diplomatic issues. With regard to Britain, it is important to note that the British delegate Arthur Balfour stressed to Prime Minister Lloyd George, "If satisfactory and durable results are to be achieved in regard to naval disarmament . . . an agreement must also be reached in regard to certain political problems which have arisen in China and the Pacific." Quoted in Goldman, 244.

56. Department of State, *Conference on the Limitation of Armament*, 4, 6.

57. Tokyo *Asahi Shinbun*, 13 July 1921; Ishii Itarō, *Gaikōkan*, 81–82.

58. Memo on the Anglo-Japanese Alliance and Japanese-American cooperation, 6 July 1921, JMFA.

59. JMFA, *NGB: Washinton kaigi,* 1:34–37.

60. Shidehara to Uchida, 14 August 1921 (No. 510); 23 July 1921 (No. 416); 14 August 1921 (No. 510); 29 September 1921.

61. Edwin L. Neville's memo, "Japan in the Far East," 1921 (in U.S. Department of State, *Papers Relating to Pacific and Far Eastern Affairs Prepared for the American Delegation to the Conference on the Limitation of Armament*); Neville's memo for Hughes, October 1921; Neville's memo on "Japan in the Far East" for the American delegation, 1921, 500.A41a/67, NA.

62. Chandler P. Anderson Diary, 28 October 1921, Anderson Papers; Roosevelt to Taft, 22 December 1910, cited in Griswold, 131–32.

63. *FRUS, 1922,* 1:1–2

64. Hoover, *Memoirs,* 3:180.

65. Anderson Diary, 26 November, 27 December 1921; Jessup, 2:447–48, 457–59.

66. J. Reuben Clark, "Some Basic Reflections of the Far Eastern Problems," 28 September 1921; "Preliminary Suggestions," n.d., 500.41a/58, NA.

67. Minutes of the Thirteenth Meeting of the U.S. Delegation, 7 December 1921, Papers of the American Delegation to the Washington Conference, 500.A41/12, NA.

68. *TSM-S,* 3.

69. Hanihara to Uchida, 5 December 1921 (Conference No. 128, urgent and confidential), JMFA.

70. For a detailed account, see Asada, "Japan's 'Special Interests'" and "Between the Old Diplomacy and the New" 224–25; Hanihara to Uchida, 5 December 1921; Anderson Diary, 26, 27 November 1921; Washburn to Root, 30 October, 26 November 1921; Washburn's memo to Root, "Japanese Situation," 26 November 1921, Washburn Papers; Jessup, 2:457–59 (italics added).

71. Anderson Diary, 18, 19 November, 27 December 1921; Jessup, 2:562; Delegates to Uchida (italics added); 26 January 1922 (Conference No. 496), JMFA (italics added).

72. Theodore Roosevelt Jr. Diary, 13 January 1922; Braisted, *The United States Navy in the Pacific, 1909–1922,* 652.

73. Beerits's memo on Far Eastern Question, Hughes Papers.

74. Shidehara to Uchida, 24 July 1921 (No. 4229); 20 December 1921 (No. 255); 9 January 1922 (No. 307) Ujita, 70.

75. Hanihara to Uchida, 25 December 1921 (No. 128, urgent and confidential) JMFA.

76. Delegates to Uchida, 29 January 1922 (Conference No. 548), JMFA.

77. Anderson Diary, 22 November 1921; 10, 21 December 1922; Delegates to Uchida, December 1921 (Conference No. 255), 9 January 1922 (Conference No. 307); Uchida to delegates, 24 December 1921 (Conference No. 237), 28 December 1921 (Conference No. 241), JMFA.

78. Shidehara to Uchida, 26 January 1922 (Conference No. 5), 28 January 1922, JMFA.

79. Katō Tomosaburō to navy vice minister, 16 January 1922, JDA.

80. Hughes, *Pathway of Peace,* 2–40; Hughes, "Foreign Policy of the United States," 575–83er 1921 (Conference No. 124), JMFA.

81. Tokyo *Asahi Shinbun,* 13 March. Delegates to Uchida, 5 December 1921 (Conference No. 1279).

82. From Watson, naval attaché, to ONI, 4 April 1922, Register No. 14746, NWC.

CHAPTER FOUR THE WASHINGTON CONFERENCE

1. *Hara Kei nikki,* 5:435; Arai, 53–54, 169; *Yamanashi ihōroku,* 68; Aoki, second foreign ministership, Part 4, 87–91, 96–98.

2. Yamanashi, *Katō Tomosaburō,* 2, 10; Itō Masanori, *Kafu kaigi to sonogo,* 351–52; Katō Gensui Denki Hensan Iin, 264–65.

3. Sagishiro Gakujin, "Kafu kaigi to Katō kaishō" [The Washington Conference and Navy Minister Katō], *Nihon oyobi Nipponjin* (1 October 1921).

4. Itō Masanori, *Kafu kaigi to sonogo,* 351–52.

5. Attaché (Tokyo) reports, 10 October 1921, GR 45, QY-Japanese; CNI's memo for CNO, 11 October 1921, RG 45, NA.

6. Attaché report from Tokyo, 23 September; 10, 21 October 1921 (Nos. 764, 769, 807), RG 45; memo for CNO, 11 October 1921, RG 45, NA. The British held an equally positive view of Katō Tomosaburō. The British ambassador to Japan, Charles Eliot, cabled the Foreign Office, "Baron Kato is reserved and silent, but has a high reputation for broad vision, calm judgment and great determination." Eliot to Arthur Balfour, 17 July 1921 (No. 412, confidential), F2693/2693/23, Foreign Office Archives, PRO.

7. Willam Pratt, "Autobiography."

8. ONI, "Memorandum for CNO," 11 October 1921 (confidential), NA.

9. Yamanashi, *Rekishi to meishō,* 156.

10. "Katō zenken dengon" [The Message of Chief Delegate Katō], full text at JDA.

11. Hughes's memo of an interview with Shidehara, 18 August 1921, 793.94/119 1/2, NA.

12. Warren to Hughes, 14 October 1921, *FRUS, 1921.*

13. Shidehara Kijūrō, *Gaikō 50-nen,* 64.

14. Attaché report, Tokyo to ONI, File No. 105–100, W-764 of 23 September 1921, and W-745 of 9 September 1921, RG 45, NA.

15. Sprout and Sprout, *Toward the New Order,* 150.

16. Yamanashi, *Rekishi to meishō,* 156.

17. Nomura to navy vice minister, 5 November 1921 (telegram No. 3), JDA.

18. The full text of the Hughes proposal appears in U.S. Department of State, *Conference on the Limitation of Armament,* 42–76. President Harding's and Hughes's case for presenting a drastic proposal—"a very large and liberal offer"— at the outset of the conference is described in Henry Cabot Lodge's "Journal of Washington Conference," 12, 24, 31 October 1921.

19. Ichihashi, 34; Theodore Roosevelt Jr. Diary, 14 December 1921.

20. Theodore Roosevelt Jr. Diary, 12 November 1921.

21. *TSM-S,* 3:23; Shidehara Heiwa Zaidan, 216; Shidehara Kijūrō, *Gaikō 50-nen,* 216. 24; Braisted, *The United States Navy in the Pacific, 1909–1922,* 598.

22. *TSM-S,* 3.

23. Shidehara Heiwa Zaidan, 216.

24. Itō Masanori, *Rengō kantai,* 259; Itō Masanori, *Gunshuku?,* 50.

25. Katō to Ide, 12 November 1921 (Conference No. 4), JDA; Katō to Uchida, received 14 November 1921 (Conference No. 18), JMFA.

26. *NGB: Washinton kaigi: gunbi seigen,* 77; Nomura Kichisaburō to Ide, 15 November 1921 (No. 6), JDA.

27. Delegates to Uchida, 16 November 1921 (Conference No. 22), JMFA; 30. Tokyo *Asahi Shinbun,* 15 November 1921.

28. Delegates to Uchida, 14 November 1921 (Conference No. 18), JMFA; Nomura Kichisaburō, "Kaiko to tenbō," 11, JDA.

29. U.S. Department of State, *Conference on the Limitation of Armament,* 106; *NGB: Washinton kaigi: gunbi seigen,* 82–83.

30. *NGB: Washinton kaigi: gunbi seigen,* 80–81; *Conference on the Limitation of Armament,* 106.

31. The *Mutsu* began its trial run after 9 October 1921, was hastily completed on 24 October before the Washington Conference, and was officially delivered to the navy on 22 November.

32. *NGB: Washinton kaigi: gunbi seigen,* 78, 79–81; Uchida to delegates, 22 November 1921 (Conference No. 44, strictly confidential and urgent), JMFA; *NGB: Washinton kaigi: gunbi seigen,* 79.

33. Interview with Enomoto, July 1972.

34. *NGB: Washinton kaigi: gunbi seigen,* 90.

35. Theodore Roosevelt Jr.: Diary, 15, 17, 30 November, 1921. Slightly different figures are given in Katō Kanji's telegram to the vice minister and vice chief, sent on November 1921, JDA. A succinct summary of the ratio question from the American viewpoint appears in William Howard Gardiner, "Memorandum of Naval Matters Connected with the Washington Conference of the Limitation of Armament, 1921–1922," Papers of William Howard Gardiner. See also William Pratt, "Autobiography," passim.

36. *NGB: Washinton kaigi: gunbi seigen,* 1, 36.

37. Ibid., 90.

38. Theodore Roosevelt Jr. Diary, 15, 17, 30 November 1921.

39. Ibid., 24 October 1921; 17, 19, 21, 30 November 1921.

40. Delegates to Uchida, arrived 19 November, 3 December 1921 (Conference No. 127), JMFA.

41. *FRUS, 1922,* 1:12.

42. Sprout and Sprout, *Toward a New Order,* 157; Hughes to Warren, 19, 27 November 1921; *FRUS, 1922,* :64–65, 67–68.

43. Quoted in Kiba, 85, 268.

44. Anderson Diary, 18, 30 November 1921.

45. Ide to Katō, 7 December 1921 (special telegram, urgent), JDA; Uchida to delegates, 22 November 1921 (Conference No. 44), JMFA.

46. Theodore Roosevelt Jr. Diary, 30 November 1921.

47. In his recent biography of Yardley, David Kahn documents that the Japanese telegram of 28 November, revealing that Japan would abandon the 10:7 ratio and accept 10:6, was available to the American delegation by 2 December. It stiffened Hughes's attitude. Kahn, 76–81.

48. Delegates to Uchida, 23 November 1921 (Conference No. 74), JMFA; interview with Enomoto, July 1975; Delegates to Uchida, arrived 26 November 1921; Hori's memo on the Washington Conference, Hori Papers, NMSDC.

49. Interview with Enomoto Jaji, July 1975.

50. "Kaigun iken" [Naval Opinion], n.d., Enomoto Papers. According to the procedures established before the conference, Katō was to direct his navy vice minister, Ide Kenji, who would explain the matter to top navy leaders. At the same time he was to keep in close touch with Katō on domestic opinion by reporting debates in the cabinet and on the Advisory Council on Foreign Relations. "Procedures of the Arms Limitation Conference," senior aide, Navy Ministry, n.d., Enomoto Papers.

51. Ide to Katō, 28 November 1921 (special telegram No. 16, urgent), JDA.

52. Rear Admiral Ichikizaka Keiichi, "Gensui Tōgō Heihachirō Kō ni kansuru hiwa" [Confidential Stories about Fleet Admiral Tōgō Heihachirō], JDA; Kiba, 227; Nomura's memo on "procedures for the naval conference," n.d., JDA; Hori's memo on the Washington Conference, Hori Papers, NMSDC.

53. Uchida to delegates, 28 November 1921 (Conference No. 73, strictly confidential and urgent), JMFA.

54. Ide to Katō, received 1, 4 December 1921 (special telegram, confidential and urgent), JDA.

55. NGB: Washinton kaigi: gunbi seigen, 122–23; Delegates to Uchida, sent 1 December 1921 (Conference No. 127, strictly confidential), JMFA.

56. NGB: Washinton kaigi: gunbi seigen, 232; Katō to Uchida, arrived 5 December 1921 (Conference No. 131), JDA.

57. Delegates to Uchida, 2 December 1921 (No. 131, strictly confidential and urgent), JMFA.

58. FRUS, 1922, 1:407–11; NGB: Washinton kaigi: gunbi seigen, 128; NGB: Washinton kaigi, 1:297–300. Katō failed to immediately report to Tokyo Hughes's agreement at this meeting to the status quo of the Philippines and Guam. Tokyo learned of this from Ambassador Charles B. Warren on 9 December. This caused some confusion between the delegates and Tokyo.

59. Katō to Uchida, 5 December 1921 (No. 127, strictly confidential), JMFA; Katō to Ide, 4 December 1921 (No. 12), JDA.

60. Katō to Ide, 4 December 1921, JDA.

61. Navy minister to vice minister, 4 December 1921, JDA; Delegates to Uchida, 5 December 1921 (No. 142, strictly confidential and urgent), JMFA.

62. Katō to Ide, 4 December 1921 (confidential, urgent), JDA; *NGB: Washinton kaigi: gunbi seigen,* 137.

63. *TSM-S,* 6–6; interview with Enomoto, July 1975.

64. "Katō zenken dengon," *TSM-S,* 3–8, Ide to Katō, 10 December, 1921 (special dispatch, No. 30, JDA).

65. *NGB: Washington Kaigi,* 1:314–16. Quoted in *Gensui Katō Tomosaburō den,* 114.

66. *TSM-S,* 3–8.

67. Quoted in *Gensui Katō Tomosaburō den,* 114. 8.

68. Quoted in *Kato Kanji taisho den,* 1008.

69. Asada, "Japanese Admirals," 142–45.

70. Katō Kanji to navy vice minister and vice chief of NGS, February 1918; navy vice minister to Katō Kanji, 30 March 1918; Katō Tomosaburō to Katō Kanji, 5 April 1918; *Nihon kaigunshi,* 2:371–91.

71. Nagai Kansei, November 1997.

72. Harada-Saionji, 1:33.

73. *Katō Kanji taishō den,* 746–49, 752–59; Katō Kanji to navy vice minister and vice chief of NGS, 24 November 1921 (No. 40), JDA; Itō Kinjirō, 191–92, 197; Katō Kanji, "Rondon kaigun jōyaku hiroku" [Secret Record of the London Naval Treaty], JDA.

74. Katō Kanji to navy vice minister and vice chief of NGS, 16, 24, 27 November; 4 December 1921 (Nos. 52, 53, strictly confidential), JDA. In his recent biography of Katō Kanji, Ian Gow fails to use Katō Kanji's crucial telegrams to the naval authorities in Tokyo. Instead, he relies exclusively on the stenographic record provided by his son, Katō Hirokazu, of the lecture Katō delivered at the Naval Staff College in "May or June 1922." Such a postconference statement, presenting ex post facto rationalizations, is worse than useless. For that matter, Gow's book does not use any Japanese archives, naval or otherwise, although he claims to have made "an extensive search of archival materials."

75. Katō Kanji to navy vice minister and chief of NGS, 4 December 1921 (No. 52, strictly confidential), JDA.

76. Katō Kanji to navy vice minister and chief of NGS, 4 December 1921 (No. 53, strictly confidential), JDA.

77. According to the regular procedure for handling telegrams at the conference, Katō Kanji, as chief naval adviser, was to show Katō Tomosaburō without delay any telegrams that he might send to the naval authorities in Tokyo. Disregarding this procedure, Katō Kanji ordered the telegraphic officer to send his dispatch directly to Tokyo. Hori's memo on the Washington Conference, NMSDC.

78. Navy minister to navy vice minister, 16 January 1922, JDA; *TSM-S,* 7.

79. Itō Masanori, *Rengō kantai no saigo,* 259; Arai, 64–65; *Gensui Katō Tomosaburō den,* 117–27; *Yamanashi ihōroku,* 78–79; Yamanashi, *Rekishi to meishō,* 160.

80. Arai, 67.

81. Asada, "Japanese Admirals," 161.

82. *Katō Kanji nikki*, 53, 55.

83. *NGB, Washinton kaigi*, 1:318.

84. *TSM-S*, 3–8.

85. Ibid., 7.

86. *FRUS, 1922*, 75–78; Delegates to Uchida, received 8 December 1921 (Conference No. 143), JMFA; Yamanashi, *Rekisho to meishō*, 162.

87. General Board, No. 438, series 1088c, 26 October 1921, NA.

88. George H. Blakeslee's memo, "The Existing Strategic Situation in the Pacific in Relation to Limitation of Armament," file of Henry Cabot Lodge, Papers of the American Delegation, NA; Hughes, Beerits's memo on Treaty for the Limitation of Naval Armament, 31–32. Mahan once wrote, "Guam held securely, with a navy superior to that of Japan, threatens every Japanese interest from Dalny and Korea to Nagasaki and Yokohama." Quoted in Buckley, 90–91.

89. Delegates to Uchida, 12 January 1922; Uchida to delegates, 12 January 1922. JMFA Relevant documents appear in *NGB: Washinton kaigi: gunbi seigen*, 239–79.

90. Quoted in Kashima, *Nichi-Bei gaikōshi*, 191–93.

91. Uchida to delegates, 14 January 1922 (Conference No. 321); Delegates to Uchida, received 12 January 1922 (Conference No. 393), JMFA; Navy Minister Katō to vice minister, 16 January 1922 (urgent and strictly confidential); Delegates to Uchida, sent 19 January 1922, JDA.

92. Vice minister to navy minister, 21 January 1922 (strictly confidential), JDA; Delegates to Uchida, 12 January 1922; Uchida to delegates, 12 January 1922; Uchida to Katō, 14 January 1922 (Conference No. 417), JMFA; Ichihashi, 90; Katō to Ide, 16 January 1922 (No. 305–6); Ide to Katō, 21 January 1922 (strictly confidential), JDA; Katō to Uchida, 27 January (No. 540), JMFA.

93. For the text of Article XIX, see *NGB: Washinton kaigi: gunbi seigen*, 278.

94. For a theoretical analysis of Katō Tomosaburō's decision making, see Asada, "Washinton kaigi o meguru Nichi-Bei no seisaku kettei," 74–81.

95. Quoted in *Gensui Katō Tomosaburō den*, 117; Itō Masanori, *Rengō kantai no saigo*, 259.

96. Mori, 50.

97. *Katō Kanji nikki*, 49–51.

98. *TSM-S*, 7.

99. A representative interpretation along this line is Tsunoda, "Nihon kaigun sandai," 90–125. See also Kobayashi Tatsuo, "The London Naval Treaty, 1930," in Morley, *Japan's Road to the Pacific War: Japan Erupts*, 3–117. I avail myself of this opportunity to revise my older interpretation that appeared in "Japanese Navy and the United States," in Borg and Okamoto, 228.

100. Baer, 103.

101. Huntington, 398.

102. Levy, 3, 90; Mahan, "Preparedness for War, 1906," in *Naval Administration and Warfare*, 193.

103. Kaufman, 15.

104. Braisted, *The United States Navy in the Pacific, 1909–1922*, 592, 670–71.

105. Joint Board, memo for CNO, 7 July 1923, J.B. No. 325, RG 80, NA.

106. Braisted, "On the United States Navy's Operational Outlook in the Pacific."

107. Braisted, *The United States Navy in the Pacific, 1909–1922*, 687.

108. Memorandum from Director of War Plans to Director of Naval Intelligence "Japanese War Plans," February 17, 1923; (RG) 80; Office of the Chief of Operations, Memorandum for the Secretary of the Navy, "Strategic Survey Pacific," 10 May 1923, (RG) 80, CNO-PD File 198-26, NA.

CHAPTER FIVE   REVOLT AGAINST THE WASHINGTON TREATY

1. Ichikizaki Keiichi, memo on secret stories about Fleet Admiral Tōgō, Ichikizaki's additional materials No. 5, JDA.

2. Takahashi, 74–75.

3. *Inoue Shigeyoshi,* 103–4.

4. Captain R. M. Colvin's report, No. 22, 1 November 1922, enclosed in Ambassador Charles Eliot's report, 9 November 1922, F 3795/25/3; Captain Marriott's report on "Administration of the Imperial Japanese Navy," enclosed in Eliot's report, British Foreign Office Archives, PRO.

5. In 1915 Rear Admiral Satō Tetsutarō, then Vice Chief of the Naval General Staff, had plotted for a similar plan and incurred the wrath of Navy Minister Katō Tomosaburō, who immediately demoted him. Katō Kanji remembered this episode. *Kato Kanji taishō den,* 769–72; Commander Takagi Sōkichi's record of his interview with Vice Admiral Takahashi Sankichi, "Circumstances Surrounding the Revision of the Naval General Staff Regulations," January 1934, JDA; Takahashi, 74, 85; Harada-Saionji, 3:116.

6. Senshishitsu, *Rengō kantai,* 1:196, 164–66.

7. The document is quoted in full in Shimanuki, "Daiichiji sekai taisen igo no kokubō hōshin," 65–74.

8. *Katō Kanji taishō den,* 767–72; Yamaji, 245–46.

9. Ōmae, 35, 37. For General Plan for Strategy, see Senshishitsu, *Rengō kantai,* 1:200–2.

10. Kurono, 126–37.

11. Ōmae, 35, 37.

12. William V. Pratt to Robert Dunn, 25 September 1921, Pratt Papers.

13. Telegram from Eliot to Foreign Office (No. 154, confidential), 12 June 1922, F43/23, British Foreign Office Archives, PRO.

14. Pratt to Rear Admiral Nomura, 25 August 1923; telegram from Eliot to Foreign Office 12 June 1922, No. 154, confidential, F 43/426/23, British Foreign Office Archives, PRO.

15. William Pratt, "Autobiography," chap. 17.

16. Cotton Diary, 25 August 1923.

17. Quoted in Yoshida, *Rengō kantai,* 247.

18. Interview with Enomoto, July 1975.

19. *Yamanashi ihōroku,* 98–99.

20. Takagi, *Jidenteki,* 50; interview with Enomoto, August 1975; Koike, "Washinton kaigi zengo," 36–37, 160.

21. U.S. Department of State, *Conference on the Limitation of Armament,* 248.

22. *TSM-S,* 7.

23. Sir J. Tilley to Austen Chamberlain, received 13 April 1927, F 3611/3611/23, British Foreign Office Archives, PRO.

24. Gunbi Seigen Kenkyū Iinkai [Investigatory Committee on Naval Limitation], "A Study on a Second Arms Limitation Conference," 18 February 1925, JDA.

25. Ibid.

26. Hori, "Explanation of ratios in auxiliary vessels," n.d. (strictly confidential), Hori Papers, NMSDC; "A Study on a Second Arms Limitation Conference"; Koike, "Taishō kōki no kaigun," 48–49; *NGB, Junēvu kaigun gunbi seigen kaigi,* 88.

27. Wheeler, *Prelude,* 80.

28. Nagai Sumitaka, "Kokubō hōshin to kaigun yōhei shisō," May 1962, Part 13, 3318–27, 3335–38, JDA; "Kōjutsu oboegaki" [Memo for an Oral Presentation], 1930, prepared by Katō Kanji, JDA.

29. *Katō Kanji taishō den,* 746–60; Satō Tetsutarō, "Daini gunshuku ni kansuru shiken" [A Private View on the Second Naval Limitation Conference], 18 February 1925, Enomoto Papers.

30. Senshishitsu, *Rengō kantai,* 1:213–15; Senshishitsu, *Kaigun gunsenbi,* 1:148–51; Senshishitsu, *Sensuikanshi,* 27–33.

31. Senshishitsu, *Kaigun gunsenbi,* 1:148–49; Katō Kanji, "Kōjutsu oboegaki."

32. NHK, 40–44; Miller, *War Plan Orange,* 79, 97–99, 115–21.

33. Katō Kanji, "Kōjutsu oboegaki"; Katō Kanji, "Gunshuki shoken"; Naval General Staff memo, "American Naval Armaments since the Washington Conference," n.d. (1930?); Saitō Papers; Nagai, "Kokubō hōshin," 13:3329–31, JDA; Senshishitsu, *Kaigun gunsenbi,* 1:150–51.

34. Senshishitsu, *Kaigun gunsenbi,* 1:150–52.

35. Miller, *War Plan Orange,* 115–26; Katō Kanji, "Kōjutsu oboegaki"; Katō Kanji, "Gunshuku shoken" [My Views on Naval Limitation]; Senshishitsu, *Kaigun gunsenbi,* 1:150–51.

36. Katō Kanji, "Gunshuku shoken"; Ōmae, 376.

37. Takagi, *Shikan,* 19; Nagai, "Kokubō hōshin," 13:3328.

38. *Katō Kanji taishō den,* 846–57, 918–19; Takahashi, 32, 77; NHK, 130–34; "Katō Kanji hiroku" [The Secret Record of Katō Kanji Concerning the London Conference], JDA (hereafter cited as "Katō Kanji hiroku"); Katō Kanji to Makino Nobuaki, 29 January 1930, Makino Papers.

39. Braisted, "Evolution of the United States Navy's Strategic Assessments," 113; Braisted, "On the United States Navy's Operational Outlook."

40. NGS secret report quoted in NHK, 119–20; Katō Kanji, "Gunshuku shoken"; Kaigunshō Gunbi Seigen Iinkai [Navy Ministry Committee on Naval Limitation], Report C-1, 1928, JDA; Braisted, "On the United States Navy's Operational Outlook"; NHK, 116–20.

41. *Kido Kōichi kankei bunsho,* 1:263–66.

42. Tanaka, "Shōwa 7-nen zengo," 11.

43. *Kobayashi Seizō oboegaki,* 12; *FRUS, 1927,* 3–14.

44. Wheeler, "The United States Navy and the Japanese 'Enemy,'" 65; Wheeler, *Pratt,* 260; Hagan, 272.

45. Ishii, *Gaikō yoroku,* 234.

46. Quoted in Nakamura Kikuo, 33–34.

47. Unno, *Nihon gaikōshi,* Vol. 16: *Kaigun gunshuku kōshō* is based only on Foreign Ministry archives. Roskill, *Naval Policy between the Wars,* 1:498–516; Wheeler, *Prelude,* 131–57.

48. Yamamoto Eisuke, *Danshaku Ōsumi Mineo,* 760.

49. Itō Masanori, "Kobayashi Seizō ron," 1–3.

50. Satō Ichirō, *Kaisōroku,* 24–25.

51. Ibid., 25–26.

52. Ibid., 27.

53. Ibid., 28–30.

54. Instructions to the chief delegate to the Geneva Conference, cabinet decision, 15 April 1927, JMFA; navy minister's instructions to chief naval adviser, 19 April 1927, JDA.

55. Saitō Shishaku Kinenkai, 3:78–79, 90–91; Takarabe to Saitō, 25 February, 17 March 1927; Saitō to Yamanashi, 2 March 1927, Saitō Papers; Aritake, 73; *Yamanashi ihōroku,* 118–19.

56. Takarabe to Saitō, 25 February, March 17, 1827; Saitō to Yamanashi, 2 March, 1927.

57. Katō Kanji to Saitō, 23 March 1927, Saitō Papers.

58. "Saitō's Conversations upon His Return," Saitō Papers; Aritake, 107–9; Saitō Shishaku Kinenkai, 3:78–79, 90–91; Satō Ichirō, 39.

59. *Yamanashi ihōroku,* 119; Kobayashi Seizō, "Report on the Geneva Conference on Naval Limitation," submitted to the navy minister and chief of NGS (1927), 191–92 (hereafter cited as "Kobayashi report"), JDA; Epstein, "Naval Disarmament," 219; Saitō Shishaku Kinenkai, 3:71–73.

60. For Kobayashi, see Itō Masanayi, "Kobayashi Seizōron."

61. Danshaku Ōsumi Mireoden, 378, 493, 506, 760.

62. Trimble, 3.

63. Kobayashi to navy vice minister and vice chief of NGS, 23 June and 18 July (Nos. 14, 39), JDA; Delegates to Foreign Minister Tanaka (concurrently prime minister), 24 July 1927 (No. 643, strictly confidential), JMFA; Kobayashi report, 101, 117–18, 134–35, 138, JDA; Satō Ichirō, 65.

64. Delegates to Foreign Minister (Prime Minister) Tanaka Giichi, 24, 25 June 1927 (Nos. 13/2 and 14/2, strictly confidential), JMFA.

65. Satō Ichirō, 43, 67.

66. Delegates to foreign minister, 25 June; 7, 16 July 1927 (Nos. 14, 28, 56), JMFA; Kobayashi report, 127, JDA.

67. Kobayashi to navy vice minister and vice chief of NGS, 15 July 1927 (No. 36, confidential); Kobayashi report, 92–93, JDA.

68. Satō Ichirō, 79, 81.

69. Navy vice minister to Kobayashi, 6 July 1927 (No. 14, confidential); Kobayashi to navy vice minister and vice chief of NGS, 18 July 1927 (Nos. 39, 41); Kobayashi report, 101–3, 115, 128–32, JDA; Itō Masanori, "Kobayashi Seizō ron," 3. Kobayashi also felt that the middle figure between Japan's demand of 70 percent and America's claim to 60 percent would be acceptable.

70. Kobayashi to navy vice minister and vice chief of NGS, 18 July 1927 (Nos. 39, 41, confidential); delegates to foreign minister, 25 June 1927; 7 July 1927 (No. 28); 18 July 1927 (No. 56); Kobayashi report, 101–3, 115, 128–32, JDA.

71. *NGB: Junēve kaigun gunbi seigen kaigi*, 186–87; navy vice minister to Kobayashi, 17 July 1927 (No. 21, confidential), 22 July 1927 (Nos. 21, 23, confidential), JDA (italics added).

72. *Kobayashi Seizō oboegaki*, 62; *Terashima Ken den*, 224.

73. Satō Ichirō, 88–90.

74. Ibid.

75. *FRUS, 1927*, 1:113–14, 130–34.

76. Delegates to foreign minister, 24 July 1927 (No. 64, strictly confidential), JMFA.

77. Navy vice minister to Kobayashi, 28 July 1927 (No. 27, confidential), JDA; Tanaka (prime minister) to the delegates, 27 July 1927, JMFA.

78. *FRUS, 1927*, 1:113–14; *DBFP*, Series IA, 3:686–87, 691–93.

79. Unno, 60.

80. Horikawa, 195.

81. Yamanashi to Saitō, 29 August 1927, Saitō Papers.

82. Summary minutes of the Privy Council, 1 October 1930.

83. Interview with Enomoto, August 1975.

84. Navy Ministry, Gunbi Seigen Kenkyū Iinkai [Investigatory Committee on Naval Limitation], "Reports on Policy Regarding Naval Limitation," prepared in August 1928, JDA (hereafter cited as "Reports"); Senshishitsu, *Kaigun gunsenbi*, 1:350–67.

85. Reports, Part B: 11–12.

86. Reports, Part B: 133–34, 169–71.

87. Reports, Part A (1): 1; Part B (1): 17.

88. Reports, Part B: 1–2, 4, 7, 12–13; Part C (1): 49–50, 132; Studies, Part B: 7.

89. Reports, Part A (1): 4–5; Part A (2): 39; Part B (1): 65–66, 99, 206–7.

90. Reports, Part A-2, 15–16, 36, 38; Part B-1, 7, 41–42.

91. "Katō Kanji hiroku."

92. Operations Division of the NGS, memo on the power of 10,000-ton, 8-inch-gun cruisers, 1 December 1929; JDA.

93. Operations Division NGS, "The formidable power of the 10,000-ton, eight-inch-gun cruiser and the need to secure 70 percent strength vis-à-vis the U.S.," 1 December 1929. A similar document is found in Saitō Papers.

94. Katō Kanji, "Gunshuku shoken"; Studies, Part A (1): 65–66.

CHAPTER SIX   THE DENOUEMENT: THE LONDON NAVAL CONFERENCE

1. Itō Masanori, *Dai kaigun*, 365.

2. Cabinet decision on policy regarding naval limitation, 28 June 1929, JMFA; Katō Kanji, "Kōjutsu oboegaki" [Memo for oral presentation], Katō Kanji Papers.

3. Telegrams to naval attachés in Washington and London, 25 July 1929 (No. 95, secret), "Main Points for the Imperial Navy's Study," JDA.

4. Captain Koga Min'eichi Diary, 8 October 1929, Hori Papers, NMSDC; Tanaka, "Shōwa 7-nen zengo," Part 1, 12.

5. Katō Kanji, "Rondon jōyaku hiroku" [Secret record of the London naval treaty], Katō Kanji Papers [hereafter cited as "Katō Kanji hiroku"].

6. Matsudaira to Shidehara, 30 August 1929 (No. 1, strictly confidential); Shidehara to Matsudaira, 16 September 1929 (No. 243, confidential), JMFA.

7. Memo of conversation between Stimson and Debuchi, 12 November 1929, in "1930-nen Rondon kaigun kaigi zenshi" [Preliminary to the 1930 London Naval Conference], JDA; Stimson's memo of conversation with Debuchi, 12 November 1929, *FRUS, 1929,* 1:274–75.

8. *FRUS, 1929,* 1:307–13; Debuchi to Shidehara, 18 December 1929 (strictly confidential and urgent), JMFA.

9. Wakatsuki (London) to Shidehara, 14 January 1930 (No. 33), JMFA.

10. Matsudaira to Shidehara, 12 August 1929 (No. 309, strictly confidential), JMFA; Matsudaira to Shidehara, 11 December 1929, *NGB,* 1:325.

11. Shidehara to Matsudaira, 23 December 1929 (No. 329, strictly confidential and urgent), JMFA.

12. "Katō Kanji hiroku"; Katō Kanji to Makino, 29 January 1930, Makino Papers; Hori Teikichi's memo on the conference and the supreme command question, 11 July 1946, Hori Papers, NMSDC.

13. Katō Kanji to Makino, 29 January 1930, Makino Papers; "Katō Kanji hiroku."

14. *Hata Shunroku nisshi,* 4.

15. "Katō Kanji hiroku."

16. Yamamoto Eisuke's memo, May 1930, Makino Papers.

17. Katō Kanji to Makino, 29 January 1930, Makino Papers.

18. NGS, "Kafu kaigi go ni okeru Beikoku no gunbi" [U.S. Naval Armaments since the Washington Conference], 14 December 1929, presented by Katō Kanji to Saitō Makoto, Saitō Papers.

19. Ibid.

20. Ikeda, "Rondon kaigun jōyaku gunreibu shiryō," 105.

21. *NGS,* "Kafu kaigi go ni okeru Beikoku no senbi," 1930.

22. Katō Kanji, "Kōjutsu oboegaki."

23. Katō Kanji to Makino, 29 January 1930, Makino Papers; Katō Kanji, "Kōjutsu oboegaki."

24. *Katō Kanji taishō den,* 890–92.

25. Ibid., 890.

26. Katō Kanji to Kaneko Kentarō, 13 December 1929 (strictly confidential), Papers of Kaneko Kentarō, DL; Ikeda, "Rondon kaigun jōyaku gunreibu shiryō," 105.

27. *Katō Kanji taishō den,* 891–92; Morley, *Japan Erupts,* 29.

28. Wakatsuki, 262–63, 334–35; *Yamanashi ihōroku,* 122; Harada-Saionji, 1:19.

29. Wakatsuki, 262–63.

30. Arima, 10:5–6, and interview with Enomoto, August 1975.

31. Cosmopolitan minded Admiral Saitō and Shidehara, regarding the naval conference as a diplomatic gathering, had advised Takarabe to take his wife with him.

32. Koga Mineichi Diary, 27 September 1929, Hori Papers, NMSDC; interview with Enomoto, August 1975.

33. Okada, *Kaikoroku,* 44.

34. *Katō Kanji taishō den,* 887.

35. Stimson to the American Embassy (Tokyo), 24 October 1929, 500/713; American Embassy (Tokyo) to Stimson, 9 November 1929, 500/713/844, Papers of Henry L. Stimson, Yale University Library (microfilm).

36. Stimson to the American Embassy (Tokyo), 24 October 1929, 500/713; U.S. Embassy (Tokyo) to Stimson, 1929, 500/713/844, Stimson Papers; Stimson, *On Active Service,* 166.

37. Ferrell, 87–88; O'Connor, 63; Stimson, 166.

38. Kaufman, 124.

39. Stimson to Hoover, 17 February 1930, Stimson Papers.

40. *Yamanashi ihōroku,* 129; Wakatsuki, 365.

41. Other moderate leaders included Admiral Taniguchi Naomi (Commander, Kure Naval District), Vice Admiral Nomura Kichisaburō (soon to succeed Taniguchi), and Vice Admiral Kobayashi Seizō (head of the Naval Construction Department). They held that there was nothing absolute about the 70 percent ratio and that Japan's position at the conference must not be governed by narrow considerations of ratios and tonnages alone. *Makino nikki,* 396; Ko-Matsudaira Tsuiokukai, 530–32.

42. Hori, "Rondon kaigi to tōsuiken mondai" [The London Conference and the Question of the Right of Supreme Command], Hori Papers, NMSDC.

43. Itō Takashi, *Shōwa shoki keijishi kenkyū,* 141; Harada-Saionji, 1:62; Arima, 5, 6, JDA.

44. Yamanashi, *Rekishi to meishō,* 172; Nakamura Kikuo, 34; Harada-Saionji, 1:19.

45. *FRUS, 1930,* 1:24.

46. Matsudaira to Shidehara, 22 March 1930 (specially ciphered), JMFA; Sakonji's statement in Arima, "Takarabe denki shiryō," 10:5, 10–78; *FRUS, 1930,* 1:24.

47. Sakonji, "The Report on the 1930 London Naval Conference" (hereafter cited as "Sakonji report"), JDA. This revealing report was a day-to-day record of the Japanese naval delegation, which was drafted by Enomoto and approved by Yamamoto Isoroku. Although the report was considerably toned down by Vice Admiral Sakonji Seizō, it was never formally submitted to the higher naval authorities in Tokyo for fear of aggravating "domestic political unrest and complications within the navy." This alluded to the controversy over the right of supreme command.

48. Sakonji report, 1, 22, 41–42, 53; Matsudaira to Foreign Minister Shidehara, 20 February 1930 (strictly confidential and specially ciphered, with a note "Destroy upon reading"), JMFA; Takarabe Diary, 25 January 1930, Takarabo Papers, DL.

49. Matsudaira to Shidehara, 20 February 1930; Shidehara to Matsudaira, 21 February 1930, JMFA.

50. Matsudaira to Shidehara, 22 March 1930 (specially ciphered), JMFA; 4 March; Koga Diary, 6, 15 March 1930, Hori Papers, NMSDC.

51. Wakatsuki to Shidehara, 18 February 1930 (No. 149), JMFA.

52. Matsudaira and Wakatsuki to Shidehara and Hamaguchi, 20 February 1930 (strictly confidential, destroy upon reading), JMFA.

53. Shidehara to Matsudaira, 21 February 1930 (confidential, to be handled by the chief of the mission), JMFA (italics added).

54. Abo to Katō Kanji, 6 March 1930; *Katō Kanji nikki,* 609.

55. "Kaigi taisaku shiken" [My Private View of Conference Strategy], 10 March 1939, Hori Papers, NMSDC; Arima, 10:5–7; Andō, 2:267; *NGB.*

56. *NGB: 1930-nen Rondon kaigun kaigi,* 2:88; *FRUS, 1930,* 56; *NGB: 1930-nen Rondon kaigun kaigi,* 1:414.

57. *NGB: Rondon kaigun kaigi keika gaiyō,* 277. The record of the Reed-Matsudaira talk appears on 277–56.

58. Hori to Sakonji, 10 March 1930, Hori Papers, NMSDC.

59. For the American side, see O'Connor, 77–81.

60. For the Reed-Matsudaira compromise, see Table 2 and *TSM,* 1.

61. Wakatsuki, 352–53.

62. Ibid., 355–56.

63. *TSM,* 1:64, 71; Sakonji report, 46–47, 63–65, 73, 78, 93; Captain Nakamura Kamesaburō, "Seikun ni itarishi jijō oyobi jigo no keika ni kansuru hōkoku" [Report on Circumstances Leading to the Request for the Final Instructions from the Government and the Developments That Followed], April 1930 (a day-to-day report of the activities of middle-echelon naval officers), entries of 13, 14, 15 March 1930, Hori Papers (hereafter cited as "Nakamura report").

64. Takarabe Diary, 13, 14 March 1930, DL; Nakamura report, 13 March 1930; Wakatsuki, 356.

65. Satō Naotake, 245–50.

66. *TSM-S,* 9–10, 11–12.

67. *TSM,* 1:71–72.

68. Sakonji to navy vice minister and vice chief of NGS, 16 March 1930, *TSM-S,* 15.

69. Wakatsuki, 355–57.

70. Yamamoto to Hori, 17 March 1930, Hori Papers, NMSDC.

71. Captain Nakamura's memo, "My Views on the London Naval Conference"; Sakonji report, 15, 16; Nakamura report, 16 March 1930, JDA; Nomura Minoru, *Yamamoto,* 179.

72. *TSM-S,* 15; Nakamura report, 13–16 March 1930; Yamamoto to Hori, 17 March 1930, NMSDC.

73. Sakonji report, 76, 93; Nakamura report, 15, 16 March 1930; *TSM-S,* 15, 17.

74. Abo to Katō Kanji, 15, 19 March 1930 (special, confidential, and personal telegram No. 3), JDA.

75. *NGS,* "Rondon kaigi kōshō keika gaiyō narabini Beikoku teian no naiyō kentō" [Summary of the Negotiations at the London Naval Conference and an Analysis of the Contents of the American Proposal] (strictly confidential), in Ikeda, "Rondon kaigun jōyaku"; Koga Mine'ichi, "Koga fukukan shuki" [Senior Aide Koga's Notes], 24 March 1930, JDA; Katō Kanji, "Memo on Various Questions on the Request for Government Instructions," Hori Papers, NMSDC; Nomura Minoru, "Tai-Bei-Ei sakusen keikaku," 223–24.

76. NGS to Takarabe, 17 March; *TSM-S,* 16–17.

77. Okada, *Kaikoroku,* 44.

78. *TSM,* 1:79.

79. Ibid., 80–82; *TSM-S,* 20, 22.

80. *TSM-S,* 22–24; TSM, 1:80–81.

81. Okada, *Kaikoroku,* 40–44.

82. Ibid., 43.

83. Ibid., 47.

84. Harada-Saionji, 1:63.

85. Yamanashi to Takarabe, 22 March 1939; Yamanashi to Abo, 21 March 1930, Hori Papers, NMSDC.

86. *TSM,* 1:74.

87. *TSM-S,* 27–28.

88. *Hamaguchi nikki,* 318, 444–45; Harada-Saionji, 1:32; "Heika no okotoba" [The Emperor's Words], contained in Hori Papers, No. 30, NMSDC.

89. Harada-Saionji, 1:18.

90. Ibid., 1:32–33.

91. *Kobayashi Seizō oboegaki,* 55.

92. *FRUS, 1930,* 1:71; *NGB: 1930 Rondon kaigun kaigi,* 2:151.

93. Okada, *Kaikoroku,* 48–49.

94. *Hamaguchi nikki,* 445–46; Hatano Masaru, "Hamaguchike shozō," 100–102.

95. Okada, *Kaikoroku,* 49–50, 174; *Okada Keisuke,* 81.

96. *TSM-S*, 36–37.

97. Ibid., 49; Takarabe Diary, 31 March 1930.

98. Nakamura report, 2 April 1930; Sakonji report, 114; Yamamoto's oral presentation to Takarabe, 2 April 1930, Hori Papers, NMSDC; Sorimachi, 301–2; Nakamura Takafusa, et al., 3:51.

99. Yamamoto's oral presentation to Takarabe, 2, 9 April 1930, Hori Papers, NMSDC.

100. *Katō Kanji nikki*, 93 (entries of 30 March 1930).

101. Quoted in Morison, *Turmoil and Tradition*, 260; Love, *History of the United States Navy*, 1:561.

102. NHK, 164.

103. Love, *History of the United States Navy*, 1:559–61; see also *TSM*, 1:95.

104. Crowley, 65.

105. Castle to acting secretary of state, 25 January, *FRUS, 1930*, 10; Symonds, 76–77, 126.

106. Cited in LaFeber, *Clash*, 58; *NGB: 1930-nen Rondon kaigun kaigi*, 2:87–88.

107. Stimson to Hoover, 17 February 1930, Stimson Papers.

108. Quoted in Wheeler, *Pratt*, 341.

109. Stimson, 168.

110. Wakatsuki, 358–59.

111. For the background, see Morley, *Japan Erupts*, 59–106.

112. Ibid., 84.

113. Sakai, 190; Harada-Saionji, 1:70.

114. *Okada Keisuke*, 161; Harada-Saionji, 1:113–14.

115. Suetsugu, "Shimatsusho" [Apologies] to Katō Kanji, 10 April 1930, JDA.

116. Takahashi, 82.

117. "Heika no non hito Kotoba" [His Majesty's Word], Hori Papers, No. 30, NMSDC.

118. Suetsugu to Katō, 17 September 1930, Katō Kanji Papers; Harada-Saionji, 1:40.

119. Harada-Saionji, 3:147.

CHAPTER SEVEN　MEN, ORGANIZATION, AND STRATEGIC VISIONS, 1931–41

1. Albion, 69, 179.

2. Yoshii, 32–43; Itō Masanori, *Dai kaigun*, 500–502; Ikeda, *Kaigun to Nihon*, 171.

3. The ethos of the Naval Academy is captured in lively contrast to Dartmouth (Royal Naval College) in Marder, 1:265–84.

4. *Inoue Shigeyoshi*, 31–2; *Mainichi gurafu: Ā Etajima*, 92, 94, 133.

5. Tomioka, *Kaisen*, 26–29, 151–52; Takagi, *Taiheiyō*, 276.

6. "Kaisen yōmurei," various versions at JDA.

7. Quoted in *Inoue Shigeyoshi*, 95.

8. Takagi, *Taiheiyō sensō*, 112–13; Chihaya, *Nihon kaigun*, 244; Senshibu, *Kaigun kaisen keii*, 1:9; Nakazawa, 238.

9. Akiyama Saneyuki, at the time of the Battle of the Sea of Japan, was 37, and Chief of Staff Katō Tomosaburō was 44. In December 1941, Chief of Staff Ugaki Matome was 52 and Head of the Operations Division Rear Admiral Fukudome Shigeru was 52. The ideal age for a rear admiral was said to be 40; that for an admiral, 50.

10. Chihaya, *Nihon kaigun*, 244; Takagi, *Taiheiyō sensō*, 112.

11. Hata Ikuhiko, "Kantaiha to Jōyakuha," 193–231.

12. Toyoda, 55–56; Nakamura Kikuo, 309; Senshibu, *Kaigun kaisen keii*, 1:8–9; Nakazawa, 238.

13. Captain R. M. Colvin's report, No. 22, 1 November 1922, in Ambassador Charles Eliot's report, 9 November 1922, F3795/25/3; Captain Marriott's report on "Administration of Imperial Japanese Navy," British Foreign Office Archives, PRO.

14. Itō Kinjirō, 168; Toyoda, 25; Nakamura Kikuo, 219; Ikeda, *Nihon no kaigun*, 2:127.

15. *Katō Kanji taishō den*, 714–18.

16. Nagai Kanseii, 87–95.

17. Krug et al., 88, 98, 103.

18. The leader of pro-German officers was Nomura Naokuni (stationed in Berlin 1929–31, 1940–43). Others were Endō Yoshikazu (1931–32, 1938), Yokoi Tadao (1932–36, 1940–43), Kami Shigenori (1935–36), Kojima Hideo (1936–37), and Shiba Katsuo (1935–37). Kojima, chief of the Seventh Section of the Intelligence Division, in charge of information about European affairs (1939–41), was especially intimate with German naval attaché Paul Wenneker. Yokoi was the war guidance officer of the Operations Division (1936–39), Kami was a member of the First Section of the Naval Affairs Bureau (1939) and the Operations Division (1939–42), and Shiba was a member of the Operations Division (1938–39) and the Naval Affairs Bureau (1939–40).

19. Chapman, *Price of Admiralty*, 1:128.

20. Quoted in Marder, 1:121.

21. Ogata, 73, 178, 256–57.

22. *Inoue Shigeyoshi*, 225.

23. Ishikawa, *Shinjuwan*, 113–22; Yoshida, *Kaigun sanbō*, 196–97.

24. Nomura Minoru, *Tennō, Fushimino miya*, 26–82.

25. Takagi, *Taiheiyō sensō*, 200; Andō, 269–70.

26. Okada, *Kaikoroku*, 143.

27. *Kido nikki*, 2:913.

28. Nomura Minoru, *Rekishi no naka no Nihon kaigun*, 74.

29. *Terashima Ken den*, 124–25.

30. *Honjō nikki*, 163.

31. Nomura Minoru, *Rekishi no naka no Nihon kaigun*, 66–67.

32. "Gunreibu kaisei no keii" [Circumstances Surrounding the Revision of the Naval General Staff Regulations], record of Commander Takagi Sōkichi's interviews with Takahashi and Inoue in January and February 1935, respectively, JDA; Harada-Saionji, 3:114–15.

33. *Inoue Shigeyoshi,* 138–44; *Inoue Shigeyoshi-S,* 8–12; Inoue, "Omoide no ki."

34. Senshishitsu, *Kaigun gunsenbi,* 1:8–10; *Inoue Shigeyoshi,* 139–49.

35. *Inoue Shigeyoshi,* 139.

36. *Terashima Ken den,* 148. The text of the revised Naval Staff Regulations appears in Senshishitsu, *Kaigun gunsenbi,* 1:8–10.

37. *Terashima Ken den,* 146, 147–48.

38. Nomura in ibid., 146.

39. Hori graduated from the Naval Academy, the Gunnery School, and Naval Staff College at the top of his class.

40. Agawa, *Reluctant Admiral,* 45.

41. Quoted in Takagi, *Yamamoto to Yonai,* 49.

42. Senshishitsu, *Rengō kantai,* 1:246; record of interview with Inoue.

43. *GS, Nitchū sensō,* 1:351–53; *Nihon kaigunshi,* 3:393–94; JMFA, *Nihon gaikō nenpyō,* 2:344–45.

44. *GS, Nitchū sensō,* 1:351–53.

45. *Kaigunshō shiryō,* 11:146–51; Senshishitsu, *Rikugun kaisen keii,* 3:309–10.

46. Ōya, quoted in Hata Ikuhiko, *Shōwashi,* 199.

47. Ishikawa Shingo, *Shinjuwan,* 113, 114, 121–22; Takagi, *Shikan,* 181.

48. "Shimada Shigetarō nikki," 360.

49. Yoshida, *Kaigun sanbō,* 244.

50. The authors of the official war history deny the importance of the First Committee. Nomura Minoru writes that it was "the arena for Ishikawa's one-man show." Senshishitsu, *Rengō kantai,* 1:496. See also *Kaigun kaisen keii,* 2:325.

51. Considerable importance is attached to the First Committee by Tsunoda Jun, author of Vol. 7 of the *TSM* series: 84–85, 95, 204–5, 95. Inoue Shigeyoshi has testified that the First Committee was extremely important. *TSM* (new ed., 1987), 7:495.

52. The file of "Various Views and Agreements: War Guidance," Takagi papers, JDA; Takagi, *Nikki to jōhō,* 1:490–91; Senshishitsu, *Rikugun kaisen keii,* 3:309–10.

53. *Inoue Shigeyoshi-S,* 286, 289.

54. The record of interview with Takada Toshitane, JMJ, cited in Senshishitsu, *Rikugun kaisen keii,* 3:310.

55. *Katō Kanji taishō den,* 824–34.

56. Suetsugu, passim; *Katō Kanji nikki,* 534–36.

57. Suetsugu's draft speech for the Supreme Military Council, 8 June 1934, Katō Kanji Papers.

58. *Katō Kanji nikki,* 490.

59. Evans and Peattie, 214.

60. Senshibu, *Shiryōshū: Kaigun nendo sakusen keikaku,* 24.

61. Senshishitsu, *Kaigun gunsenbi,* 1:160–62, 174–77; Senshishitsu, *Sensuikanshi,* 27–54; Fukudome, *Shikan,* 124; Nakayama, 22.

62. Toyoda, 88; Yamamoto Eisuke's memo, 1930, Saitō Papers.

63. Goldstein and Dillon, 324.

64. Senshishitsu, *Rengō kantai,* 1:322–23.

65. Senshibu, *Shiryōshū: Kaigun nendo sakusen keikaku,* 22–25, 775; Senshishitsu, *Rengō kantai,* 1:322, 328–29; Nagai, "Kokubō hōshin," Part 13:3327–28, JDA; Nakazawa, 9.

66. Senshibu, *Shiryōshū: Kaigun nendo sakusen keikaku,* 795–800.

67. Sorimachi, 450–51; Agawa, *Yamamoto,* 131 (italics added).

68. Peattie, *Sunburst,* 129ff.; Takagi, *Yamamoto to Yonai,* passim.

69. Senshishitsu, *Hawai sakusen,* 7, 73–74, 82–86.

70. *Inoue Shigeyoshi,* 287–91; *Inoue Shigeyoshi-S,* 34–38.

71. *Inoue Shigeyoshi-S,* 126–32.

72. *Inoue Shigeyoshi,* 300.

73. Ibid., 301.

74. Genda, *Pāru Hāba,* 105–10; Goldstein and Dillon, 6–7.

75. Staff study, "Strategy and Tactics against Enemy 'A,'" November 1936, JDA.

76. Senshishitsu, *Hawai sakusen,* 39–44, 512–33.

CHAPTER EIGHT   ABROGATION OF THE WASHINGTON
TREATY AND AFTER

1. *TSM-S,* 64–65; *Kaigunshō shiryō,* 1:378–79.

2. Study by the investigating committee on arms limitation, 1935 (strictly confidential), Enomoto Papers; *Kaigunshō shiryō,* 1:160–63.

3. *Kaigunshō shiryō,* 1:160–63.

4. *TSM-S,* 55–56; *Okada Keisuke,* 147, 154–65, 187–88.

5. Ibid., 167–68.

6. The first supplemental building program provided for building each category of ship to treaty limits, construction of ships not covered by the treaty, and expansion of naval aviation. Senshishitsu, *Kaigun gunsenbi,* 1:396–413; *Kaigunshi,* 3:219.

7. By March 1933 Japan had built up to 95 percent of the treaty strength, while the United States had built up to merely 65 percent. Hull, 1:287.

8. Levine, 43–44.

9. Love, *History of the United States Navy,* 1:581.

10. *Katō Kanji nikki,* 167.

11. Naval attaché (in Washington) to navy vice minister, 10 June 1932 (No. 57, confidential); naval attaché to adjunct, Navy Ministry, 14 July 1932 (No. 67, confidential); naval attaché to vice chief of NGS, August 1932, JDA; *Kido nikki,* 1:198; Senshishitsu, *Kaigun gunsenbi,* 1:4.

12. Quoted in Higuchi, *Nihon kaigun,* 162–63; Ishikawa Shingo, *Shinjuwan,* 1.

13. Shinmyō, 178–79.

14. Higuchi, *Nihon kaigun,* 173.

15. *Kaigunshō shiryō,* 1:100, 102, 160.

16. Chief of NGS to navy minister, "Consultations Regarding Arms Replenishment to Be Carried Out after 1934" (No. 154, confidential), 6 May 1933, JDA; Navy Ministry memo, "A View on the International Situation from the Standpoint of National Defense," 3 October 1933, Saitō Papers, navy minister's oral statement at the Five Ministers Conference, 21 September 1933; navy minister's draft statement at the cabinet meeting, "Policy Regarding the 1935 Naval Conference," 6 October 1933, Saitō Papers and JMFA; *GS: Nitchū sensō,* 4:35.

17. Grew, *Ten Years in Japan,* 116.

18. Quoted in Senshishitsu, *Rengō kantai,* 1:279.

19. Ishikawa to Katō, "Memo on policy for the forthcoming naval conference," *Katō Kanji nikki,* 480–83.

20. Ibid., 535–36.

21. Ibid., 481.

22. Ibid., 480.

23. Tōgō Shigenori, *Jidai no ichi men,* 2–93; Tōgō Shigehiko, 138–39.

24. Navy minister's statement at the Five Ministers Conference, "My View on the Empire's Foreign Policy to Cope with the International Situation in the Future," 16 October 1933; "Navy's Revised Draft Policy toward the United States," n.d., JMFA.

25. *Kaigunshō shiryō,* 1:26.

26. *Katō Kanji nikki,* 540–41.

27. Harada-Saionji, 3:155, 198–99; Shigemitsu, *Shōwa no dōran,* 1:81.

28. Sakai, 103, 106.

29. *GS: Nitchū sensō,* 4:16–18, 25–26, 28–36; Harada-Saionji, 4:24; Tōgō Shigenori, *Jidai no ichi men,* 92–93.

30. Memo of the first section of the Naval Affairs Bureau, July 1934, JDA; *GS, Nitchū sensō,* 4:16–18, 25–26, 28–29, 30–36; Harada-Saionji, 4:24; Tōgō Shigenori, 92–93.

31. Senshishitsu, *Rengō kantai,* 1:280; Nakazawa, 20.

32. Okada, *Kaikoroku,* 88.

33. *Kido nikki,* 1:346; Saionji-Harada, 4:16–171; Okada, *Kaikoroku,* 88.

34. *Kido nikki,* 1:346; Saionji-Harada, 4:16–17 (italics added).

35. *Kido nikki,* 1:350.

36. *Honjō nikki,* 1:191–92, 328, 330, 346; Harada-Saionji, 4:16–19, 22–23; *Makino nikki,* 581; *Kido nikki,* 1:347.

37. Harada-Saionji, 3:322.

38. Harada-Saionji, 4:24, 27–28; Minutes of the Five Ministers Conference, 24 July 1934, JMFA.

39. Harada-Saionji, 4:34–35; *Kido nikki,* 1:350; 196; Pelz, *Race,* 60.

40. *Okada Keisuke*, 180; Pelz, "Rondon gunshuku kaigi," 64; record of Yoshida Zengo's statement, December 1956, Suikō Kai, Tokyo.

41. *Makino nikki*, 580–82; Harada Saionji, 3:321–22; *Kido nikki*, 1:350; *Katō Kanji taishō den*, 903–4; *Katō Kanji nikki*, 536.

42. Harada-Saionji, 4:45; Shōda, 1:277; *Makino nikki*, 580–83.

43. Senshishitsu, *Rengō kantai*, 1:281–82.

44. *Kaigunshō shiryō*, 1:125; *Okada Keisuke*, 260; *GS, Vol. 12, Nitchū sensō*, 4:40; Harada-Saionji, 4:44–48.

45. *Makino nikki*, 582.

46. Ibid., 583; *Honjō nikki*, 194 (italics added).

47. Suetsugu, "Gunshuku taisalku shiken," 8 June 1934, Katō Kanji Papers; Harada-Saionji, 3:211–12, 4:46–47, 53.

48. Finance ministry memo, "Policy Toward the Naval Limitation Conference," n.d. (strictly confidential), Saitō Papers.

49. Harada-Saionji, 4:20–22; *Honjō nikki*, 193–94, 198.

50. Sakai, 23.

51. *TSM*, 1:159.

52. *Honjō nikki*, 193, 196; *GS: Nitchū sensō*, 4:60–61, 63.

53. *Katō Kanji nikki*, 270.

54. The instructions appear in *NGB: 1935-nen Rondon kaigun kaigi*, 109–12.

55. *Inoue Shigeyoshi*, 126.

56. *Inoue Shigeyoshi-S*, 281.

57. *NGB: 1935-nen Rondon kaigun kaigi*, 8–9.

58. *Kaigunshō shiryō*, 1:160–62.

59. *NGB: 1935-nen Rondon kaigun kaigi*, 344–53.

60. Ibid., 281.

61. *Kaigunshō shiryō*, 1:160–62; *GS: Nitchū sensō*, 4:41.

62. Heinrichs, *Threshold*, 36.

63. Kaufman, 168; Heinrichs, *Threshold*, 36.

64. *DBFP*, Second Series, Vol. 13, 54–55.

65. Quoted in Pelz, *Race*, 127.

66. Roskill, 2:315; Pelz, *Race*, 52.

67. *FRUS, 1934*, 1:315; *NGB: 1935-nen Rondon kaigun kaigi*, 136, 156, 161.

68. *DBFP*, Second Series, Vol. 13, 52, 371.

69. Julius Pratt, *Hull*, 1:102.

70. *DBFP*, Second Series, Vol. 13, 134, 141, 143.

71. Quoted in Nomura Minoru, *Yamamoto*, 176.

72. Quoted in Pelz, *Race*, 149.

73. *FRUS, 1935*, 65.

74. *GS: Nitchū sensō*, 4:85.

75. Agawa, *Yamamoto*, 131.

76. *FRUS, 1935*, 1:68.

77. *Kaigunshō shiryō*, 4:85.

78. The instructions to Nagano appear in *NGB: 1935-nen Rondon kaigun kaigi keika hōkokusho*, 211–13.

79. *DBFP*, Second Series, Vol. 13, 736.

80. Ibid., 740; *FRUS, Japan: 1931–1941*, 1:287; JMFA, *Nihon gaikō nenpyō*, 2:319; *NGB: 1935-nen Rondon kaigun kaigi keika hōkokusho*, 266–67.

81. Richardson, 80.

82. *Takamatsu no miya nikki*, 2:361.

83. Shigemitsu, *Gaikō kaikoroku*, 156; Shigemitsu, *Shōwa no dōran*, 1:82–83.

84. *Nihon kaigunshi*, 3:381, 365–66.

85. Suetsugu, 82.

86. *Inoue Shigeyoshi*, 258.

87. Ishikawa Shingo's memo to Katō Kanji, "My private view on policy toward the next arms limitation," strictly confidential, Katō Kanji Papers; *Katō Kanji nikki*, 483–84.

88. Ishikawa Shingo, 78–81.

89. Quoted in Agawa, *Reluctant Admiral*, 93.

90. Toyama, 21.

91. *Kaigunshō shiryō*, 1:282–92.

92. Hatano, "Nihon kaigun to nanshin," 218–22.

93. Senshishitsu, *Daihon'ei rikugunbu*, 1:381; *GS: Nitchū sensō*, 1:351–53.

94. *GS: Nitchū sensō*, 1:354–355, 359–61.

95. Yokoyama, 47–49, *GS: Nitchū sensō*, 1:361–65; Crowley, 278–300, 351–52; Hatano, "Nihon kaigun to nanshin," 217–2.

96. *GS: Nitchū sensō*, 1:358–60; JMFA, *Nihon gaikō nenpyō*, 2:344–47; Senshishitsu, *Rengō kantai*, 1:299.

97. Senshishitsu, *Rengō kantai*, 1:315–318.

98. Senshishitsu, *Rengō kantai*, 1:322–324.

99. *Kaigunshō shiryō*, 2:286–89, 4:274–75; Ishikawa Shingo, 113, 122.

100. *Kaigunshō shiryō*, 2:286–89; Ishikawa Shingo, *Shinjuwan*, 113, 112.

101. *GS: Nitchū sensō*, 1:9, 217–19, 221–26, 231–33; Shimada Toshihiko, 55–68, 84; Akagi, 133–45.

102. *GS: Nitchū sensō*, 4:375–92; Senshishitsu, *Kaigun gunsenbi*, 1:778, 783; Tomioka, "Taiheiyō sensō zenshi," 1:778, 783.

103. *GS: Nitchū sensō*, 4:375–92; Senshishitsu, *Kaigun gunsenbi*, 1:778, 783.

104. Senshibu, *Kaigun kaisen keii*, 1:343–45.

105. Aizawa, *Kaigun no sentaku*, 139.

106. Ibid., 139, 179–88.

107. *Inoue Shigeyoshi-S*, 24.

CHAPTER NINE   THE JAPANESE NAVY AND
THE TRIPARTITE PACT

1. Takada, *Yonai Mitsumasa no tegami*, 63–65, 92; Takagi, *Nikki to jōhō*, 1:308.

2. Ogata, 37; Takada, *Shizuka naru tate*, 348–49. In January 1937 there was talk of appointing Suetsugu navy minister, but Yamamoto squashed the idea, saying that the emperor and Prince Fushimi distrusted him. Harada-Saionji, 5:228–29.

3. Harada-Saionji, 7:39.

4. Okada, *Kaikoroku*, 131.

5. Ogata, 59–60.

6. Record of interview with Yokoi Tadao, JDA.

7. *Inoue Shigeyoshi*, 238. "Miraculously" is Admiral Takagi Sōkichi's word quoted in Agawa, *Yonai*, 1:77.

8. Chapman, *The Price*, 1:xxi.

9. Ibid., 161.

10. *DGFP*, Series D, 6:623–24, 737, 858; Harada-Saionji, 8:37–38, 189, 198.

11. Harada-Saionji, 7:34, 35, 189, 198.

12. Takagi, *Nikki to jōhō*, 1:162–64, 237.

13. *Inoue Shigeyoshi*, 239.

14. *GS: Nitchū sensō*, 3:153–54, 156, 160, 177, 183–84.

15. Ibid., 339–42.

16. Ibid., 343, 174–76.

17. Ibid., 156 (italics added).

18. Harada-Saionji, 7:267–69; Captain Takagi, "My view on a Japanese-German-Italian pact," 17 December 1938; Takagi's memo on a Japanese-German-Italian agreement, April 1939, Takagi Papers; *Takagi nikki*, 197.

19. *GS: Nitchū sensō*, 3:153–65; Takada, *Yonai Mitsumasa no tegami*, 138–39.

20. Ogata, 41.

21. Ibid., 40–42, 54, 58.

22. *GS: Nitchū sensō*, 3:161–65 and passim.

23. Quoted in Takada, *Shizuka naru tate*, 1:338–39.

24. *Inoue Shigeyoshi*, 228–30; *Inoue Shigeyoshi-S*, 27.

25. *Inoue Shigeyoshi*, 225.

26. Ibid., 225–29.

27. Height.

28. Grew, *Ten Years in Japan*, 280–81.

29. Takada, *Shizuka naru tate*, 1:346–47.

30. *GS: China*, 3:164, 169.

31. Harada-Saionji, 7:249, 8:30.

32. Sanematsu Yuzuru, *Saigo no toride* is a favorable but well-documented biography of Yoshida.

33. Chapman, 1:168.

34. Ogata, 61.

35. "Outline of Policy toward the United States," 22 October 1940, JDA; *TSM-S,* 318–19; Meeting of the prospective cabinet members.

36. *TSM,* 5:182–86; Morley, *Deterrent Diplomacy,* 216–19, 220–21.

37. Chapman, 1:168.

38. *TSM,* 5:182–85; Sanematsu, *Saigo no toride,* 76–77.

39. Sanematsu, *Saigo no toride,* 79.

40. Imperial Headquarters–Government Liaison Conferences (*Daihon'ei seifu renraku kaigi*) were established to coordinate the action of the cabinet and the high command. The chiefs of staff and ministers of two services met with the prime minister and civilian members of the cabinet twice a week to thrash out major questions of grand strategy. This conference series became the highest decision-making body. When especially important matters were discussed the emperor attended, thus creating Imperial Conferences (*Gozen kaigi*).

41. *TSM,* 5:185–86, 196 (italics added); *Kimitsu sensō nisshi,* 1, 18.

42. *TSM,* 5:184.

43. Sanematsu, *Saigo no toride,* 78–79.

44. Senshibu, *Kaigun kaisen keii,* 2:70–71.

45. Ishikawa Shingo, 229–30.

46. *Inoue Shigeyoshi,* 276–77.

47. The text of the Tripartite Pact appears in JMFA, *Nihon gaikō nenpyō,* 2:459–62.

48. *TSM-S,* 333.

49. Ibid., 338–41.

50. Konoe, 30–31; Yabe, 2:161–62; Shinmyō, 79.

51. *TSM-S,* 338–41.

52. Shinmyō, 178–79

53. *TSM-S,* 333.

54. Ugaki, 2; Senshishitsu, *Rengō kantai,* 1:485.

55. Record of interview with Toyoda Teijirō, JDA.

56. Senshishitsu, *Rikugun kaisen keii,* 2:214.

57. Ibid.; Fukudome, *Shikan,* 139.

58. Harada-Saionji, 8:365–66.

59. Senshibu, *Kaigun kaisen keii,* 2:108–9.

60. *Kaigunshō shiryō,* 11:270–73.

61. Third (Intelligence) Division, "Estimate of the Situation," 7 September 1940; "Attitude of the United States toward the Tripartite Pact and Our Policy," 29 September 1940, JDA.

62. Third Division, "Estimate of the Situation," 7 September 1940.

63. Genda, *Kaigun kōkūtai,* 23.

64. Langer and Gleason, *Undeclared War,* 35–38.

65. Quoted in Utley, *Going to War,* 110.

66. Grew, *Ten Years in Japan,* 333–34; Grew, *Turbulent Era,* 2:1231, 1254–55.

67. Roosevelt to Grew, 21 January 1941; *FRUS, 1941,* 1:68.

68. Quoted in Utley, *Going to War,* 68, 109.

69. Roosevelt to Grew, 21 January 1941.

70. Pratt to Nomura, as told to Captain Takagi Sōkichi, 18 February 1939, Takagi, *Nikki to jōhō,* 1:241.

71. Quoted in Utley, *Going to War,* 110.

72. Intelligence Division, "Estimate of the Situation," 7 September 1940, JDA.

73. Intelligence Division, "American Reaction to the Tripartite Pact and Policies to Cope with It," 28 September 1940; *Kaigunshō shiryō,* 11:270–73; Senshishitsu, *Rengō kantai,* 1:494.

CHAPTER TEN   THE SOUTHWARD ADVANCE AND THE AMERICAN EMBARGO

1. Nakahara Diary, 3, 29 September 1939, 15 January 1940, JDA.

2. Morley, *Fateful Choice,* 242.

3. Hatano and Asada, 386.

4. Utley, *Going to War,* 79.

5. Quoted in Feis, 23.

6. Senshibu, *Kaigun kaisen keii,* 1:357.

7. Quoted in Utley, "Franklin Roosevelt and Naval Strategy," 54.

8. Anderson, "1941 De Facto Embargo," 3.

9. *Kaigunshō shiryō,* 2:555–57.

10. Hatano, "Nihon kaigun to 'Nanshin,'" 230.

11. *Pearl Harbor Attack,* Part 12, 932; Richardson, 330–33.

12. Quoted in *Pearl Harbor,* 112. For the Japanese response, see Fukudome, *Shikan,* 158.

13. *TSM,* 7:19; Nakazawa, 19, 42–47.

14. It was only in October 1942 that an expert in convoy escort was appointed by the naval high command (Ōi Atsushi, 26, 59–60, 64; Senshishitsu, *Kaijō goeisen,* 74–75, 76). In slighting a convoy escort the Japanese navy was influenced by Mahan. For the United States, a largely self-sufficient nation, protection of sea communications and merchant shipping was not as important as it was for Britain or Japan. Mahan, with his obsession with the decisive battle encounter, considered a convoy escort of secondary importance.

15. *TSM,* 7:20.

16. Nakazawa, 43–47.

17. Senshishitsu, *Daihon'ei rikugunbu*, 2:71; Sanematsu, *Saigo no toride*, 6–77.

18. Senshibu, *Kaigun kaisen keii*, 2:63.

19. *TSM*, 6:159.

20. *TSM-S*, 315–16.

21. Ibid.; JMFA, *Nihon gaikō nenpyō*, 2:437–38.

22. *TSM-S*, 323.

23. Senshishitsu, *Rikugun kaisen keii*, 1:440–42.

24. Ibid., 446.

25. Ibid., 1:390, 441.

26. Senshishitsu, *Rikugun kaisen keii*, 3:79.

27. Senshishitsu, *Rikugun kaisen keii*, 1:464–65.

28. *Inoue Shigeyoshi*, 285; Senshitsu, *Rengō kantai*, 1:320.

29. Ibid., 285–87.

30. Senshishitsu, *Kaigun gunsenbi*, 1:594–98; Navy Ministry paper on "The Present Status of Armaments," 1941, JDA; Ōmae, 60.

31. Senshishitsu, *Kaigun gunsenbi*, 1:594; Pelz, *Race*, 217.

32. Langer and Gleason, *Undeclared War*, 35.

33. *GS: Nitchū sensō*, 3:369–71; *TSM-S*, 325.

34. *TSM-S*, 325; *GS: Nitchū sensō*, 3:497–500.

35. Utley, *Going to War*, 105, 107.

36. Senshishitsu, *Rengō kantai*, 1:480–81.

37. *Inoue Shigeyoshi*, 269; Senshibu, *Rigun kaisen keii*, 3:304.

38. (Italics added.) Naval planners had estimated that by mid-April 1941, with the progress of wartime mobilization, the Japanese navy would attain operational strength of 75 percent compared to the United States, a 5 percent increase over the navy's traditional 70 percent target. Senshibu, *Rikugun kaisen keii*, 3:304; *TSM*, 6:216–17.

39. *TSM-S*, 333.

40. Yamamoto to Shimada, 10 December 1949, "Gohōroku," JDA.

41. Fujii Diary, 11 February 1941.

42. *Kido nikki*, 2:851.

43. *Kimitsu sensō nisshi*, 1:66–75; Fujii Diary, 11 February 1941.

44. *TSM*, 7:86–87.

45. JMFA, *Nihon gaikō nenpyō*, 2:495.

46. *Kimitsu sensō nisshi*, 1:75.

47. Fujii Diary, n.d.

48. Kobayashi Seizō, "Kaisōroku," JDA; Hoshina et al., *Taiheiyō sensō hishi*, 237.

49. *TSM*, 7:202.

50. Record of interview with Shiba Katsuo, JDA.

51. Senshibu, *Rikugun kaisen keii*, 4:122–23; recollections of Vice Admiral Maeda Minoru, JDA (italics added).

52. *TSM-S*, 427–39.

53. Captain Ōno of the Operations Division testified that there was a general fear that the United States was building a military base in southern Indochina to forestall Japan.

54. Quoted in Spector, *Eagle*, 75; Prange, *At Dawn*, 292–93.

55. Nakahara Diary, 19 June 1941. The report was presented to Navy Minister Oikawa and Vice Minister Sawamoto and the chief of the Naval General Staff and its leaders.

56. Fujii Diary, 2 July 1941.

57. *TSM-S*, 442; *Kimitsu sensō nisshi*, 1:115–16; Fujii Diary, 11 June 1941.

58. Ishikawa Diary, 19 June 1941.

59. Ickes, 567.

60. *Kimitsu sensō nisshi*, 1:121.

61. Heinrichs, *Threshold*, 145.

62. *TSM-S*, 467–69; Shinmyō, 133–34.

63. Senshishitsu, *Rikugun kaisen keii*, 4:124; record of interview with Oka Takazumi, JMJ; staff studies, JDA.

64. "Sawamoto Yorio nikki," 438–40; "Ishikawa nikki," 287–88; Shinmyō, 131, 133–34; Hatano, Bakuryō.

65. Senshishitsu, *Rikugun kaisen keii*, 4:167.

66. Yoshizawa, 211.

67. *Inoue Shigeyoshi*, 441; *TSM-S*, 481.

68. *TSM-S*, 481; "Sawamoto nikki," 442, 444; Fujii Diary, 21 July 1941.

69. "Sawamoto nikki," 442; *TSM-S*, 481.

70. *TSM-S*, 481; record of interview with Oka Takazumi, JMJ (italics added).

71. Tomioke, *Kaisen*, 59; Shiryō Chōsa Kai, 268; Senshishitsu, *Rengō kantai*, 1:528; *Kimitsu sensō nisshi*, 1:138; quoted in Prange, *At Dawn*, 166; record of interview with Oka Takazumi, JMJ; Senshishitsu *Rikugun kaisen keii*, 4:124.

72. Record of interview with Maeda Minoru, JDA; Senshibu, *Kaigun kaisen keii*, 2:331; *Nihon kaigunshi*, 4:298.

73. Record of interview with Oka Takazumi, JDA.

74. "Kobayashi kaisōroku," JDA; *Nihon kaigunshi*, 4:294; *Inoue Shigeyoshi*, 308–9.

75. *Kobayashi Seizō oboegaki*, 90–93.

76. *Kido nikki*, 2:895–96; *Sugiyama memo*, 286. For example, Herbert Bix maintains: "From late 1940 . . . [Hirohito] made important contributions during each stage of policy review, culminating in the opening of hostilities against the United States and Great Britain in December 1941." *Hirohito and the Making of Modern Japan* (New York: HarperCollins, 2000), 12, 23. This thesis is not supported by documentary evidence.

77. See Mauch.

78. ONI, "Memorandum for CNO," 11 October 1921 (confidential) NA.

79. William Pratt, "Autobiography."

80. Quoted in Agawa, *Yonai*, 1:237.

81. Takagi, *Nikki to jōhō*, 1:241.

82. Quoted in Senshibu, *Kaigun kaisen keii*, 2:278–79.

83. *Nomura Kichisaburō*, 15–17; Takagi's memo on Admiral Nomura's appointment, Seikai jōhō, S12 2/2, Takagi Sōkichi Papers, JDA; Senshishitsu, *Rikugun kaisen keii*, 3:452–53.

84. Hull, 2:987.

85. *Inoue Shigeyoshi*, 304–5; *NGB: Nichi-Bei kōshō*, 1:24–28; *Nihon kaigunshi*, 4:248–50. Hoshina; et al., 229; Senshishitsu, *Rikugun kaisen keii*, 3:548–49.

86. *Nomura Kichisaburō*, 548, 848; Nomura, 184–85, 186–87; *NGB: Nichi-Bei kōshō*, 1:30–31, 167; Mauch, 369; Kobayashi Seizō, "Kaisōroku," JDA.

87. *NGB: Nichi-Bei kōshō*, 1:166.

88. Miwa Munehiro, ed., "Nomura chū-Bei taishi nikki" [The Diary of Nomura, Ambassador to the United States, 3 June–30 August], *Kyūshū Kyōritsu daigaku keizai gakubu kiyō* 66 (December 1996), 97.

89. Ibid., 130; *Pearl Harbor Attack*, Exhibit No. 1, 1–2.

90. Japanese Consul General Takashi Tomio cabled false information to Tokyo: "What comes next to an advance into French Indochina will be an ultimatum to the Dutch East Indies." The limit of Japan's southward advance at this time was southern Indochina. Senshishitsu, *Rikugun kaisen keii*, 4:346–48.

91. Langer and Gleason, *Undeclared War*, 649–55.

92. Ickes, 588.

93. Albion, "1941 De Facto Embargo"; Anderson, *Standard Vacuum Oil Company*.

94. *Kobayashi Seizō oboegaki*, 93.

95. For Hornbeck's mentality, see Thomson, 103–04.

96. Record of interview with Takada Toshitane, JMJ; Tomioka, "Zenshi," 3:37.

97. Senshibu, *Rikugun kaisen keii*, 5:31–32.

98. Butow, 223.

CHAPTER ELEVEN   DECISION FOR WAR

1. Senshishitsu, *Kaigun gunsenbi*, 1:730–31.

2. The fish metaphor appears in Butow, 245.

3. Ibid., 223, 225; Heinrichs, *Threshold*, 182.

4. *Kimitsu sensō nisshi*, 1:145.

5. *Kido nikki*, 2:895–96; Sawada, 116–18.

6. For example, Bix, 23.

7. Senshishitsu, *Rikugun kaisen keii*, 4:468; Nomura Minoru, *Yamamoto*, 222–23.

8. Senshibu, *Kaigun kaisen keii,* 2:402; Senshishitsu, *Rikugun kaisen keii,* 4:464; *Nihon kaigunshi,* 4:3–21.

9. Hatano Sumio, *"Daitōa sensō,"* 207–8.

10. Senshishitsu, *Rengō kantai,* 1:485.

11. Senshishitsu, *Rikugun kaisen keii,* 1:450.

12. *Kimitsu sensō nisshi,* 1:147.

13. Ibid., 148.

14. Senshishitsu, *Daihon'ei rikugunbu,* 2:410–11, 414; Senshishitsu, *Rikugun kaisen keii,* 1:450.

15. *TSM-S,* 507.

16. Record of Fukudome's talks, 3:101–3, JDA.

17. *TSM-S,* 507, 510 (italics added).

18. *Kimitsu sensō nisshi,* 1:153.

19. *TSM-S,* 508–13; *Sugiyama memo,* 1:303–4, 310; "Takagi hiroku bassui," 8 September 1941, Takagi Papers.

20. *Sugiyama memo,* 1:314–15; Ike, 138–49, 512–13.

21. Okada, *Kaikoroku,* 136.

22. "Sawamoto nikki," 444.

23. *TSM-S,* 512; record of Fukudome's talks, 3:91. According to Fukudome's recollection, Nagano anticipated that a chance for interceptive operations would occur within one year of the opening of hostilities.

24. Record of interview with Miyo Kazunari, JDA.

25. There is no written record of this statement by Nagano, but Fukudome Shigeru writes that he heard something to this effect. Fukudome, *Kaigun no hansei,* 90–91; record of interview with Fukudome, JDA; *TSM-S,* 12; Shinmyō, 28; Fujii Diary 6 September 1941.

26. Fukudome, *Kaigun seikatsu,* 202–03.

27. *Sugiyama memo,* 1:311.

28. For a theoretical formulation, see Snyder and Diesing, 393, 397; Ole R. Holsti, "Crisis Management," in Betty Glad, 125–27, 175.

29. Senshibu, *Kaigun kaisen keii,* 2:484–85.

30. *Nihon kaigunshi,* 3:234; Senshishitsu, *Hawai sakusen,* 6–7.

31. Senshibu, *Kaigun kaisen keii,* 2:491–92; "Sawamoto nikki," 460; Senshishitsu, *Rikugun kaisen keii,* 5:109.

32. *Sugiyama memo,* 1:116–17.

33. Senshibu, *Kaigun kaisen keii,* 2:498–99.

34. Shinmyō, 168–69; Konoe, 92.

35. Senshibu, *Rikugun kaisen keii,* 5:114–15; *Kido nikki,* 1:913.

36. Senshishitsu, *Rikugun kaisen keii,* 5:120–21; Yabe, 2:379.

37. Senshishitsu, *Rikugun kaisen keii,* 5:128–29; Yabe, 2:387–88; *Kido nikki,* 2:913.

38. Senshishitsu, *Rikugun kaisen keii,* 5:129–31.

39. Shinmyō, 178–79.

40. "Sawamoto nikki," 474; Senshibu, *Kaigun kaisen keii,* 2:506.

41. Toyoda, 62.

42. Chihaya, quoted in Goldstein and Dillon, *Pearl Harbor Papers,* 330.

43. Yamamoto to Shimada, 24 October 1941, in "Gohōroku," JDA; *Shimada's talk, Suikō Kai;* Shimada Diary, 17 October 1941.

44. "Shimada nikki," 360.

45. Shimada Diary, 1 November 1941; "Shimada nikki," 360, 362, 474; record of Admiral Shimada Shigetarō's talks, Suikō Kai; *Kaigun kaisen keii,* 2:531–32; Hoshina et al., 266; Hoshina, *Daitōa sensō hishi,* 45; 1; Nomura Minoru, *Yamamoto,* 113; *Kimitsu sensō nisshi,* 1:178–80; *Sugiyama memo,* 1, 370–72.

46. Quoted in Langer and Gleason, *Undeclared War,* 845.

47. Shimada Diary, 1 November 1941.

48. *Sugiyama memo,* 1:370–71; *TSM–S,* 550, 560–61, 568.

49. *Kimitsu sensō nisshi,* 180.

50. *TSM-S,* 554.

51. Ibid., 550.

52. Ibid., 568.

53. Ibid., 571.

54. Quoted in Prange, *At Dawn,* 291.

55. Ibid., 344.

56. Yamamoto to Shimada, 10 December 1940, "Gohōroku," JDA.

57. *TSM,* 7:207.

58. Agawa, *Reluctant Admiral,* 186.

59. Yamamoto to Shimada, 24 October 1941, "Gohōroku," JDA.

60. Harada-Saionji, 8:365–66.

61. Konoe, 32; *Inoue Shigeyoshi,* 241; Nomura Minoru, *Yamamoto,* 257.

62. Yamamoto to Hori, 11 November 1941, "Gohōroku," JDA; Nomura, *Yamamoto,* 257, 260; *TSM,* 7:202.

63. Morley, *Final Confrontation,* 287.

64. Takagi, *Yamamoto,* 76.

65. Senshishitsu, *Hawai sakusen,* 78, 230–31.

66. Senshishitsu, *Hawai sakusen,* 7, 73–75, 230–31.

67. Yamamoto to Hori, 11 October 1941, "Gohōroku," JDA; Senshishitsu, *Hawai Sakusen,* 73–74, 78.

68. Senshishitsu, *Hawai Sakusen,* 74, 76–77; Fukudome, Shikan, 151.

69. Ibid., 80.

70. Yamamoto to Oikawa, 24 November 1940, printed in Senshishitsu, *Hawai Sakusen,* 534–35.

71. Yamamoto's memo on armaments, 7 January 1941, sent to Oikawa; cited in Senshishitsu, *Kaigun kaisen keii,* 2:144–47 (italics added).

72. Yamamoto to Shimada, 24 October 1941, "Gohōroku," JDA (italics added).

73. Kobayashi Seizō, "Kaisōroku," JDA. Yamamoto's chief of staff, Rear Admiral Ōnishi Takijirō, believed that a Hawaiian attack, which would strongly provoke the United States, must be avoided. Such an attack would militate against a quick war of short duration. Yamamoto should have known of his chief of staff's idea. Senshishitsu, *Hawai sakusen,* 109.

74. Senshishitsu, *Hawai sakusen,* 81; Senshibu, *Kaigun kaisen keii,* 2:458.

75. Senshishitsu, *Hawai sakusen,* 97–98.

76. Prange, *At Dawn,* 302.

77. Senshishitsu, *Hawai sakusen,* 113.

78. *TSM-S,* 585 (italics added).

79. Senshishitsu, *Hawai sakusen,* 115; Senshibu, *Kaigun kaisen keii,* 2:458.

80. Fukudome, *Shikan,* 267 (italics added).

81. Prange, *At Dawn,* 582.

82. Fukudome, *Shikan,* 356–57.

83. JMFA, *Nihon gaikō nenpyō,* 2:563–64.

84. *Kimitsu sensō nisshi,* 1:192; Senshibu, *Rikugun kaisen keii,* 5:488–90.

85. *Okada Keisuke,* 364–65; *Kido nikki,* 2:926–27; Senshibu, *Kaigun kaisen keii,* 2:546.

86. *Kido nikki,* 2:926–27.

87. *Kido nikki,* 2:928; Shimada shuki, 30 November 1941; Senshibu, *Kaigun kaisen keii,* 2:848–49.

88. Terasaki, 71–72, 75–76.

89. JMFA, *Nihon gaikō nenpyō,* 2:573; Senshibu, *Rikugun kaisen keii,* 5:341.

90. Senshishitsu, *Hawai sakusen,* 262.

91. Itō Kinjirō, 222, 261–62.

92. Asada in Borg and Okamoto, 259.

93. Ibid.

CONCLUSION

1. Tomioka, *Kaisen,* 42, 55–56; Shiryō Chōsa Kai, 169, 312; Tomioka quoted in Yoshida, *Kaigun sanbō,* 183.

2. Nomura Minoru, *Taiheiyō sensō,* 21.

3. Nakazawa, 42.

4. Senshishitsu, *Hawai sakusen,* 96; record of Fukudome's talks, 3:23.

5. Morimatsu, 9, 42, 84; *Kaigunshō shiryō,* 12:33.

6. *Kaigunshō shiryō,* 11:474–77, 12:33; Shinmyō, 166.

7. *Kaigunshō shiryō*, 12:33; Tomioka, "Taiheiyō sensō zenshi," 4:5, 93–94; Tomioka, *Kaisen*, 55, 58; Shiryō Chōsa Kai, 166, 466; Barnhart, "Japanese Intelligence," 450; Okada, *Kaikoroku*, 135; Shinmyō, 66.

8. Tomioka, "Taiheiyō sensō zenshi," 5, 93–94; "Sawamoto nikki," 471; Bureau of Naval Ordnance to chief of NGS, 31 October 1941, JDA; Hoshina, 28, 46; Nakazawa, 44–45; record of interview with Hashimoto Shōzō, JMJ.

9. Hoshina, *Daitōa sensō hishi*, 21–22; Andō, 2:287–88; Ishikawa, 338–41; Okada, *Kaikoroku*, 135; *Okada Keisuke*, 365; Shinmyō, 166.

10. Yokoyamo, 99–100.

11. Ibid., 82–83; Yokoyama in Nakamura Kikuo, 143–45.

12. Yokoyama, 82–83, 91, 94, 97–98; record of interviews with Yokoyama, JMJ; Yokoyama, in Nakamura Kikuo, 151–52.

13. Prados, 64–65, 70, 100.

14. Ishikawa, *Shinjuwan*, 114; records of interview with Ishikawa.

15. Toyoda, 57; Hoshina, 2; Hoshina, et al, 4.

16. Fudome, *Shikan*, 112; Nakazawa, 209.

17. Fukudome, *Shikan*, 97–98; *Kaigun seikatsu*, 204; record of interview with Shimada, Suikō Kai; Shinmyō, 26.

18. Janis, 37, 39.

19. Butow, 315–16.

20. Senshishitsu, *Rikugun kaisen keii*, 3:77, 4:494; Hatano, "Yokushi senryak," 95–96.

21. *Kimitsu sensō nisshi*, I:8, 75, 77, 86, 121, 147, 170, 179.

22. Record of interview with Inoue Shigeyoshi, JMJ.

23. Hara Shirō, 64, 66.

24. "Sawamoto nikki," 21 July 1941, 442; Fujii Diary, 21 July 10.

25. Quoted in Takagi, *Yamamoto to Yonai*, 247; Harada-Saionji, 5:96; taped interview with Miyo Kazunari, JDA.

26. Record of interview with Miyo Kazurari, JDA.

27. Quoted in Senshishitsu, *Rengō kantai*, 1:246.

28. Quoted in Yoshida, *Kaigun sanbō*, 312–13.

29. Letter from Inoue Shigeyoshi, quoted in *TSM* (new ed.), 7:494.

BIBLIOGRAPHY

ARCHIVES

Britain, Foreign Office Archives, Public Record Office. Kew, UK

Enomoto Jūji Papers. Contained in the "Senbi gunshuku" [Naval Armanent and Limitation] group, JDA (see "Notes on Principal Sources")

Hori Teikichi, Library, NMSDC (see "Notes on Principal Sources")

Japan, Library, Institute of Defense Studies, Japanese Defense Agency

Japan, Ministry of Foreign Affairs Archives, Diplomatic Record Office

Japan, Ministry of Justice, Senpan Shiryō Shitsu (Office of War Crimes Materials)

United States, Department of the Navy Archives, National Archives. College Park, Md.

United States, Department of State Archives, National Archives. College Park, Md.

United States, Naval Historical Collections, Naval War College. Newport, R.I.

United States, Records of the General Board. Record Group 45, Modern Military Record, NA

PRIVATE PAPERS

Anderson, Chandler P., LC.

Cotton, Lyman A., diary. University of North Carolina, Chapel Hill, N.C.

Fujii Shigeru, diary. Copy in private hands.

Gardiner, William Howard. Houghton Library, Harvard University.

Hughes, Charles Evans, LC.

Ishikawa Shingo, diary. In private hands.

Katō Kanji, Institute of Social Science, the University of Tokyo.

Kobayashi Seizō, "Kaisōroku" [Memoirs]. JDA.

Konoe Fumimaro. Copies at JDA.

Lodge, Henry Cabot. Massachusetts Historical Society, Boston.

Mahan, Alfred Thayer. LC.

Makino Nobuaki. DL.

Nakahara Yoshimasa, "Nisshi kaisō" [Diary]. JDA.

Pratt, William V. Operational Archives, Naval History Division, Washington Navy Yard.

Roosevelt, Theodore, Jr. LC.

Saitō Makoto. DL.

"Sawamoto Yorio shuki" [Manuscript Notes]. JDA.

"Shimada Shigetarō taishō bōbiroku" [Memos and Diary]. JDA.

"Shimada Shigetarō taishō shuki" [Manuscript Notes]. Suikō Kai, Tokyo.

Stimson, Henry L., microfilmed diary. Yale University Library.

Takagi Sōkichi. JDA.

Takarabe Takeshi, DL.

Washburn, Stanley. LC; Washburn Oral History, Columbia University Library.

Yamamoto Isoroku's letters ("Gohō Roru"). JDA.

Yoshida Zengo, "Shuki" [Manuscript Notes]. Suikō Kai.

GOVERNMENT PUBLICATIONS*

Britain. *Documents on British Foreign Policy, 1919–1939 [DBFP]*, First Series, Vol. 14. Edited by Rohan Butler, J. P. T. Bury, and M. E. Lambert. London: HMSO, 1966.

———. *DBFP*, Second Series, Vol. 1. Edited by E. L. Woodward and Rohan Butler. London: HMSO, 1947.

———. *DBFP*, Second Series, Vol. 13. Edited by Rohan Butler. London: HMSO, 1973.

Germany. *Documents on German Foreign Policy*, Series D (1937–1945). Vol. 6, *The Last Months of Peace, March–August 1939*. London: HMSO, 1956.

Japan. Daihon'ei Rikugunbu Sensō Shidōhan [War Guidance Office of the Imperial Headquarters, Army]. *Kimitsu sensō nisshi* [Confidential War Journal]. Edited by Gunjishi Gakkai [Association of Military History]. 2 vols. Kinshōsha, 1998.

Japan (JMFA). *Nihon gaikō nenpyō narabini shuyō bunsho, 1840–1945* [Chronology and Major Documents of Japanese Diplomacy, 1840–1945]. 2 vols. Reprinted by Hara Shobō, 1966.

———. *NGB: 1930-nen Rondon kaigun kaigi* [1930 London Naval Conference]. 2 vols. 1983–84.

———. *NGB: 1935-nen Rondon kaigun kaigi* [1935 London Naval Conference]. 1986.

———. *NGB: Junēvu kaigun gunbi seigen kaigi* [Geneva Naval Conference]. 1982.

———. *NGB: Nichi-Bei kōshō, 1941* [Japanese-American Negotiations, 1941]. 2 vols. 1990.

———. *NGB: Rondon kaigun kaigi keika gaiyō* [A Summary Account of the Developments at the London Naval Conference]. 1979.

---

*Place of publication for Japanese books is Tokyo unless otherwise noted.

———. *NGB: Rondon kaigun kaigi oyobi kōshō, jōyaku setsumeisho* [Preliminary Negotiations for the London Naval Conference and Explanations of the Treaty]. 1982.

———. *NGB: Washinton kaigi* [Documents on Japanese Foreign Policy: Washington Conference]. 2 vols. Gannandō, 1977–78.

———. *NGB: Washinton kaigi gunbi seigen mondai* [Washington Conference: The Problem of Naval Limitation]. 1974. (Abbreviated as *NGM: Washinton kaigi: gunbi seigen*)

———. *NGB: Washinton kaigi kyokutō mondai* [Washington Conference: Far Eastern Questions]. 1976.

United States. *FRUS (Papers Relating to the Foreign Relations of the United States), 1921* (Washington, D.C: GPO, 1922); *1921*, 2 vols. (1936); *1922*, Vol. 1 (1938); *1927*, Vol. 1 (1942); *1929*, Vol. 1 (1943); *1930*, Vol. 1 (1945); *1934*, Vol. 1: *General, The British Commonwealth* (1951); *1935*, Vols. 1, 3 (1952–53); *1939*, Vol. 3: *Far East* (1955); *1941*, Vols. 4–5: *Far East* (1956–58); *Japan, 1931–1941*, 2 vols. (1943).

U.S. Congress. *Hearings before the Joint Committee of Investigation of the Pearl Harbor Attack*. 79th Cong., 1st sess., Part 12, Washington, D.C.: GPO, 1946.

U.S. Department of State. *Conference on the Limitation of Armament: Washington, November 12, 1921–February 6, 1922*. Washington, D.C.: GPO, 1922.

———. *Papers Relating to Pacific and Far Eastern Affairs Prepared for the Use of the American Delegation to the Conference on the Limitation of Armament, Washington, 1921–1922*. Washington, D.C.: GPO, 1922.

PRINTED DOCUMENTS

Bōeichō Bōei Kenkyūjo Senshibu [War History Department, Institute of Defense Studies, Defense Agency], ed. *Shiryōshū: Kaigun nendo sakusen keikaku* [Collected Documents: The Navy's Annual Operational Plans]. Asagumo Shimbunsha, 1987.

Gendaishi shiryō (GS) [Documents on Contemporary History]. Vol. 7, *Manshū jihen* [The Manchurian Incident]. Edited by Kobayashi Tatsuo and Shimada Toshihiko. Misuzu Shobō, 1964.

———. Vol. 8, *Nitchū sensō, 1* [China War, 1]. Edited by Shimada Toshihiko and Inaba Masao. Misuzu Shobō,1964.

———. Vol. 10, *Nitchū sensō, 3* [China War, 3]. Edited by Tsunoda Jun. Misuzu Shobō, 1964.

———. Vol. 11, *Zoku Manshū jihen* [Sequel Volume on the Manchurian Incident]. Eds. Inaba Masao, Kobayashi Tatsuo, and Shimada Toshihiko. Misuzu Shobō, 1965.

———. Vol. 12, *Nitchū sensō, 4* [China War, 4]. Edited by Kobayashi Tatsuo, Inaba Masao, Shimada Toshihiko, and Usui Katsumi. Misuzu Shobō, 1965.

Ike Nobutaka, ed. and trans. *Japan's Decision for War: Records of the 1941 Policy Conferences*. Stanford, Calif.: Stanford University Press, 1967.

Kobayashi Tatsuo, ed. *Suiusō nikki: Rinji Gaikō Chōsa Iinkai kaigi hikki nado* [Record of the Advisory Council on Foreign Relations, etc.]. Hara Shobō, 1966.

Nihon Kokusai Seiji Gakkai [Japan Association of International Relations], ed. *Taiheiyō Sensō e no michi: Bekkan shiryōhen* [The Road to the Pacific War: Supplementary Volume of Documents]. Edited by Inaba Masao, Kobayashi Tatsuo, Shimada Toshihiko, and Tsunoda Jun. Asahi Shimbunsha, 1963. Reprinted 1988.

Ōkubo Tatsumasa et al., eds. (Doi Akira, supervisor). *Shōwa shakai keizai shiryō shūsei: Kaigunshō shiryō* [Collection of Documents on Social and Economic History of the Shōwa Period: Navy Ministry Documents]. 12 vols. Ochanomizu Shobō, 1978–1987. (Abbreviated as *Kaigunshō shiryō*)

Ross, Steven T., ed. *American War Plans, 1919–1941*, Vol. 2, *Plans for War against the British Empire and Japan: The Red, Orange, and Red-Orange Plans, 1923–1938*. New York: Garland, 1992.

Sanbō Honbu [Army General Staff], ed. *Sugiyama memo: Daihon' ei-seifu renraku kaigi nado hikki* [Sugiyama Memo: Record of Imperial Headquarters–Government Liaison Conferences, etc.]. Hara Shobō, 1967.

INTERVIEWS AND ORAL HISTORY

Records of Interviews

Fukudome Shigeru (JDA); Hashimoto Shōzō (JMJ); Inoue Shigeyoshi (JDA); Maeda Minoru (JDA); Miyo Kazunari (JMJ and JDA); Oka Takazumi (JMJ); Shiba Katsuo (JDA); Takada Toshitane (JDA); Takahashi Sankichi (JDA); Toyoda Teijirō (JDA); Yokoi Tadao (JDA).

Fukudome Shigeru talks, March 1960 (Suikō Kai, Tokyo); Shimada Shigetarō. Record of conversations. Suikō Kai.

My Own Interviews

Enomoto Jūji. July and August 1975.

Stanley K. Hornbeck. February 1961.

Mrs. Theodore Roosevelt Jr. October 1960.

Tomioka Sadatoshi. November 1968.

BOOKS, ARTICLES, AND UNPUBLISHED STUDIES

Agawa Hiroyuki. *Gunkan* Nagato *no shōgai* [The Life of the Battleship *Nagato*]. 2 vols. Shinchōsha, 1975.

———. *Inoue Shigeyoshi*. Shinchōsha, 1986.

———. *Reluctant Admiral: Yamamoto and the Imperial Navy*. Translated by John Bester. Kōdansha International, 1979.

———. *Yamamoto Isoroku* (new ed.). Shinchō Bunko, 1973.

———. *Yonai Mitsumasa*. 2 vols. Shinchōsha, 1978.

Aizawa Kiyoshi. *Kaigun no sentaku: Saikō Shinjuwan e no michi* [The Navy's Choice: The Road to Pearl Harbor Reconsidered]. Chūō Kōronsha, 2002.

————. "Kaigun ryōshikiha to nanshin: Kainantō shinshutsu mondai o chūshin ni shite" [The Pro-Anglo-American Faction of the Japanese Navy and the Advance to Hainan Island]. In *Dainiji sekai taisen: Hassei to kakudai,* edited by Gunjishi Gakkai. Kinseisha, 1990.

————. "Nihon kaigun no gunshuku ridatsu no sentaku" [The Japanese Navy's Choice to Withdraw from Naval Limitation]. *Kokusaigaku ronshū* 21 (July 1988).

Akagi Kanji. "Nihon kaigun to Hokkai jiken" [The Japanese Navy and the Pakhoi Incident]. *Keiō Daigaku Hōgakubu Kenkyūka ronbunshū.* 1977.

Akiyama Saneyuki. *Kaigun ōyō senjutsu* [Applied Naval Tactics] (secret). Typed copy at the Library, NMSDC.

Akiyama Saneyuki senjutsu ronshū. [Collection of Akiyama Saneyuki's treatises on strategy]. Chūō Kōron shinsha, 2005.

Akiyama Saneyuki Kai. *Akiyama Saneyuki.* Akiyama Saneyuki Kai, 1933.

Albion, Robert Greenhalgh. *Naval Policy, 1798–1947.* Edited by Rowena Reed. Annapolis, Md.: Naval Institute Press, 1980.

Anderson, Irvine H. *Standard Vacuum Oil Company and United States East Asian Policy, 1933–1941.* Princeton, N.J.: Princeton University Press, 1973.

————. "1941 De Facto Embargo on Oil to Japan: A Bureaucratic Reflex." *Pacific Historical Review* 44 (May 1975).

Andō Yoshio, ed. *Shōwa keizaishi e no shōgen* [Witnesses to the Economic History of the Showa Period], Vol. 2. Mainichi Shinbunsha, 1966.

Aoki Arata. "Uchida Yasuya denki sōkō" [Manuscript Biography of Uchida Yasuya]. (unpublished manuscript) JMFA.

Arai Tatsuo. *Katō Tomosaburō.* Jiji Tsūshinsha, 1959.

Arima Kaoru. "Takarabe denki shiryō" [Materials for a Biography of Admiral Takarabe] (unpublished manuscript). JDA.

Aritake Shūji. *Saitō Makoto.* Jiji Tsūshinsha, 1958.

Asada Sadao. "Amerika no tai-Nichi kan to 'Washinton taisei'" [American images of Japan and the 'Washington system']. In *Kokusai Seiji,* Vol. 34, *Nichi-Bei kankei no imēji.* Yūhikaku, 1966.

————, ed. and trans. *Arufureddo T. Mahan* [Anthology]. Kenkyūsha, 1977.

————. "Between the Old Diplomacy and the New, 1918–1922: The Washington System and the Origins of Japanese-American Rapprochement." *Diplomatic History* 30 (April 2006).

————. "From Washington to London: The Imperial Japanese Navy and the Politics of Naval Limitation, 1921–30." *Diplomacy & Statecraft* 4 (November 1993). Reprinted in *The Washington Conference, 1921–22,* edited by Erik Goldstein and John Maurer. Ilford, Essex, UK: Frank Cass, 1994.

————. "Japan and the United States, 1915–1925." Ph.D. thesis, Yale University, 1963.

————, ed. *Japan and the World, 1853–1952: A Bibliographic Guide to Japanese Scholarship in Foreign Relations*. New York: Columbia University Press, 1989.

————. "Japanese Admirals and the Politics of Naval Limitation: Katō Tomosaburō vs. Katō Kanji." In *Naval Warfare in the Twentieth Century: Essays in Honour of Arthur Marder*, edited by Gerald Jordan. London: Croom Helm, 1977.

————. "The Japanese Navy and the United States." In *Pearl Harbor as History*, edited by Dorothy Borg and Shumpei Okamoto. New York: Columbia University Press, 1973.

————. "Japan's 'Special Interests' and the Washington Conference, 1921–22." *American Historical Review* 67 (October 1961). Reprinted in *Japan and North America*, Vol. 1, *First Contacts to the Pacific War*, edited by Ellis Krauss and Benjamin Nyblade. London: RoutledgeCurzon, 2004.

————. "Jinshu to bunka no sōkoku: Imin mondai to Nichi-Bei kankei" [Race and Culture: The Immigration Question and Japanese-American Relations]. In *Nihon to Amerika*, Vol. 2, *Demokurashī to Nichi-Bei kankei*, edited by Saitō Makoto. Nan'undō, 1973.

————. "Kaigun seisaku no hen'yō to tai-Bei kaisen e no michi, 1930–41" [Transformations of Japanese Naval Policy and the Road to War with the United States]. In *Ryōtaisenkan no Nichi-Bei kankei*. Tokyo Daigaku Shuppankai, 1993.

————. "Kyū gaikō to shin gaikō no hazama, 1918–22: Nichi-Bei detanto to Washinton taisei no seiritsu" [Between the Old Diplomacy and the New, 1918–22: Japanese-American Détente and the Emergence of the Washington System]. In *Senkanki no Nihon gaikō*, edited by Iriye Akira and Aruga Tadashi. Tokyo Daigaku Shuppankai, 1984.

————. "Nichi-Bei kankei no naka no Mahan: Kaijō kenryokuron to Taiheiyō bōchō o megutte" [Mahan and Japanese-American Relations: Centering on Sea Power Theory and Expansion in the Pacific]. In *Ryōtaisenkan no Nichi-Bei kankei*. Tokyo Daigaku Shuppankai, 1993.

————. "Nihon kaigun to gunshuku: Tai-Bei seisaku o meguru seiji katei" [The Japanese Navy and Naval Limitation: Political Process of Policy toward the United States]. In *Washinton taisei to Nichi-Bei kankei*, edited by Hosoya Chihiro and Saitō Makoto. Tokyo Daigaku Shuppankai, 1978.

————. "Nihon kaigun to tai-Bei seisaku oyobi senryaku" [The Japanese Navy and Its Policy and Strategy toward the United States]. In *Nichi-Bei kankeishi*, Vol. 2, edited by Hosoya Chihiro et al. Tokyo Daigaku Shuppankai, 1971.

————. "1920-nendai ni okeru Amerika no Nihonzō: 'Imēji kenkyū' no ichi shiron" [American Images of Japan during the 1920s: An Approach to "Image Studies"]. *Doshisha Amerika kenkyū 2* (March 1965).

————. "The Revolt against the Washington Treaty: The Imperial Japanese Navy and Naval Limitation, 1921–1927." *Naval War College Review* 46 (Summer 1993).

————. *Ryōtaisenkan no Nichi-Bei kankei: Kaigun to seisaku kettei katei* [Japanese-American Relations between the Wars: Naval Policy and the Decision-Making Process]. Tokyo Daigaku Shuppankai, 1993.

————. "Washinton kaigi" [Washington Conference] and "Washinton taisei" [Washington system]. In *Shinpan Nihon gaikōshi jiten* [Encyclopedia of Japanese

Diplomatic History] (new ed.), edited by Gaimushō Gaikō Shiryōkan *Nihon Gaikōshi Jiten Hensan Iinkai*. Yamakawa Shuppansha, 1992, 1093–1102.

———. "Washinton kaigi o meguru Nichi-Bei no seisaku kettei katei no hikaku: Hito to kikō" [Comparison between the Japanese and American Decision-Making Processes at the Time of the Washington Conference: Policy Makers and Organizations]. In *Taigai seisaku kettei katei no Nichi-Bei hikaku*, edited by Hosoya Chihiro and Watanuki Jōji. Tokyo Daigaku Shuppankai, 1977.

———. "Washinton kaigi to Nihon no taiō: 'Kyū gaikō' to 'shin gaikō' no hazama" [Japan's Response to the Washington Conference: Between the 'Old Diplomacy' and the 'New Diplomacy']. In *Senkanki no Nihon gaikō*, edited by Iriye Akira and Aruga Tadashi. Tokyo Daigaku Shuppankai, 1984.

———. "Washinton kaigun gunshuku no seiji katei: Futari no Katō o megutte" [The Political Process of the Washington Naval Limitation: Centering on the Two Katōs]. *Doshisha hōgaku* [Doshisha Law Review] 49 (March 1998).

Baer, George W. *One Hundred Years of Sea Power: The U.S. Navy, 1890–1990*. Stanford, Calif.: Stanford University Press, 1994.

Barnhart, Michael A. "Japanese Intelligence before the Second World War: 'Best Case' Analysis." In *Knowing One's Enemies: Intelligence Assessment before the Two World Wars*, edited by Ernest May. Princeton, N.J.: Princeton University Press, 1984.

———. *Japan Prepares for Total War: A Search for Economic Security*. Ithaca, N.Y.: Cornell University Press, 1987.

Bix, Herbert. *Hirohito and the Making of Modern Japan*. New York: HarperCollins, 2000.

Bōeichō Boei Kenshūjo Senshibu: *Senshi sōsho Daihon'ei Kaigunbu: Dai Tōa Sensō kaisen keii* [Imperial Headquarters, Navy Circumstances Leading to the Outbreak of the Greater East Asian War]. 2 vols. Asagumo Shuppansha, 1979. (Abbreviated as Senshibu, *Kaigun kaisen keii*)

———. *Senshishitsu Daihon'ei Rikugunbu* [Imperial Headquarters, Army]. Vol. 1 [up to May 1940]. Asagumo Shinbunsha, 1967.

———. *Daihon'ei Rikugunbu* [Imperial Headquarters, Army]. Vol. 2 [up to December 1941]. Asagumo Shinbunsha, 1968.

———. *Senshishitsu, Hawai sakusen* [Hawaii Operation]. Asagumo Shinbunsha, 1967.

———. *Kaigun kōkū gaishi* [A General History of Naval Aviation]. Asagumo Shinbunsha, 1976.

———. *Kaijō goeisen* [Conroy Escort]. Asagumo Shinbusha, 1971.

——— [Nomura Minoru]. *Daihon'ei Kaigunbu, Rengō kantai, 1: Kaisen made* [The Imperial Headquarters, Navy Combined Fleet, Vol. 1, Up to the Outbreak of Hostilities]. Asagumo Shinbunsha, 1975.

———, *Senshibu, Daihon'ei Rikugunbu. Dai Tōa sensō kaisen keii* [Circumstances Leading to the Outbreak of the Greater East Asian War]. 5 vols. Asagumo Shinbunsha, 1973–74. (Abbreviated as Senshishitsu, *Rikugun kaisen keii*)

———. *Sensuikan shi* [A History of Submarine Warfare]. Asagumo Shinbunsha, 1979.

———— [Suekuni Masao]. *Kaigun gunsenbi* [Naval Armament and War Preparations], Vol. 1. Asagumo Shinbunsha, 1969.

Borg, Dorothy, and Shumpei Okamoto, eds. *Pearl Harbor as History: Japanese-American Relations, 1931–1941.* New York: Columbia University Press, 1973.

Bowling, Roland Alfred. "The Negative Influence of Mahan on the Protection of Shipping in Wartime: The Convoy Controversy in the Twentieth Century." Ph.D. thesis, University of Maine at Orono, 1980.

Braisted, William R. "Evolution of the United States Navy's Strategic Assessments in the Pacific, 1919–31." In *The Washington Conference, 1921–22*, edited by Erik Goldstein and John Maurer. Ilford, Essex, UK: Frank Cass, 1994.

————. "On the American Red and Red-Orange Plans, 1919–1939." In *Naval Warfare in the Twentieth Century, 1900–1945: Essays in Honour of Arthur Marder*, edited by Gerald Jordan. London: Croom Helm, 1977.

————. "On the United States Navy's Operational Outlook in the Pacific, 1919–1931." Paper presented at the Kauai Conference on the History of Japanese-American Relations, January 1976.

————. *The United States Navy in the Pacific, 1897–1909.* Austin: University of Texas Press, 1958.

————. *The United States Navy in the Pacific, 1909–1922.* Austin: University of Texas Press, 1971.

Buckley, Thomas A., *The United States and the Washington Conference.* Knoxville: University of Tennessee Press, 1970.

Bull, Headley. "The Objectives of Arms Control." In *The Use of Force: International Politics and Foreign Policy*, edited by Robert J. Art and Kenneth N. Waltz. Boston: Little, Brown, 1971.

Butow, Robert J. C. *Tojo and the Coming of the War.* Stanford, Calif.: Stanford University Press, 1961.

Bywater, Hector C. *Sea Power in the Pacific: A Study of American-Japanese Problems.* Boston: Houghton Mifflin, 1921.

————. *Taiheiyō sensō.* Translated by Hori Kazuichi. Min'yūsha, 1925. Originally published as *The Great Pacific War: A History of the American-Japanese Campaign of 1931–33.* New York: Houghton Mifflin, 1925. Reprinted by Wilfrid Laurier University Press, 1988.

Chapman, John W. M. "The Pacific in the Interception and Policies of the German Navy, 1919–1945." In *War and Diplomacy across the Pacific, 1919–1952*, edited by A. Hamish Ion and Barry D. Hunt. Waterloo, Ont.: Wilfrid Laurier University Press, 1988.

————, ed. and trans. *The Price of Admiralty: The War Diary of the German Naval Attaché in Japan* [Paul Wenneker]. Vol. 1, *25 August 1939–23 August 1940.* East Sussex, UK: Saltire, 1982.

Chihaya Masataka. *Nihon Kaigun no kōzai* [The Strengths and Failures of the Japanese Navy]. Purejidentosha, 1994.

———. *Nihon kaigun no senryaku hassō* [Strategic Thought of the Japanese Navy]. Purejidentosha, 1982.

———. *Rengō kantai kōbōki* [The Rise and Decline of the Combined Fleet]. Chūō Bunko, 1996.

Clemensen, A. "The Geneva Conference of 1927 in Japanese-American Relations." Ph.D. thesis, University of Arizona, 1975.

Coletta, Paolo E. "Prelude to War: Japan, the United States, and the Aircraft Carrier." *Prologue* 23 (Winter 1991).

Conroy, Hilary, and Harry Wray, eds. *Pearl Harbor Reexamined: Prologue to the Pacific War*. Honolulu: University of Hawaii, 1990.

Crowl, Philip A. "Alfred Thayer Mahan: The Naval Historian." In *Makers of Modern Strategy from Machiavelli to the Nuclear Age*, edited by Peter Paret. Princeton, N.J.: Princeton University Press, 1986.

Crowley, James B. *Japan's Quest for Autonomy: National Security and Foreign Policy, 1930–1938*. Princeton, N.J.: Princeton University Press, 1966.

Daihon'ei Rikugunbu Sensō Shidō Han [War Guidance Office, Imperial Headquarters, Army Section]. *Kimitsu sensō nisshi* [Confidential War Journal]. Edited by Gunjishi Gakkai. 2 vols. Kinseisha, 1998. (Abbreviated as *Kimitsu sensō nisshi*)

Daini Fukuinkyoku Zanmu Shoribu, ed. *Taiheiyō sensō kaisen zenshi: Kaisen made no seiryaku senryaku* [History Preceding the Outbreak of the Pacific War: Politics and Strategy up to the Outbreak of War]. Ryokuin Shobō, 2001.

Davis, George T. *A Navy Second to None: The Development of Modern American Naval Policy*. New York: Harcourt, Brace, 1940.

Davis, Vincent. *Admirals Lobby*. Chapel Hill: University of North Carolina Press, 1967.

Dingman, Roger. "Japan and Mahan." In *The Influence of History on Mahan: The Proceedings of a Conference Marking the Centenary of Alfred Thayer Mahan's* The Influence of Sea Power upon History, 1660–1783, edited by John B. Hattendorf. Newport, R.I.: Naval War College Press, 1991.

———. *Power in the Pacific: The Origins of Naval Arms Limitation, 1914–1922*. Chicago: University of Chicago Press, 1978.

Dockrill, Saki, ed. *From Pearl Harbor to Hiroshima: The Second World War in Asia and the Pacific: 1941–45*. London: Macmillan, 1994.

Doyle, Michael K. "The United States Navy—Strategy and Far Eastern Policy, 1931–1941." *Naval War College Review* 29 (March 1977).

Ellicott, J. M. "Japanese Students at the United States Naval Academy." United States Naval Institute, *Proceedings* 73 (March 1947).

Epstein, Marc Alan. "The Historians and the Geneva Naval Conference." In *Arms Limitation and Disarmament: Restraint on War, 1899–1939*, edited by B. J. C. McKercher. Westport, Conn.: Praeger, 1992.

———. "Naval Disarmament and the Japanese: Geneva 1927." Ph.D. thesis, State University of New York at Buffalo, 1995.

Evans, David C., and Mark R. Peattie. *Kaigun: Strategy, Tactics, and Technology of the Imperial Japanese Navy, 1887–1941*. Annapolis, Md.: Naval Institute Press, 1997.

Feis, Herbert. *Road to Pearl Harbor: The Coming of the War between the United States and Japan*. Princeton, N.J.: Princeton University Press, 1950.

Ferrell, Robert H. *American Diplomacy in the Great Depression: Hoover-Stimson Foreign Policy, 1929–1933*. New Haven, Conn.: Yale University Press, 1957.

Freidel, Frank. *Franklin D. Roosevelt: The Apprenticeship*. Boston: Little, Brown, 1952.

Fujioka Taishū. *Kaigun shōshō Takagi Sōkichi* [Rear Admiral Takagi Sōkichi]. Kōjinsha, 1986.

Fukudome Shigeru. *Kaigun no hansei* [Reflections on the Navy]. Nihon Shuppan Kyōdō, 1951.

———. *Kaigun seikatsu 40-nen* [Forty Years of Naval Life]. Jiji Tsūshinsha, 1971.

———. *Shikan Shinjuwan kōgeki* [A Historical View of the Pearl Harbor Attack]. Jiyū Ajiasha, 1955.

Fukui Shizuo. *Nihon no gunkan* [Japanese Warships]. Shuppan Kyōdōsha, 1956.

Genda Minoru. *Kaigun kōkūtai shimatsuki: Sentōhen* [An Account of Naval Air Corps: Battles]. Bungei Shunjū, 1962.

———. *Pāru Hābā: Unmei no hi* [Pearl Harbor: The Fateful Day]. Gentōsha, 2001.

Glad, Betty, ed. *Psychological Dimensions of War*. London: Sage Publications, 1990.

Goldman, Emily O. *Sunken Treaties: Naval Arms Control between the Wars*. University Park: Pennsylvania State University Press, 1994.

Goldstein, Donald M., and Katherine V. Dillon, eds. *The Pearl Harbor Papers: Inside the Japanese Plans*. Dulles, Va.: Brassey's, 1993.

Goldstein, Erik, and John Maurer, ed. *The Washington Conference, 1921–22: Naval Rivalry, East Asian Stability and the Road to Pearl Harbor*. Ilford, Essex, UK: Frank Cass, 1994.

Gow, Ian. *Military Intervention in Pre-War Japanese Politics: Admiral Katō Kanji and the "Washington System."* Richmond, Surrey, UK: Routledge Curzon, 2004.

Grew, Joseph C. *Ten Years in Japan: A Contemporary Record Drawn from Diaries and Private and Official Papers*. New York: Simon and Schuster, 1944.

———. *Turbulent Era: A Diplomatic Record of Forty Years, 1904–1945*, Vol. 2. Boston: Houghton Mifflin, 1952.

Griswold, A. Whitney. *Far Eastern Policy of the United States*. Reprinted by New Haven, Conn.: Yale University Press, 1962.

Gunjishi Gakkai, ed. *Dainiji sekai taisen: Hassei to kakudai* [The Second World War: Its Outbreak and Escalation]. Kinseisha, 1990.

———, ed. *Dainiji sekai taisen*, Vol. 2, *Shinjuwan zengo* [The Second World War, Vol. 2, Circa the Pearl Harbor Attack]. Kinseisha, 1991.

————, ed. *Manshū jihen saikō* [The Manchurian Incident Reconsidered].
Kinseisha, 2001.

Hagan, Kenneth J. "Alfred Thayer Mahan: Turning America Back to the Sea." In *Makers of American Diplomacy from Benjamin Franklin to Alfred Thayer Mahan,* edited by Frank J. Merle and Theodore A. Wilson. New York: Scribner, 1974.

————. *This People's Navy: The Making of American Sea Power.* New York: Free Press, 1991.

Hamaguchi Osachi. *Hamaguchi Osachi nikki, zuikanroku* [Diary and Memos]. Edited by Ikei Masaru, Hatano Masaru, and Kurosawa Fumitaka. Misuzu Shobō, 1991.

Handō Kazutoshi. *Nihon kaigun no eikō to zasetsu* [The Glories and Defeat of the Japanese Navy]. PHP Kenkyūjo, 1994.

Hara Kei. *Hara Kei nikki* [Diary], Vol. 5. Edited by Hara Keiichirō. Reprinted by Fukumura Shuppan, 1965.

Hara Shirō. *Dai senryaku naki kaisen* [Starting a War without a Grand Strategy]. Hara Shobō, 1987.

Harada Kumao. *Fragile Victory: Prince Saionji and the 1930 London Treaty Issue from the Memoirs of Baron Harada Kumao.* Trans. Thomas Francis Mayer Oakes. Detroit, Mich.: Wayne State University Press, 1968.

————. *Saionjikō to seikyoku* [Prince Saionji and Politics]. 9 vols. Iwanami Shoten, 1950–52. (Abbreviated as Harada-Saionji)

Hata Ikuhiko. "Admiral Yamamoto's Surprise Attack and the Japanese Navy's War Strategy." In *From Pearl Harbor to Hiroshima: The Second World War in Asia and the Pacific, 1941–45,* edited by Saki Dockrill. London: Macmillan. 1994.

————. "Futsuin shinchū to gun no nanshin seisaku, 1940–41" [The Advance to French Indochina and the Military's Southward Advance Policy, 1940–41]. In *TSM,* Vol. 6, *Nanpō shinshutsu.* [Advance Southward], edited by Nihon Kokusai Seiji Gakkai. Asahi Shinbunsha, 1963.

————. "Kantaiha to Jōyakuha: Kaigun no habatsu keifu" [The Fleet Faction and the Treaty Faction: Genealogy of Naval Factionalism]. In *Shōwashi no gunbu to seiji, 1: Gunbu shihai no kaimaku,* edited by Miyake Masaki et al. Daiichi Hōki, 1983.

————. *Nihon rikukaigun sōgō jiten* [Comprehensive Encyclopedia of the Japanese Army and Navy]. Tokyo Daigaku Shuppankai, 1991.

————, ed. *Shinjuwan moeru* [Pearl Harbor Burning]. 2 vols. Hara Shobō, 1991.

————. *Shōwashi no gunjintachi* [Military and Naval Leaders during the Showa Period]. Bungei Shunjū, 1982.

————. "Suetsugu Nobumasa—Kantaiha no yū" [Suetsugu Nobumasa: The Hero of the Fleet Faction]. *Keizai Ōrai* (June 1979).

Hata Shunroku. *Zoku Gendaishi shiryō 4: Rikugun, Hata Shunroku nisshi* [*GS* Sequel Volume 4: Army: Diary of Hata Shunroku]. Misuzu Shobō, 1983.

Hatano Masaru. "Hamaguchike shozō no 'Hamaguchi Osachi bunsho'" [Papers of Hamaguchi Osachi in the Possession of the Hamaguchi Family]. Keiō University, *Hōgaku kenkyū* 67 (July 1994).

———. *Hamaguchi Osachi.* Chūō Kōronsha, 1993.

Hatano Sumio. *Bakuryō tachi no Shinjuwan* [The Pearl Harbor Attack and Staff Officers]. Asahi Shinbunsha, 1991.

———. *"Daitōa sensō" no jidai: Nitchū sensō kara Nichi-Bei-Ei sensō e* [The Age of the "Greater East Asian War": From the China War to the Japanese-American-British War]. Asahi Shuppansha, 1988.

———. "Nanshin e no tenkai, 1940 [Swing to "Southward Drive," 1940]. *Ajia keizai* 26 (May 1985).

———. "Nihon kaigun no seijiryoku" [The Political Influence of the Japanese Navy]. *Rekishi to tabi* (September 1999).

———. "Nihon kaigun to 'Nanshin': Sono seisaku to riron no tenkai" [Japanese Navy and Southward Advance: Historical Developments of Its Policy and Theory]. In *Ryōtaisenkanki Nihon-Tōnan Ajia kankei no shosō,* edited by Shimizu Hajime. Ajia Keizai Kenkyūjo, 1986.

———. "'Shinjuwan e no michi' saikō" ["The Road to Pearl Harbor" Reconsidered]. *Gaikō jihō* 1283 (November/December 1991).

———. "Shōwa kaigun no nanshin ron" [The Navy's Southward Advance in the Showa Period]. *Rekishi to jinbutsu,* special issue, *Hishi: Taiheiyō sensō* (December 1984).

———. "'Yokushi senryaku' no hatan: Nichi-Bei kaisen to bakuryō tachi" [The Failure of "Deterrent Strategy": The Outbreak of the Japanese-American War and Japan's Staff Officers]. In *Seikimatsu kara mita Daitōa sensō: Sensō wa naze okottanoka.* Purejidentosha, 1991.

Hatano Sumio and Asada Sadao. "The Japanese Decision to Move South." In *Paths to War: New Essays on the Origins of the Second World War,* edited by Robert Boyce and Esmonde M. Robertson. London: Macmillan, 1989.

Hattendorf, John B., ed. *Mahan on Naval Strategy: Selections from the Writings of Rear Admiral Alfred Thayer Mahan.* Annapolis, Md.: Naval Institute Press, 1991.

Hattendorf, John B., and Lynn C. Hattendorf, comps. *A Bibliography of the Works of Alfred Thayer Mahan.* Newport, R.I.: Naval War College Press, 1986.

Hattori Takushirō. *Daitōa sensō zenshi* [Complete History of the Great East Asian War], Vol. 1. Masu Shobō, 1953.

Height, John M. "Franklin D. Roosevelt and the Naval Quarantine of Japan." *Pacific Historical Review* 40 (May 1971).

Heinrichs, Waldo H., Jr. "Franklin D. Roosevelt and the Risks of War, 1939–1941." In *American, Chinese, and Japanese Perspectives on Wartime Asia, 1931–1949,* edited by Iriye Akira and Warren Cohen. Wilmington, Del.: Scholarly Resources, 1990.

———. "The Role of the United States Navy." In *Pearl Harbor as History,* edited by Dorothy Borg and Shumpei Okamoto. New York: Columbia University Press, 1973.

————. *Threshold of War: Franklin D. Roosevelt and American Entry into World War II.* New York: Oxford University Press, 1988.

Herzog, James H. *Closing of the Open Door: American-Japanese Diplomatic Negotiations, 1936–1941.* Annapolis, Md.: Naval Institute Press, 1973.

————. "Influence of the United States Navy in the Embargo of Oil to Japan, 1940–1941." *Pacific Historical Review* 35 (August 1966).

Higuchi Hidemi. *Nihon kaigun kara mita Nitchū kankeishi kenkyū* [A Study of the History of Sino-Japanese Relations Focusing on the Japanese Navy]. Fuyō Shobō, 2002.

————. "Nihon kaigun no tairiku seisaku no ichi sokumen, 1906–21" [An Aspect of the Continental Policy of the Japanese Navy, 1906–21]. *Kokushigaku* 147 (May 1992).

"Hijōji hyaku jinbutsu" [One Hundred Leaders in Crisis]. *Bungei shunju* (January 1934).

Hirama Yōichi. *Daiichiji sekai taisen to Nihon kaigun* [The First World War and the Japanese Navy]. Keiō Gijuku Daigaku Shuppankai, 1998.

Hirose Junkō, ed. *Kindai gaikō kaikoroku* [Modern Diplomatic Memoirs], Vol. 3. Yumani Shobō, 2000.

Hone, Thomas C., and Mark D. Mandeles. "Interwar Innovation in Three Navies." *Naval War College Review* 40 (Spring 1987).

Honjō Shigeru. *Honjō nikki* [Diary]. Hara Shobō, 1967.

————. *Emperor Hirohito and His Chief Aide-de-Camp: 1933–36.* University of Tokyo Press, 1974.

Hoover, Herbert C. *Memoirs of Herbert Hoover.* Vol. 3, *1920–33.* New York: Macmillan, 1952.

Horikawa Jun'ichirō. *Jufu sangoku kaigi to sonogo* [The Geneva Conference and After]. Hōbunkan, 1929.

Hoshina Zenshirō. *Daitōa sensō hishi: Ushinawareta wahei kōsaku* [A Secret History of the Greater East Asian War: Failure of Peace Maneuvers]. Hara Shobō, 1975.

Hoshina Zenshirō, Ōi Atsushi, and Suekuni Masao. *Taiheiyō sensō hishi* [A Secret History of the Pacific War]. Nihon Kokubō Kyōkai, 1987.

Hosoya Chihiro. "Miscalculations in Deterrent Policy: U.S.-Japanese Relations, 1938–1941." In *Pearl Harbor Reexamined: Prologue to the Pacific War,* edited by Hilary Conroy and Harry Wray. Honolulu: University of Hawaii Press, 1990.

————. "Nichi-Bei kankei no hakyoku: Yokushi seisaku to sono gosan, 1939–1941" [The Collapse of Japanese-American Relations: Deterrent Policy and Its Miscalculations, 1939–1941]. In Hosoya Chihiro, *Ryōtaisenkan no Nihon gaikō.* Iwanami Shoten, 1988.

————. "Sangoku dōmei to Nisso chūritsu jōyaku" [The Tripartite Pact and the Japan-Soviet Neutrality Pact]. In *TSM,* Vol. 5, *Sangoku dōmei, Nisso chūritsu jōyaku.* Asahi Shimbunsha, 1963.

Hosoya Chihiro and Saitō Makoto, eds. *Washinton taisei to Nichi-Bei kankei* [The Washington System and Japanese-American Relations]. Tokyo Daigaku Shuppankai, 1978.

Hosoya Chihiro, Saitō Makoto, Imai Seiichi, and Rōyama Michio, eds. *Nichi-Bei kankeishi: Kaisen ni itsaru 10-nen (1931–41)* [History of Japanese-American Relations: Ten Years Prior to the War, 1931–41]. 4 vols. Tokyo Daigaku Shuppankai, 1971–72.

Hughes, Charles Evans. *The Autobiographical Notes of Charles Evans Hughes.* Edited by David J. Danelaki and Joseph S. Tulchin. Cambridge, Mass.: Harvard University Press, 1973.

———. "The Foreign Policy of the United States." *Current History* (January 1924).

———. *The Pathway of Peace.* New York: Harper, 1925.

Hull, Cordell. *Memoirs of Cordell Hull.* 2 vols. New York: Macmillan, 1948.

Huntington, Samuel. "Arms Races: Prerequisites and Results." In *The Use of Force: International Politics and Foreign Policy*, edited by Robert J. Art and Kenneth N. Waltz. Boston: Little, Brown, 1971.

Ichihashi, Yamato. *The Washington Conference and After.* Stanford, Calif.: Stanford University Press, 1928.

Ickes, Harold L. *The Secret Diary of Harold L. Ickes: The Lowering Clouds, 1939–1941.* New York: Simon and Schuster, 1955.

Ikeda Kiyoshi. "Kaigun no taishitsu" [The Naval Temperament]. *Suikō* (December 1992).

———. *Kaigun to Nihon* [The Navy and Japan]. Chūō Kōronsha, 1981.

———. *Nihon no kaigun* [The Japanese Navy] (new ed.). Asahi Sonorama, 1987.

———. "Nihon no sensō shidō keikaku: Kaisenji no sensō shūketsu o chūshin ni shite [Japan's War Guidance: With Particular Reference to the Plan to End the War]. Tōhoku University, *Hōgaku* 43 (July 1979).

———. "Rondon kaigun jōyaku ni kansuru Gunreibu gawa no shiryō 3-pen" [Three Documents of the Naval General Staff Regarding the London Naval Treaty]. Osaka Shiritsu Daigaku, *Hōgaku zasshi* 15 (December 1968).

———. "Rondon kaigun jōyaku to tōsuiken mondai [The London Naval Treaty and the Problem of the Supreme Command]. *Hōgaku zasshi* 15 (October 1968).

Inoue Shigeyoshi "Omoide no Ki" [Reminiscences]. In private hands.

Inoue Shigeyoshi Denki Kankō Kai, ed. *Inoue Shigeyoshi* [Biography]. Editor, 1982.

Iriye Akira. "Japan against ABCD Powers." In *American, Chinese, and Japanese Perceptions on Wartime Asia, 1931–1949*, edited by Iriye Akira and Warren Cohen. Wilmington, Del.: Scholarly Resources, 1990.

———. *The Origins of the Second World War in Asia and the Pacific.* London: Longman, 1987.

———. *Pacific Estrangement: Japanese and American Expansion, 1897–1911*, Cambridge, Mass.: Harvard University Press, 1972.

Iriye Akira and Aruga Tadashi, eds. *Senkanki no Nihon gaikō* [Japanese Diplomacy between the Wars]. Tokyo Daigaku Shuppankai, 1984.

Ishii Itarō. *Gaikōkan no isshō*. [Diplomatic Memoris]. Yomiuri Shinbunsha, 1972.

Ishii Kikujirō. *Gaikō yoroku*. Iwanami Shosten, 1930. Translated as *Diplomatic Commentaries*. Baltimore: Johns Hopkins Press, 1936.

———. *Gaikō zuisō* [Essays on Diplomacy]. Kashima Shuppankai, 1967.

Ishikawa Shingo. "Ishikawa Shingo nikki: Kaisen zen'ya no 6-kagetsu" [The Diary of Ishikawa Shingo: Six Months Preceding the Commencement of the War]. Edited by Moriyama Atsushi. *Chūō Kōron* (January 1992).

———. *Shinjuwan made no keii: Kaisen no shinsō* [Circumstances Leading to Pearl Harbor: The Truth about the Commencement of the War]. Jiji Tsūshinsha, 1960.

Ishikawa Yasushi. *Satō Tetsutarō kaigun chūjō den* [Biography]. Hara Shobō, 2000.

Itō Kinjirō. *Ikiteiru kaishō Katō Kanji* [The Living Admiral Katō Kanji]. Shōwa Shobō, 1942.

Itō Kōbun. "Satō Tetsutarō no kokubō riron" [National Defense Theory of Satō Tetsutarō]. *Kaikankō hyōron* 4 (September 1966).

Itō Masanori. *Dai kaigun o omou* [Recollections of the Great Navy]. Bungei Shunjū Shinsha, 1956.

———. *Gunshuku?* [Naval Limitation?]. Shun'yōdō, 1930.

———. *Kafu kaigi to sonogo* [The Washington Conference and After]. Tōhō Jironsha, 1928.

———. "Kobayashi Seizō ron" [An Essay on Kobayashi Seizō]. *Kaizō* (October 1936).

———. *Rengō kantai no saigo* [The Last of the Combined Fleet]. Bungei Shunjū, 1968.

Itō Takashi. "Kantaiha sōsui Suetsugu Nobumasa" [The Leader of the Fleet Faction Suetsugu Nobumasa]. *Rekishi to jinbutsu* 60 (August 1976).

———. *Shōwa shoki seijishi kenkyū: Rondon kaigun gunshuku mondai o meguru seiji shūdan no taikō to teikei* [A Study of the Political History of the Early Showa Period: Conflicts and Alignments of Political Groups over the Issue of the London Naval Limitation]. Tokyo Daigaku Shuppankai, 1969.

Janis, Irvin. *Groupthink: Psychological Studies of Policy Decisions and Fiascoes* (2nd ed.). Boston: Houghton Mifflin, 1982.

Jessup, Philip. *Elihu Root*, Vol. 2. New York: Dodd, Mead, 1938.

Kahn, David. *The Reader of Gentlemen's Mail: Herbert O. Yardley and the Birth of American Codebreaking*. New Haven, Conn.: Yale University Press, 2004.

Kaigun Daijin Kanbō [Navy Minister's Secretariat], ed. *Kaigun gunbi enkaku* [A History of Naval Armaments]. Reprinted by Gan'nandō, 1970.

Kaigun Rekishi Hozonkai, comp. *Nihon kaigunshi* [Japanese Naval History], Vols. 1–4. Daiichi Hōki Shuppan, 1995. (Abbreviated as *Nihon kaigunshi*.)

Kaigunshō Kaigun Gunji Fukyūbu [Publicity Division, Navy Ministry]. *Kokumin no seikatsu to gunshuku* [National Life and Naval Limitation]. October 1934.

Kanazawa Masao. *Waga kaigun to Takahashi Sankichi* [Our Navy and Takahashi Sankichi]. Takahashi Shin'ichi, 1970.

Karsten, Peter. "The Nature of 'Influence': Roosevelt, Mahan and the Concept of Sea Power." *American Quarterly* 23 (October 1971).

———. *The Naval Aristocracy: The Golden Age of Annapolis and the Emergence of Modern American Navalism.* New York: Free Press, 1972.

Katō Gensui Denki Hensan Iin. *Gensui Katō Tomosaburō den* [Biography]. Editor, 1928.

Katō Kanji. "Katō Kanji kankei Bunsho: Shōwa" 8–9nen o chūshin ni [Papers Relating to Katō Kanji: With Special Reference to 1933–34]. Tokyo Toritsu Daigaku, *Hōgakkai zasshi* 10 (March 1970).

———. *Zoku gendaishi shiryō.* Vol. 5, *Kaigun: Katō Kanji nikki* [Second Series of *GS*, Vol. 5, Navy, Diary of Katō Kanji]. Misuzu Shobō, 1994.

Katō Kanji Taishō Denki Hensankai, ed. *Katō Kanji taishō den* [Biography]. Hensankai, 1928.

Kaufman, Robert Gordon. *Arms Control during the Pre-Nuclear Era: The United States and Naval Limitation between the Two World Wars.* New York: Columbia University Press, 1990.

Kaya Okinori. *Senzen sengo 80-nen* [Eighty Years before and after the War]. Rōman, 1975.

Kennedy, Malcolm D. *The Estrangement of Great Britain and Japan, 1917–35.* Manchester, UK: University of Manchester Press, 1969.

Kiba Kōsuke. *Nomura Kichisaburō* [Biography]. Nomura Kichisaburō Denki Kankō Kai, 1961.

Kido Kōichi. *Kido Kōichi kankei bunsho* [Papers Relating to Kido Kōichi]. Edited by Kido Nikki Kenkyūkai. Tokyo Daigaku Shuppankai, 1966.

———. *Kido Kōichi nikki* [Diary]. Edited by Kido Kōichi Kenkyūkai. 2 vols. Tokyo Daigaku Shuppankai, 1966.

Knudsen, L. T. "A Note on Walter LaFeber, Captain Mahan, and the Use of Historical Sources." *Pacific Historical Review* 40 (November 1971).

Ko-Matsudaira Tsuneo Tsuiokukai, ed. *Matsudaira Tsuneo tsuiokushū* [Reminiscences of Tsuneo Matsudaira]. Editor, 1961.

Kobayashi Michihiko. "Teikoku kokubō hōshin no dōyō" [Commotions about the Imperial National Defense Policy]. *Nihon rekishi* 507 (August 1990).

———. "Teikoku kokubō hōshin saikō [Imperial National Defense Policy Reconsidered]. *Shigaku zasshi* 98 (March 1989).

Kobayashi Seizō. *Kaigun taishō Kobayashi Seizō oboegaki* [Memoranda of Admiral Kobayashi Seizō]. Edited by Itō Takashi and Nomura Minoru. Yamakawa Shuppansha, 1981.

Kobayashi Tatsuo. "Kaigun gunshuku jōyaku (1921–1936)" [Treaties of Naval Limitation, 1921–1936]. *TSM*, Vol. 1, *Manshū jihen zen'ya.* Asahi Shinbunsha, 1963.

Kodera Kenkichi. *Dai-Ajia shugiron* [On Greater Asianism]. Hōbunkan, 1916.

Koike Seiichi. "Taishō kōki no kaigun ni tsuiteno ichi kōsatsu" [A Study on the Japanese Navy in the Late Taishō Period]. *Gunji shigaku* 25 (June 1998).

———. "Washinton kaigun gunshuku kaigi zengo no kaigun bunai jōkyō" [Conditions in the Navy around the Time of the Washington Conference]. *Nihon rekishi* 480 (May 1980).

Konoe Fumimaro. *Heiwa e no doryoku* [My Efforts for Peace]. Denpō Tsūshinsha, 1946.

Koyama Hirotake. *Zōho gunji shisō no kenkyū* [A Study on Military Thought] (enlarged ed.). Shinsensha, 1977.

Krug, Hans-Joachim, Hirama Yōichi, Berthold J. Sander-Nagashima, and Axel Niestlé. *Reluctant Allies: German-Japanese Naval Relations in World War II*. Annapolis, Md.: Naval Institute Press, 2001.

Kurono Taeru. *Teikoku kokubō hōshin no kenkyū* [A Study of the Imperial National Defense Policy]. Sōwasha, 2000.

Kusumi Tadao. "Akiyama Saneyuki to Nihonkai kaisen" [Akiyama Saneyuki and the Battle of the Sea of Japan]. *Chūō kōron* (August 1965).

LaFeber, Walter. *The Clash: U.S.-Japanese Relations throughout History*. New York: Norton, 1997.

———. *The New Empire: An Interpretation of American Expansionism, 1860–1898*. Ithaca, N.Y.: Cornell University Press, 1963.

———. "A Note on the 'Mercantilistic Imperialism' of Alfred Thayer Mahan." *Mississippi Valley Historical Review* 48 (March 1962).

Langer, William L., and S. Everett Gleason. *The Challenge to Isolation: The World Crisis of 1937–1940 and American Foreign Policy*. New York: Harper and Row, 1952.

———. *The Undeclared War: The World Crisis and American Foreign Policy, 1940–1941*. New York: Harper and Row, 1953.

Leopold, Richard. *Elihu Root and the Conservative Tradition*. Boston: Little, Brown, 1954.

Levine, Robert H. *The Politics of American Naval Rearmament, 1930–1938*. New York: Garland, 1988.

Levy, Morris. "Alfred Thayer Mahan and United States Foreign Policy." Ph.D. thesis, New York University, 1965.

Livezey, William E. *Mahan on Sea Power*. Norman: University of Oklahoma Press, 1947.

Love, Robert E., Jr. *History of the United States Navy*, Vol. 1, *1775–1941*. Harrisburg, Penn.: Stackpole Books, 1992.

———, ed. *Pearl Harbor Revisited*. New York: St. Martin's, 1995.

Mahan, Alfred Thayer. *Arufureddo T. Mahan* [Anthology]. Edited and translated by Asada Sadao. Kenkyūsha, 1977.

———. *Beikoku kaigun senryaku* [Translation of *Naval Strategy*]. Translated by Ozaki Shuzei. Kōa Nihonsha, 1932. Reprinted as *Kaigun senryaku*, 1942.

———. *From Sail to Steam: Recollection of Naval Life*. New York: Harper and Brothers, 1907.

————. *The Influence of Sea Power upon History, 1660–1783.* Boston: Little, Brown, 1890.

————. *The Interest of America in International Conditions.* Boston: Little, Brown, 1910.

————. *The Interest of America in Sea Power, Present and Future.* Boston: Little, Brown. 1897.

————. *Kaijō kenryoku shiron* [Partial translation of *The Influence of Sea Power*]. Translated by Kitamura Ken'ichi. Hara Shobō, 1982.

————. *Kaijō kenryoku shiron* [Translation of *The Influence of Sea Power*]. Translated by Suikōsha. Tōhō Kyōkai, 1896.

————. *Letters and Papers of Alfred Thayer Mahan.* Edited by Robert Seager II and Doris Maguire. 3 vols. Annapolis, Md.: Naval Institute Press, 1975.

————. *Naval Administration and Warfare.* Boston: Little, Brown, 1908.

————. *Naval Strategy Compared and Contrasted with the Principles and Practices of Military Operations on Land.* Boston: Little, Brown, 1911.

————. "The Open Door." In Alfred Thayer Mahan, *The Interest of America in International Conditions.* Boston: Little, Brown, 1910.

————. "Preparedness for War, 1906." In Alfred Thayer Mahan, *Naval Administration and Warfare.* Boston: Little, Brown, 1908.

————. *The Problem of Asia and Its Effect upon International Policies.* Boston: Little, Brown, 1900.

————. "Retrospect upon the War between Japan and Russia." Reprinted in Alfred Thayer Mahan, *Naval Administration and Warfare.* Boston: Little, Brown, 1908.

————. "Some Reflections upon the Far Eastern War." In Alfred Thayer Mahan, *Naval Administration and Warfare.* Boston: Little, Brown, 1908.

————. *Taiheiyō kaiken ron* [Translation of *The Interest of America in Sea Power*]. Translated by Minakami Umehiko. Kobayashi Matashichi, 1900.

————. "The Value of the Pacific Cruise of the United States Fleet 1908: Prospect" and "The Value of the Pacific Cruise of the United States Fleet 1908: Retrospect." Reprinted in Alfred Thayer Mahan, *Naval Administration and Warfare.* Boston: Little, Brown, 1908.

Mahan, Lyle Evans. "My Parents, Rear Admiral and Mrs. Alfred Thayer Mahan." *Naval War College Review* 43 (Autum 1990).

Mainichi gurafu. Special issue, *Aa Etajima* [Ah! Etajima]. 1 August 1969.

Makino Nobuaki. *Makino Nobuaki nikki* [Diary]. Edited by Itō Takashi. Chūō Kōronsha, 1990.

Mandel, Richard. "The Struggle for East Asia's Rimlands: Franklin D. Roosevelt, the Joint Chiefs of Staff, and U.S. Far Eastern Policy, 1921–1945." Ph.D. thesis. Cornell University, 1990.

Marder, Arthur J. *Old Friends, New Enemies: The Royal Navy and the Imperial Japanese Navy.* Vol. 1, *Strategic Illusions, 1936–1941.* New York: Oxford University Press, 1981.

Mauch, Peter. "Revisiting Nomura's Diplomacy: Ambassador Nomura's Role in the Japanese-American Negotiations, 1941." *Diplomatic History* 28 (June 2004).

Merrill, James M. "Successors of Mahan: A Survey of Writings on American Naval History, 1914–1960." *Mississippi Valley Historical Review* 50 (March 1964).

Miller, Edward S. "War Plan Orange, 1897–1941: The Blue Thrust through the Pacific." In *Naval History: The Seventh Symposium of the U.S. Naval Academy,* edited by William B. Cogar. Wilmington, Del.: Scholarly Resources, 1988.

———. *War Plan Orange: The U.S. Strategy to Defeat Japan, 1897–1945.* Annapolis, Md.: Naval Institute Press, 1991.

Miwa Kimitada. "Japanese Images of War with the United States." In *Mutual Images: Essays in American-Japanese Relations,* edited by Akira Iriye. Cambridge, Mass.: Harvard University Press, 1975.

Miwa Munehiro, ed. "Nomura chū-Bei taishi nikki, 3 June–30 August 1941" [Diary of Ambassador Nomura to the United States]. *Kyūshū Kyōritsu Daigaku keizai gakubu kiyō* 66 (December 1996).

Mizuno Hironori. "Ā Akiyama kaigun chūjō" [Ah! Vice Admiral Akiyama]. *Chūō Kōron* (March 1918).

Mori Shōzō. *Senpū nijūnen* [Twenty Tumultuous Years]. Reprinted by Kōjinsha, 1968.

Morimatsu Toshio. *Sōryokusen kenkyūjo* [Total War Research Institute]. Hakuteisha, 1983.

Morison, Elting E. *Turmoil and Tradition: A Study of the Life and Times of Henry L. Stimson.* New York: Houghton Mifflin.

Moriyama Atsushi. "Daisanji Konoe naikaku to 'Teikoku kokusaku suikō yōryō'" [The Political Process of Drafting 'Guidelines for Implementing National Policy,' 6 September 1941]. *Shigaku zasshi* 101 (September 1992).

———. "'Hikettei' no kōzu: Dainiji, daisanji Konoe naikaku no taigai seisaku o chūshin ni" [Evasion of Decision Making: The Diplomacy of the Second and Third Konoe Cabinets]. In *Dainiji sekai taisen,* Vol. 2: *Shinjuwan Zengo.* Kinseisha, 2003.

———. "Kaigun chūkensō to Nichi-Bei kōshō: Gunmu nika no kōsō o chūshin ni" [Middle-Echelon Naval Officers and the Japanese-American Negotiations: With Particular Reference to the Second Section of the Naval Affairs Bureau]. *Kyūshū shigaku* 99 (March 1991).

———. "Kōki nanshin buryoku shinshutsu to 'kokusaku'" [Opportunistic Armed Advance into the South and "national policy"]. *Nihon rekishi* 531 (August 1992).

———. *Nichi-Bei kaisen no seiji katei* [The Political Process Leading to the War against the United States]. Yoshikawa Kōbunkan, 1998.

Morley, James William, ed. *Deterrent Diplomacy: Japan, Germany, and the USSR, 1935–1940.* Japan's Road to the Pacific War. New York: Columbia University Press, 1976.

———, ed. *The Fateful Choice: Japan's Advance into Southeast Asia, 1939–1941.* New York: Columbia University Press, 1980.

———, ed. *The Final Confrontation: Japan's Negotiations with the United States, 1941.* Translated by David A. Titus. New York: Columbia University Press, 1994.

———, ed. *Japan Erupts: The London Naval Conference and the Manchurian Incident, 1928–1932.* New York: Columbia University Press, 1984.

Murakami Sachiko. *Futsu-In shinchū* [Japan's Thrust into French-Indochina, 1940–1945]. Privately printed, 1984.

Murakami Teiichi, ed., *Kaigun shōshō Akiyama Saneyuki: Gundan* [Rear Admiral Akiyama Saneyuki: A War Story]. Jitsugyō no Nihonsha, 1917.

Nagai Kansei. "Katō Kanji shōshō ikkō no hō-Doku gunji chōsa" [Rear Admiral Katō Kanji Visit to Germany for Military Investigations]. *Hatō* 23:1 (September 1997), 23:2 (November 1997).

Nagai Sumitaka. "Kokubō hōshin to kaigun yōhei shisō no hensen" [Development of the National Defense Policy and Naval Strategic Thought], Nos. 1–13. Staff study. JDA.

Nakahara Yoshimasa. "Dainiji sekai taisenshi" [A History of the Second World War], Unpublished. Vol. 1. JDA.

Nakamura Kikuo. *Shōwa Nihon kaigun hishi* [A Secret History of the Japanese Navy in the Showa Period]. Banchō Shobō, 1969.

Nakamura Takafusa et al., eds. *Gendaishi o tsukuru hitobito* [Men Who Shaped Contemporary Japanese History]. Mainichi Shinbunsha, 1971.

Nakayama Sadayoshi. *Ichi Kaigun shikan no kaisō* [Recollections of a Naval Officer]. Mainichi Shinbunsha, 1981.

Nakazawa Tasukō Kankō Kai. *Kaigun chūjō Nakazawa Tasuku: Sakusen buchō, jinji kyokuchō* [Vice Admiral Nakazawa Tasuku, the Chief of the Operations Division and Personnel Bureau]. Hara Shobō, 1979.

Neu, Charles E. *The Troubled Encounter: The United States and Japan.* New York: Wiley, 1975.

Neumann, William L. *America Encounters Japan: From Perry to MacArthur.* Baltimore: Johns Hopkins Press, 1963.

———. "Franklin Delano Roosevelt: A Disciple of Admiral Mahan." United States Naval Institute, *Proceedings* 78 (July 1952).

NHK "Dokyumento Shōwa" Shuzaihan, ed. *Dokyumento Shōwa 5: Orenji sakusen* [A Documentary on the Showa Era, Vol. 5: War Plan Orange]. Kadokawa Shoten, 1986.

Niimi Masaichi Kankō Kai, ed. *Teitoku Niimi Masaichi* [Autobiography and Reminiscences]. Hara Shobō, 1995.

Nish, Ian. *Alliance in Decline: A Study of Anglo-Japanese Relations, 1908–1923.* London: Athlone, 1972.

———. *Japanese Foreign Policy, 1869–1942: From Kasumigaseki to Miyakezaka.* London: Routledge and Kegan Paul, 1977.

———. *Japanese Foreign Policy in the Interwar Period.* Westport, Conn.: Praeger, 2002.

Nomura Kichisaburō. *Beikoku ni tsukai shite: Nichi-Bei kōshō no kaiko* [My Mission to the United States: Recollections of the Japanese-American Negotiations]. Iwanami Shoten, 1946.

———. "Kaiko to tenbō" [Retrospection and Prospect]. Unpublished. NMSDC, 1957.

Nomura Minoru. "Kaigun no Taiheiyō sensō kaisen ketsui" [The Navy's Decision to Commence the Pacific War]. Keio University, *Shigaku* 56 (February 1987).

———. *Nihon kaigun no rekishi* [Japanese Naval History]. Yoshikawa Kōbunkan, 2002.

———. *Rekishi no naka no Nihon kaigun* [The Japanese Navy in History]. Hara Shobō, 1980.

———. "Tai-Bei-Ei kaisen to kaigun no tai-Bei 7-wari shisō" [The Outbreak of the War with the United States and Great Britain, and the Idea of a 70 Percent Ratio]. *Gunji shigaku* 9 (September 1973).

———. *Taiheiyō sensō to Nihon gunbu* [The Pacific War and the Japanese Military]. Yamakawa Shuppan, 1983.

———. *Tennō, Fushimi no miya to Nihon kaigun* [The Emperor, Prince Fushimi, and the Japanese Navy]. Bungei Shunjū, 1988.

———. *Yamamoto Isoroku saikō* [Yamamoto Isoroku Reconsidered]. Chūō Kōronsha, 1996.

O'Connor, Raymond G. *Perilous Equilibrium: The United States and the London Naval Conference of 1930*. Lawrence: University of Kansas Press, 1962.

Ogasawara Naganari. *Teikoku kaigun shiron* [On the History of the Imperial Japanese Navy]. Shun'yōdō, 1898. Republished as *Nihon Teikoku kaigun kaijō kenryokushi kōgi* [Lectures on the History of Sea Power of the Imperial Navy]. Shun'yōdō, 1903.

Ogata Taketora. *Ichi gunjin no shōgai* [The Life of a Sailor (Yonai Mitsumasa)]. Bungei Shunjū Shinsha, 1955.

Ōi Atsushi. *Kaijō goeisen* [Convoy Operations]. Gakushū Kenkyūsha, 2001.

Okada Sadahiro, ed. *Okada Keisuke kaikoroku fu Rondon gunshuku mondai nikki* [Memoirs of Okada Keisuke and Diary of the London Naval Limitation Problem]. Mainichi Shinbunsha, 1977. (Abbreviated as Okada, *Kaikoroku*)

Okada Taishō Kiroku Hensai Kai [Aritake Shūji], ed. *Okada Keisuke*. Editor, 1956. (Abbreviated as *Okada Keisuke*)

Ōmae Toshikazu. "Kyū Nihon kaigun no hējutsuteki hensen to koreni tomonau gunbu narabini sakusen, 1: Daitōa sensō kaishi made [Tactical Development of the Japanese Navy: Armaments and Operations up to the Opening of the Greater East Asian War]. Staff study. JDA.

Ōsumi Taishō Denki Kankō Kai. *Danshaku Ōsumi Mineo den* [Biography]. Kaigun Yūshūkai, 1943.

Ōya Hayato [Ishikawa Shingo]. *Nihon no kiki* [Japan's Crisis]. Moriyama Shoten, 1931.

Peattie, Mark R. "Akiyama Saneyuki and Emergence of Modern Japanese Naval Doctrine." United States Naval Institute, *Proceedings* 103 (January 1977).

———. *Sunburst: The Rise of Japanese Naval Air Power, 1909–1941*. Annapolis, Md.: Naval Institute Press, 2001.

Peattie, Mark R., and David C. Evans. "Satō Tetsutarō and Japanese Strategy." *Naval History* 4 (Fall 1990).

Pelz, Stephen E. *Race to Pearl Harbor: The Failure of the Second London Naval Conference and the Onset of World War II*. Cambridge, Mass.: Harvard University Press, 1974.

———. "Rondon gunshuku kaigi to yoron" [London Naval Disarmament Conference and Japanese Public Opinion]. *Kokusai seiji: Nihon gaikōshi kenkyū—Gaikō to yoron*, 1970.

Prados, John. *Combined Fleet Decoded: The Secret History of American Intelligence and the Japanese Navy in World War II*. New York: Random House, 1995.

Prange, Gordon W. *At Dawn We Slept: The Untold Story of Pearl Harbor*. In collaboration with Donald M. Goldstein and Katherine V. Dillon. New York: McGraw-Hill, 1981.

Prange, Gordon, with Donald M. Goldstein and Katherine V. Dillon. *Pearl Harbor: The Verdict of History*. New York: Viking Penguin, 1986.

Pratt, Julius W. *Cordell Hull*, Vol. 1. New York: Cooper Square, 1964.

———. *Expansionists of 1898: The Acquisition of Hawaii and the Spanish Islands*. Baltimore: Johns Hopkins Press, 1936.

Pratt, William V. "Autobiography." In Pratt Papers, Operational Archives, Naval History Division, Washington Navy Yard.

Puleston, William D. *Mahan: The Life and Work of Captain Alfred Thayer Mahan, U.S.N.* New Haven, Conn.: Yale University Press, 1939.

Rapoport, Anatol, ed. *Clausewitz on War*. Middlesex, UK: Penguin Books, 1968.

Reitzel, William. "Mahan on Use of the Sea." In *War, Strategy, and Maritime Power*, edited by Benjamin M. Simpson. New Brunswick, N.J.: Rutgers University Press, 1977.

Richardson, James O. *On the Treadmill to Pearl Harbor: The Memoirs of Admiral J. O. Richardson as told to George C. Dyer*. Washington, D.C.: GPO, 1973.

Rigler, Frank V. "Our Alumni from Other Nations." *Shipmate* (October 1965).

Rivera, Carlos R. "Big Stick and Short Sword: The American and Japanese Navies as Hypothetical Enemies." Ph.D. dissertation, Ohio State University, 1995.

Roosevelt, Theodore. *Letters of Theodore Roosevelt*, Vol. 1. Edited by Elting E. Morison. Cambridge, Mass.: Harvard University Press, 1951.

Roskill, Stephen. *Naval Policy Between the Wars*. Vol. 1, *The Period of Anglo-American Antagonism, 1919–1929*. New York: Walker, 1968.

———. *Naval Policy Between the Wars*. Vol. 2, *The Period of Reluctant Rearmament, 1930–1939*. London: Collins, 1976.

Ross, Steven T., ed. *American War Plans, 1919–1941*. Vol. 2, *Plans for War against the British Empire and Japan: The Red, Orange, and Red-Orange Plans, 1923–1938*. New York: Garland, 1992.

———, ed. *American War Plans, 1919–1941*. Vol. 3, *Plans to Meet the Axis Threat, 1939–1940*. New York: Garland, 1992.

Saeki Shōichi. "Images of the United States as a Hypothetical Enemy." In *Mutual Images: Essays in American-Japanese Relations*, edited by Akira Iriye. Cambridge, Mass.: Harvard University Press, 1975.

Sagan, Scott D. "The Origins of the Pacific War." *Journal of Interdisciplinary History* 18 (Spring 1988).

Sagishiro Gakujin. "Kafu Kaigi to Katō Kaishō" [The Washington Conference and Navy Minister Katō Tomosaburō]. *Nippon oyobi Nipponjin* (1 October 1921).

Saitō Seiji. "Kaigun ni okeru daiichiji sensō kenkyū to sono hadō" [The Japanese Navy's Study of World War I and Its Impacts]. *Rekishigaku kenkyū* 530 (July 1984).

Saitō Shishaku Kinenkai, ed. *Shishaku Saitō Makoto den* [Biography]. Editor, 1942.

Sakai Keinan. *Eiketsu Katō Kanji* [Katō Kanji, a Great Man]. Nōberu Shobō, 1983.

Sakurai Masakiyo. *Teitoku Akiyama Saneyuki* [Admiral Akiyama Saneyuki]. Iwanami Shoten, 1934.

Sanematsu Yuzuru. *Aa Nihon kaigun* [Ah, the Japanese Navy], Vol. 2. Kōjinsha, 1977.

———. "Hachi-hachi kantai to Katō Tomosaburō" [The eight-eight fleet and Katō Tomosaburō]. *Rekishi to jinbutsu* (1 August 1976).

———. *Kaigun Daigaku kyōiku: Senryaku senjutsu dōjō no kōzai* [Education of the Naval Staff College: The Merits and Demerits of Its Strategic-Tactical Training]. Kōjinsha, 1993.

———. *Saigo no toride: Teitoku Yoshida Zengo no shōgai* [The Last Fortress: Life of Admiral Yoshida Zengo]. Kōjinsha, 1974.

Satō Ichirō. *Satō Ichirō gunshuku kaigi kaisōroku, shōgai* [Memoirs of Naval Limitation Conferences and My Life]. Edited by Satō Tama and Satō Shintarō. Privately printed, 1991.

Satō Naotake. *Kaiko 80-nen* [Recollection of 80 Years of Diplomacy]. Jiji Tsūshinsha, 1964.

Satō Tetsutarō. "Kokubō sakugi" [A Proposal for National Defense] (Navy Ministry, secret, 1912). Unpublished, JDA.

———. *Teikoku kokubō shiron* [On the History of Imperial National Defense]. Suikōsha, 1908. Reprinted by Hara Shobō, 1979.

———. *Teikoku kokubō shironshō* [Abbreviated History of Imperial National Defense]. Suikōsha, 1912.

Satō Tetsutarō et al. *Kokubō mondai no kenkyū* [A Study of the National Defense Problem]. Navy Ministry? 1913. Unpublished, JDA.

Sawada Shigeru. *Sanbō jichō Sawada Shigeru kaisōroku* [Recollections]. Fuyō Shobō, 1982.

Sawamoto, Yorio. "Sawamoto Yorio kaigun jikan nikki: Nichi-Bei kaisen zen'ya" [Diary of Navy Vice Minister Yorio Sawamoto: On the Eve of the Japanese-American War]. *Chūō kōron* (January 1988).

Seager, Robert, II. "Alfred Thayer Mahan: Navalist and Historian." In *Quarterdeck and Bridge: Two Centuries of American Naval Leadership*, edited by James C. Bradford. Annapolis, Md.: Naval Institute Press, 1997.

———. ed., *Alfred Thayer Mahan: The Man and His Letters*. 3 vols. Annapolis, Md.: Naval Institute Press, 1977.

Segawa Yoshinobu, "Washinton kaigi (1921–1922) to 7-wari kaigun mondai" [The Washington Conference and the Question of the 70 Percent Naval Ratio]. *Hōgaku shinpō* 91 (June 1984).

Senshishitsu. *See* Bōeichō.

Shidehara Heiwa Zaidan, ed. *Shidehara Kijūrō* [Biography]. Editor, 1955.

Shidehara Kijūrō. *Gaikō 50-nen* [Fifty Years of my Diplomacy]. Yomiuiri Shinbunsha, 1951.

Shigemitsu Mamoru. *Gaikō kaikoroku* [Diplomatic Memoirs]. Mainichi Shinbunsha, 1978.

———. *Japan and Her Destiny: My Struggle for Peace.* Edited by F. S. G. Piggott. New York: Dutton, 1958.

———. *Shōwa no dōran* [Turbulence during the Showa Period]. 2 vols. Chūō Kōronsha, 1952.

Shimada Kinji. *Amerika ni okeru Akiyama Saneyuki* [Akiyama Saneyuki in America]. Asahi Shimbunsha, 1969.

———. *Roshia sensō zen'ya no Akiyama Saneyuki* [Akiyama Saneyuki on the Eve of the War with Russia]. Asahi Shimbunsha, 1990.

Shimeda Shigetarō. "Shimada Shigetarō taishō kaisen nikki" [Diary Immediately Prior to the Opening of Hostilities]. *Bungei Shunjū* (December 1976).

Shimada Toshihiko. "Kawagoe-Chō gun kaidan no butaiura" [The Secret Background of Kawagoe-Chang Chun Negotiations]. Part 1. *Ajia kenkyū* (10 April 1963).

Shimanuki Takeji. "Daiichiji sekai taisen igo no kokubō hōshin, shoyō heiryoku, yōhei kōryō no hensen" [The Development of the National Defense Policy, the Naval Strenth Requirement, and the General Plan for Strategy since World War I]. *Gunji shigaku* 9 (June 1973).

———. "Nichiro sensō ikō ni okeru kokubō hōshin, shōyō heiryoku, yōhei kōryō no hensen" [The Development of the National Defense Policy, the Naval Strength Requirement, and the General Plan for Strategy since the Russo-Japanese War]. *Gunji shigaku* 8 (March 1973).

Shinmyō Takeo, ed. *Kaigun sensō kentō kaigi kiroku: Taiheiyō kaisen no keii* [A Record of the Conference of Former Naval Leaders: Examining the Circumstances Leading to the Opening of the Pacific War]. Mainichi Shinbunsha, 1976.

Shinohara Hiroshi. *Kaigun sōsetsushi: Igirisu gunji komondan no kage* [History of the Founding of the Japanese Navy: The Shadows of the British Naval Advisory Group]. Ribupōto, 1986.

Shiozaki Hiroaki. "Gunbu to nanpō shinshutsu" [The Military and the Southward Advance]. In *Shōwashi no gunbu to seiji*, Vol. 3, *Taiheiyō sensō zen'ya*, edited by Masaki Miyake et al. Daiichi Hōki: Shuppan, 1991.

Shiryō Chōsa Kai, ed. *Taiheiyo sensō to Tomioka Sadatoshi* [The Pacific War and Tomioka Sadatoshi]. Gunji Kenkyūsha, 1971.

Shōda Tatsuo. *Jūshin tachi no Shōwashi* [A History of the Showa Period Centering on Senior Statesmen]. Bungei Shunjū, 1981.

Snyder, Glenn H., and Paul Diesing. *Conflict among Nations: Bargaining, Decision Making, and System Structure in International Crises.* Princeton, N.J.: Princeton University Press, 1977.

Sorimachi Eiichi. *Ningen Yamamoto Isoroku gensui no shōgai* [Personal Biography of Fleet Admiral Yamamoto Isoroku]. Kōwadō, 1964.

Spector, Ronald H. *At War at Sea: Sailors and Naval Combat in the Twentieth Century.* New York: Viking, 2001.

———. *Eagle against the Sun: The American War with Japan.* New York: Free Press, 1985.

————. *Professors of War: The Naval War College and the Development of the Naval Profession*. Newport, R. I.: Naval War College Press, 1977.

Sprout, Harold, and Margaret Sprout. *The Rise of American Naval Power, 1776–1918*. Princeton, N.J.: Princeton University Press, 1966.

————. *Toward a New Order of Sea Power: American Naval Policy and the World Scene, 1918–1922*. Princeton, N.J.: Princeton University Press, 1946.

Sprout, Margaret T. "Mahan: Evangelist of Sea Power." In *Makers of Modern Strategy: Military Thought from Machiavelli to Hitler*, edited by Edward Mead Earle. Princeton, N.J.: Princeton University Press, 1942.

Stephan, John. *Hawaii under the Rising Sun: Japan's Plans for Conquest after Pearl Harbor*. Honolulu: University of Hawaii Press, 1984.

Stimson, Henry L. *On Active Service in Peace and War*. New York: Harper, 1947.

Suekuni Masao. "Katō Tomosaburō: Washinton gunshuku jōyaku teiketsu no eidan" [Katō Tomosaburō: Resolution to Conclude the Washington Naval Treaty]. In *Nihon kaigun no meishō to meisanbō*, edited by Yoshida Toshio et al. Shin Jinbutsu Ōraisha, 1986.

Suetsugu Nobumasa. *Sekaisen to Nihon* [The World War and Japan]. Heibonsha, 1940.

Sullivan, Mark. *The Great Adventure at Washington: The Story of the Conference*. Garden City, N.Y.: Doubleday, 1922.

Sumida, Jon Tetsuro. *Inventing Grand Strategy and Teaching Command: The Classic Works of Alfred Thayer Mahan Reconsidered*. Baltimore: Johns Hopkins University Press, 1997.

Suzuki Kantarō. *Suzuki Kantarō jiden* [Autobiography]. Ōgiku Kai Shuppanbu, 1949.

Symonds, Craig L. "William Veazie Pratt." In *Chiefs of Naval Operations*, edited by Robert W. Love Jr. Annapolis, Md.: Naval Institute Press, 1980.

Takada Makiko. *Shizukanaru tate: Yonai Mitsumasa* [The Silent Shield: Yonai Mitsumasa], Vol. 1. Hara Shobō, 1990.

————. *Yonai Mitsumasa no tegami* [Yonai Mitsumasa's Letters]. Hara Shobō, 1993.

Takagi Sōkichi. *Jidenteki Nihon kaigun shimatsuki* [Autobiographical Account of the Japanese Navy]. Kōjinsha, 1971.

————. *Nikki to jōhō* [Diary and Reports]. Edited by Itō Takashi et al. 2 vols. Misuzu Shobō, 2000.

————. *Shikan Taiheiyō sensō* [A Personal View of the Pacific War]. Bungei Shunjū, 1969.

————. *Taiheiyō sensō to riku-kaigun no kōsō* [The Pacific War and the Army-Navy Conflict]. Keizai Ōraisha, 1967.

————. *Takagi Sōkichi nikki: Nichi-Doku-I sangoku dōmei to Tōjō naikaku datō* [Diary: The Tripartite Pact Question and the Overthrow of the Tōjō Cabinet]. Mainichi Shinbunsha, 1985.

————. *Yamamoto Isoroku to Yonai Mitsumasa* (new ed.). Bungei Shunjū, 1950.

Takahashi Shinichi, ed. *Waga kaigun to Takahashi Sankichi* [Our Navy and Takahashi Sankichi]. Editor, 1970.

Takamatsu no miya Nobuhito. *Takamatsu no miya nikki* [Diary], Vols. 1–3. Chūō Kōronsha, 1995–96.

Takarabe Takeshi. *Takarabe Takeshi nikki, 1, Kaigun jikan jidai* [Diary of navy vice minister days], Vol. 1. Edited by Banno Junji et al. Yamakawa Shuppan, 1983.

Takeshita Isamu. *Kaigun no gaikōkan Takeshita Isamu nikki* [Diary of Takeshita Isamu, the Naval Diplomat]. Edited by Hatano Masaru et al. Fuō Shobō, 1998.

Tanaka Hiromi. "Shōwa 7-nen zengo ni okeru Tōgō gurūpu no katsudō: Ogasawara Naganari nikki o tōshite" [The Activities of the Tōgō Group: Through the Diary of Ogasawara Naganari]. 2 parts. *Boei Daigakkō kiyō: Jinbun kagaku hen* 51 (September 1985), 53 (March 1986).

———. *Tōgō Heihachirō*. Chikuma Shobō, 1999.

Taylor, Charles C. *The Life of Admiral Alfred Thayer Mahan, Naval Philosopher, Rear Admiral United States Navy*. London: Doran, 1920.

Terasaki Hidenara and Mariko Terasaki Miller, eds. *Shōwa tennō dokuhakuroku* [The Monologues of the Showa Emperor]. Bungei shyujū, 1991.

Terashima Ken Denki Kankō Kai, ed. *Terashima Ken den* [Biography]. Editor, 1973.

Thomson, James, Jr. "The Role of the Department of State." In *Pearl Harbor as History*. New York: Columbia University Press, 1972.

Tobe Ryōichi. "Hokubu Futsu-In shinchū: 'Nanshin' no ichi danmen to shite no kōsatsu" [A Study on Advance to Northern Indochina]. *Bōei Daigakkō kiyō (Shakai kagaku hen)* 37 (November 1978).

———. "Nihon no nanshin to tai-Bei kaisen" [Japan's Southward Advance and Opening of Hostilities with the United States]. In *Nihon gaikō to taigai funsō* [Japanese Diplomacy and External Conflicts], edited by Gomi Toshiki and Hasegawa Yūichi. Renga Shobō, 1984.

Tōgō Shigehiko. *Sofu Tōgō Shigenori no shōgai* [The Life of My Grandfather Tōgō Shigenori]. Bungei Shunju, 1993.

Tōgō Shigenori. *The Cause of Japan*. Translated and edited by Tōgō Fumihiko and B. B. Blakeney. New York: Simon and Schuster, 1956.

———. *Jidai no ichi men* [An Aspect of the Showa Era]. Kaizōsha, 1952.

Tomioka Sadatoshi. *Kaisen to shūsen: Hito to kikō to keikaku* [Commencing and Terminating a War: Men, Organization, and Planning]. Mainichi Shinbunsha, 1968.

———. "Taiheiyō sensō zenshi" [History of the Era Preceding the Pacific War]. (unpublished). Vols. 1–4. Shiryō Chōsa Kai, n.d.

Toyama Saburō. *Dai tōa sensō to senshi no kyōkun* [The Greater East Asian War and the Lessons of War History]. Hara Shobō, 1978.

Toyoda Soemu. *Saigo no teikoku kaigun* [The Last of the Imperial Navy]. Sekai no Nihonsha, 1950.

Trimble, William F. "Admiral Hilary P. Jones and the 1927 Geneva Naval Conference." *Military Affairs* 43 (February 1979).

Tsunoda Jun. *Manshū mondai to kokubō hōshin: Meiji kōki ni okeru kokubō kankyō no hendō* [The Manchurian Question and Japan's Defense Policy: Changes in the Defense Setting of Japan after the Late Meiji Period]. Hara Shobō, 1967.

———. "Nihon kaigun sandai no rekishi" [History of Three Generations of the Japanese Navy]. *Jiyū* (January 1969).

———. "Nihon no tai-Bei kaisen (1940–1941)" [Japan's initiation of War with the United States]. *TSM*, Vol. 7, Asahi Shinbunsha, 1963.

Tuleja, Thaddeus V. *Statesmen and Admirals: Quest for a Far Eastern Naval Policy*. New York: Norton, 1963.

Turk, Richard W. *The Ambiguous Relationship: Theodore Roosevelt and Alfred Thayer Mahan*. New York: Greenwood, 1987.

Ugaki Matome. *Sensōroku* [War Diary]. Hara Shobō, 1968.

Ujita Naoyoshi. *Shidehara Kijūrō* [Biography]. Jiji Tsūshinsha, 1955.

Unno Yoshirō (Horinouchi Kensuke, supervisor). *Nihon gaikōshi*. Vol. 16, *Kaigun gunshuku kōshō, fusen jōyaku* [Japanese Diplomatic history, Vol. 16, Negotiations for Naval Limitation and the Kellogg-Briand Pact]. Kashimna Shuppankai, 1973.

Utley, Jonathan G. "Franklin Roosevelt and Naval Strategy, 1933–1941." In *FDR and the U.S. Navy*, edited by Edward J. Marolda. New York: St. Martin's, 1998.

———. *Going to War with Japan, 1937–1941*. Knoxville: University of Tennessee Press, 1985.

———. "Upstairs, Downstairs at Foggy Bottom: Oil Exports to Japan, 1940–41." *Prologue* 8 (Spring 1976).

Vlahos, Michael. *The Blue Sword: The Naval War College and the American Mission, 1919–1941*. Newport, R.I.: Naval War College Press, 1980.

———. "The Naval War College and the Origins of War-Planning against Japan." *Naval War College Review* 33 (July–August 1980).

———. "Wargaming: An Enforcer of Strategic Realism, 1919–1942." *Naval War College Review* 39 (March–April 1986).

Wakatsuki Reijirō. *Kofūan kaikoroku* [Memoirs]. Yomiuri Shinbunsha, 1950.

Weigley, Russell F. *The American Way of War: A History of United States Military Strategy and Policy*. Bloomington: Indiana University Press, 1973.

———. "The Role of the War Department and the Army." In *Pearl Harbor as History*, edited by Dorothy Borg and Shumpei Okamoto. New York: Columbia University Press, 1973.

Wheeler, Gerald E. *Admiral William Veazie Pratt, U.S. Navy: A Sailor's Life*. Washington, D.C.: Naval History Division, Department of the Navy, 1974.

———. *Prelude to Pearl Harbor: The United States Navy and the Far East, 1921–1931*. Columbia: University of Missouri Press, 1963.

———. "The Roads to War: The United States and Japan, 1931–1941." In *American Diplomacy in the Twentieth Century*, edited by Warren F. Kimball. St. Louis: Forum, 1980.

———. "The United States Navy and the Japanese 'Enemy': 1919–1931." *Military Affairs* 21 (Summer 1957).

Yabe Teiji. *Konoe Fumimaro* [Biography], Vol. 2. Kōbundō, 1952.

Yamada Akira. *Gunbi kakuchō no kindaishi: Nihongun no bōchō to hōkai* [Arms Expansion in Modern History: Expansion and Collapse of Japanese Armed Forces]. Yoshikawa Kōbunkan, 1997.

Yamaji Kazuyoshi. *Nihon kaigun no kōbō to sekininsha tachi* [The Rise and Fall of the Japanese Navy and the Responsible Persons]. Tsukudo Shobō, 1959.

Yamamoto Eisuke, ed. *Danshaku Ōsumi Mineo den* [Biography]. Kaigun Yūshūkai, 1943.

"Yamamoto Isoroku no kaisen zengo no shokan" [Yamamoto Isoroku's Letters Prior to and Following the Outbreak of Hostilities]. In *Dainiji sekai taisen, 2: Shinjuwan zengo,* edited by Gunjishi Gakkai. Kinseisha, 1991.

Yamanashi Katsunoshin. *Katō Tomosaburō gensui o shinobu* [In Remembrance of Fleet Admiral Katō Tomosaburō]. Suikōkai, 1967.

———. *Rekishi to meishō: Senshi ni miru rīdāshippu no jōken* [History and Great Admirals: The Conditions for Leadership as Seen in Naval History]. Mainichi Shimbunsha, 1981.

Yamanashi Katsunoshin Sensei Kinen Shuppan Iinkai, ed. *Yamanashi Katsunoshin ihōroku* [Legacies of Admiral Yamanashi Katsunoshin]. Suikōkai, 1968.

Yasui Sōmei. "Yo no mitaru Akiyama Saneyuki chūjō" [Vice Admiral Akiyama as I Saw Him]. *Taiyō* (March 1918).

Yokoyama Ichirō. *Umi e kaeru: Kaigun shōshō Yokoyama Ichirō kaikoroku* [Back to the Sea: Memoirs]. Hara Shobō, 1980.

Yokoyama Ryūsuke. "Washinton kaigi to taiheiyō bōbi mondai" [The Washington Conference and the Pacific Fortification Problem]. *Bōei kenkyōjo kiyō* 1–2 (December 1998).

Yonai Mitsumasa. *Kaigun taishō Yonai Mitsumasa oboegaki* [Memos of Admiral Yonai Mitsumasa]. Transcribed by Takagi Sōkichi and edited by Sanematsu Yuzuru. Kōjinsha, 1978.

Yoshida Toshio. *Kaigun sanbō* [Navy Staff Officers]. Bungei Shunjū, 1989.

———. *Nihon teikoku kaigun wa naze yaburetaka* [Why Was the Imperial Japanese Navy Vanquished?]. Bungei Shunjū, 1995.

———. *Rengō kantai: Tōgō Heihachirō to Yamamoto Isoroku* [The Combined Fleet: Tōgō Heihachirō and Yamamoto Isoroku]. Akita Shoten, 1968.

———. *Shikikan to wa nanika: Nihon kaigun yonin no mei shidōsha* [Conditions for a Commander: Four Great Leaders of the Japanese Navy]. Kōjinsha, 2001.

Yoshida Toshio, Chihaya Masataka, et al. *Nihon kaigun no meishō to meisanbō* [Great Admirals and Great Staff Officers of the Japanese Navy]. Shin Jinbutsu Ōraisha, 1986.

Yoshii Hiroshi. "Kaigun habatsu no kenkyū" [A Study of Naval Factionalism]. *Rekishi to jinbutsu* (May 1978).

Yoshizawa Minami. *Sensō kakudai no kōzu: Nihongun no "Futsu-In shinchū"* [The Structure of War Escalation: The Japanese Troops' Advance into French Indochina]. Aoki Shoten, 1986.

INDEX

Index

Index entries follow.

ABOUT THE AUTHOR

SADAO ASADA graduated from Carleton College and received a Ph.D. in American history from Yale University. He taught diplomatic history at Doshisha University, Kyoto, from 1963 until his retirement in March 2006. His *Japanese-American Relations between the Wars* (in Japanese) won the prestigious Yoshino Sakuzo Prize in 1994. He has edited *Japan and the World, 1853–1952: A Bibliographic Guide* (Columbia University Press). For his articles he has been awarded the Edward Miller History Prize from the president of the U.S. Naval War College and the Louis Knott Koontz Memorial Award from the American Historical Association (PCB). He has widely contributed to the *American Historical Review, Journal of American History, Pacific Historical Review, Diplomatic History, Naval War College Review, Journal of Strategic Studies,* and *Journal of American-East Asian Relations.* He lives in Kyoto.

The Naval Institute Press is the book-publishing arm of the U.S. Naval Institute, a private, nonprofit, membership society for sea service professionals and others who share an interest in naval and maritime affairs. Established in 1873 at the U.S. Naval Academy in Annapolis, Maryland, where its offices remain today, the Naval Institute has members worldwide.

Members of the Naval Institute support the education programs of the society and receive the influential monthly magazine *Proceedings* and discounts on fine nautical prints and on ship and aircraft photos. They also have access to the transcripts of the Institute's Oral History Program and get discounted admission to any of the Institute-sponsored seminars offered around the country.

The Naval Institute also publishes *Naval History* magazine. This colorful bimonthly is filled with entertaining and thought-provoking articles, first-person reminiscences, and dramatic art and photography. Members receive a discount on *Naval History* subscriptions.

The Naval Institute's book-publishing program, begun in 1898 with basic guides to naval practices, has broadened its scope to include books of more general interest. Now the Naval Institute Press publishes about one hundred titles each year, ranging from how-to books on boating and navigation to battle histories, biographies, ship and aircraft guides, and novels. Institute members receive significant discounts on the Press's more than eight hundred books in print.

Full-time students are eligible for special half-price membership rates. Life memberships are also available.

For a free catalog describing Naval Institute Press books currently available, and for further information about subscribing to *Naval History* magazine or about joining the U.S. Naval Institute, please write to:

Member Services
U.S. NAVAL INSTITUTE
291 Wood Road
Annapolis, MD 21402-5034
Telephone: (800) 233-8764
Fax: (410) 571-1703
Web address: www.navalinstitute.org